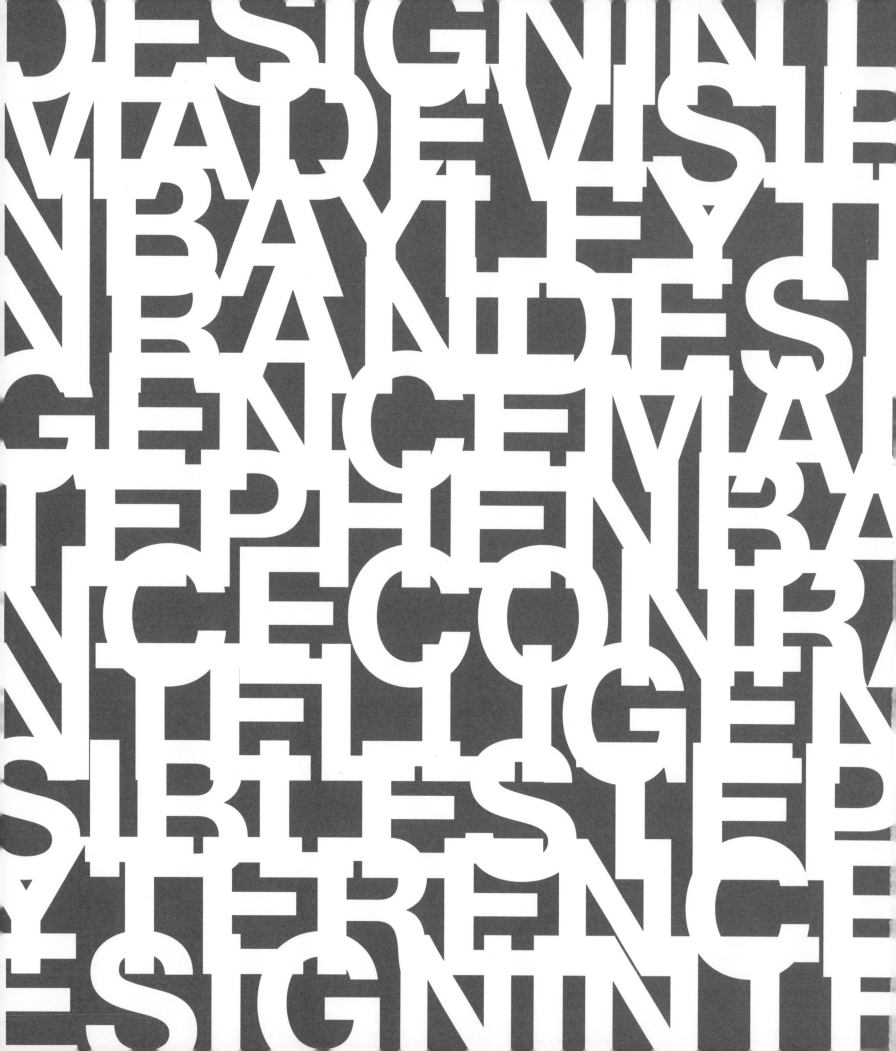

It is the purpose of art to improve on Nature
Voltaire

It is the purpose of Design to improve on industry
Stephen Bayley & Terence Conran

It is the purpose of art to improve on Nature
Voltaire

Published in 2007 by Conran Octopus Limited
a part of the Octopus Publishing Group
2–4 Heron Quays, London E14 4JP
www.conran-octopus.co.uk

Text copyright © 2007 Conran Octopus Ltd
Book design and layout copyright © 2007 Conran Octopus Ltd

British Library Cataloguing-in-Publication Data.
A catalogue record for this book is available from
the British Library.

ISBN: 978-1-84091-477-1

Publishing Director Lorraine Dickey
Editor Sybella Marlow
Copy Editor Sian Parkhouse
Researcher Michelle Danso

Art Direction & Design Jonathan Christie
Picture Researcher Anne-Marie Hoines

Production Manager Angela Young

Printed in China

Authors' Acknowledgements
A word of thanks to Lorraine Dickey, Sybella Marlow,
Anne-Marie Hoines, Michelle Danso and all the editorial
team at Conran Octopus who managed monster egos
and a complicated project with astonishing dignity and calm.
And special thanks to Jonathan Christie, the designer, who
made such elegant sense of the title.

Page 3: John Vaaler,
paperclip, design first
registered in 1899.
Page 4–5: FIAT's Lingotto
factory on Turin's Via Nizza,
1916–1923. Matte-Trusco's
epic building was a symbol of
Futurist dynamism by the
integration of machines into
cities. Le Corbusier called it
'one of the most impressive
sights in industry… a guideline
for town planning.'

Design: Intelligence Made Visible
Stephen Bayley & Terence Conran

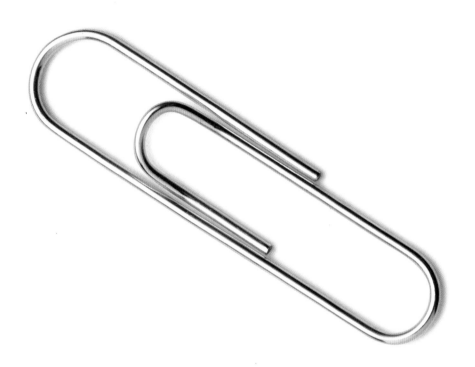

 conran OCTOPUS

Contents

A note on good design
Terence Conran

What is good design? This is a question asked very often, but rarely answered successfully. The answer is that it is immediately visible: something that has not been intelligently designed will not work properly. It will be uncomfortable to use. It will be badly made, look depressing and be poor value for money. And what's more, if it doesn't give you pleasure, it is bad design. You would be stupid to want bad design. Good design really is intelligence made visible.

Everything that is made betrays the beliefs and convictions of the person who made it. Everything has been designed. Conscious or unconscious decisions have always been made which affect the way a product is manufactured, how it will be used and what it looks like. This applies to a flint arrowhead or a cruise missile. Even arranging food on a plate is a design decision. As is your signature, a very important one in fact as it shows how you want people to perceive you.

My answer about good design, or thoughtful design as I'd prefer to call it, is that it comprises 98 per cent commonsense and 2 per cent of a mysterious component which we might as well call art or aesthetics. A good design has to work well, be made at a price the consumer finds acceptable and it must give the consumer practical and aesthetic pleasure. It also must be of a quality that justifies the price paid. If the design has some innovatory qualities then, at least in my opinion, it becomes an even better design. In addition, well-designed products tend to have a long lifespan and usually acquire an attractive patina of usage. Which is to say, it gets better as it gets older: old Levis, a legible printed page, a leather club chair, good shoes, table and chairs would all be examples.

I believe a designer has to research his subject before he puts pen to paper or mouse to computer. The car designer Peter Horbury pins-up photographs of all his inspirations before he starts work. On a new Ford pick-up truck, for instance, he used archive shots of

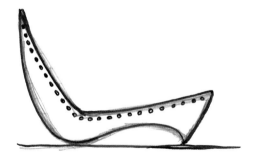

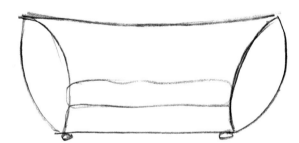

Airstream trailers and steam locomotives. He says 'you need to tell a story'. You need to know history. Not least because those who do not know history are condemned to repeat it. You learn from history, but you aim for the future. The designer's job is not to repeat history, but to make it. It is also essential in my opinion to know your market : how people live, where they live, their income and their aspirations. You must also have a clear idea of why and how what you are designing will improve their lives.

All this relates to the manufacturing process, the materials you use and the methods of distribution. No designer can work effectively if he does not understand the capability of the machinery he must use. The same can be said of cost structure and the humdrum facts of distribution and sales. How the product will be sold, displayed and packaged are all vital parts of the designer's task and must be fully understood at the beginning of any project.

Innovation is a defining characteristic of good design. The capacity to see a new solution to an existing problem is what a designer does. But that is not the same as saying good design involves a restless search for novelty. Good design tends to be enduring. It's this tension between finding effective innovations and achieving lasting values that, so far as I am concerned, gives the designer so much of his creative energy. The designer always needs a proper working relationship with the engineer, the materials technologist. This sort of collaboration is going to be ever more important in future, as established definitions and distinctions about design, art and architecture become ever more blurred in a world where the most significant activity is the invisible organization of electrons in the information economy.

In a changing world, some things remain the same. I firmly believe it is the designer's responsibility to help improve the quality of people's lives through products that work well, are affordable and look beautiful.

That seems to me an intelligent solution.

Below: Early sketches of some of Terence's ideas for furniture designs for Benchmark and The Conran Shop. The hand and the brain connect – sometimes!

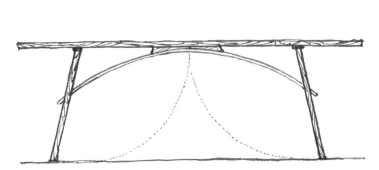
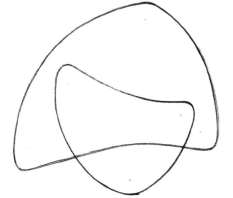

THOUGH HUMAN GENIUS IN
ITS VARIOUS INVENTIONS
WITH VARIOUS INSTRUMENTS
MAY ANSWER THE SAME END,
IT WILL NEVER FIND AN
INVENTION MORE BEAUTIFUL OR
MORE SIMPLE OR DIRECT THAN

NATURE, BECAUSE IN
HER INVENTIONS
NOTHING IS LACKING
AND NOTHING
SUPERFLUOUS.

LEONARDO DA VINCI

A note on *disegno*
Stephen Bayley

In the Renaissance, draughtsmen did what was called *disegno*. For Leonardo da Vinci, the greatest draughtsman of them all, *disegno* meant not just the art and craft of drawing itself, but the ability to communicate ideas graphically. Leonardo's broad interpretation of *disegno* was very close to what we call 'design': an ability to conceptualise an idea, express it in materials and prove it by demonstration. When the word *disegno* migrated into English in the sixteenth century, it came to mean not merely 'drawing', but intention.

Today, design has both these senses : a useful mixture of creative expression and intellectual purpose. Leonardo knew that already. In his letter of application to Lodovico Sforza, Duke of Milan, he listed his talents and achievements, putting the design of useful canals far in front of mere decorative painting or sculpture. Design is an art that works.

1: The sculptor, Eduardo Paolozzi, pays homage to the master. When Leonardo da Vinci wrote a job application to Lodovico Sforza, he gave priority to his skills as a designer over his genius as a painter.

An industrious love of art
The beginnings of design

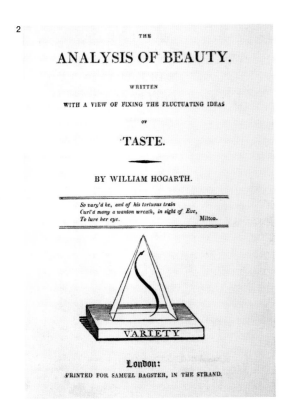

2

1: Louis Jacquard's loom mechanized manual work with a system of punched cards, a pioneering form of software. Here Jacquard shows his invention to Lazare Carnot in Lyon, 1801.

2: The painter William Hogarth published his *Analysis of Beauty* in 1753. It includes one of the first discussions of aesthetics in manufactured goods. Hogarth's abstract 'line of beauty' (shown in the pyramid) suggests that in the coming industrial age art and design will escape classical constraints.

Modern design is, culturally speaking, rather old. It is rooted in two distinct historic developments. One was the division of labour, the industrial process of breaking down manufacturing into its component tasks, which the eighteenth-century Scottish economist Adam Smith said could make manufacturing more profitable. The other was the refinement of techniques of high-volume production prompted by the assumed correlation between high-volume and low-unit costs. The consequences – long lead times and standardized products – imposed a discipline that called for careful product planning. The technological and social changes that arose around these developments are familiarly known as the Industrial Revolution. They occurred when certain technological processes were noticed and exploited by engineers and entrepreneurs in Britain. Although these same technological processes were known to men of science in all Europe, the British enjoyed a background of political stability, a centralized government, a tradition of free enterprise and of utilitarian philosophy, and also an abundance of natural resources, which together enabled these engineers and entrepreneurs to take the first commercial advantage of industry. And because Britain faced the artistic and social consequences of the Industrial Revolution before any other nation, it was in Britain that design developed first.

In the eighteenth century there was a dominant belief in the power of reason. It went hand in hand with a desire to enquire into the nature of both the natural world and the man-made one. Literature was alive with metaphors of industry, the earliest factories offering poets spectacular visions of the future world. For example, in *The Seasons* (1726–30) James Thomson wrote, 'These are thy blessings, Industry, rough power!' It was this sort of investigative, artistic awareness that led the painter William Hogarth to write his book, *The Analysis of Beauty* (1753), in which he set out to quantify the laws which govern our responses to art. Elements of appropriateness and fitness dominate the texts; he is aware that forms that are in themselves elegant can excite disgust if they are misapplied.

The book exhibits a new element of informed criticism of the arts such as in its views on Rococo architecture: 'Twisted columns are undoubtedly ornamental; but as they convey an idea of weakness, they always displease, when they are improperly made use of as supports to anything that is bulky.' But he also commented on the emergent phenomenon of consumer products. For his frontispiece he chose to use an illustration of John Cheere's sculpture yards at Hyde Park Corner, where reproduction lead statues of ancient Greek and Roman originals were being fabricated to cater for the demands of the growing middle-class market. Their purchasers could not afford to go on the Grand Tour to buy real antiques with the milordi, but nonetheless wanted to show that they were people of taste and discrimination.

1

'We must endeavour to work out the foundations on which to build a new style and in my opinion the origin clearly lies in never creating anything which has no valid reason for existing, even with the almighty sanction of history and the manifold consequences of its powerful machines.'
Henry van de Velde

These reproduction classical statues were among the first tokens of taste in the modern world. Later, Tom Wolfe would call their equivalents status details. They were symbols of an age when art met industry, and showed that when mass-production began, manufacturers and artists became self-conscious about the style and meaning of what they were making. The development was crucial because the introduction of culture into industry was the beginning of design and marked the start of the process that was to see the disappearance of the simple working craftsman from the economy. This also indicated that the reproduction classes were born and copies of pretentious taste reigned supreme for many a year.

While Hogarth considered these issues at an abstract level in London, in Britain's soon-to-be industrial Midlands Josiah Wedgwood was coming to terms with the reality of the early Industrial Revolution. The sculptor John Flaxman was to inscribe on his monument to Wedgwood in Burslem church: 'He converted a rude and inconsiderable manufactory into an elegant Art and an important part of National commerce.' Before mass-production

'Design is first and foremost an attitude.' Roger Tallon

1: Joseph Wright of Derby was one of the first artists to sense (ands then record) the drama and romance of the industrial revolution. His *Arkwright's Cotton Mill by Night* (1782–3) is the first ever oil painting of an industrial scene.

2: William Shipley, founder of the Society of Arts.
3: The frontispiece to Hogarth's *Analysis of Beauty* shows John Cheere's sculpture yard at Hyde Park Corner. Cheere ran a business reproducing classical statues in lead, feeding a new taste for 'antiques' to the emerging middle-class consumer.

craftsmen controlled every aspect of making, from invention to merchandising, whether individually or in groups. After the Industrial Revolution the designer assumed the role of planner, as distinct from the craftsman 'maker', in the manufacturer-to-consumer cycle, and the new manufacturing and commercial processes had the effect of separating inventing from making and making from selling. Wedgwood was the first to exploit this division of labour in the production of consumer goods. To design his wares he employed practising artists, such as the sculptor John Flaxman, the painter George Stubbs, and countless anonymous Italian modellers, all of whom worked out the appearance of the goods but were not actually involved in making them. In so doing he was the first man to introduce working artists into the industrial process, and he called into existence a new class of being: the designer.

Although where marketing was concerned Wedgwood's achievements all looked forward, there was a substantial element of revivalism in his business because the style his fine artists followed was the current fashion of neo-classicism. This is typical of the age, for although there was a widespread belief in the necessity of progress, artists in the later eighteenth century could only see 'progress' as an interpretation of the art of Greece and Rome. Wedgwood's most famous production was appropriately the reproduction 'Portland' vase of 1790, and he named his Staffordshire factory 'Etruria' in order to evoke the Etruscan art that was in part his model.

Wedgwood made prodigious contributions to the techniques of mass-production (he kept an 'Experiment Book' where he catalogued his various technical innovations), and was made a Fellow of the Royal Society to acknowledge his work on the development of the pyrometer. It has been said that Wedgwood's research and self-education were inseparable from his commercial ambitions. In this respect, he was a pioneer of marketing, too. To realize the potential of what he had achieved in mass-production he opened a shop to sell his wares in London. These wares were separated by Wedgwood into 'useful' and 'beautiful' ones, evidence that to this eighteenth-century mind a distinction existed between the aesthetic and the practical aspects of design.

Both the moral and the mercantile components of the new phenomenon were sensed simultaneously at an 'official' level. In an ambitious programme to unite commerce with art, William Shipley founded the Society of Arts in 1754 (granted a Royal charter in 1908 and since known as the Royal Society of Arts). Its objectives were 'to embolden enterprise, to enlarge Science, to refine Art, to improve Manufactures and extend Commerce', thus summarizing the material and metaphysical aims of Britain's Industrial Enlightenment. It was established in imitation of the more exclusive Royal Society, an elected academy of distinguished scientists, but with more democratic, popular and practical aspirations. As such it gave Britain an institution which did justice to her international industrial lead, and the Society set about administering the Industrial Revolution and regulating its aesthetics.

However, the Society of Arts' results were sadly and ironically more cerebral than practical. Eighty years after the Society was founded, Great Britain's arts might have been doing well enough, and her manufactures and commerce were well-established, but her products were not setting standards which provided models for future generations. When France, Germany (and later the United States) industrialized they proved better able to make fine consumer products than Britain. A Parliamentary Select Committee was appointed in the 1830s to consider the problem of an increase in foreign imports and to find the answer to 'the best means of extending knowledge of the Arts and of the Principles of Design among the People (especially the manufacturing population)'. Distinguished foreigners

'The Christian architect should gladly avail himself of those improvements and increased facilities that are suggested from time to time. The steam engine is a most valuable power for sawing, raising and cleansing stone, timber and other materials… we do not want to arrest the course of inventions, but to confine these inventions to their legitimate use.' A.W.N. Pugin

were called in to give evidence to the committee, which had the doleful business of hearing a formidable weight of evidence suggesting that the quality of French and German education and manufacturing was so far in front of Britain's that there could be little chance of her ever catching up. France and Germany's better design owed much to their schools, where models of excellence were collected together to provide examples for the new industrial classes, and where young designers were given training and manufacturers exposed to models for imitation. When the committee published its Report on Arts and Manufactures in 1836 its conclusions were that the only chance of saving Britain's industrial future must be 'to infuse, even remotely, into an industrious and enterprising people a love of art'. The Westminster Review remarked, 'Enough! and more than enough of testimony to the combined degradation of taste and national profits! The admonition it conveys is bitter, but wholesome.'

The 1836 Report was the beginning of a Government initiative to sponsor new Schools of Design in Ornamental Art. (It also prompted the creation of the first museums in the belief that definite benefits would accrue from gathering together artefacts of high quality from across the ages and exposing the nation's youth to them.) In 1837 the old premises of the Royal Academy in Somerset House were made available for the first School of Design (which was one of the origins of the Royal College of Art). Some of the more perceptive critics saw this as a substantial symbol that in the new machine age, fine art would have to move over for industrial design; the painter William Dyce even set up a Jacquard loom in the London School of Design and his successor abolished life drawing in favour of painting on glass and ceramics. But despite these heroic initiatives, and despite the 17 other Schools of Design set up across the country, by 1846 another Parliamentary Committee was announcing the bold experiment a failure. The initiative had failed to such a degree that when the Prime Minister asked the painter Benjamin Robert Haydon whether the 'people will ever have any taste' his answer was, 'How should they, if no means are taken to educate them?'

Among the reasons for the failure was the fact that the teachers at the Schools of Design were mostly fine artists who had little idea of real commercial needs, and that increasingly, where 'official' opinion was concerned, industry and culture were thought to occupy different areas of social life. Thus, while designers did begin working at ground level within the new ceramic, textile and metal industries, they were not given the same status or titles as fine

1: Josiah Wedgwood built his Staffordshire factory in 1769. In pursuit of a classical ideal, he named this industrial monument 'Etruria'. The canal it was built beside was the information super-highway of its day.
2: John Flaxman, the sculptor modelled the 'Dancing Hours' for Wedgwood's white on blue Jasperware in 1778.

3: The Wiener Werkstaette was founded in 1903. Its metalware, including this 1909 coffee service, was made by hand, although its strict geometrical form anticipated the machine aesthetic.
4: Peter Behrens designed AEG's graphics as well as its buildings and products. This price list for electric kettles was in use during 1910-13. His search for clarity in typography took him back to a fifteenth century Venetian original.

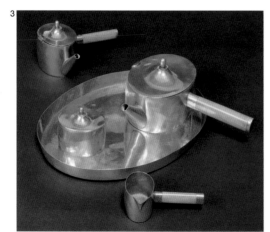

artists and architects. The expansion of trade during the nineteenth century should have enabled British designers to become fully integrated with the processes of mass-production and marketing, but because the authorities were more concerned with public taste and with the promotion of exports, little was done to realize the practical opportunities for artists working in industry.

The same cannot be said of Germany and the United States. These countries industrialized very rapidly during the second half of the nineteenth century and were more able, or at least more inclined, to adopt a practical approach to design. From the start they were more willing to integrate design into manufacturing, particularly in the emergent electrical industries (where Britain lagged far behind). It was in Germany that for the first time an architect, Peter Behrens, took entire control of the appearance of an industrial corporation. For the Allgemeine Elektrizitäts Gesellschaft (AEG), Behrens designed everything from posters through kettles to buildings. This ambitious venture, sometimes seen as the first ever corporate identity programme, marked Britain's industrial decline relative to her neighbours. Corporate identity is the informal name for the visual character of a company. Its practitioners maintain that it is not only products and services that help their clients become successful, but also their visible character, from the letterhead to the livery of the trucks.

Peter Behrens, with his work for AEG, was a pioneer, but it is in the United States that corporate identity has really flourished. Eliot Noyes, who undertook a vastly successful corporate identity programme for IBM in the Fifties, described the business when he said: 'Clothes may not make the man, but they do tell you something about him.'

Most American design consultancies specialize in corporate identity as opposed to product design. Among the leaders are Anspach Grossman Portugal, Lippincott & Margulies and Landor Associates. (See also Saul Bass, Henri Henrion, Wolff Olins and American design and British design page 319.) At some point in the later Nineties, conversations about corporate identity turned into conversations about branding.

'We don't expect everyone to become expert designers; that is neither possible nor desirable. We cannot all become accountants, but we can learn enough to read a balance sheet.' Gordon Russell

Lawful prey
Mass-consumption

The story of taste in the nineteenth century is one of confusion and crisis. It can be seen as a two-part drama. The first act was the undermining by archaeology of the classical values which sustained Sir Joshua Reynolds and his academicians, especially when an expedition to Sicily by the Franco-German architect Jakob-lgnaz Hittorff (1792–1867), designer of Paris' Gare du Nord, discovered that the ancient temples of the Greeks were not the austere, white edifices which the neo-classicists and academicians had fancied, but were in fact garish and polychrome. The second act was the opening up of consumerism to more than one social class as manufacturing exploded.

The reasons for the growth in consumerism were multiple: they included huge increases in the mass-production of consumer goods because of technological improvements in manufacturing, a rapid rate of increase in population during the second third of the century, a generally improving standard of living, and the growth of urbanization which brought with it the implications of increased consumption of material goods, especially as status objects. By roughly 1860 more people from more social classes were regularly buying more products than ever before. The implications for design were enormous.

It was no longer possible to maintain, as Reynolds had done a century earlier, that there was a single standard of taste and that any man could achieve it; quite evidently, there were many standards. Artistic and philosophic attempts to rationalize these different standards form a fundamental part of the story of design in the following century.

Under the influence of mass-consumption the refined, confident elegance of Regency style, which was essentially aristocratic, gave way to a multiplicity of styles that reflected the social and industrial upheavals of the age of Queen Victoria.

With the loss of classical standards, many nineteenth-century designers began to look to other sources for authority for their ideas. Some were led into eclecticism, deriving inspiration from this or that style of the past, while others chose to be guided by 'moral' standards rather than archaeology. Among the first to react to the explosion in housing and consumer design was the eccentric architect <u>Augustus Pugin</u>, who turned to an idealized model of the Middle Ages (which he imagined as an era of perfect social harmony) to serve as a didactic contrast to the world of the 'depressed people' which he saw all around him. He was the major intellectual force behind, and perhaps the greatest creative genius of, an ethical campaign, concentrated on architecture, which we call the Gothic Revival.

Although essentially less practical than <u>Henry Cole</u>, the Victorian official who was most active in promoting design as a solution to Britain's export problem, Pugin's thought was a profound influence on Cole and his group: the *Journal of Design and Manufactures*, founded

1: The architect Jakob-Ignaz Hittorff's archaeological investigations showed that ancient Greek temples were brightly coloured, not the austere monochrome of neo-classical fantasy. This blew apart all existing assumptions about taste and anticipated the imminent excesses of High Victoriana. The illustration is from Hittorff's Restituton du temple d'Empedocle a Selinonte (1828).

2: Until the last quarter of the nineteenth century, soap had been a generic product. But when William Hesketh Lever created Sunlight, the story of branding had begun.

'How many things can you do to enhance and how do you avoid those things which do not? If there is a moral commitment – or an opportunity – for a designer, that is it.' George Nelson

by Cole in 1849, is full of Pugin's thought translated into 'sound principles', but contained a hard, commercial sense quite alien to Pugin's medievalism. Both men were implacable critics of the Government's Schools of Design. Pugin wrote:

'I have almost given up my hope of seeing any real good effected by the Schools of Design…[they are] a hindrance to the revival of true taste and feeling, for the minds of the students are perverted by copying the same stale models that have been used for years without producing a single artist capable of designing anything original or appropriate.'

Henry Cole shared his view.

Pugin's solution to the disorders of the day was a happy rediscovery of the architecture of the Middle Ages. He believed that 'good' societies produced 'good' people and that 'good' people necessarily produced 'good' design. But this was not merely backward-looking romanticism: Pugin had sophisticated ideas about the propriety of form. In his book, *Christian Architecture* (1841), he wrote:

'It is impossible to enumerate half the absurdities of modern metal workers; but all these proceed from the false notion of disguising instead of beautifying articles of utility. How many objects of ordinary use are rendered monstrous and ridiculous, simply because the artist, instead of seeking the most convenient form, and then decorating it, has embodied some extravagance to conceal the real purpose for which the article was made!'

This strain of thought passed directly to <u>William Morris</u>, who absorbed the ideas wholesale. Pugin thus has a claim to be the founder of the entire sensibility that was later to give nineteenth-century design theorists their views on propriety and from there fed

1

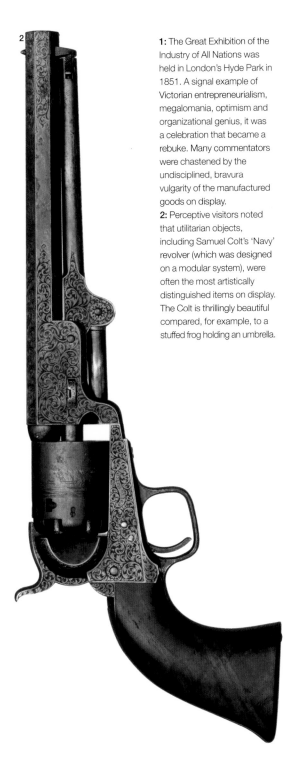

1: The Great Exhibition of the Industry of All Nations was held in London's Hyde Park in 1851. A signal example of Victorian entrepreneurialism, megalomania, optimism and organizational genius, it was a celebration that became a rebuke. Many commentators were chastened by the undisciplined, bravura vulgarity of the manufactured goods on display.

2: Perceptive visitors noted that utilitarian objects, including Samuel Colt's 'Navy' revolver (which was designed on a modular system), were often the most artistically distinguished items on display. The Colt is thrillingly beautiful compared, for example, to a stuffed frog holding an umbrella.

'You cannot bore people into buying your product, you can only interest them in buying it. You cannot save souls in an empty church.' David Ogilvy

directly into the Modern Movement, but he also has a claim to be the creator of that backward-looking sentiment which ultimately sucked life out of it. That he could do both is a testament to the fecundity of his thought and its influence.

Pugin was also a major influence in the form and the content of the Great Exhibition of 1851, a lesson in taste conceived for the British nation by Prince Albert, Henry Cole and their circle of friends. It was to be a didactic tableau vivant, one of the first major trade exhibitions, but it proved to be something of a shock. Just as Pugin had said, industry appeared to be out of control: the mass-produced objects on display were scarred by vulgar and inappropriate ornament and too many of them were concerned with extravagances that concealed their real purpose. While many of the Indian products were 'rude' in workmanship, it was agreed that they very often displayed an understanding of the 'correct principles of ornament' superior to anything made in Britain.

Gottfried Semper, a German architect resident in England, noticed (as Horatio Greenough had in America) that it was only purely utilitarian objects, like Samuel Colt's .36 'Navy' revolver from the United States, which was also being manufactured on a small scale in Pimlico, that seemed to be pleasing and appropriate. Colt's treatise *On the Application of Machining to the Manufacture of Rotating Chamber-Breeched Firearms and their Peculiarities* enjoyed a surprisingly wide readership in High Victorian Britain. It was much more than a study of weapons design; it was a philosophical system.

One result of the Great Exhibition was that sensitive individuals in the circle of Prince Albert were prompted, a century after Hogarth, to analyze anew the aesthetic principles which govern our reaction to pattern and design. The most remarkable and influential publication to result from this was a book called *The Grammar of Ornament*, compiled by a Welsh architect called Owen Jones. Another result was a renewed impetus to create an educational institution that would cater for Britain's needs in the area of design. This was to be a museum run by Henry Cole.

A committee, which included Pugin, was set up to select exhibits from the Great Exhibition to put into Henry Cole's new museum. They were chosen in order to counter the malaise which they considered to have afflicted contemporary industry, and in order to teach the public some lessons in taste. Of £5,000 made available, almost twice as much was spent on Indian products as on British ones selected 'without reference to styles, but entirely for the excellence of their art or workmanship'. Under the auspices of the Government's Department of Practical Art (which became the Department of Science and Art in 1853), this collection was assembled into the Museum of Manufactures at Marlborough House on Pall Mall in central London the year after the exhibition closed.

The germ of the collection in Henry Cole's museum gradually grew by gifts and acquisitions, all the time maintaining adherence to its founding idea that, 'Each specimen has been selected for its merits in exemplifying some right principle of construction or ornament… to which it appeared desirable that the attention of our Students and Manufacturers should be directed.' In addition, in order to emphasize some lessons in design, Henry Cole set up a 'Chamber of Horrors' in the Museum of Manufactures. Here he would demonstrate how the mass-produced metalware of Birmingham (which Pugin called an 'inexhaustible mine of bad taste') was inferior to the 'rude scarfs of Tunis'. It was an inspired reversal of the principles of the traditional academy: instead of setting up good examples to be seen for imitation, Cole set up some examples for avoidance, 'bad' designs, full of false principles, put on display to be reviled and to excite higher ambitions.

'Fine art deals with internally imposed problems. But if there's no external problem, there's no design.' Milton Glaser

'Mass-production demands a search for standards. Standards lead to perfection.' Le Corbusier

1: The Victorian Society was founded in 1958 in the Kensington house of the *Punch* magazine illustrator Linley Samborne.
2: Mass-distribution was as influential as branding in the development of consumer goods. Sears Roebuck used the new railroads as sales arteries. Its famous catalogue (this example from Fall, 1897) provided even the inhabitants of remote rural communities with the same choice as a vast urban department store. It was an informal encyclopaedia of design.

3: Gustave Dore's experience of London slums inspired his later work on Dante's Inferno. 'Over London By Rail' (1872) was an indictment of unplanned urban expansion, a haunting illustration of John Ruskin's apocalyptic critiques of urban life.

With all the moral certainty of the age, Cole and his colleagues set out to look for some aesthetic certainties too. They were absolutely sure that they knew what was good and what was bad in design, and what was bad was lack of symmetry, disregard of structure, formless confusion and superficial decoration. Although Cole's efforts aroused public ridicule (and most of the manufacturers insisted on having their products withdrawn), he got the sort of response that betrayed deeply suppressed instincts and fears. Five years after the 'Chamber of Horrors', he was able to set up his grander museum in rural Brompton on land owned by the Commissioners of the 1851 exhibition.

With great clarity of vision he wanted his new museum to be 'specially commercial in so commercial an age'. At first known as the South Kensington Museum and then as the 'Brompton Boilers' (on account of its apparently makeshift construction in iron), the Museum which Cole founded was renamed the <u>Victoria and Albert Museum</u> in 1899. But Cole and his fellows did not realize that the emerging world economy meant that the market was likely to dominate taste and that it was no longer possible for a small elite, no matter how well-intentioned, to set universal standards.

While in Britain the problems of design reform and public taste preoccupied the authorities, in the United States a less self-conscious attitude towards mass-production and consumption developed. While Britain led in the manufacture of goods in some traditional applied art industries (ceramics and textiles, for instance), during the second half of the nineteenth century new companies in the United States surged ahead in the making of mechanical and electrical goods. Add to this the relative wealth and homogeneous character of a population sharing the same basic economic circumstances, and the picture of a country ready for huge innovations in mass-consumption is complete.

The United States was the first nation to produce and consume new appliances such as vacuum cleaners, sewing machines, typewriters and washing machines. At the same time it developed a 'culture' of these goods for the home and the office. The early emancipation of women and the smaller numbers of servants after the Civil War encouraged the growth of these manufacturing industries and meant that new merchandise was to acquire a role in everyday life three quarters of a century before it happened in Europe.

At first the design of the new American products was determined by the manufacturing processes by which they were made. Samuel Colt's elemental 'Navy' model revolver which had shocked the British in 1851 was a remarkable example of how the aesthetic character of the product could be determined by machine-made, standardized parts. This approach pervaded the early production of all mechanical and electrical goods in the United States, but was moderated as mass-consumption increased. Soon the new products were decorated with surface patterns, applied as a marketing strategy to enhance their appeal to female consumers.

American design was to develop in a more pragmatic way than in Europe, and designers and manufacturers were always aware of the demands of the market place and were quite unashamed to respond to them. In early American design theory, there was none of the need to make moral statements, as did Pugin, Morris and their followers. From this moment, design in America had a special quality. The United States was uninhibited by the cultural and political boundaries that constrained the Europeans. Influenced only by manufacturing processes and motivated by marketing needs, American industry enjoyed the opportunity of supplying a vast, homogeneous market with unique modern products. It is not surprising that when the first industrial design studios appeared, they were in America.

'Two innocent articles of American life – the Sears Roebuck catalog and the phonograph record – are the most powerful pieces of foreign propaganda in Russia… the catalog comes first.'
Franklin D. Roosevelt

3

A kilogram of stone or a kilogram of gold?
Survival and revival of craft values

In the later nineteenth century British design became more involved with morals and ideology than even <u>Pugin</u> could have envisaged. To the leading writers of the age, the major challenge was to establish a simple and rational way of life but, in contrast, the most celebrated contemporary designer <u>William Morris</u> offered what was basically an exclusive and elitist pseudo-medieval fantasy world.

Morris and his contemporaries inherited a considerable amount of their theory from Pugin, especially his hatred of the city (whose image he liked to draw as a stack of sooty factory chimneys, a soulless non-conformist chapel and tenement housing). Pugin and, later, <u>John Ruskin</u> were High Tories who despised the crude middle classes and the modern innovation of joint-stock capitalism, and each found distant prospects (of either the Middle Ages or the countryside) to act as symbolic cures for contemporary ills. Their views took root to such an extent that in the next generation the leaders of taste in Britain became spokesmen of the back-to-the-land disposition, inspired by culturally complex and essentially fanciful rural ideals.

From Pugin via Ruskin and Morris a movement called the Arts and Crafts arose. The name came from an off-shoot of the <u>Art Workers' Guild</u> which first showed in a shopping street in London's West End in 1888. A collective of painters and craftsmen, it was intended to be called 'The Combined Arts', but a zealous bookbinder member called T.J. Cobden Sanderson proposed 'Arts and Crafts' as an alternative label and it stuck. Until he was called away in 1893 to be Director of Design at Manchester School of Art, the first President of the Arts and Crafts Exhibition Society was the Liverpudlian illustrator <u>Walter Crane</u>. In 1893 <u>William Morris</u> took over. It was through Morris' influence and direction that the Arts and Crafts movement – originally a selling exhibition of this and that – established <u>John Ruskin</u>'s barmy philosophy in the damaging and dominant place it retains in English imaginative life.

The good things about the philosophy are easily explained. A belief in the primacy of art and the nobility of honest labour are two to start with. Then there is a quintessential, and inflexible, moralism, wrong-headed perhaps, but noble nonetheless. Ordinary things – a salt cellar, a chair, a rug – were to be taken seriously. The bad things are easily explained too. Through the Arts and Crafts, the English were taught to believe that modern was bad, that excellence only existed in the past. Its exponents spoke of novelty, but were entirely backwards looking. It was a philosophy of defeat, based on ideas of sentiment and retreat. They intended to dignify labour – Ruskin spoke of the 'life and liberty of every workman' – but it never occurred to Ruskin and the rest of them that the same workman might, in

1: William Morris' love of nature made him the spiritual leader of the Crafts Revival of the later twentieth century. His 'Fruit' wallpaper of 1864 (which was still in production in the 1980s) is typical of his genius at turning natural forms into flat pattern.

1: William Morris' Merton Abbey workshops began selling William de Morgan's painted earthenware tiles in 1872. In the 1880s de Morgan set-up his own pottery nearby.

2: The Viennese architect and pamphleteer, Adolf Loos' strident views on the vicousness of decoration and ornamnent made him an inspirational figure of Modernism.

'There is hardly anything in the world that some person cannot make a little worse and sell a little cheaper and people who consider price alone are this person's lawful prey.' John Ruskin

fact, like to have a car and an electric light bulb instead of a schlock medieval pastiche tapestry, a minstrel's gallery or a stained-glass windows.

The architecture and design of the Arts and Crafts Movement is based on a rejection of technology. It is also based on privilege. Alan Powers, apparently without irony, wrote that 'The Arts and Crafts house will typically be found in a grand suburb.' Of course, the idea of smocked makers doing slipware in candlelit studios is charming, but elsewhere Siemens, Ford and Edison had a different and, some would say, more positive view of the potential of the new century. True, the Bauhaus acquired some of the Arts and Crafts rhetoric when Walter Gropius used as its slogan 'Art and Technology: a new unity', but the Arts and Crafts had a woefully retarding effect on English taste. To look at an Arts and Crafts artefact and to understand it is to appreciate, or be shocked by, the paralysing backwardness of England's view of the future.

Worse, when the blinkers of art history are removed, the ham-fisted ugliness of Arts and Crafts becomes horribly obvious. Never in the history of art have so many useless, awkward things been produced in support of a fragile and irrelevant belief. Look without prejudice at a C.R. Ashbee salt cellar of circa 1899. In hand-bashed silver set with carnelian gems, a winged figure supports a sphere with a contrived, and exhausted, floral motif atop. It is precious, inappropriate, ill-proportioned, expensive, silly, sad and wrong. Did no one ever ask why you want a winged figure supporting your salt? Who bought it? Or take a chair by Charles Rennie Mackintosh. What is the point of a chair you cannot sit on? It is a dramatic diagram, certainly. But that diagram is a drama about a sentimental view of the past, not an optimistic view of the future.

Arts and Crafts designers enjoyed, for example, the Cotswolds. This was because it combined the opportunity of maximum picturesque charm with the temptation of nearby train links to the fleshpots of the capital city, and the heroes of the Arts and Crafts, Ashbee, Ernest Gimson and William Lethaby, did not disdain to use the railway. Similarly, there were few active Arts and Crafts practices exposed to the meteorological rigours of the Yorkshire Dales (or the scorn and ridicule of the real workmen of Sheffield and Doncaster).

The Arts and Crafts practitioners aimed to produce designs for furniture, glass, silver and other areas of the applied arts inspired by the craft values of 'truth to materials' and fitness for purpose. Simplification and honesty of decoration, derived at all times from the natural world, were essential to all Arts and Crafts activity. However, the Arts and Crafts

'Not only is ornament produced by criminals, but also a crime is committed through the fact that ornament inflicts serious injury on people's health, on the national budget and hence on cultural evolution.' Adolf Loos

was not really one style, but many. At its base was a social experiment intended to reform society through art and design and to establish handcrafting as the dominant mode of manufacture. It grew out of Pugin's Gothic Revival, but absorbed the japonisme of Edward Godwin and the Queen Anne of Philip Webb on the way. In the 1890s it merged stylistically with Art Nouveau.

The polemics of the Arts and Crafts were more influential than its actual products. The romantic notions of Ruskin, Morris and Ashbee were balanced by an attention to detail and the attitude of truth to materials. As its historian, Gillian Naylor, has said, the movement was 'based in part on a generation's preoccupation with doctrine and "style" in architecture and design, and in part on reactions ... to the facts of life in a machine age'. When translated to Germany by Hermann Muthesius these elements laid the basis for a more practical revolution in production and education that found its fullest expression in Walter Gropius's curriculum at the Bauhaus.

Arts and Crafts principles reached the public with the work of Ambrose Heal, a shopkeeper and furniture-maker and founder member of the Design and Industries Association (DIA). His store in London's Tottenham Court Road was seen as an island of civilized values in an ocean of reproduction mediocrity – indeed, *The Artist* called the furniture stores neighbouring Heal's 'slurs on civilization'. Heal's honest designs of unpolished, unstained oak were the expression in furniture of the taste for things natural and simple that had made the socialist thinker Edward Carpenter wear sandals and a Saxon tunic, and turned George Bernard Shaw into a disciple of Gustav Jaeger's sanitary woollen systems, which declared that animal fibres were more healthy to wear than dead vegetable ones. Heal was himself exposed to these theories, but was particularly inspired by the theories of W. R. Lethaby, the architect-educationalist and pioneer member of the DIA. Lethaby looked around at the products of High Victorian mass-consumption and observed that the chief characteristics were 'extravagant expenditure on the worthless; the lowering of our demands to a penny picture postcard level; and overcrowding with trivialities'.

Although Heal's introduction of simplicity into the market was a radical departure for a conservative industry, the fact that his Arts and Crafts inspiration was, however distantly, derived from the past drove British taste, because of its very success, down a blind alley of nostalgia. This prevented it in subsequent decades from responding to the more modern impulses coming from Continental Europe. Although ideas about fitness and propriety that had originated in Britain were taken up with enthusiasm in the German-speaking countries and in Scandinavia, where they were translated into the Modern Movement, there was so little response in their native country that Nikolaus Pevsner could declare in the mid-Thirties that Britain was at least 12 years behind the rest of Europe in accepting modern design. The British heritage was a rag-bag of clubs and guilds, sentimental relics left behind after the wave of Arts and Crafts enthusiasm had receded.

Perhaps the keenest response to the demand for simplicity was found in Austria, a country whose relative industrial primitiveness offered a firmer basis for innovation. It was in Austria that Michael Thonet had begun his successful manufacture of bentwood furniture in the middle of the nineteenth century. It was also in Austria that the architect Adolf Loos adapted the Arts and Crafts view about simple materials, blended it with his own slick and idiosyncratic view of manners and style, and turned it into a 'philosophy' that was to be profoundly influential on the Modern Movement. He wrote in 1898, 'What is worth more, a kilogram of stone or a kilogram of gold? The question probably seems ridiculous. But only to the merchant. The artist will answer: all materials are equally valuable as far as I am concerned.'

2

1: A Swedish interior of 1885.
2: The Lygon Arms in Broadway, Gloucestershire, was the family business of Gordon Russell, the furniture-maker who became Britain's first design guru.

3: Although its parentage was in the Arts and Crafts movement, Art Nouveau designers showed no interest in simplicity. Rather, Art Nouveau was the last hurrah of an exhausted decorative tradition. The picture shows a lizard doing service as a door knocker on a 1900 house in Paris' Avenue Rapp.

'Forget the spreading of the hideous town/Think rather of the pack-horse on the down.'
William Morris

This taste for simplicity reached such an extreme state with Loos that in 1908 he wrote an esssay that he entitled 'Ornament and Crime'. His thought became one of the strongest esoteric influences on Le Corbusier and the others who used Loos' fevered proclamations as the ideological basis for 'progressive' European architecture and design between the Wars.

The impact of British ideas was felt strongly in Germany. One of the transmitters of the influence was the diplomat Hermann Muthesius, whose book, *Das Englische Haus* (1905), with its explanation of the Arts and Crafts, contributed to the climate of ideas surrounding the creation of the Deutsche Werkbund in 1907. However, the German Werkbund was far more committed to industrial production than were any of the British design reformers, and Muthesius himself made a profound contribution to German design and education in his elaboration of the theory of Typisierung (standardization). This theory ultimately emerged in Walter Gropius's syllabus at the Bauhaus together with some Arts and Crafts principles about form and materials, which meant that in a roundabout way the backward-looking theories of the British craft enthusiasts contributed directly to the chief creative group of the Modern Movement.

Arts and Crafts principles were imported, too, into the United States at the turn of the century, influencing the ideas and work of Frank Lloyd Wright, whose maverick ideas and inspired leadership were to have a fundamental effect on design theory in the twentieth century. Although there has been very little theoretical writing devoted to design, nonetheless many attempts have been made to reconcile the design process with various areas of philosophical speculation. In the nineteenth century John Ruskin and Gottfried Semper related design to architecture, while William Morris related it to social theory. At the same time, Christopher Dresser, a botanist, and Owen Jones, an architect, tried to draw up vocabularies of visual ideas according to the categorizations of their particular disciplines.

The first years of the twentieth century were dominated by Functionalism in its various versions. The German Hermann Muthesius campaigned for standardization in contrast to the Belgian Henry van de Velde's theories for artistic individualism. The most profound and far-reaching declarations of a design theory for the twentieth century were made by

Walter Gropius and Le Corbusier. Both men were devotees of the machine aesthetic, and each was in his individual way influenced by the ideals of the <u>Deutsche Werkbund</u>. Le Corbusier developed a theory about the 'objets-types' (standardized objects), but it was little more than a poetic re-working of Muthesius' standardization. Although presenting them as the inevitable end to the quest for a relevant design theory for the century, Le Corbusier was, in fact, only offering subjective opinions based on his own preferred aesthetic. Many other <u>Modern Movement</u> theorists claimed to ground their thoughts in the objective discipline of engineering, but their motivation was, nevertheless, more poetic than scientific.

After the Second World War design theory developed strongly in favour of a systematic approach so as to ally design with the governing principles of mass-production and business management. A considerable amount of effort was expended to determine the rules of ergonomics, while a movement called 'design methods' attempted to systematize the creative parts of the design process so that (at least in principle) anybody bright enough to read could design a new product. This application of pseudo-rational (and always obfuscatory) thinking was a reaction against the commercial success of styling. While <u>Raymond Loewy</u> said his only conception of beauty was an upwardly rising sales curve, <u>Bruce Archer</u>, Christopher Alexander and Geoffrey Broadbent wrote unreadable tomes on systematic method.

Meanwhile, an alliance in the real world between popular culture and taste meant that design was shifting its base from Functionalism. This was noticed by <u>Peter Reyner Banham</u>, <u>Robert Venturi</u>, <u>Gillo Dorfles</u> and <u>Roland Barthes</u>, who all set out to analyse not so much the process of design, as the meaning of the object used. This entailed a much less systematic and a more intuitive approach, borrowing methods and techniques from art history, anthropology and sociology. Design theory, like design practice, has in recent years become eclectic. It is no longer concerned to advance a monolithic theory about either an aesthetic or a process, but simply aims to understand design in its social context.

The Scandinavian countries were deeply influenced by British ideas. They all had equivalent indigenous craft movements and, as in Britain, the promotion of craft ideals became a sort of statement about national values. In Finland the craft movement centred around Eliel Saarinen, in Denmark around the silversmith <u>Georg Jensen</u>, and in Sweden (which was more industrially advanced than its neighbours) around the industries of <u>Gustavsberg</u>, <u>Orrefors</u> and <u>Rörstrand</u>.

The Scandinavian interpretation of the craft ideal was, perhaps, the most genuinely successful one. These countries succeeded in forming a genuine alliance between craft practice and industrial production, at the same time evolving a democratic, modern design that respected traditional materials and production techniques, but which responded, nonetheless, to the social and economic requirements of the twentieth century.

Scandinavian furniture designers never entirely rejected wood in favour of tubular steel, nor did they do away with natural patterns or colour. Their solution was to combine the best of the old with the best of the new and to move gently and gracefully into the twentieth century.

Crafts ideals still exist today, having been artificially stimulated by the Crafts Revival of the late twentieth century. In reality craft and design can never be entirely separated: the craft ideal remains a means of moderating the loss of humanism in mass-production, while providing objective standards of quality for industrial designers to emulate. And in the early twenty-first century, when so many advanced economies are entering a post-industrial phase (and manufacturing is itself exported), distinctions between craft and design are becoming ever less rigid and less clear.

3

4

Hygiene of the optical
The romance of the machine

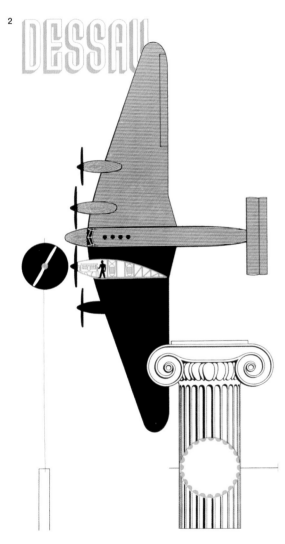

2: Brochure for Verkehrsburo, Dessau, by Joost Schmidt, 1930. Elements of classicism and modernism are mixed in this design for the transport authority in the Bauhaus' home town. Junkers aircraft were made in Dessau too, but the ionic column was included to suggest traditional culture.

1: Charles Sheeler was the outstanding painter of mechanical romanticism, abstracting machines and factories into idealized formal compositions of compelling abstract beauty. This is his 'Upper Deck' of 1929.

The taste for simplicity and for first principles in matters of design predisposed many architects and designers throughout Europe and the United States to an awareness of the machine, both as a means of achieving rational modern design (in mass-production) and as a metaphor of that achievement (when mechanistic details were adapted for everyday things).

Although the proponents of this machine style believed they represented the unalterably correct expression of the modern world, like Functionalism (with which machine romanticism is sometimes confused) the style was itself no more than an expression of a particular taste. But unlike Functionalism, which is a philosophical attitude more than 200 years old, the romance of the machine developed solely in the twentieth century. The Victorians believed that when machines were consumer products they should be disguised; the promoters of the Modern Movement believed that machines should speak for themselves (and, occasionally, for other things too). The rationale was that the visual character of any product should be determined by the internal logic of its construction and mechanism. In architecture this approach had deep-seated and strong social and aesthetic implications, in product design it was usually interpreted more in terms of symbolically effective styling.

The First World War brought about major structural changes in industrial production. The military demand for high-quality, mass-produced components created a need for standardization that after the War provided a tangible ideal for modern mass-produced consumer products. Even before the war the Deutsche Werkbund had promoted the idea of Typisierung (standardization of objects) and the architect Bruno Paul had produced Typenmobel (standardized furniture); but the most vigorous innovations came about in 1927–8 when the Deutscher Normen Ausschuss (German Standards Commission) produced proposals for the A-standard paper sizes which were used by the Reichskuratorium für Wirtschaftlichkeit (State Efficiency Board) in its programmatic introduction of standardized procedures into book-keeping.

Although the Germans had the greatest practical successes with the impulse to standardize and to tidy up, it was with a Swiss architect, Le Corbusier, that the same impulse reached its extreme. Le Corbusier was heavily influenced by his contact with German architects, but his work was to exceed theirs to an immeasurable extent in romance and poetry. To the German industrial ethic he added style, verve and wit. He made houses look like aeroplanes and ships and he analysed eighteenth-century architecture in pseudo-scientific terms so as to demonstrate that a taste for order was omnipresent in beautiful things. In his magazine, *L'Esprit nouveau*, he liked to publish cut-away drawings of stub axles, presenting a banal

component from a modern car factory as an image as worthy of contemplation and as likely to exalt as great sculpture or great painting.

Le Corbusier followed the Werkbund's austere Typisierung in looking for objects suitable as the chic French objet-type: he used the café wine glass and the Thonet chair both in his architectural interiors and in his Purist paintings. He believed that engineers were 'healthy and virile, active and useful, balanced and happy in their work', and he coined the ultimate expression of the machine-romantic sentiment when he declared that 'a house is a machine for living in'. Misquoted and taken out of context this remark brought about such abuse that Frank Lloyd Wright rejoined, 'Yes, but only insofar as the human heart is a suction pump', and Marcel Breuer added, 'and you don't want to get greasy if you lean against a wall'.

The machine aesthetic influenced fine art and art education. In Holland a group of architects and painters called De Stijl evolved a simple visual language based on primary colours and black and white horizontal and vertical (and, only later, diagonal) lines. Gerrit Rietveld's 'Red-Blue' chair of 1918 was the supreme example of this aesthetic, a rigorous language which made furniture design into a theorem: the overlapping planes of this remarkable and unlikely chair were intended as a demonstration of chair construction and as a diagram of the route of forces. Early contacts with members of the De Stijl group influenced the development of the foundation course at the Bauhaus, where students were

'The Machine Aesthetic… was… selective and classicising, one limb of the reaction against the excesses of Art Nouveau, and it came nowhere near an acceptance of machines on their own terms or for their own sakes.' Peter Reyner Banham

'All too much of the man-made is an ugly, inefficient, depressing chaos.' Dieter Rams

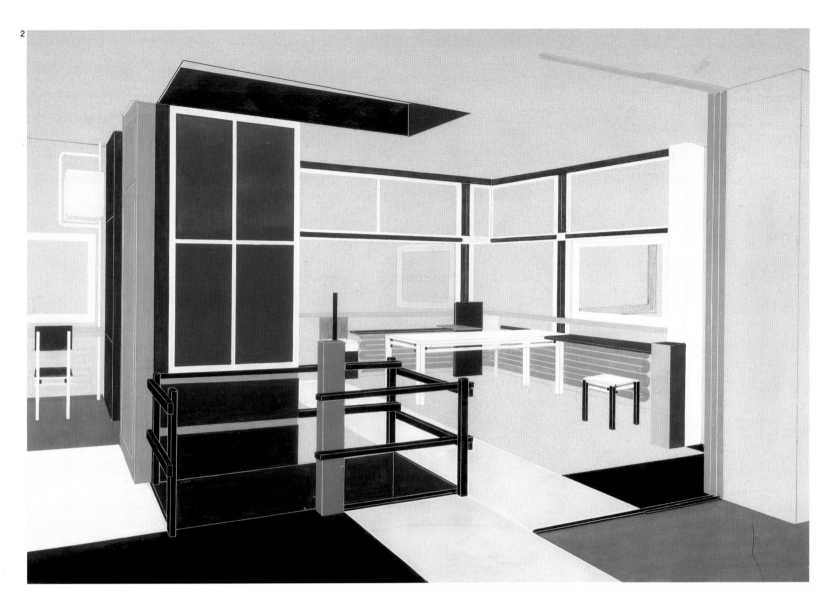

introduced to ideas about 'basic' design, to geometrical shapes which, at least in metaphorical terms, suggested the rationality of the machine. Conducted by painters such as Wassily Kandinsky and Paul Klee, and guided by the mystic pedagogue Johannes Itten, students at the Bauhaus were taught how to construct two- and three-dimensional compositions from basic geometrical units in simple, yet expressive, ways. It was these pseudo-mechanistic forms that the students later translated into objects – desk lights and kettles – which they made in the craft workshops of the Bauhaus where the philosophy of their early training was put into practice.

The taste for machine living was never fully accepted in the United States, despite the success of the 1934 'Machine Art' exhibition at New York's Museum of Modern Art. Nor was it ever fully accepted in Britain (except by local authority architects who imitated only the superficial aspects of Le Corbusier's architecture, ignoring his refinements and lacking his sophisticated cultural references). Sir Reginald Blomfield said that most modern interiors designed on the Le Corbusier model looked as though they were fit only for 'vegetarian bacteriologists'. At about the same time Heath-Robinson and K.R.G. Browne published a satire, *How To Live in a Flat*, finding tubular steel furniture the most risible of all the machine-romantics' inventions. Indeed, the tubular steel chair, derived from the technology of aircraft production, was, as both its champions and its enemies agreed,

1: The first generation of aircraft excited the admiration of designers in the Twenties, but few were the sleek machines of the artists' imagination. An exception was the Air Pullman by William B. Stout, pioneer of all-metal construction. The strict geometry of its duralumin fuselage was a real world equivalent of Bauhaus design theory.

2: Gerrit Rietveld was the leading architect of the radical Dutch group De Stijl, founded in 1917. His Schroeder House in Utrecht was built in 1923. It was a manifesto more than a realistic residential proposition, an architectural expression of Piet Mondrian's primary coloured non-objective paintings.

1: 'How To Live in a Flat' by W. Heath-Robinson and K. R. G. Browne, 1936. Humourists, including Evelyn Waugh and Heath-Robinson, often found the affectations of Modernism ridiculous. Tubular steel was only in limited respects a rational material for domestic furniture and became an easy target for lampoon. The authors suggest that if conversation at table lapses, a diversion might be found in trying to find the joins in the metalwork.

2: Marcel Breuer's 'Wassily' chair was, appropriately for so diagramatic a design, named after the abstract painter and Bauhaus teacher, Wassily Kandinsky.

3: Henry J. Kaiser's Boulder Dam, Colorado, 1936, was often illustrated in contemporary books and magazines when Modernist partisans needed a heroic illustration of the possibilities of industrial art.

'If the artist is really to function in the modern world, he must feel himself a part of it, and to have this sense of social integration he must command the instruments and materials of that world.'
Laszlo Moholy-Nagy

'The school is the servant of the workshop.'
Walter Gropius on the Bauhaus

'The Bauhaus was not an institution… it was an idea.'
Ludwig Mies van der Rohe

the most characteristic symbol of a taste for the machine… and the absurdities that sometimes arose from it.

There is a sense in which the roots of the Modern Movement can be found in neo-classicism. Not just in the way in which Le Corbusier ascribed to Blondel the same impetus that inspired him, but also in the sense that both the neo-classical architects and the designers of the Modern Movement were searching for authority. One looked for it to the past, the other looked around and saw it in the unself-conscious products of industry.

Ironically, it was some time before the machine aesthetic was actually applied to machines themselves. It first found expression in architecture (and paradoxically in some applied art industries) where the references to 'the machine' were really little more than a justification of a taste for simple, abstract forms.

After the Second World War the machine style reached its most highly developed state, especially in the products of the Frankfurt electrical company <u>Braun</u> and those of all its imitators from Britain through the United States to Japan. It fell to <u>Dieter Rams</u>, Braun's chief designer, to introduce some Bauhaus principles to the consumer. Rams believes that appliances should be discreet, 'like the good English butler', and not dominate their surroundings. Preferably, they should be black, white or grey. This refined minimalism was the starting point of the phenomenon of the 'black box' in industrial design. Successive reductions of detail created an anonymity that was, in fact, a curious reversal of the expressive principles which had originally inspired the campaigners for the machine style. Taken to its *reductio ad absurdum*, Rams's spare, angular designs showed that the machine style did not produce 'rational' consumer products, that somehow reflected the function of the machine itself, but only very stylized ones.

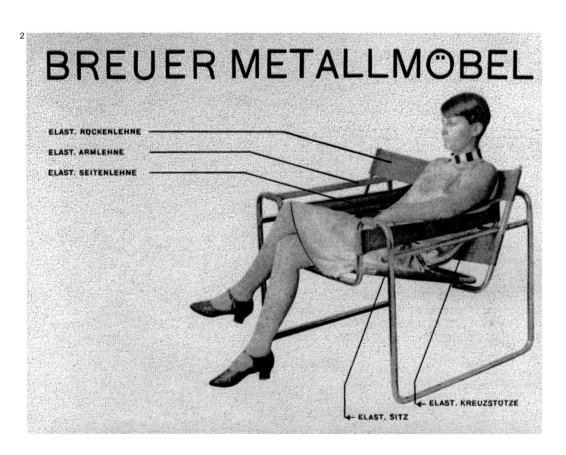

Come aboard THE 707

5

The cash value of art
America

2

The concept of design in the USA has always been somewhat different to that held in Europe. Edgar Allan Poe outlined the American attitude in an essay, 'The Philosophy of Furniture': 'We have no aristocracy of blood, and having therefore as a natural, and indeed as an inevitable thing, fashioned for ourselves an aristocracy of dollars, the display of wealth has… to take the place and perform the office of heraldic display in monarchical countries.'

Around the time of the First World War, what professional design there had been in consumer products was directed at what was imagined to be, and unself-consciously declared as, 'women's tastes'. This taste was assumed to be wantonly eclectic, decorative and superficial, but represented a significant market. When the publisher Condé Nast took over *House & Garden* in 1915 it was with the intention of showing women that the home could be just as effective an expression of self as fashion. It was these 'tastes' and this market that the first generation of professional industrial designers began to attack.

At the end of the War America began to sense some of the symbolic requirements of the new machine age. The Metropolitan Museum in New York appointed a young curator, Richard F. Bach, with a special brief to encourage 'the application of arts to manufactures and practical life', rather as Henry Cole's Museum of Practical Art had striven to do in London 60 years before. In Bach's imagination factories were to become provinces of art and imagination, the assembly lines empty canvases. By 1925 he had assembled more than a thousand examples of industrial art in the Met and arranged them to demonstrate his passionately held belief that the relevant medium of the twentieth century was not oil on canvas or sculptured marble, but mass-produced consumer goods. At a time when the department stores were filled with ugly, crude, revivalist styles – apparently reflecting 'women's tastes' and ironically looking rather like conventional museums – Bach was pleased to be able to claim that his department at the Met was beginning to look more and more like a real, modern store. A colleague of Bach's at New Jersey's Newark Museum called John Cotton Dana also sensed the spirit of the age and in an emotional appeal to businessmen, published in *Forbes* magazine in 1928, spoke of the importance of design to a lively economy and coined the memorable phrase 'the cash value of art' to describe to *Forbes*' readers what might be gained from applying design to manufacturing.

The problem that Dana was addressing was that the success of the mail-order businesses of Sears, Roebuck and others had satisfied the day-to-day material needs of the nation and the production/consumption cycle had become static. There was no growth in output so manufacturers had to compete among themselves to capture whatever was available of the consumer's disposable income. The situation worsened during the Depression; then the

'**Affluence offers the kind of
freedom I am deeply suspicious
of. It offers freedom from restraint
and virtually it is impossible to do
something without restraints.**'
Charles Eames

'**Keats wrote a few immortal lines
about a Grecian urn. Had he
known about it and felt like it, he
would have written them about an
aeroplane.**' Norman Bel Geddes

National Recovery Act stabilized prices, removing even price differential from the customer's horizon of choice. Manufacturers could now compete on appearance alone and, hence, the concept of design was introduced. 'Design' here meant determining the appearance of a product not only along aesthetic lines but with a view to stimulating sales – a characteristically American compromise between idealism and profiteering.

Soon the idea got around and American magazines frequently ran articles with headlines like 'Best Dressed Products Sell Best'. One of the pioneer designers who first established a New York studio, Henry Dreyfuss, said that design was 'the silent salesman' – he might have added that beauty was his business tool. The term 'industrial design' first appeared in around 1919, and George Nelson tartly observed what it meant in reality when he said that the first generation of American designers were business consultants who specialized in taste.

Dreyfuss was introduced to design while working with Norman Bel Geddes on the stage set of the play *The Miracle*, whose successful Broadway run in 1923 translated the protean Bel Geddes into a national celebrity. Although the theatre offered Bel Geddes a broad canvas for his liberal imagination, being the 'first American to feel the cultural surge of the twentieth century', as Arthur Pulos put it, he soon began to look for opportunities 'more akin to life' than the stage. He met the German architect Erich Mendelssohn, and his influence together with a well-thumbed copy of Le Corbusier's *Vers une architecture* introduced this first twentieth-century American to European culture – and incidentally brought an element of social responsibility into a reckless life.

Under Bel Geddes' influence, Dreyfuss set up his own design practice in 1929, but had very little work until one day in 1930, according to a well-used anecdote, a representative

1: Edward Hopper was, in the words of poet Langston Hughes, 'Riveted to reality's image.' Hopper's 'Nighthawks' of 1942 captures the tawdry reality of the American dream, yet is rich in an equivocal romanticism.

2: Henry Dreyfuss' Bell '300' telephone of 1937 was one of the most distinguished exercises in consumer design of the period. First models were made in metal, plastic was used later. Manufactured in huge numbers to meet wartime demand, the '300' became a universal symbol of American competence. It also became a classic of industrial design.

'The boundless evil caused by shoddy mass-produced goods and by the uncritical imitation of earlier styles is like a tidal wave sweeping across the world.'
Josef Hoffmann & Koloman Moser

2

'I don't remember being forced to accept compromises, but I've willingly accepted constraints.'
Charles Eames

of the Bell Telephone Company walked into his office and announced a $1,000 prize for the design of a new telephone. Somewhat influenced by the stylistic excesses of his mentor Bel Geddes, Dreyfuss tried the opposite approach and said that he believed in human engineering and that a machine should be designed from the inside out. The Bell rep took him to be insane and left, believing that such a mechanistic strategy of design would rob the telephone of the popular appeal it would need to be successful during the era when 'women's taste' was still influential. However, it was Dreyfuss' conviction that you could make a consumer product every bit as seductive if you paid attention to the details and to the performance. Working on this basis, Dreyfuss prepared a design for the Bell desk telephone that remained in all its essentials the standard American phone for the next 40 years.

Dreyfuss had become aware that to be successful in a flamboyant world he had to offer his clients a commodity more enduring than the ephemeral glitter of a tinsel styling job. He offered them human engineering, or anthropometrics, the study of human physical dimensions in relationship to the objects used on a daily basis. It is purely concerned with measurements; whether, for example, a chair is high enough or a knife handle long enough to fit the palm of the hand. Only a few designers apart from Dreyfuss have made a study of anthropometrics, most notably the Scandinavian furniture designers in the Twenties (especially Kaare Klint) and Ergonomi Design Gruppen in Sweden. In his book *Designing for People* (1955), Dreyfuss described how he used maquettes of a male and female – whom he called Joe and Josephine – to determine the functional layout of various designs, whether a control console for the Bell telephone, a tractor seat or an aeroplane seat.

The importance of human factors in design was trumpeted by Dreyfuss and his press agents in routine announcements about convenience, utility and safety in design: an example of his approach was the headlight he incorporated in his design of the Hoover upright vacuum cleaner for the benefit of the woman of taste pursuing dust in gloomy corners.

Unlike his pioneering contemporaries Raymond Loewy and Walter Dorwin Teague, Dreyfuss was never completely seduced by streamlining, the glib and facile use of the language of aerodynamics purely for the sake of appearance. The streamlined style developed into a popular automobile aesthetic, but it also penetrated the world of domestic appliances, affecting the shapes of irons, toasters and refrigerators. It became the most familiar product style of the mid-century, its dissemination aided by the popularity of plastics, which could easily be shaped into the characteristic curved and furrowed forms. But Dreyfuss did not succumb; his office was run with strict controls and a lot of probity: to ensure that a conflict of interests might never arise, he restricted his client list to a mere dozen or so major companies. Raymond Loewy did quite the opposite.

Loewy combined in one publicized and stage-managed personality the flair of Bel Geddes and the practicality of Dreyfuss (but added to the severe bone structure and muscle tissue of anthropometrics the seductive flesh of styling). As an immigrant, Loewy could see America afresh and he found the experience moving:

'There is something about a large up-to-date American plant in action that deserves the descriptive attention of some great writer. It is one of the most exciting sights in the world, and one that America alone can offer. A remarkable thing, and one that impresses me still after thirty years, is the natural elegance of the American workman… In their well-cut overalls, gauntlets and peaked caps, they look like the ambassadors of a great industrial nation… I have seen assembly line or spray booth operators that would make movie stars look like tired head waiters. They have poise and dignity. They… represent the working aristocracy of the world.'

'The reception of Gropius [at Harvard]… was like a certain stock scene from the jungle movies of that period. Bruce Cabot and Myrna Loy make a crash landing in the jungle… They are surrounded by savages… who immediately bow down and commence a strange, moaning chant. The White Gods! Come from the skies at last!' Tom Wolfe

1

With his career comes the great distinction, whether real or assumed, between styling and design. In his first major design job, in 1929 for the English reprographic machine manufacturer Sigmund Gestetner, he fused the spirit of the times with 50lbs of modelling clay and made the first piece of office equipment to rely on streamlining. Of all the pioneer consultant designers who set up their studios in New York in the late Twenties it was Loewy who realized to the fullest extent the commercial possibilities of the new trade. He also commanded fees to match. His clients all paid him retainers of between $10,000 and $60,000, plus royalties. By 1946, the year when he told the *London Times*, 'I do not ever remember designing anything purely for appearance,' Loewy had built up an enormous client list of 75 international corporations for whom his designs were grossing, he claimed, $900 million annually. He shared the attitude of the normally less business-like Bel Geddes who, in a letter to his lawyer, summed up the character of the pioneer American designers when, referring to some dealings with a client, he wrote: 'You misunderstand the point of my letter. Perhaps if I state it more briefly, you will not. Get as much money out of them as you can.'

The Thirties in America was a decade when licensed artists went out and sold themselves, and their vision of the future, to their clients. This commercial phenomenon was paralleled in a reflective way by the Museum of Modern Art in New York, which was far more interested in European than in American design.

Alfred H. Barr, the Museum's director, considered streamlining an absurdity and criticized Loewy for being highly paid and having a 'blind concern with fashion'. His response was the celebrated 'Machine Art' exhibition in 1934, organized by Philip Johnson. This exhibition was based on some rarefied assumptions about the inevitable beauty of pure engineering products derived from the books and manifestos of the machine-romantics of Europe. It made no reference to commercial, popular or industrial considerations in design, but was instead an elegant essay by an aesthete temporarily consumed by a taste for ships' propellers, ball races and gears.

The distinction implied in the exhibition between styling and design was becoming more clear. It became clearer still when Walter Gropius and Marcel Breuer arrived in New York from London and made the Museum their spiritual home. They carried with them the principles of European Modernism, firmly founded on morals and not on Mammon. It was into this atmosphere that Eliot Noyes turned up for his first job. He absorbed at first hand the Bauhaus ethic and after that he could never be satisfied with pioneer American industrial designers because he said they were 'not motivated by a high enough intent'. Then he went on to apply the Bauhaus to big business… and could never again use the word styling without wincing.

Whatever conservative feelings Europeans had about styling, America's contribution to twentieth-century design was the crucial one of allowing the professional designer to develop as an integral part of the process of making mass-produced consumer goods. The involvement became yet greater after the Second World War when European (and European-trained American) designers, men such as Eero Saarinen and Charles Eames, began designing furniture eventually put into production by Herman Miller and Knoll. There was an element of commercial realism to design that was always missing in Britain, and irrelevant to the more severe concerns of the Germans. Just as in architecture Pierre Konig on the West coast and Norman Jaffe on the east, made the severe tectonic strictures of Le Corbusier available to rich, hedonistic tastemakers, so Herman Miller and Knoll did with furniture. Americans consumerized Europe's intellectualized and politicized design and turned it into democratic luxury goods.

1: Raymond Loewy's Gestetner duplicator of 1929. The transformation of a clunky old relic into a sleek, successful modern product was the stock-in-trade of the first generation of consultant designers.
2: Walter Dorwin Teague's NCR pavilion at the New York World's Fair, 1939, was an unwitting monument to design as 'the cash value of art'. Daily attendances were rung-up on a seven storey model of NCR's new Model 100 cash register.

3: Eliot Noyes trained as an architect at Harvard. From his teachers, Walter Gropius and Marcel Breuer, he acquired a European Puritanism to complement his own New England tastes. Noyes had no time for consumerist vulgarity and was committed to reforming American design. In his New Canaan studios he kept a child's model of a car dashboard (in the style of Harley Earl) to teach staff and clients about false principles in design.

'It was the first time I had ever seen people who exuded a sense of the world.'
Niels Diffrient (born Star, Minnesota) on meeting the Knolls

In the United States design has been a fundamental part of modern business. At one extreme this degenerated into the crass commercialism of planned obsolescence. There were two views about it. To an industrial designer like Harley Earl it was one of the springs of wealth and the greatest possible stimulus to designers; he actually called it the 'dynamic economy'. Similarly enthusiastic, Brooks Stevens said, 'Our whole economy is based on planned obsolescence, and everybody who can read without moving his lips should know it by now. We make good products, we induce people to buy them, and the next year we deliberately introduce something that will make those products old-fashioned, out of date, obsolete… It isn't organized waste. It's a sound contribution to the American economy.'

But to consumer activists like Vance Packard obsolescence was a social evil, providing the opportunity for manipulation as soon as production began to outstrip demand. He identified three types of obsolescence in his book *The Waste Makers* (1960): of function, quality and desirability. The obsolescence of function was when a new product came along to do the job better, of desirability when fashion changed. Of that of quality, this was what made Willy Loman in Arthur Miller's *Death of a Salesman* says, 'Once in my life I would like to own something outright before it's broken! I just finish paying for the car and it's on its last legs. The refrigerator consumes belts like a goddam maniac. They time those things. They time them so when you've finally paid for them, they're used up…'

Manufacturers still 'life' a product, predicting how long it will last: the consequences of an economic system where durability means people out of work have still to be faced and it is not in any manufacturer's interests to design an everlasting light bulb. The problem with creating perfectly beautiful and functional objects is that there is no point in doing anything else. If the word culture contains concepts of growth and evolution, then maybe a modicum of obsolescence is a good thing.

Whatever the criticisms of American consumerism, it has enabled the designer to become a serious professional, with an efficient business-like structure to support him, and with status conferred on his work. Knoll was the first furniture manufacturer to sell its wares under designers' names, ('the Mies chair' and 'the Breuer chair'). When the cult of 'the designer' emerged in the Seventies as an important marketing tool it was the Americans who led the field.

2

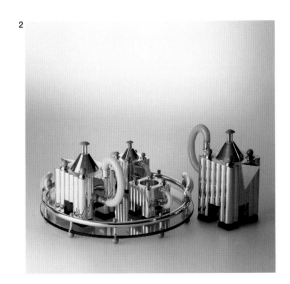

1: Dante Giacosa's Fiat Nuova Cinquecento was, with the Vespa, the perfect symbol of Italy's post-War ricostruzione: democratic mass transport, smothered in charm. It went on sale in 1957 at a pricey 465,000 lire.

2: In 1979-80 Alessi invited eleven top architects and designers to make a Post-Modern coffee service. One response was by Princeton architect Michael Graves, put into very limited production three years later.

If Britain had her industrial revolution in the middle of the eighteenth century, and gave the world an example for imitation, then Italy had its industrial revolution two centuries later and gave the world something different to imitate: the first coherent design style for consumers – a culture of design so complete in its embrace of fashion, products, cars and business equipment that Lombardy and Piedmont produced what amounted to a modern renaissance.

In terms of the international market, Italian design only emerged after 1945, during the period which the Italians call la ricostruzione. It was a period of industrial and social renovation that was a spiritual and practical rejection of the pompous absurdities of Fascism. Typical of its spirit was <u>Gio Ponti</u>'s magazine <u>*Domus*</u>, edited by the architect <u>Ernesto Rogers</u>. <u>*Domus*</u> promoted Rationalism (the Italian version of the <u>Modern Movement</u>) in architecture as the antidote to what remained of the collapsed social order. In the first edition in 1947 Ponti wrote, 'Our ideal of the good life and a level of taste and thought expressed by our homes and manner of living are all part of the same thing.' This was not indulgent philosophizing, for the mood in post-War Italy invited speculation about how best to organize life and art together. The great thing about Italy is that they have never successfully distinguished between life and art.

Although there were isolated examples of design excellence from Italy before the Second World War – <u>Marcello Nizzoli</u>'s work for <u>Olivetti</u> is one example, <u>Franco Albini</u>'s another – it is only since 1945 that it has been possible to speak of 'Italian design' and summon up an image that is universally understood. Although the post-War generation was heavily influenced by the pictures of American products, such as <u>Charles Eames</u>' chairs, and by Henry Moore's sculptures, the synthesis they created was uniquely Italian. Alberto Rosselli typified the aims of the new generation in a *Stile Industria* editorial: 'Industrial design in the United States represents one of the fruits of a free competition system in which peculiar economic and production conditions have led to a continuous market expansion… In Italy, by contrast, the true nature of design… results from a harmonic relationship between production and culture.'

Milan, and to a lesser extent Turin, enjoyed a particular set of socio-economic circumstances which nurtured the creation of this sophisticated material culture. Milan not only had an enlightened business class which was prepared to use the fruits of its industry to realize some social objectives that the Italian state was likely to ignore, but the city also produced waves of architect-designers from its Polytechnic. Moreover, 'official' culture was poor and this encouraged the development of strong architecture-based subcultures.

'I despise provincial utopia. I know that every man has his memories… Other people too have lived in particular circumstances… but there is absolutely no reason, for me or for them, to immure ourselves in defensive fortresses in which to play and replay ad nauseam the scratchy record of our singularity.'
Ettore Sottsass Jnr

Similarly, the *carrozzerie* of Turin gave form to a nation's artistic traditions and future industrial aspirations in a succession of exquisite car designs that emerged from the shops of Pininfarina and the factories of FIAT. On a visit to Italy in 1950 the American designer Walter Dorwin Teague was so taken aback by the energy displayed by the Milanese that he said, 'Since the War the artists have been frolicking like boys let out of school.'

By the late Forties Italy had developed a design style which was characterized by an elegant modification of American streamlining, found in a range of products from Nizzoli's 'Lexikon 80' typewriter to Piaggio's 'Vespa' motor scooter.

Between 1951 and 1957 Italian design became firmly institutionalized: Alberto Rosselli founded the journal Stile Industria in 1953 (it folded in 1962); the Associazione Disegno Industriale was set up in 1956; in 1954 the large department store chain La Rinascente inaugurated the Compasso d'Oro awards, following a successful in store exhibition of 1953 called 'The Aesthetics of the Product'. The idea was originally Gio Ponti's and Alberto Rosselli's. The jury for the first year included Ponti and Marco Zanuso. Awards were given to Marcello Nizzolli for his Necchi 'Bu' sewing machine, to Sottsass for the Olivetti 'Lettera', as well as to Bruno Munari for foam rubber toys and to Mario Antonio Franchi for a now forgotten automatic rifle. At the ninth, tenth and eleventh Triennales the new Italian designs were shown to the world in a stimulating atmosphere of criticism, discussion and demand.

By the Fifties the style of the Forties had been consolidated and was joined by a rich and complex furniture aesthetic which owed a debt to Surrealism and to organic sculpture.

1

1: The Lingotto factory was designed for FIAT by Matte-Trusco in 1914. It is both an audacious experiment in concrete construction (with vast uninterrupted floorplates and superlative helical ramps), but also a fine demonstration of Futurism made functional: a hymn to the dynamism of daily life. The roof features a high-speed test track, later made even more famous by Peter Collinson's cult 1969 movie *The Italian Job* (recently voted 27th most successful British film of all time).

2: Piero Fornasetti's whimsical reworking of everyday objects, including this 1984 hand-printed bicycle, was a streetwise response to Surrealism.

Certain designers became associated with specific manufacturers, producing a fertile marriage of art and industry (although Vittoriano Gregotti pointed out that, at first, as far as the companies were concerned this was more of an exercise in public relations than in enlightened sponsorship): Marcello Nizzoli continued his association with Olivetti, but also worked for Necchi, the sewing machine manufacturer; Marco Zanuso worked for furniture manufacturer Arflex; and a younger generation of designers, including Ettore Sottsass (who once said 'industry should not *buy* culture, industry should *be* culture'), established their own connections with manufacturers. The degree to which the Milanese designers identified with and showed affection for local industry even brought about a temporary split in the Italian radical establishment, with the more doctrinaire Roman Rationalists accusing the urbane Milanese of selling out to the agents of capitalism – the dispute was resolved in favour of the North.

As the designer and writer Andrea Branzi wrote, the styles of the winners of the Compasso d'Oro and of the goods shown at smart exhibitions of the Triennales filtered down through products made for all levels of Italian society:

'Even the smallest joiner's shop soon learnt how to make bar counters that looked like Gio Ponti's own designs, the smallest electric workshop soon learnt to make lamps that looked like Viganò's, and upholsterers played on armchair models that might be reminiscent of Zanuso's. This sort of indiscriminate profane looting afforded a formal renovation of the entire middle layer of Italian society. It was a style that finally replaced Fascist tinsel, and the provincial neo-classical, thus creating an opportunity to shape our first draft of a modern Italy, in a temporary but complete manner.'

During the Sixties, a chasm appeared in Italian design between chic mainstream products and the more experimental pieces created in the interests of radical design. But by the Seventies the same workshops which helped spread Italian 'high' design across the country also sustained the avant-garde furniture makers Studio Alchymia and Memphis, which emerged in the late Seventies from a background established by the radical-Pop groups Archizoom and Superstudio in the previous decade. Without the artisan-based workshop facilities that support even the big design-based manufacturers like Artemide, Kartell and

'Industry should not buy culture, industry should be culture.'
Ettore Sottsass

'One could revolutionize not only the system of upholstery, but also the structural manufacturing and formal potential.'
Ettore Sottsass

1: Ettore Sottsass, 'Beverly' console from the first Memphis collection, 1981.

2: Zanuso's 'lady' chair was given first prize at the 1951 Milan Triennale.

Flos, Memphis' extravagant ideas would have remained sketches or conversation pieces, but instead they have achieved international celebrity. For Sottsass, who once said, 'I have never made monuments for the public drama, only fragile sets for private theatre, for private meditation and solitude,' the success of Memphis was acutely ironic.

In fashion progress has been equally great. When an Emilio Pucci dress was first photographed for *Harper's Bazaar* in St Moritz in 1947, Paris was scandalized, but the centre of gravity has switched to Milan now to such an extent that when a conference was held in the spring of 1981 to discuss the setting up of a Museum of Fashion, the unchallenged assumption was that the city had become 'the unrivalled fashion capital, not just of Italy, but of the world'. And again in this there is a unique fusion of big business and design: Montecatini Edison, one of Italy's great industrial concerns, became a major shareholder in Elio Fiorucci's chain of clothes shops.

Like the radical objects of Archizoom, Fiorucci's fashion design was greatly influenced by the England of the Sixties: Mary Quant, Mr Freedom and the King's Road (or, at least, a particularly vigorous interpretation of it). Fiorucci's style was what he called 'discomoda'; he interpreted American blue jeans for Italian youth. During the early Seventies these became the most familiar symbol of the increasing domination of Italy – and in particular of Milan – over the world of fashion. The Venice-based Benetton family, with their standardized shops filled with budget knitwear in strong, sophisticated colours brought a representative of Italian design to high streets and main streets across Europe, the United States and Japan. In 1975 the Italian National Chamber of Fashion emphasized the increasing importance of ready-to-wear over haute couture by moving the nation's premiere dress show to Milan from Florence.

By the beginning of the Eighties Italian design had emerged from what now looks like a period of febrile experimentation during the Fifties and Sixties, into a position where it was perhaps the major influence in international material culture. For so long as Italy retained any capacity to manufacture advanced consumer electronics, Italian industrial designers were able to provide an appropriately advanced formal language for consumers to read. The last great typewriter, Mario Bellini's ET121 for Olivetti, was a perfect reconciliation of a century's progress in manufacturing, technology and design.

The prestige of Italian design was further enhanced by the success of the new generation of car-body studios, in particular Giorgetto Giugiaro's ItalDesign which was responsible for such important products as Volkswagen's Golf, and which has ever since been retained by manufacturers from Korea, Japan, Sweden and the United States. Giugiaro was able to provide workmanlike, well-proportioned solutions to everyday needs, often anonymously, while keeping the imagination of the global consumer alive with ever more audacious concept cars appearing at the regular motor shows in Turin, Paris, Frankfurt, Detroit and Tokyo.

The hard-edged success of these international businesses provided a backdrop for the experimentation of Studio Alchymia and its less pretentiously intellectual rival Memphis. Just when Italian design appeared to be reaching a plateau of respectability, the appearance of these two remarkable and highly provocative groups proved that the restless creative vigour apparent since the Forties, still existed. Memphis might have appeared dementedly radical, but was only possible with the support of Milan's very well-organized, middle-sized manufacturing concerns. Although the precise differences between the products and the manners of each will, to future historians, be topics providing a rich subject for debate, both really represented the same thing: evidence that within Italian industrial culture there were still all the resources, both practical and creative, for new ideas about design to flourish.

7

Ugly, inefficient, depressing chaos
Symbolism and consumer psychology

In the 200 or so years since 'design' emerged from the crafts of the pre-industrial world to its present position as a major force in all mature economies, one central phenomenon is very apparent: Sir Joshua Reynolds' certainty about standards of taste, which was being eroded 100 years after his death, has in recent times disappeared altogether.

'Good taste' and 'bad taste' are relatively modern terms. They have emerged because a plurality of values has made it necessary to distinguish what constitutes 'good' in design. The English word 'taste' derives from an old French term meaning 'to touch' or 'to feel', a sense that is preserved in the modern Italian word *tastiera*, which means 'keyboard'. The modern concept of taste seems to have originated in France, and was first taken up in England by eighteenth-century men of letters, who no longer used it only to mean sensation in the mouth but as a metaphor for judgment. In the later eighteenth century, at the time when Josiah Wedgwood was separating his wares into 'useful' pieces, and 'ornamental' ones designed in the fashionable neo-classical manner, philosophical discussion of the nature of judgment became involved with the practical business of manufacture.

In the nineteenth century many efforts were made, some perverse, some wildly optimistic, to understand and control popular taste. Henry Cole was the first man brave enough to teach about 'bad' design. Later Elsie de Wolfe introduced the term 'good taste', but her definition had more to do with status than with academic standards, for her 'good taste' denoted the choice of a style of interior design that she felt had social *cachet*. At the same time the thinkers of the Modern Movement attempted to restore the academic standards that were lost in the commercial and spiritual confusion of the Victorian age, and tried to establish precepts for design in answer to the morally loaded question, 'What is good design?' Since the Second World War, with the explosion of mass communications, taste has become a fundamental, if unspoken, issue in all design. However, the standards of taste are even more uncertain than before the Modern Movement. 'Good taste' itself is held in suspicion in some quarters, where an excess of it is regarded as being as unwelcome as careless vulgarity, and many radical designers set out deliberately to offend against traditional standards.

When Reynolds spoke of there being one standard of taste, the processes which brought about the Industrial Revolution had only just begun. Although in his day the ceramic industries of Staffordshire were using some power machines and semi-mechanized transfer printing, most manufacturers of consumer goods were using processes no different to those employed in the Middle Ages. But with the subsequent industrialization and the depopulation of the countryside, mass-production accompanied by mass-consumption has come to mean that for the first time in history every social class could be consumers. With the growth of

1: Gaetano Pesce,
'Up 5 & 6', 1969.

1: Braun electric razors, 1950, 1962, 1984: a fine demonstration of design evolution. The S50 was introduced at the Frankfurt Spring Fair, the company's first post-War product. Hans Gugelot's 'Sixtant' of 1962 showed the influence of the Hochschule für Gestaltung's principles of systematic design. Dieter Rams' 1984 model is very nearly the last possible refinement of the type.

'There are a lot of museums of the automobile, none of refrigerators.'
Patrick Le Quement

consumerism the taste for moral and critical certainties, beloved by classicists of Reynolds' colour and set by the educated minority, was lost.

In a sense, the Modern Movement can be seen as an attempt to restore that lost order. It was necessary in the struggle to clear the air for the Modernists to overstate their case, and like all overstatements their argument has been susceptible to parody, as it was in the satire of the Anglo-American designer-decorator T. H. Robsjohn-Gibbings. *Homes of the Brave* (1954) made fun of a number of Modernist darlings, including Horatio Greenough, the Victorian itinerant sculptor of Modernism, of whom Robsjohn-Gibbings wrote, 'Greenough believed that form should follow function as in nature and as in the sailing ships. Though hardly news to American shipbuilders, to American architects it was a startling idea.'

In recent years, Modernism has seen much more criticism, especially from Post-Modernists. Progress in technology has dated some of the Movement's assumptions, for 'truth to materials' makes some sense when you are dealing with elemental substances like marble or iron which have properties made familiar by tradition, but Teflon or Kevlar pose awkward questions about exactly what their natures are that designs can be 'true' to them. Although Functionalism attempted to re-establish standards of 'good form', now it is seen, as Gaetano Pesce has noted, that function 'is only one facet of the materials which men use and achieve'.

The most stimulating achievement of Post-Modernism is that it has forced a revival of interest in symbolism, an element of Western culture which the Modernists (although not Le Corbusier) overlooked in their enthusiasm to prove their point. Symbolism underwrites the majority of our attitudes to material culture: the Vitruvian tradition in architecture, for example, is based on a language of forms which identifies the Doric order with manly beauty and the Ionic with feminine charm. Even Eliot Noyes, the man who created the corporate identity for IBM, and who inherited the ethic of the Bauhaus from his teachers Walter Gropius and Marcel Breuer, actually told the company that its buildings lacked symbolic value. Without betraying any of his principles, he then went about – in Ursula McHugh's memorable expression – applying the Bauhaus to big business and turned the German Modern Movement into the style of corporate America.

Now it is possible to see that just as it was sentimental cultural provincialism that made spokesmen for the Arts and Crafts movement anti-machine, so it was a reductive fanaticism that led the Modern Movement to see machines as ends in themselves. Henry Ford said, 'A piece of machinery or anything that is made is like a book, if you can read it', and now we can see that the most successful manufacturers of consumer products have adapted their design policies to allow for symbolism. The degree to which manufacturers such as Porsche, Sony, Braun, Audi and Ford understand consumer psychology and use design as an important aspect of their marketing (as well as their production) processes is shown by the elements of metaphor in the design of their products. In producing one of the world's most desirable sports cars, Porsche is justly proud of the company's unimpeachable engineering credentials. But none of the elements in Porsche's design are dictated by functional considerations alone. Anatole Lapine, head of the studio, says that his assignment is to design a car that will still be visually interesting in 20 years' time. This is a reversal of Mies van der Rohe's celebrated remark that when it came to the appearance of things he didn't want to be interesting, he just wanted to be good. Moreover, Lapine (who was trained at General Motors) has none of the horror of styling that would have been expected of a purist of the previous generation: 'What is the difference between a stylist, a designer or a what-have-you? I don't think it's so important what we call each other, but what we do and what we have to show for it… I know just as many bad designers as I know good stylists.'

'Less is more.' Mies van der Rohe
'More for less.' Richard
Buckminster Fuller
'Less is a bore.' Robert Venturi

2: The poster to launch Sony's
Walkman in Japan in 1980
suggested how this influential
new product embraced old
and new, men and women,
east and west.

It is not only makers of exclusive products like Porsche who are aware of visual metaphor. The Japanese, manufacturers to the entire world, have produced remarkable achievements in consumer psychology: they know exactly how to make their products speak to their consumers. It is perhaps Sony more than any other manufacturer that has dangled the carrot of appearance before the consumer. Being smaller than most Japanese electronic companies, Sony has been forced to compete not only by complementing the product lines of its rivals, but by concentrating on the special language of successful consumer products. It was the first Japanese company, and the first mass-market producer anywhere, to realize how appealing the *semantics* of technology were to the customer. First of all Sony pioneered the selling of unusual new products (sometimes not containing any special technical novelty, but always employing a novel synthesis, the first clock-radio being an obvious example) and then complemented this marketing strategy with bold innovations in appearance. These innovations always evoked some technical mystique and gave a Sony product a special presence denied to other manufacturers, but which the other manufacturers soon copied. For instance, Sony provided VU-meters for the first domestic stereo tape-recorder so that a suburban drawing room might look a little bit like a studio console. At the same time the company invented the satin anodized aluminium hi-fi amplifier with its familiar array of knobs, flick switches, tumblers, levers and dials which, while fully satisfying the customer's taste for symbolism, often paid no attention whatsoever to the mechanism within.

Sony designers understood completely how to arouse the customer's desire by an artful display of textures and details, and other Japanese manufacturers have learnt the same trick. Their culture's traditional preference for miniature forms has given to cameras and other high-quality consumer durables an almost obsessive attention to tiny details, an attention extended from small to large objects when Honda interior designers were briefed to look at Nikon cameras before starting to sketch. Whether it is a car, a camera or a tape-recorder, the single element which unites all successful Japanese designs is that the customer is always flattered by being made the possessor of an optimistic, sophisticated product where minute attention to detail gives him the satisfying feeling of rubbing up against professionalism.

German product designers, more than any others, have acquired a reputation for working within the inflexible rules of function. Inheriting some of the tradition of the Bauhaus and a lot of the practice of Ulm's Hochschule für Gestaltung, the Germans have been able to maintain the widespread belief that the study of the end-use of a product and a consideration of the materials available will, as if by some semi-mystical process, reveal the perfect form of a timeless, unimprovable design.

However, the evolution of Braun electric razors over the past 30 years betrays this philosophy for what it really is, an exercise in style. Since about 1950 there have been no fundamental changes in the mechanism of the electric razor or, indeed, in the landscape of the human face, but the fact that the form of their razors has changed since then demonstrates that they, as much as any other interested group, are sensitive to subtle aspects of appearance. Dieter Rams, Braun's chief designer, has even admitted making last-minute adjustments to a razor design because the almost finished product did not achieve the effect he had in mind. He did not admit to having *styled* it, but that was what he meant. This fact that German Functionalism is a style and not an austere result of engineering is further demonstrated by the Braun ET44 electronic calculator and the Braun Pl, Al, Tl, Cl hi-fi system. Both are impressive and attractive machines but the 'functionalism' has been reduced to a stylistic language. The designer, no matter what he says, cannot claim to have studied at any very great length the engineering components within either the hi-fi or the calculator and to

1: Paul Jaray's streamlined design was given the Reichspatent No. 442111. The patent application dates from 1921–26. This photograph was taken in Berlin, 1935.

2: The 1982 Ford Sierra. Aerodynamics became part of the branding proposition when designer Uwe Bahnsen proposed the most radical Ford product ever.

'It is futile to pretend that industrial design or styling has any other function than to support marketing.' A Ford executive

have evolved from them a corresponding form to fit the function: both machines were actually made in Japan. The designers at Braun dressed them up.

There is no better case study of the increasing significance of design in corporate life during the Eighties than Ford. The Cortina brought Detroit glitz to suburban England, but within a package of European dimensions. It was a technically crude car, but an effective consumer product. And it went through interesting artistic evolutions: the fourth and last generation Cortina, a fine razor-edged conception of neat proportions and elegant standing, was, in fact, drawn by Patrick Le Quement who later at Renault became the most radical mainstream car designer of them all.

But by the Eighties, it was felt the consumer was ready for a tad more sophistication. Equally, considerations of safety and environmental responsibility had shown up in research as increasingly significant influences on consumer choice. So Ford, the biggest, crudest, most successful manufacturer of them all decided to design a car that conveyed advanced messages for the consumer to deconstruct.

Yet this goal was not a purely scientific one, susceptible to a single scientific solution, but involved emotion and intuition. The designers decided to make the body of the Sierra a semantic vehicle for announcing a new commitment to technology, design and aerodynamics, or the scientific study of how bodies pass through air. Certain superficial elements of the science passed into the repertoire of design when streamlining became fashionable during the Thirties. Streamlining applied some of the features of aerodynamic bodies to objects that were not aerodynamic, and often never could be.

The first aerodynamic car was patented in 1922 by Paul Jaray, who made revolutionary claims for the enhanced fuel economy that his efficient shape would produce. Jaray's influence was passed directly into the Porsche studio by Erwin Komenda, who had also known the work of Wunibald Kamm; but after the commercial failure of Carl Breer's Airflow design for Chrysler, aerodynamics was not taken as a serious option for popular cars for many years. Although Citroën has continuously experimented with aerodynamically efficient shapes, it was not until Ford introduced the Sierra in 1982 that a mass-market vehicle was designed with aerodynamic efficiency in mind; the Sierra's designer, Uwe Bahnsen, said, 'I believe we might even have underestimated… the willingness of the public to accept the effect of functional requirements in the aesthetic execution of a motor car.' To the more design-literate consumer, aerodynamics was known to be technically important so it gave the consumer a receipt for his investment, in Harley Earl's memorable words. In the quarter of a century since the Sierra, efficient aerodynamics have become an assumption of vehicle design.

Yet aerodynamics was itself something of a black art, as the general physics of airflow were well known, but the specific behaviour of air over a moving car was not understood. This left the designers a great deal of creative scope. From concept sketches through to clay models, aerodynamic theories were teased out but only scientifically tested after the shape had been determined on subjective, aesthetic grounds. Only when management had approved the full-scale models which the designers offered, was the car passed through a computerized bridge called a scan mill so that accurate technical drawings could be generated.

Throughout the process of modern car body design, symbolism, allusion and metaphor are the bases of management discussion. The question of how light falls on curved surfaces, and of how 'gentleness, tautness and strength', to use the Ford designer's words, might be invested in a windscreen pillar, are everyday considerations in a car design studio. The consumer learns aesthetics from car design. This is not to say that car design is art, only that it has usurped the conventional role of art.

3

'If today somebody comes to me for a new lighting fixture, we will work on it for at least two to three months. There was a time when I would have known at once what this fixture should look like. It was enough to know what the product was supposed to do and what were the production facilities and… avanti! Today I am not sure I know what to do and in what style to work… the relationship with the public which is going to use the product has grown so complex… that I simply don't know how to touch people I am not familiar with.'
Ettore Sottsass, Jnr.

3: A Monroe calculator of 1964 by Graham & Gillies, one of the last of its kind before intelligent, miniature electronics revolutionized both form and fuction.

Bob Lutz, who was chairman of Ford of Europe when the Sierra programme was going through, has spoken of the mystical component in successful car design. His words apply with equal validity to all product design: 'There's a very fine line between doing a movie that gets out there and fails and doing a movie that's *Star Wars* … and yet the celluloid's the same, the actors are the same and so is the amount spent on special effects. One film's good, the other isn't because there is that creative and psychological content in any product programme that defies a totally systematic approach.'

The design of consumer products is a partly rational, partly artistic process. BMW's superb reputation for technocratic rationalism was dramatically undermined at the beginning of the twenty-first century by the audacious, illogical and irrational *Formgebung* of Chris Bangle. Now jittery surfaces, complex curves and wilful expression of complexity have entered the mainstream of car body design.

Of course, machines should work efficiently, economically and safely; furniture should be comfortable and, if possible, inexpensive. But design is more than a matter of catering for essential needs: just as important is its aesthetic function. Frank Lloyd Wright once said he didn't care much about the essentials of life – provided that he had an adequate supply of its luxuries.

In a sense, thoughtful design is a democratic luxury, but it is a luxury that no civilized person can afford to be without. It is a form of communication that takes place without words.

In the first chapter there was a quotation from Hogarth's *Analysis of Beauty*, a book that was an early and successful attempt to discriminate about the material world. In the 200 and more years since that essay, mass-production has evolved and has been perfected, and in the course of this evolution the designer has been variously an artist, an architect, a social reformer, a mystic, an engineer, a management consultant, a public relations man and, perhaps, now a computer engineer. In this way design reflects the preoccupations of its age.

Certainly, design in the future will change in accordance with technology and social conditions, but in important respects it also remains the same as it was in Hogarth's day. Just as no form of communication has ever entirely replaced the one it succeeded (so that today we have books *and* television), so whatever new machines will come along to pose design problems, the designer will still also have to think about things for people to sit on, eat with, drink from, and so on. The designs of the past have contributed ideas about form which are a part of our language of objects, and which are the bases for solutions to these problems.

New developments in technology and in production are going to mean an enhanced role for the designer, not a diminished one. He will still have to find forms to express new ideas for objects as yet unforeseen. The example of the calculator shows just how rapidly technology can create new mass-market products: in 1957 a calculator weighed 130kg, cost more than $2,000 and was produced at an annual rate of no more than 1,200 units. By 1983 a technically superior machine weighed less than 0.02kg, cost $26 and more than 30 million were made in the year. Moreover, advancing technology is tightening the loop between the manufacturer, the retailer and the consumer. As product lifecycles become shorter, the designer is in ever more demand to interpret the products of industry for the public. As new products emerge, markets expand. Each new product and each new market needs a 'language' and in the Eighties it became well understood that it was the designer's job to provide it.

It was a decade when design achieved unprecedented prominence. But it was also the decade when, first, the IBM PC and then the Apple Mac introduced consumers to an expanding world of varied choice that made the hierarchic assumptions of rust-bucket industries with their transfer lines and five-year plans, high volumes, fixed costs and standardized products seem as archaic as bootblack or ducking stools.

All that is solid melts into air
Design since the Eighties

2

1: The 2007 iPhone. The ultimate in technological convergence and disciplined product design.

2: Karl Marx, 1818–1883. Making the case for the consumer, 1867.

Karl Marx's memorable words provide a gloss for the status of industrial design in a world where the most important commodity, gigabytes of information, is invisible.

The first edition of this book appeared in the middle of the Eighties, now known, not always derisively, as 'the design decade'. That first edition was intended as a bible for London's Design Museum, which opened in 1989. Since then an extraordinary enlargement of interest in design has not necessarily kept pace with the subject itself. The technological, cultural, financial and commercial environments have changed with unpredictable speed in the past 20 years. All the old fixed assumptions about mass-production, sales, national characteristics, desire and status have dissolved into a miasma of new media, global markets, and fragmented tribes with very long tails.

Voltaire said it is the purpose of art to improve on nature. It was the purpose of design to improve on industry. The problem is that in usage the word 'design' has recently deteriorated from signifying the meritorious to suggesting the meretricious: a rapid descent from saint to sinner, from ennobling and exalting industrial art to the silly 'designer' chair only destined to be sold at auction.

The architect Le Corbusier rightly said that design is 'intelligence made visible'. For a long time that was magnificently true, but nowadays all too often less attractive characteristics are on display when the 'designer' is at work. Attention-seeking frivolity would be an example. Once, the greatest designers gave speed and direction to a century's thoughts, creating furniture, machines and devices by which their age will be remembered. Now, too often too many designers are busy with feckless neophilia, a restless quest for novelty cynically separated from purpose or need.

There are interesting parallels from the world of fashion. It is 100 years or so since Paul Poiret virtually invented the fashion designer, casting him as an entrepreneur and a characterful creative genius. Chanel, Dior and St-Laurent were successive evolutions of the prototype. And then in the Eighties Calvin Klein, Giorgio Armani and Ralph Lauren assumed the status of the designer, but in different business circumstances. The product was not *haute-couture*, but global branding. It seems unlikely that similarly ambitious brand-building will ever happen again.

The achievement of the Eighties in democratizing fashion on an international basis undermined the integrity of design. The world of fashion is now dominated not by maestros of the catwalk, but by low-cost, immediate fashion empires. In design, the circumstances are similar. In the middle of the twentieth century great designers – whether Harley Earl, Charles Eames or Dieter Rams – laboured mightily to impose their art and their intellect

1: Jurgen Bey of Droog Design, the 'Kokon' wall-chair in PVC, 1997. This is curiously reminiscent of a medieval misericord.

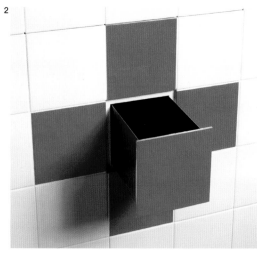

2: Peter van der Jagt, Erik-Jan Kwakkel and Arnout Visser of Droog Design: another multifunctional *objet*, a bathroom tile that is also a drawer, 1997.

onto old-fashioned, focussed industries. They aimed to improve, to invent, to beautify.

Their achievement was magisterial, impressive, influential and lasting, creating classics of design that transcend time. These were works of synoptic brilliance. But now, any product can be reverse-engineered (a polite term for 'copied') overnight in Asia. It's a vampirical process, made worse by the vagaries of dealing with global markets. 'Fashion,' says the world's most thoughtful commentator on clothing, Suzy Menkes, 'is no longer the defining badge of social acceptability.' And it is the same with design. Although design's most articulate priesthood made claims about fitness and function, so many of their assumptions were (to be honest) based in stale, pale, male ideas about status which could not always survive exposure to the global markets design so assiduously courted. Since 2001 we have been in the age of the iPod. In one sense, it is a design classic, a very slick way of packaging downloads, but it is something else as well. It shuffles not just songs, but perceptions. Alex Ross wrote in *The New Yorker*; 'A lot of younger listeners think the way the iPod thinks. They are no longer so invested in a single way of seeing the world.' A single interpretation of design may now be history.

To understand how this happened, you have to chase the idea through history. From the Italian *disegno*, meaning drawing, the word emigrated to England where it first meant 'intention'. For an object to be designed, it had to have good intentions. And with the invocation of that loaded G-word you enter the moral maze of art. Design was a sort of reform, a desire to make things tidy, more beautiful and, if at all possible, more useful as well.

There were two sources. First, the chaos of Victorian Britain, when the astonishing reach of mass-production tastelessly exceeded the aesthetic grasp of both the manufacturers and the consumers by a very unhealthy margin. This forced Henry Cole to open his 'Chamber of Horrors' to humiliate manufacturers and divert the public from error. Exhibits included a decorative stoat holding an umbrella. Second, the triumphant rise of international consumerism in the middle of the last century, when reach and grasp had the same uneasy relationship. In the first instance you got the furniture of J. H. Belter, Gothic gasoliers (so derided by Nikolaus Pevsner) and fish knives (tokens of gentility so derided by Nancy Mitford and John Betjeman). In the second, you got the 1959 Cadillac Fleetwood Eldorado Biarritz with its 390 cubic inch V-8.

In the days when 'design' suggests meretricious novelty, it is elegiac to write that it was one of the great ordering and reforming processes of the twentieth century, policing the vast multinational corporations which were created to exploit both new technologies and new consumers. In 1970 Jay Doblin could write:

'His use of the largest tool available – the factory – has been ingenious at times, but regretfully we are both benefited and victimized by its enormous output and by the accumulating of its product.'

Design was a remedy to cure these industrial ills, a road map for more enlightened consumption. This was empowering and ambitious. When Eliot Noyes told IBM's Thomas Watson, Jnr 'You would prefer neatness' he soon after tidied up a global industry, designing its products, buildings and graphics. In this way from New York to Tokyo, via Frankfurt and Milan, entire corporations were slickly packaged and neatness was imposed. To help them do this, hero designers traded in sonorous verities that were seldom tested, but often repeated. Form followed function. Problems had solutions and they were meant to be permanent. Materials possessed a truth… but this was before translucent polycarbonate (a material inclined to dissimulation). In this way, aesthetic privilege was democratized as individuals of genius imposed personal visions on

'The decisive factor is fanatical care beyond the obvious stuff.'
Jonathan Ive

'The eighteenth century Age of Reason was followed by the nineteenth century Age of Scientific Inquiry. Which exploded, in the twentieth century into the Age of Perfectability through Science and Art. It was, of course, an impossible dream.'
Ada Louise Huxtable

3: Design Museum, London, 1989. An initiative by the authors to raise the status and enhance the understanding of design.
4: Google is the ultimate rematerialized business. Since its first appearance in 1998, designer Dennis Hwang alters the company's logo to match anniversaries and significant events. Now that logos are mostly electrons, not signwriting, the application can become dynamic.

computers, furniture, appliances and cars. It was a beautiful, if illusory moment.

The great designers had their equivalents in other great reforming voices of the mid-century. Rachel Carson's *Silent Spring* (1962) began popular environmental awareness. *Unsafe at Any Speed* (1965) was <u>Ralph Nader</u>'s launch of militant consumerism. <u>Vance Packard</u> was a critique of social ambition. And Jane Jacobs' *Death and Life of Great American Cities* (1961) re-wrote the assumptions of town-planning. But this magnificent theology for consumers could not outlast the decline of the great corporations that were design's Medici. That same IBM has abandoned manufacturing and <u>General Motors</u> is technically bankrupt.

The corporations are gone, markets are fragmented. We are dematerialized and the world is flat. Anything or anybody can be anywhere else instantaneously. Centres of excellence are not Ulm, the corso Vittorio Emmanuele or New Canaan, but Guangzhou. Taste is directed not by *Domus* or *The Architectural Review*, still less the sclerotic Design Council, but by what comes through the broadband connection: unmediated, unedited, populist not elitist. The forces directing consumer culture have changed from push to pull, notably described in James Surowiecki's *The Wisdom of Crowds* (2006). The most powerful forces in the world are the organized electrons of modern communications. And they are invisible. Everyone knows that 60 gigabytes is important, but no one has a clue what they look like.

And designers, in search of meaning and justification, have turned themselves into commodities and then into brands, aping the process once applied to products, but applied now to personalities. <u>Philippe Starck</u> is better known than the manufacturers he works for. No longer the puritanical, possibly even prissy, reformer, here-today's successful designer is a breezy adventurer who may soon be as gone-tomorrow as a Cadillac's tail fins.

The celebrity designer is a problem case. Recent research in the United States showed that the share price of major corporations moved inversely to the CEO's aggregate of media appearances or newsprint namechecks. There is an absurdity in this quest for celebrity because when designers were less well-known they were more influential. And the inverse applies: Philippe Starck's visibility is huge, his influence insignificant, at least in positive terms. The same applies to the other performers in the designer circus. As a result, 'designer' has become attenuated beyond meaning. If, as is sometimes claimed, everything has been designed, then everybody can be a designer. Now, anyone who can rag-roll an old Irish pine dresser claims the title. When anything goes, so little often does. No longer is the designer helping to edit dross from the universe; he is contributing to the excess.

More than 100 years ago <u>Thorstein Veblen</u> (once described as the last man who knew everything) coined the expressions 'conspicuous consumption' and 'the pecuniary canons of taste'. And in a brilliant rhetorical flip he added 'invention is the mother of necessity'. If you can make it, you can, if you are lucky and you have effective PR representation, find some poor fool who will buy it. As a result, designers today are not telling us to prefer neatness, but are busy inventing things we do not need to buy with money we do not have to impress people we have not met.

So far from being the factory's moralizer, designers are now subverting rather than assisting the consumer. We buy things to express ourselves, but as Daniel Boorstin once mused, 'everything we do to make life more interesting, more varied, more exciting, more "fabulous", more promising, in the long run has the opposite effect.' So, while designers once chose names that sounded like Wall Street (<u>Cermayeff & Geismar</u> would be an example), today they choose names that sound more like hippy bands (Tangerine, Droog) or venues for mobile clubbing (Experimental Jetset, Rockstar Games, Timorous Beasties).

'You know a design is good when you want to lick it.' Steve Jobs, founder of Apple Computer

'I have personally found that persons who had studied painting least were the best judgers of it.' William Hogarth

2: Mazda is based in Japan, owned by Americans, and make cars at the China First Auto Works in Haikou. In twenty-first century design, all boundaries are blurred.

1: Studio Job, 'Biscuit' collection for Royal Tichelaar Makkum, Netherlands, 2006.

The invention of design assumed that objects have a character, indeed, a morality. They really do mean something. That is still a valuable, even precious, insight. Indeed, anything that is made betrays the beliefs and preoccupations of the person who made it – and they are usually passed onto the person who acquires it.

But the formal language of design has now changed to reflect more general changed circumstances. Disciplined grids seem archaic while new materials and new computer-controlled cutting techniques and advanced bonding technologies make it, quite literally, possible to make anything you can imagine. As a result, the tens of thousands of designers working at the beginning of the twenty-first century are not struggling to find an aesthetic cure for the ills of industrialization, but rather indulging in making fantastical techno-organic shapes out of photo-sensitive polymers.

The spirit of the age is anti-industrial even as its guardians exploit advanced technologies. And as an example of its uncertainties, no one knows if Thomas Heatherwick is a sculptor, an architect or a designer. Perhaps it does not matter. But while an earlier generation of designers were determined to clear clutter and mess from the world, to reform and energize industry, by 2006 the 'product designers' of Studio Job were happy to pose in a fashion shoot in Comme des Garcons jackets and Converse trainers tricked out by Junya Watanabe. Eliot Noyes posed for magazine photography as well, but he was more interested in showing journalists his house and his matching pairs of Porsches, Land-Rovers or Thunderbirds (depending on the year).

And the great business model that twentieth-century design established is no longer relevant. Pioneer industrial designers argued forcefully that there was 'a cash value of art', to use Norman Bel Geddes' expression, that artful transformations of banale objects could win sales and make beautiful profits. Nowadays, there are very few ugly products left to transform. A single rule-proving exception is Jonathan Ive's iPod. High-density data storage has been turned into an almost erotically attractive fetish by superb quality white polycarbonate and polished alloy, exciting cupidity even amongst the cynical or the sophisticated. It is perhaps an even better and certainly more optimistic monument to product design – described as *The Perfect Thing* in Steven Levy's 2006 book – than Carlo Scarpa's hauntingly elegant 1970 tomb of Giuseppe Brion and Onorina Vega at San Vito d'Altivole in the Veneto.

The alphabet, vocabulary and language of design are all changing, but the desire to invent, to beautify and to sell are fixed. The Pleasure Principle and the Profit Motive are not going away. But design is perplexing because it is so contrary. Notions of quality and utility are, ultimately, as subjective as beauty. Designers talk of solving problems, but what they really do is put the problem in a new form, as Paola Antonelli wittily put it. And that question of novelty is infuriatingly fugitive. There's a paradox at the heart of design: the designer's instinct is to improve and change things, yet he claims his own improvements and changes have lasting value.

Design is as maddening to define as it is pleasing to enjoy. E. H. Gombrich once said there is no such thing as art, only artists. Maybe you could apply that to design and designers. This book is about the very best of them.

Alvar Aalto 1898–1976

Alvar Aalto is one of the heroes of <u>Modernism</u>, but it would be wrong to see him as an austere mechanic of design: in his life and work there were strong romantic elements. In the years after 1917, when Finland gained its independence from Russia, its designers were trying to find an expression for their national identity. Alvar Aalto was an important part of this movement. During the period up to the end of the Thirties he produced his best designs, combining natural materials and romantic values.

Aalto set up an architectural office in Helsinki in 1923 and made his reputation with two public buildings, a sanatorium at Paimio (l929–33) and a library at Viipuri (1927–35). The sanatorium in particular was widely publicized throughout the world, and dramatic monochrome pictures in the *Architectural Review* and elsewhere helped establish Aalto's architecture as a symbol of the <u>International Style</u> in Finland. However, the real essence of his work is somewhat different from pure Modernism.

Although Finland had a small and vociferous <u>Functionalist</u> lobby (known as the Funkis), Aalto did not belong to it, and was never driven to any extremes: his architecture mediated between modern forms and traditional materials, and his furniture followed the same path. Nonetheless, it is significant that in so very publicly working on a sanatorium and a library, Aalto made the connection between Modernism and social purpose.

In 1927 Aalto met Otto Korhonen, the owner of the Oy Huonekalu-ja furniture factory, and while working for him on a design for the firm's stand for the 700th birthday of the town of Turku, Korhonen introduced him to the techniques of the furniture industry. They were to work together on both Paimio and Viipuri. For the sanatorium, Aalto designed a chair with a birch frame and a moulded plywood seat, reminiscent of the 'Luterma' seats produced by an Estonian company called Luther and used in tramcars and railway carriages throughout Europe and America. With his concept of a seat 'hanging' in a frame Aalto may have been influenced by <u>Marcel Breuer</u>'s metal 'Wassily' chair, although he was not attracted to tubular steel because 'the rational methods of creating this furniture style have been on the right track, but the result will be good only if rationalization is exercised in the selection of materials.'

To Aalto this meant using wood. Four designs for the sanatorium furniture were shown at the Buildings Congress for the Nordic Countries held in Helsinki in summer 1932. The high-back armchair with its complicatedly bent birchwood laminated ebonized seat was, for technical reasons, only produced in a very short run (estimated by Christie's in a 2006 London sales catalogue as perhaps no more than 25 examples). But it was frequently used in Aalto articles and promotional literature, offering through the media a convincing impression of mass-production.

For the library furniture Aalto again collaborated with Korhonen, designing a new stacking stool with legs of solid wood, bent at the top to form an attenuated 'L' shape by an ingenious new technique of sawing and gluing. The 'L' legs were fastened directly to the stool seats (which were available in a variety of materials and finishes). This 'L' leg provided a basis for a whole range of furniture, including cocktail cabinets and side chairs, which was developed between 1933 and 1935. The furniture was typical of Aalto's design in the Thirties: functional, but not utilitarian, and while the 'L' leg was a standardized component (allowing for high-volume production at low unit cost), its flexibility did not compromise either the designer's or the consumer's range of options.

1: Alvar Aalto, cantilevered armchair in bent, laminated and lacquered plywood, 1931–2.
2: Aalto's tea trolley was designed in 1936 for Artek in Helsinki. Again it uses bent, laminated plywood in a structure both practical and decorative. It has been in production continuously.
3: Eero Aarnio, 'Ball' chair, 1965.

4: The evolution of the AEG logotype from 1896 through 1900, 1907, 1908 to 1912 shows the company's increasing awareness of clarity in design. The original curlicue device was by Franz Schwechten. For the Paris exhibition of 1900 Otto Eckmann produced a new logo inspired by fashionable Art Nouveau. Peter Behrens' first logo appeared in 1907. An entirely different design appeared the following year, but by 1912 AEG's logo, based on Aldus Manutius' Venetian typeface of the quattrocento, was established and has remained essentially unchanged.

In 1934 Finmar, a business established by two British architectural critics to promote Finnish Design, showed the first exhibition of Aalto's furniture in London, at Fortnum & Mason on Piccadilly, helping establish a clear view of Aalto among the metropolitan artistic elite. This was an early example of how inspired entrepreneurialism helped fix a notion of 'design' in the public imagination. The next year Aalto met his future wife, Maire Gullichsen, and together they established Artek, a store in Helsinki that still sells Aalto furniture made by Korhonen's factory.

During the Thirties Aalto also designed glassware. The most celebrated piece was a 1936 entry in a competition organized to celebrate the Karhula Glassworks' 50th birthday. Shown in the Paris exhibition of 1937, it was first known as Eskimoerins skinnbuxa ('Eskimo's skin trousers'), but is better known now as the 'Savoy' series of vases, after the exclusive Helsinki hotel interior which Aalto designed. The asymmetrical, organic, irrational design of the glassware was a refutation of geometric formalism.

Aalto's later buildings include students' quarters at Boston's MIT (1947–9) and a Pensions Building in Helsinki (1952–7). Around 1947 he tried developing his furniture ideas of the Thirties, but none had the poetry and purity of his earlier designs. Aalto remains one of the most significant figures in the public's recognition of Modernism.
Bibliography Paul David Pearson *Alvar Aalto and the International Style* Watson-Guptill, New York, 1977; Secker & Warburg, London, 1978; Karl Flieg *Alvar Aalto* Praeger, New York, 1975; Thames & Hudson, London, 1975; Malcolm Quantrill Alvar Aalto: a critical study Secker & Warburg, London, 1982; *Alvar Aalto* exhibition catalogue, Museum of Modern Art, New York, 1997; H. Cantz *Alvar and Aino Aalto Design*, Bischofsberger, Bielefeld, 2004

Eero Aarnio born 1932

Eero Aarnio is a Finnish furniture designer, who became famous for his chairs during the Sixties. The 'Ball' (1965) and 'Gyro' (1968), both designed for Asko, were, according to the *New York Times*, 'the most comfortable forms to hold up the human body'. However, they now look like essays in period style, props from *Barbarella*. While in the Sixties Aarnio was interested in developing a new aesthetic for plastic furniture, his recent return from Finland to Germany has found him concentrating on computer models for chair design.

AEG

AEG stands for Allgemeine Elektrizitäts Gesellschaft. It grew out of DEG (the German Edison Company for Applied Electricity), formed by Emil Rathenau in 1883 after he had seen, and been impressed by, Edison's light bulb at the 'Exposition Internationale d'Electricité' in Paris in 1881. The company hired <u>Peter Behrens</u> to execute the first ever corporate identity programme. Behrens took the old logotype by the curlicues and turned AEG into one of the first modern companies, with a fully integrated and designed range of products, buildings and graphics.

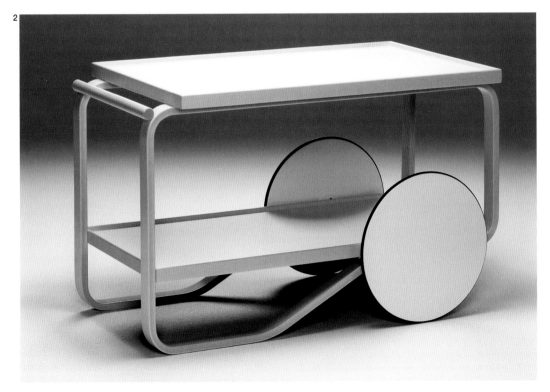

Otl Aicher 1922–91

The German graphic designer Otl Aicher studied in Munich and was involved in the planning of Ulm's Hochschule für Gestaltung, where he became a professor in 1955 and was rector 1962–4. He had already married Inge Scholl, the school's founder. At Ulm, Aicher helped develop a highly rational approach to design, which was to characterize the work of the school.

Aicher taught at Yale from 1958 and in 1972 received the commission to design the graphics for the Munich Olympic Games. His professional objective has always been to devise clear, rationalized graphics, integrating imagery with typography, and for the Munich Olympics job he designed a system of symbols which was effective but not intrusive. From 1952 to 1954 he was a consultant to Braun, and has subsequently been retained by the Dresdner Bank, Frankfurt Airport, Erco and BMW, where he has used graphics to create the public character of his clients. His name has become synonymous with the restrained, austere school of German typography. Although considered dated by some, Aicher's graphics are a monument to clarity.
Bibliography Markus Rathgeb *Otl Aicher* Phaidon, London, 2007

Josef Albers 1888–1976

Josef Albers became an art teacher after graduating from Berlin's Konigliche Kunstschule in 1915. Five years later he joined the Bauhaus and in 1923 began teaching on the Vorkurs, or foundation course, becoming a full professor in 1925. Of all the Bauhaus teachers, Albers was most concerned with the systematic investigation of visual phenomena. As well as re-organizing the glass workshop, Albers designed type and furniture, but is best known for taking Bauhaus teaching techniques and ideals to the United States. In 1933 he became head of the art department at the experimental Black Mountain College in Asheville, North Carolina. Between 1950 and 1958 he was head of the Department of Design at Yale University. He began his influential (and often copied) series of 'Homage to the Square' pictures in 1950. Apparently simple, these squares play with perceptions and were the beginning of that moment in art, continuing today, that assumes the active collaboration of the viewer. Albers's 'Squares' were both a stimulus to and a reflection of Fifties and Sixties interior design as well being significant influences on the irreverent Pop of Robert Rauschenberg and the severe minimalism of Donald Judd.
Bibliography *Albers and Moholy Nagy* exhibition catalogue, Tate Modern, London, 2006

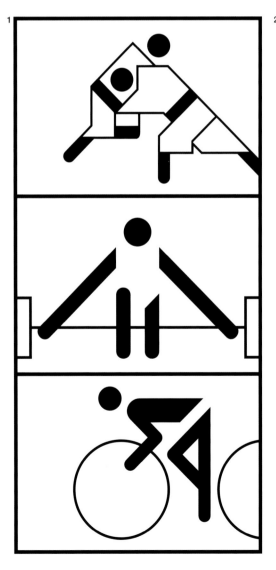

Franco Albini 1905–77

Franco Albini was born near Como, north of Milan, and graduated in architecture from Milan Polytechnic in 1929. Until the end of the Second World War he concentrated on interior and exhibition design, only later broadening his concerns to cover town-planning, architecture and product design. He was professor of architectural design at Milan Polytechnic from 1963 to 1975.

Albini was one of the first Italian rational architects to apply his skills to products. He designed a remarkable 'Mobile Radio' in 1941, with the components squeezed between glass, and a 'tensistructure' bookcase – in which the essence of the structure was tautened wires – that was frequently illustrated in Italian architectural magazines. It was after a meeting with Albini that Cassina decided to devote its corporate energies to 'innovative modern design'.

Albini's major architectural works were the La Rinascente department store in Rome and the interior of the Milan underground station (1962–3). In 1950 he won the 'Low Cost Furniture Competition' in New York. For him modern taste was 'against exceptional things, the search for novelty for novelty's sake, technical acrobatics,

unique pieces, and, on the contrary, prefers ordinary and poor materials, simple and neat technical solutions, mass-produced objects', and his own designs always employed an economy of means, their structure being an expressive part of the design.

Bibliography G.C. Argan *Franco Albini* Mini, 1962; 'Il disegno del mobile razionale in Italia 1928/1948' *Rassegna*, number 4

Don Albinson born 1915

Don Albinson studied in Sweden at the Cranbrook Academy and at Yale. He was Charles Eames's assistant and made the prototypes of many of his master's celebrated chairs. The contact with Eames also brought Albinson in touch with George Nelson. Albinson became design director of Knoll in 1964, where he stayed until 1971. He was especially skilled in production engineering, and his work at Knoll involved not only producing his own stacking chair but mainly getting other people's tricky designs – he cites Warren Plattner's 'wire stuff' – through the engineering process and into stores.

3

1: Otl Aicher, pictograms for the 1972 Munich Olympics. Aicher developed a core set of graphic elements for all the event's print and signage.
2: Josef Albers, Homage to the Square: Joy, 1964.

3: Franco Albini's apartment, Milan, 1940. Apparent here are the two elements of Albini's personal style, expressively sculptural furniture and a delightful mixture of ancient and modern.

Studio Alchymia

Studio Alchymia was founded in Milan in 1979 by the architect Alessandro Guerrero, but its moving spirit has been Alessandro Mendini, an architect who is editor of *Domus*. It was intended to function as a gallery for designers, where avant-garde prototypes could be exhibited free from industrial constraints. The name was chosen so as to confront the assumptions of Modernism: a title that was mystical and suggested magic, although Alchymia has also promoted what it called the 'banale', the design of the everyday.

Alchymia inherited both ideas and personnel, including Andrea Branzi, from the Italian radicalism of the Sixties. Its first two collections were self-consciously intellectual and given the ironic names 'Bauhaus I' and 'Bauhaus 2'; they consisted of a group of bizarre furniture pieces characterized by expressive forms and covered with plastic laminates. Since one of the original participants of the studio, Ettore Sottsass, left in 1981 to form a more commercial avant-garde group called Memphis, Studio Alchymia has become less concerned with three-dimensional design and more with sub-political radicalizing and performance art, under the increasing influence of Mendini.

Bibliography Barbara Radice *Elogio del banale* Studio Alchymia, Milan, 1980; Andrea Branzi *The Hot House: Italian New Wave Design* MIT, Cambridge, Mass., 1984

Alessi

Alessi is a firm typical in many ways of Italian culture. Family-owned, with a clear sense of its own traditions and its debt to locality (in this case Omegna on the beautiful Lago d'Orta), since 1921 it has been committed to making everyday things more agreeable. Italians have failed to make a sensible distinction between art and life and Alessi is an attractive demonstration of that. Originally focused on hand-crafted metalware for the table, during the *ricostruzione* Alessi became committed to mass-production. Carlo Alessi's inox Bombe coffee service became a period classic. In recent years Alessi has continually commissioned imaginative work from designer galacticos: Richard Sapper, Achille Castiglioni, Ettore Sottsass, Michael Graves and Philippe Starck have all contributed to its catalogue. Some see in Alessi's recent commitment to playfulness a tiresome frivolity and neophilia, but energy and enterprise remain a part of the company's commitment to providing attractive everyday goods at affordable prices.

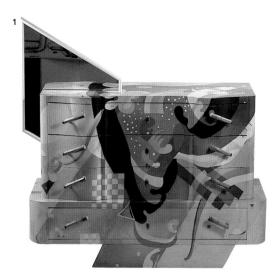

1: Alessandro Mendini, Sideboard for Juliette's House, 1978. This example of 're-design' is typical of the cavalier approach of Studio Alchymia and its ironic celebration of the everyday. Mendini found a banale second-hand sideboard in a junkshop, then decorated it in a sophisticated pattern derived from Kandinsky.

2: Carlo Alessi's original 'Bombe' coffee service, circa 1945. Used in almost every Italian caffe, this was the basis of the company's fortunes.

3: Michael Graves' bollitore had a whistle that sounded like an Amtrak train and a handle too hot to handle: Post Modern design ignored rationality.

Alfa Romeo

Henry Ford, of all people, used to raise his hat any time he saw an Alfa Romeo. This is the second largest Italian car manufacturer and has a long tradition of employing outstanding coachbuilders and designers. Unlike FIAT, which is based in Turin, Alfa Romeo's home is Milan and the city's seal is used on the manufacturer's badge. 'Alfa' stands for the Anonima Lombardi Fabbrica Automobili, which took on the engineer Niccolò Romeo in 1914 (although his name was not incorporated until after the Second World War).

Alfa Romeo gained considerable mystique from its involvement in motor-racing in the years immediately before and after the Second World War. Although the once nationalized concern has usually been in a parlous financial state for decades, its commitment to excellence in engineering and its continued patronage only of outstanding body designers, including Touring, Nuccio Bertone and Giorgetto Giugiaro, have won it a high critical reputation. Its sophisticated automotive image epitomizes the European 'sculptured' approach to car design. The 1949 6C 2500 'Villa d'Este' with body by Touring is proof, if proof were ever needed, that in the twentieth century car design easily surpassed studio sculpture in its easy transactions with physical beauty.

The company's first volume car was the Giulietta Sprint, with body by Bertone, which appeared in 1954.

It established standards for the small sports coupé that lasted a decade. Similarly, the Alfasud, which began a long-term association with Giugiaro, defined the small advanced European car for more than a decade after its introduction in 1971.

Bibliography *Sustaining Beauty – 90 years of art in engineering* exhibition catalogue, National Museum of Science and Industry, London, 2001–2002

4: 1951, Alfa-Romeo 159 Grand Prix racing car. The 1479cc straight eight had twin superchargers and produced 425hp.
5: 1949, Alfa-Romeo, 6C 2500 'Villa d'Este', with a body by Carrozzeria Touring of Milan.

Emilio Ambasz born 1943

Emilio Ambasz was born in Argentina and studied architecture at Princeton. He was curator of design at New York's Museum of Modern Art from 1970 to 1976, where in 1973 he mounted the influential exhibition 'Italy: The New Domestic Landscape'. It was the first celebration of the ongoing cult for Italian design and designers.

After leaving MoMA Ambasz became an independent industrial designer, rather as Eliot Noyes had done 30 years before. In 1977 he designed the 'Vertebra' chair with Giancarlo Piretti, which represented a radical re-think about the essential properties of and problems presented by the design of an office chair, and combined these with a pleasing aesthetic; it won a Compasso d'Oro award in 1981. His 'Osiris' low-voltage spotlight, also designed with Piretti for Erco, won a 'Designers' Choice Award for Excellence' in 1983.

Ambasz is a quixotic and mercurial figure: he finished the undergraduate course at Princeton in just one year and, at MoMA and with his own Institute of Architecture and Urban Studies, has been a strong, though independent, creative force in the New York design world.

He has summed up his view of design: 'I believe the designer's real task begins once functional and behavioural needs have been satisfied. We create objects not only because we hope to satisfy the pragmatic needs of man, but mainly because we need to satisfy the demands of our passions and imagination… The designer's milieu may have changed but the task, I believe, remains the same: to give poetic form to the pragmatic.'

'The designer's milieu may have changed but the task, I believe, remains the same: to give poetic form to the pragmatic'

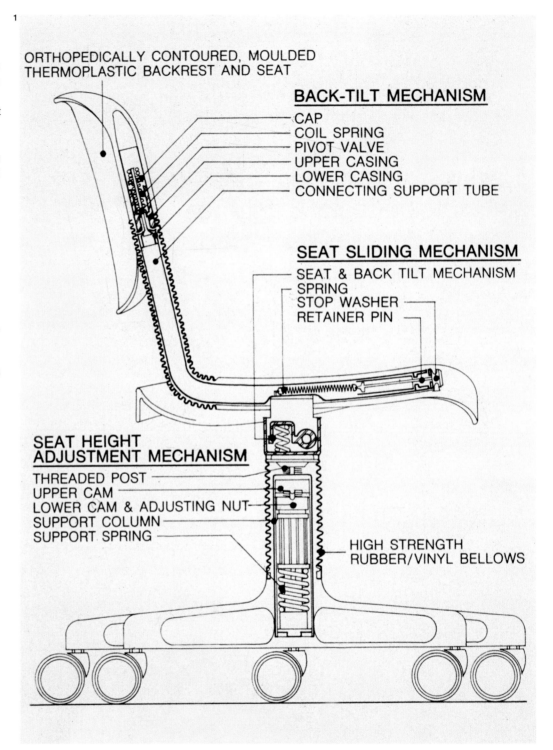

1

ORTHOPEDICALLY CONTOURED, MOULDED THERMOPLASTIC BACKREST AND SEAT

BACK-TILT MECHANISM
CAP
COIL SPRING
PIVOT VALVE
UPPER CASING
LOWER CASING
CONNECTING SUPPORT TUBE

SEAT SLIDING MECHANISM
SEAT & BACK TILT MECHANISM
SPRING
STOP WASHER
RETAINER PIN

SEAT HEIGHT ADJUSTMENT MECHANISM
THREADED POST
UPPER CAM
LOWER CAM & ADJUSTING NUT
SUPPORT COLUMN
SUPPORT SPRING

HIGH STRENGTH RUBBER/VINYL BELLOWS

Arabia

The Arabia pottery factory was founded in Finland in 1874 by the Swedish firm Rörstrand, and took its name from the Helsinki suburb where it was based. By 1916 it had broken away from Rörstrand. Although it had been producing table and kitchenware in undecorated, glazed stoneware for some time it was not until the Thirties that it began to gain an international reputation for promoting modern commercial ceramics. In 1946 Kaj Franck became chief designer, and Arabia began to produce textured stoneware in natural, earthy colours which (with its oven-to-table practicality) did much to persuade the rest of the world about the character of Scandinavian modern design. As chief designer, Franck also commissioned work from Ulla Procopé. Like Rörstrand and Gustavsberg, Arabia practises a sophisticated sort of design patronage, allowing ceramic artists studio space in its factories as well as involving them in the design and manufacture of mass-produced ware.

Bruce Archer born 1922

L. Bruce Archer has been a pioneer in England of systematic design. He was educated as a mechanical engineer and taught at London's Central School of Arts and Crafts and at Ulm's Hochschule für Gestaltung. In 1964 he published *Systematic Method for Designers*, an attempt to quantify and analyze every step in the process of design, but his method has not been widely adopted. Archer was inspired by the 1951 Festival of Britain which showed him 'I could be an artist and an engineer at one and the same time'. At one point his Design Research Department in the Royal College of Art had a staff of 30. Its bureaucracy was as systematized as its design processes, with a proper methodology (very unusual in art colleges) for student reviews. In 1984, after 25 years, the then rector Jocelyn Stevens gracelessly closed down the department.

Archigram

Formed in 1961, Archigram was a group of architects consisting of Warren Chalk (born 1927), Peter Cook (born 1936), Dennis Crompton (born 1935) and David Greene (born 1937). They married Fifties Pop with what later became known as High-Tech, in an attempt to integrate architecture with mass culture. Archigram, despite its commitment to Pop and technology, did not construct edifices, but drew imaginative, even cartoonish, Utopian essays of what might be. Their most published project was the Plug-in-City of 1965. Archigram was a major influence on Italian radical designers in the Sixties and on the Richard Rogers and Norman Foster schools in the following decades.

2

3
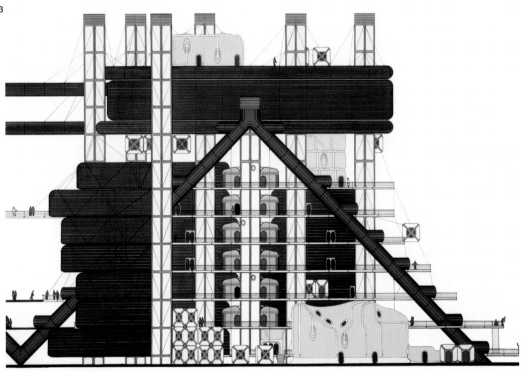

1: Emilio Ambasz, 'Vertebra' office chair, 1977.
2: Pitcher for Arabia by Heikki Orvola: Finnish purity.
3: Peter Cook of Archigram, the University Node from Plug-In-City, 1965: the influential complexity of English Pop.

Architectural Review

The *Architectural Review* is Britain's premier journal of architectural criticism. It was founded in 1896 and at the time of its first issue was remarkable in that, unlike existing popular journals such as *The Builder*, it was concerned with the creative rather than the technical aspects of building. At first, in the hands of editor Mervyn Macartney, its bias was to the classical, but around 1930 it became directly connected with the promotion of <u>Modernism</u> in Britain. It is in this respect that the *Review*'s importance to design lies: it was a very substantial influence on the history of taste through its tireless and polemical proselytizing for <u>The Modern Movement</u>. The proprietor, a reclusive man called Hubert de Cronin Hastings, was responsible for bringing in a highly distinguished range of writers to the *Review*'s pages: poet John Betjeman, oenologist Philip Morton Shand and Byzantine enthusiast Robert Byron; <u>Nikolaus Pevsner</u> was on the editorial board. Even D. H. Lawrence and Evelyn Waugh contributed articles. <u>Laszlo Moholy-Nagy</u> took photographs and did layouts, while the *Review*'s house photographers, Dell and Wainwright, used panchromatic film and red filters to make <u>International Style</u> buildings in Harrow and south London look as though they were photographed in the strong sunlight and shadows of the Mediterranean.

The *Architectural Review* continued as a campaigning journal throughout the Fifties, when its star writers included Pevsner, <u>Peter Reyner Banham</u> and Ian Nairn, but by the Sixties the formula was becoming tired and the lack of conviction throughout architecture was reflected in lacklustre and directionless features.

Bibliography David Watkin *The Rise of Architectural History* The Architectural Press, London, 1980; Eastview, New York, 1980

Archizoom

Archizoom was founded in Florence in 1966. Together with the other radical groups of architects, <u>Gruppo Strum</u>, <u>Superstudio</u> and NNN, it formed the basis for the sophisticated Italian response to <u>Pop</u>. It was greatly influenced by the English group of architectural designers <u>Archigram</u>.

Archizoom's founders included <u>Andrea Branzi</u> and <u>Paolo Deganello</u>. It promoted what they chose to call 'anti-design', and for the 1968 Milan <u>Triennale</u>, the year of the *événements* in Paris, they established a 'Centre for Eclectic Conspiracy'. Archizoom's 'Mies' chair of 1970 was typical of their work: it was uncompromisingly irreverent, both to <u>Mies van der Rohe</u>'s memory and to the nature of sitting. Upholstered Dacron was slung across a triangular, chromium-plated frame. Their aim was design that was anti-status, anti-consumer and anti-chic. Archizoom was dissolved in 1974, but was an influence on the later Italian radical furniture designers, <u>Studio Alchymia</u> and <u>Memphis</u>.

Bibliography *Italy: The New Domestic Landscape* exhibition catalogue, Museum of Modern Art, New York, 1973

1

HOUSE AT WIMBLEDON

E. C. KAUFMANN (OF TOWNDROW AND KAUFMANN) AND R. E. BENJAMIN, ARCHITECTS

The site of this house is on a corner, with streets running along its southern and western boundaries. The site is 150 ft. wide by 110 ft. long. It was decided to place the house in the far north-north-west corner—in order that the main rooms should have a southern aspect and at the same time face the bulk of the garden. The building line enforced was 40 ft. The overall depth of the house is a further 45 ft. The remaining piece of land overlooked by the kitchen only is utilized as a small kitchen garden. All trees that could be spared have been preserved and fresh trees planted in place of those removed. Illustrations 1 and 2 show the corner of the house overlooking the garden, with the double window of the lounge and the balcony over it. The front door is on the left.

127

2

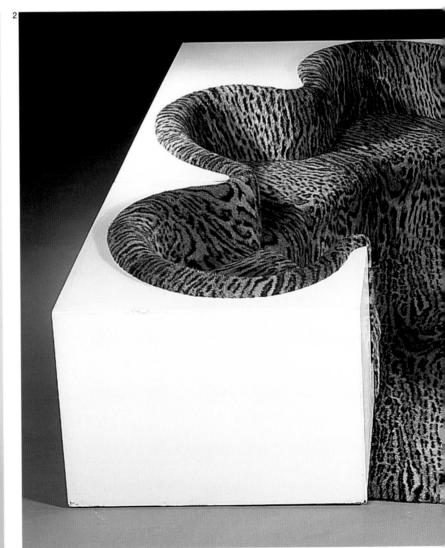

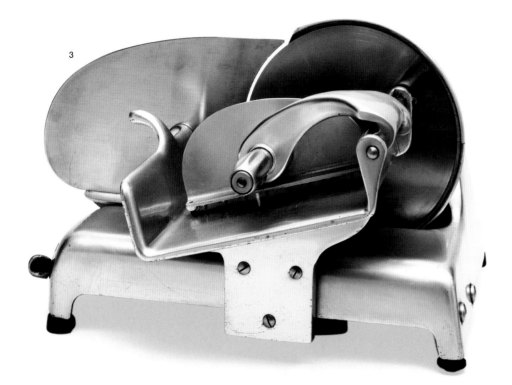

Egmont Arens 1888–1966

Egmont Arens typified the American commitment to the style of streamlining and to the marriage of design with commerce. Like the other first generation American pioneer consultant designers, he started by doing something completely different, and only became a packaging and product designer after a career in journalism. He worked for a number of short-lived firms desperate to design themselves out of the Depression. He designed several spun-aluminium saucepan sets and wrote a book, *25 Years of Progress in Package Design*.

Bibliography Arthur J. Pulos *The American Design Ethic* MIT, Cambridge, Mass., 1983

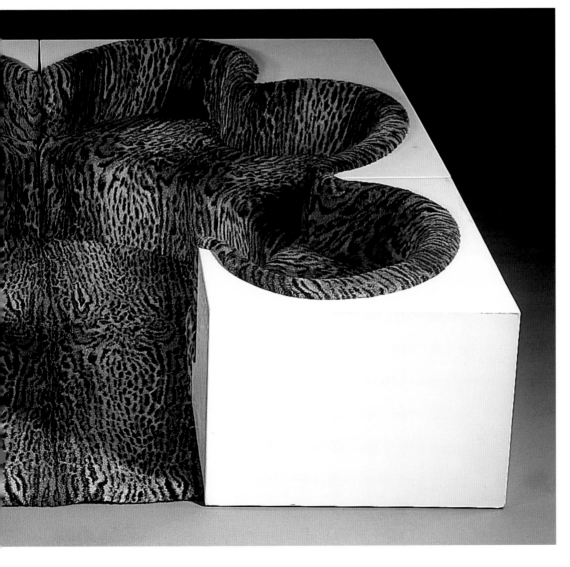

Egmont Arens typified the American commitment to the style of streamlining and to the marriage of design with commerce

1: *Architectural Review*, an English champion of Modernism and a singular influence on national taste.

2: Archizoom, 'safari' seating for Poltronova, 1968.
3: Egmont Arens, Model 410 streamlined meat slicer, circa 1940. As if kitchen equipment was going to fly!

Giorgio Armani born 1935

A fashion writer in the English newspaper *The Guardian* once claimed: 'If Chanel means the Twenties, Dior the Fifties and Quant the Sixties, Armani could come to mean the Eighties.' If this has proved true, it is because of his propagation of a casually elegant, formal-informal style in fashion, typified by his unstructured jacket, which produces a sloppy refinement that only bespoke tailoring could achieve before, and by unconventional combinations such as gilets worn over coats.

He was born in Piacenza and studied medicine, but instead of practising as a doctor, took a job as a window display artist at La Rinascente, Italy's leading chain of stores. He worked his way up to Rinascente's fashion and style department and then joined Nino Cerrutti as a designer in 1961. At Cerrutti's textile factory Armani learnt to respect materials: 'That's why today whenever I see anyone throwing away a sample of cloth, it's like cutting off my hand.' In 1970 he set up a salon of his own and started trading under his own name in 1975: 'My clothes are for women who have money. They are not for a teenager who expects novelty,' he writes. Elio Fiorucci added that they are 'over serious and not for the many who like to have fun'.

L. & C. Arnold

With Berliner Metallgewerbe and Thonet, the Arnold company was one of the pioneer manufacturers of tubular steel furniture in Germany in the Twenties.

2

Art Deco

In the histories of design which see progress as just a succession of style labels, Art Deco has, since the later Sixties, been seen as the successor to the Arts and Crafts movement and to Art Nouveau. This is to overestimate the importance of Art Deco itself and, by extension, of journalistic taxonomy.

Art Deco is not really a single style, but the name given to the fashions which dominated the decorative arts in the years between the First and Second World Wars. It is also known as Jazz Modern, and as moderne; in both incarnations it derives its force from the more philosophically severe experiments in art and design taking place at the time in such places as the Bauhaus, as well as from the contemporary influences of Cubism, Diaghilev's 'Ballet Russe' and Egyptology. But Art Deco was at the same time another phenomenon as well: much of what the sale rooms now call Art Deco is in fact not the popularization of Modernism but the decadent furniture of the French classes who consumed luxury chairs by E. J. Ruhlmann, interiors by Süe et Mare and silver by Jean Puiforcat.

The name Art Deco derived from the 'Exposition Internationale des Arts Décoratifs et Industriels Modernes', held in Paris in 1925, where the architecture was characterized for the most part by faceted forms, complex silhouettes and decorated surfaces. Art Deco is in origin a French style; it was imported en masse into a number of other countries, particularly Britain and the USA, where it can be seen, for example, in the ceramics of Clarice Cliff and in Donald Deskey's interiors for Radio City Music Hall.

Bibliography *Art Deco* exhibition catalogue, Victoria and Albert Museum, London, 2003

Art Deco is in origin a French style; it was imported en masse into other countries, particularly Britain and the USA

3

1: Giorgio Armani, 1979. Fashion becomes design then branding.
2: Oliver Hill's The Midland Hotel, Morecambe, 1933.
3: Exhibition flat above the Park Lane branch of Coutts Bank by Betty Joel.

Art Nouveau

Art Nouveau was the first twentieth-century popular style, a mass-produced and effete successor to the rustic-biased Arts and Crafts movement. The name derived from a shop, opened in Paris in 1895 by the publisher of Artistic Japan, Samuel Bing; in Italy it is called Stile Liberty, after the London shop, while in Germany and Scandinavia it is known as Jugendstil (literally, 'youth style').

Art Nouveau reached its climax in the goods and architecture on display at the Paris Exhibition of 1900. When the official English collector brought back prize selections and presented them to the South Kensington Museum, official attitude was so outraged that they were banished to the outstation at Bethnal Green on the basis that the fire screens by Emile Gallé might deprave the workers and provide, contrary to Henry Cole's wishes, inferior models for imitation. Walter Crane saw Art Nouveau as the last manifestation of the nineteenth-century interest in decoration and described it as 'a strange, decadent disease'.

The chief characteristics of Art Nouveau appeared in a curvilinear version, recognizable by a 'whiplash line' and represented in France by Hector Guimard and in Spain by Gaudì, and in a more rectilinear version represented in Britain by Charles Rennie Mackintosh and in Austria by Josef Hoffmann. Art Nouveau responded to new materials – particularly wrought iron in architecture – and was well adapted to glass, a medium in which Gallé in France and Louis Comfort Tiffany in the USA excelled. But despite the use of new materials, Art Nouveau was also the last manifestation of the interest in decoration and its sinuous shapes look like overcooked asparagus or organisms viewed through a microscope. Tendrils abound, and there is an occasional sperm-like detail. In France these tendrils were applied to everything from vases to fire stations. At its most refined, Art Nouveau approaches the elegant simplicity of Josef Hoffmann who transformed the style into a disciplined repertoire of geometric forms.

Bibliography Robert Schmutzler *Art Nouveau* Thames & Hudson, London, 1964; *Art Nouveau* exhibition catalogue, Victoria and Albert Museum, London, 2000

1: Art Nouveau (or 'Stile Liberty') stucco at Villa Ruggei, Pesaro, 1902–7.
2: Gustav Klimt, Judith II, 1901.
3: Paris Art Nouveau by Hector Guimard. Whether in private property, erotic art or public service, Art Nouveau made vegetable forms lascivious.
4: The limits of lacquered birch: Ben af Schulten, Baby chair 616 for Artek, 1965.
5: Alvar Aalto, Screen 100 for Artek, 1933–36.

Art Workers' Guild

The Art Workers' Guild is a private club founded in 1884 by five assistants working in the studios of the architect Norman Shaw, including W. R. Lethaby. They were united in the conviction that architecture was an art rather than a profession, and this was the theme of an important tract they published in 1892, intended to state their implacable opposition to the Royal Institute of British Architects.

The Art Workers' Guild was formed, in Gillian Naylor's words, to promote 'the breakdown of relations between the artist, the architect and the craftsman'. It was responsible for the Arts and Crafts Exhibition Society, which held its first exhibition at the New Gallery in Regent Street in 1888 under the presidency of Walter Crane. Like Freemasonry, there is a lot of ritual and paraphernalia attached to the mystique of being a Guildsman: the Master and his acolytes all wear ceremonial robes (designed by C. F. A. Voysey) and there used to be a virtual vow of secrecy.
Bibliography Gillian Naylor *The Arts and Crafts Movement* Studio Vista, London, 1971; MIT, Cambridge, Mass., 1971

> **The Art Workers' Guild was formed, in Gillian Naylor's words, to promote 'the breakdown of relations between the artist, the architect and the craftsman'**

4

Artek

Artek is a Helsinki furniture store set up by the architect Alvar Aalto and Maire Gullichsen in 1935.

5

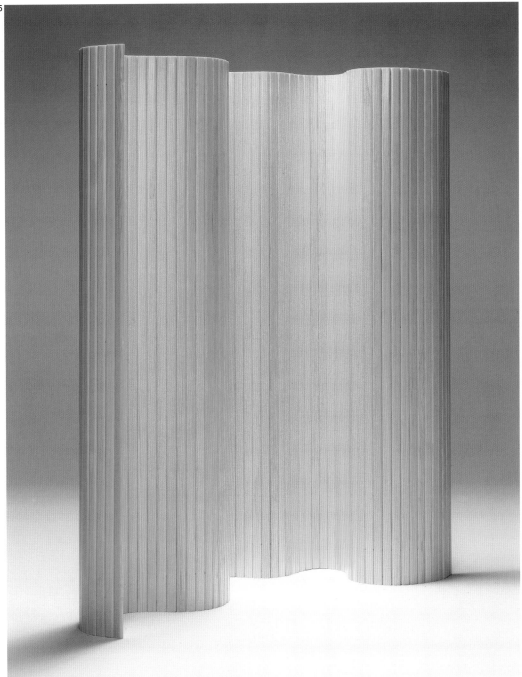

Arteluce

Arteluce is a firm in Milan, active since the Forties, which specializes in lighting. Together with some other Milanese companies, it has been an influential patron of designers during Italy's modern renaissance. Its first designer was its founder, Gino Sarfatti, who made highly expressive lighting inspired by the contemporary sculpture of Alexander Calder.

Sarfatti was born in Venice in 1912 and studied aero-naval engineering. He was continuously interested in novelty: plexiglas, neon and halogen designs followed each other. A troubled Arteluce was sold to Flos in 1974 and Sarfatti, who died in 1984, became a stamp dealer in Como.

Artemide

Artemide is a Milan furniture store and manufacturer, owned by Ernesto Gismondi, professor of rocket technology at Milan Polytechnic. It was established in 1951 and committed itself from the outset to modern design. Since then it has employed the leading product designers in Italy, including Vico Magistretti, Ettore Sottsass and Richard Sapper. Gismondi also gave financial support to Memphis.

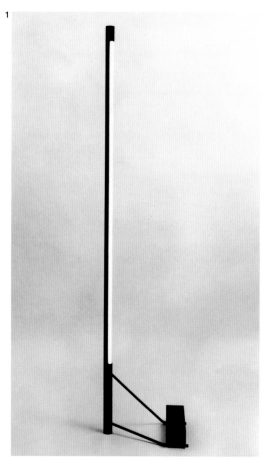

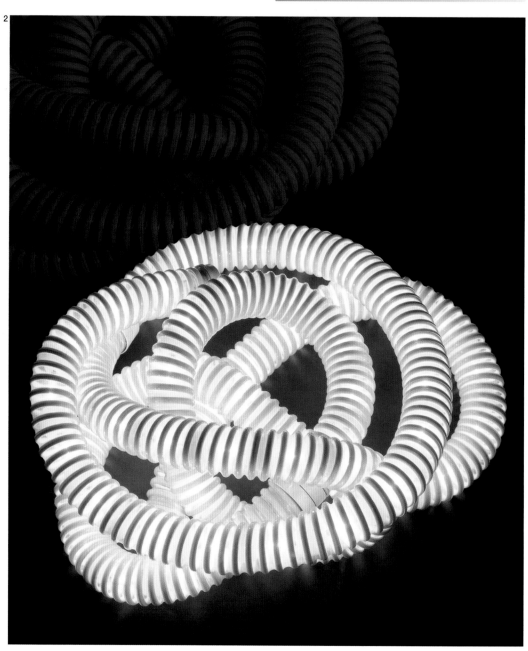

1: Gino Sarfetti, '1063' lamp in lacquered aluminium with neon tube, 1954.
2: Livio Castiglioni and Gianfranco Frattini, 'Boalum' lamp for Artemide, 1970. The 'Boalum' adapts its shape to different conditions.
3: Vico Magistretti, 'Eclisse' bedside table lamp in lacquered steel for Artemide, 1967.

4: Charles Robert Ashbee, silver loop-handled dish for The Guild of Handicraft, 1901.
5: Herbert Bayer, Aspen Institute, Aspen, Colorado, 1950. Corporate America in the form of Walter Paepcke's Container Corporation, pays homage to the Bauhaus in the Rocky Mountains.

Charles Robert Ashbee 1863–1942

Charles Robert Ashbee was one of the principal forces in the Arts and Crafts movement. The son of a bibliophile erotomaniac, in 1888, after an apprenticeship to the architect G.F. Bodley, he founded the Guild and School of Handicrafts at Toynbee Hall, moving it in 1891 to premises in the Mile End Road in London's East End. His mission, derived from reading <u>John Ruskin</u> and <u>William Morris</u>, was to teach what he called the British Working Man about the finer things in life, at least as they were understood in Chelsea. It was from there that he cycled to the Mile End Road every day, to read his British Working Men extracts from Ruskin. He would also tell them that manual labour was an exalting activity and that a revival of medieval trade practices was the best way to counter the evils of industrialization.

In 1902 he left London altogether and moved to Chipping Campden in the Cotswolds, where he established a School of Arts and Crafts, and continued to design furniture and silver in an effete variation of the style of William Morris. Here his Guild of Handicrafts satisfied the market's temporary demand for the products of 'art workers', while Ashbee himself satisfied his own demand for comradeship with sturdy British Working Men. The astonished townsfolk of Chipping Campden watched the bemused urban workers, led by a daffy intellectual, descend on their sleepy main street, taking part in a social and artistic experiment that was to become the prototype of the Crafts Revival in Britain and in America. It lasted seven years before it went bankrupt. By 1915 Ashbee had become disillusioned with handicrafts and went to Cairo University to be a lecturer in English.

Ashbee's designs themselves were derivative and not especially significant, but his Chipping Campden experiment and his writings on art and society had considerable influence, particularly in Austria, on <u>Josef Hoffmann</u> and the other designers of the <u>Wiener Werkstätte</u>, and in Germany, Scandinavia and the USA. In many ways Ashbee's importance is in giving form to Arts and Crafts principles, inspiring others to fight against the alienating aspects of industrialization and to base twentieth-century design values upon an ethical system inherited from an imaginary world of the crafts. From this complex net of ideas that lasted so briefly, Britain has inherited the country cottage cult, the attire of the artistic radical and a reinforcement of the picturesque.

Bibliography Fiona MacCarthy *The Simple Life: C.R. Ashbee in the Cotswolds*, Lund Humphries, London, 1981; Alan Crawford *C.R. Ashbee* Yale University Press, New Haven & London, 1985

Aspen

Aspen was a defunct silver-mining town in Colorado when Walter Paepcke, founder of the Container Corporation of America, decided in 1946 to develop it as a centre for civilized resort. Paepcke employed <u>Herbert Bayer</u> (who had come to the United States from the <u>Bauhaus</u> in Germany) to design the Aspen Institute for Humanistic Studies. From this base Aspen became the centre for a major international design conference, organized every year by the IDCA (International Design Conference at Aspen), which, being to the United States what the <u>Royal Society of Arts</u> is to Britain, represents the entire American design profession.

Bibliography Peter Reyner Banham *The Aspen Papers* Praeger, New York, 1974; James Sloan Allen *The Romance of Commerce and Culture* University of Chicago Press, Chicago, 1984

Aspen became the centre for a major international design conference

Gunnar Asplund 1885–1940

A Swedish architect, Gunnar Asplund first became known as a designer for room sets he designed for a 'Home' exhibition at Stockholm's Liljevalch's Gallery in 1917. They attracted attention because of their crisp blue-and-white wallpaper and curtains, simple spruce furniture and cupboards filled with Wilhelm Kåge's working man's dinner services. He was then commissioned by Gregor Paulsson to be the architectural designer of the highly influential Stockholm Exhibition of 1930 and was, therefore, responsible for helping publicize international modern architecture to an entire generation. Earlier, Asplund also designed furniture for the Nordiska Kompaniet, in which he revived neo-classicism as a decorative style. Cassina has recently reissued some of his pieces from this period.

1: Gunnar Asplund, interior for the 'Home' exhibition, Stockholm, 1917.
2: Gunnar Asplund, the main restaurant at the Stockholm exhibition of the Modern Decorative and Industrial Arts, 1930.

Sergio Asti born 1926

Sergio Asti graduated in architecture from Milan Polytechnic in 1953. Of all the Milanese designers of his generation, he has been the most independent, apparently unwilling to align himself with any particular group or theory (although he was one of the founders of the Italian Association of Industrial Designers in 1956). His designs have been predominantly for ceramic tableware and each has a strong sculptural character. He has designed light fittings for Arteluce, Artemide and Kartell and his 'Marco' glass vase for Salviati won a Compasso d'Oro award in 1962. Ettore Sottsass says that Asti's designs 'explain to you what you are doing while you are doing something; they are provisions, diagrams for your life, they disclose possibilities, they let you participate'. On the other hand, Vittorio Gregotti wrote, 'Obsession with quality has been the essence of Sergio Asti's work for 30 years…', and added that his work 'opposes the proletarian trend of the Modern Movement' and that it exemplifies 'that state of confusion which is typical of the middle class today'.
Bibliography *The World of Sergio Asti* exhibition catalogue, International Craft Center, Kyoto, 1983

3: Gae Aulenti, interior of the Gare d'Orsay, Paris 7eme, was transformed into a museum 1980–86.

Gae Aulenti born 1927

Gae Aulenti was born near Udine and graduated in architecture from Milan Polytechnic in 1954. She first worked in the neo-Liberty style, a Pop version of Art Nouveau, then as an unpaid assistant to Ernesto Rogers, and then in exhibition design on her own account until 1967, when she began to undertake the same work for Olivetti. It is as an exhibition designer that she has made the greatest impact, and her work combines a purity of line with the use of rich textured materials. She designed the Olivetti showroom in the rue Faubourg St Honoré in Paris in her first year with the company, and then, in 1969, the travelling exhibition 'Concept and Form', which showed many people the role that Olivetti has played in modern design. In 1968, 1969, 1970, 1976 and 1978 she designed stands for FIAT at the Turin Motor Show and in 1968, 1969 and 1970 at Geneva. In 1975 she designed a range of furniture for Knoll.
Bibliography *Gae Aulenti* exhibition catalogue, Padiglione d'Arte Contemporanea, Milan, 1979

4: An interior view of the Olivetti showroom in Paris, renovated by Gae Aulenti in 1967.

David Bache 1926–94

David Bache is the only British car body designer ever to have achieved international celebrity. His career as an apprentice began in Britain's industrial Midlands in the late Forties, in the context of the merger in 1949 of the Austin and Nuffield manufacturing concerns. Austin already had an Italian designer, Riccardo Burzi, on the pay-roll; he had joined the Birmingham outfit from Lancia in the Twenties. Burzi was responsible for the astonishingly extravagant Austin Atlantic and the delightfully minimal Austin A30, for which Bache designed the instrument panel. This was one of Britain's first serious small cars, making a credible rival to Issigonis' Morris Minor.

Bache joined Rover in 1954. His first cars to go into production were the cleaned-up Series II Land-Rover and the Rover P5 of 1959, known familiarly as the Three Litre. It was followed by the P6, or Rover 2000 of 1963, perhaps the most sophisticated British production car ever. Like his other designs, the P6 was invested with much symbolism, conscious and unconscious: the Citroën DS that he admired and the Ferrari that he drove both donated details.

Although this was a brilliant start, Bache's position as Britain's leading car designer was compromised by the catastrophic series of mergers that brought all the disparate manufacturing groups into a mismatched, muddle-headed and under-financed assemblage called British Leyland. This merger meant that 126 separate product lines from Austin, Morris, Rover, Triumph and Jaguar had to be rationalized and some brilliant designs by Bache and his engineering partner Spen King were casualties. Two lost designs included the P8, a 4.4 litre V8 saloon, and the P9, a re-energized sports car that was judged to be superior to the Porsche 911. However, Bache produced two designs in the autumn of Britain's motor industry which were excellent by even the most severe competitive standards: the Range Rover of 1970 and the P10, or Rover SDI, of 1975. In any other country Bache would be a national hero, but in Britain his name is scarcely known. Besides the much-admired products which went into production, Bache can claim impressive innovation in many details of car design, including instrument logic and aerodynamics.

M.H. Baillie Scott 1865–1945

Mackay Hugh Baillie Scott was an English architect of the Arts and Crafts movement whose work became well known in Germany and Austria after he built a palace for the Grand Duke of Hesse at Darmstadt in 1898 and furnished it with furniture made to his own designs by the Guild of Handicrafts. From the Künstlerkolonie (artists' colony) the influence of Baillie Scott's monumental yet folksy style spread across the German-speaking world at a time when English art and the English gentleman were idols revered by the Continental avant-garde. One further influence of Baillie Scott's work in Europe was the publication in two volumes of the drawings for a competition organized by the magazine *Innen-Dekoration* called *Haus eines Kunstfreundes* (A House of an Art Lover) in a series edited by Hermann Muthesius.

However, in spite of his strong influence abroad, his individual designs were unremarkable. His main contribution to the history of style was to legitimize the English domestic villa.

Bibliography James D. Kornwulf *M. H. Baillie Scott and the Arts and Crafts* Johns Hopkins University Press, Baltimore, 1971

Bakelite

Bakelite was one of the first-generation plastics, invented by a Belgian-American chemist called Leo Henricus Baekeland (1863–1944) in 1907. 'Bakelit' was the German form of his family name.

Used at first only in electrical engineering, Bakelite soon began to appear in consumer products. In the Thirties its malleable properties were ideal for designers looking for new materials to give dramatic presence to the first generation of self-consciously 'designed' consumer products. With Bakelite rapid variation was possible, and it facilitated the production of many new shapes. Without its technical properties, <u>Jean Heiberg</u>'s telephone and <u>Wells Coates</u>' radio would not have been possible. Bakelite was also significant in that it was used to make luxury items, such as bangles and cigarette cases that had hitherto been made out of ebony or ivory, available in vast numbers for the mass market.

Bibliography *Bakeliet, techniek, vormgeving, gebruik* exhibition catalogue, Boymans-van Beuningen Museum, Rotterdam, 1981; Sylvia Katz *Plastics* Studio Vista, London, 1978

1: David Bache's 1963 Rover 2000 was the first car with an ergonomic interior.
2: M.H. Baillie-Scott, Waterlow Court, Hampstead Garden Suburb, London, 1910.

3: Ekco SH25 console wireless in bakelite, by J.K. White, 1931–2.
4: A 1951 Time-Life shoot of Balenciaga evening dresses, inspired by Toulouse-Lautrec.

3

Cristobal Balenciaga 1895–1972

Cristobal Balenciaga was a Basque who opened a couture house in Paris in 1936, after tailoring in San Sebastian and Madrid. He soon established a reputation there for his 'demanding' clothes of supreme cut and elegance. In his personal and his business affairs Balenciaga brought *hauteur* to new heights. He was indifferent to the press, to certain potential customers who did not reach his standards of perfection, and to the protocol of the Paris fashion season, but his clothes transcended criticism. They had a strong Spanish influence, evident in the use of lace, satins and brocades, and in shapes reminiscent of a bull-fighter's cape. Balenciaga was also entirely indifferent to fashions in fashion and created gowns that have a timeless artistry; his colour sense was strong, and he frequently used reds, rich browns, turquoises and black. In 1957 he introduced the 'sack' dress, prefiguring fashions of the Sixties. He retired in 1968.

4

Chris Bangle born 1955

Chris Bangle was born in Wausau, Wisconsin. He studied liberal arts at the University of Wisconsin and car design at the Art Center, Pasadena. Bangle read about the latter on the box of a plastic model car kit. At first he was tempted to work for <u>Disney</u>, but instead joined <u>General Motors</u>' German subsidiary, Opel. Bangle then went to <u>FIAT</u>. In Turin he produced the strange Coupe Fiat, which announced his preference for irrational expressionistic details and curious shapes and radii: he claims a woman's bottom inspired the cleft on the Fiat's headlamp lens. The car's ludic shape may betray a lasting influence of cartoons. At <u>BMW</u> in Munich Bangle has controversially revolutionized a design inheritance that had its origins in <u>Bauhaus</u> severity. He cites Monet and Cezanne as influences and says of his favourite architect: 'When you go into (Frank Lloyd) <u>Wright</u>'s studio, you want to go down on your knees because you are in the presence of a God.'

1

1: Under Chris Bangle, BMW has shown ever more radical concept cars at international motor shows.

2: Before the ur-Leica photographic negatives were the same size as prints, but Oskar Barnack's use of miniature 35mm film created the concept of enlargement. The compact size of successive Leicas made photo-journalism possible.
3: Alfred H. Barr, 'Cubism and Abstract Art' exhibition catalogue, Museum of Modern Art, New York, 1936. MoMA presents itself as the epicentre of modern art.

Peter Reyner Banham 1920–88

With <u>Sigfried Giedion</u> and <u>Nikolaus Pevsner</u>, Peter Reyner Banham was the most important twentieth-century writer on design.

Before the war he served an apprenticeship with the Bristol Aeroplane Company, where he gained a familiarity with technical objects that has seen him through many a tortuous metaphor. Banham became a staff writer on the <u>*Architectural Review*</u> during the Fifties and in successive milestone articles rethought the entire history of <u>Modernism</u> from first principles. These same articles were published in 1960 as *Theory and Design in the First Machine Age*, which was also the subject of his doctoral dissertation. Although Banham has no sympathy with <u>Post-Modernism</u>, his book was the first to undermine the credentials of <u>Functionalism</u>. Banham was associated with the founding of <u>Pop</u> at London's Institute of Contemporary Arts in 1956, and all his subsequent articles have explored various themes concerned with everyday architecture and design, in particular expendability and symbolism.

Banham can be said to have inaugurated the serious study of design and popular culture in Britain. In the late Seventies he moved to the United States.

Bibliography Peter Reyner Banham *Design By Choice* Rizzoli, New York, 1981; Academy Editions, London, 1982

Oscar Barnack 1879–1936

Oscar Barnack was the designer of the first effective 35mm camera. Put into production by Leitz, it became known as the Leica (Leitz camera). The prototype appeared in 1913, the production model 12 years later. Using film in a rigid cassette, it was light and portable. Max Berck's 'Elmar' lenses made it optically superb, and all subsequent developments in photography depended on the standard he established. In the design of the camera, Barnack made no concessions to aesthetics, but his scrupulous attention to detail and his engineer's reluctance to indulge in meretricious ornament made the Leica a symbol of the Machine Age. Furthermore, the camera's ingenuity and precision construction made it the model for all cameras of its type.

2

Barnsley Brothers

Sidney (1865–1926) and Ernest (1863–1926) Barnsley were craftsmen-designers of furniture who set up a Cotswold workshop with <u>Ernest Gimson</u> in 1895. They represented the most vernacular end of the British Arts and Crafts movement, self-consciously using traditional materials, techniques and furniture types in their work.

Alfred H. Barr 1902–81

Alfred H. Barr was born in Detroit, the son of a Presbyterian minister. As director of New York's <u>Museum of Modern Art</u> from 1929 to 1943 he played an important role in the drama of unveiling European modern art and design to the American people. He set up the architecture and design department in 1932 (split, in 1940, into its two halves). It was Barr who was chiefly responsible for MoMA's 'Machine Art' exhibition of 1934 (see page 42), which looked at the design of anonymous machine parts, and he was behind the movement towards collecting and exhibiting 'good design' for which the museum was known in the Forties and Fifties. Under Barr the museum also put on two other highly important shows. He gave <u>Philip Johnson</u> the chance to introduce European modern architecture to America with the 'International Style' show in 1932, whose title is the origin of the label; and

in 1940 <u>Eliot Noyes</u> organized the exhibition 'Organic Design in Home Furnishings', with chairs by <u>Charles Eames</u> and <u>Eero Saarinen</u> that have since become classics (see page 320).

Greeted in the American press as 'that whorehouse on 53rd Street', Barr's museum became vital in introducing new art to a stratum of American society. But with its evolution into a sleek Manhattan institution with its rites of fundraising and its curatorial solemnities, modern art, or MoMA's version of it, became stultified. It is, as many observers noted, impossible for something founded by Rockefellers to be radical.

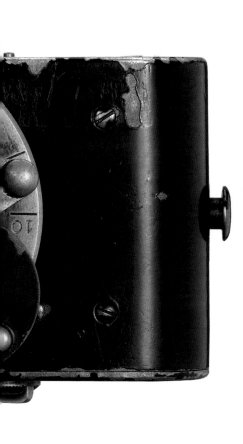

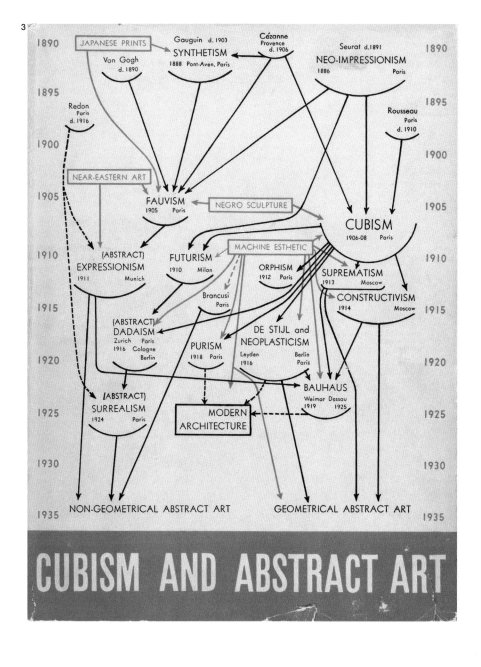

Roland Barthes 1915–80

Roland Barthes was born in Cherbourg in 1915 and became France's most successful intellectual. He interrogated the everyday world, moving from formal literary criticism to writing brilliantly on the meaning of things, for example steak and chips, the Tour de France and, most memorably, the new Citroën. For Barthes, dealing with a text or an object was an erotic transaction: reading was 'jouissance', a word which means both joy and 'coming' in the sexual sense. To experience this enjoyable sense of escape, Barthes argued, you need to get in deeper.

He began writing in 1947 in Albert Camus' little magazine *Combat*, essays subsequently published in 1953 as *Le Degre Zero de l'ecriture*. 'Degre Zero' may be translated as bottom line. This quest for the essence preoccupied Barthes. When later he wrote about 'Etat Zero' he meant neutrality and to Barthes there could never be such a thing. In the modern world everything has meaning and it is the critic's job to chase down that fugitive essence and explain it to the public.

The French intellectual tradition made this revolution in perception possible. In the late Twenties the historians Marc Bloch and Lucien Febvre declared that real history should not concern the battles and the politicians (which they called '*L'histoire evenementielle*'), but should be concerned with large patterns of behaviour ('*la longue durée*') and with the passions and beliefs of individuals ('*mentalites*'). This led to various histories of private life and studies of the mundane; of these Barthes became a consummate master through his refinement of Structuralism, an approach to the world that combines the methodologies of literary criticism, anthropology, linguistics and Freud. The most important aspect of Structuralism is semiotics, the study of signs, a specialism Barthes made his own. Edmund Leach explained semiotics when he wrote:

'Any human creative act starts as a mental operation which is then projected onto the external world… The mental operations of any human designer are circumscribed not only by the qualities of his material and his objectives, but by the design of the human brain itself.'

Mythologies, 1957, was his affectionate satire of bourgeois taste, a selection of sly ruminations that turned him into a public figure. In London we had kitchen sink drama, in Paris they had kitchen sink analysis. The most significant essay in *Mythologies* was about a car. The introduction of the radical new Citroën DS19 at the Paris Salon de l'Automobile in 1955 had caused a significant media flurry. So keen was Citroën to demonstrate the sensational sculpture of this astonishing vehicle that it was originally shown on a pylon, without wheels lest the rude intrusion of tyres compromise the public's pure aesthetic response to its divine shape. In French 'DS' sounds like the word for 'goddess' and this happy accident put Barthes into a mood of mock piety. No one has ever explained the significance of industrial design better than Barthes in this bravura opening sentence:

'I think that cars today are almost the exact equivalent of the great Gothic cathedrals: I mean the supreme creation of an era, conceived with passion by unknown artists, and consumed in image if not in usage by a whole population which appropriates them as a purely magical object.'

Here we have the essential elements of Barthes' approach to his material. There is a sensuality in the writing, but there is also something contrarian. Like Flaubert, Barthes detested '*l'opinion courante*'. He said current opinion was like Medusa: if you acknowledged it, you became petrified. So, instead, with the '*puissance de subversion*' he set about debunking it. But he was not hostile: his instincts were celebratory, not combative.

Through Roland Barthes, the structuralist view of the world has passed effortlessly into the mainstream of modern thought, so much so that it is difficult to appreciate now the freshness of his insights. But there are discrepancies in Barthes. As one who set out to clarify the designed world, he ended up obfuscating it. For instance, writing of voile and muslin in his 1967 book *The Fashion System*:

'Formally, the assertion of species is simply a binary opposition of the type a/(A-a); strictly speaking therefore, the genus is not a paradigm of various species, but only the grouping which limits the substantial possibilities of opposition.'

Selective quotation does Barthes no favours. His best books are the suggestive essays, not the theoretical postulates. He was a master of generalization. (Later he admitted he only wrote *The Fashion System* for money).

Was Roland Barthes a bit of a fraud or one of the most original thinkers of the twentieth century? It plays both ways. His semiotic analysis of a *ballon de rouge* included finger-wagging digressions into third world debt and why the Algerians would be better off with cash crops other than vines. Meanwhile, he ordered soft-boiled eggs, sausages and bordeaux at Café Flore. He admitted early in his career:

'What I claim is to live to the full the contradictions of my time, which may well make sarcasm the condition of truth.'

1

Re-read Barthes now and you realize that there was no great methodology, no great Theory with a capital 'T'. Rather, he makes his point through cumulative aphorism and shrewd observation. His great feat? To make us take ordinary things seriously. As Professor Morris Zapp says in David Lodge's academic satire *Small World* : 'I'm a bit of a deconstructionist myself.'

With his uniquely intelligent vision, Barthes helped us to read the world.

Bibliography *Mythologies Editions du Seuil*, Paris, 1957; *Elements de semiologie* Denoel, Paris, 1965; *Systeme de la Mode Editions du Seuil*, Paris, 1967: *L'Empire des signes Skira*, Geneva, 1970: *Roland Barthes* exhibition catalogue, Centre Pompidou, Paris, 2002

Saul Bass 1920–96

American graphic designer and film-maker Saul Bass was born in New York, but ran his office in Los Angeles. Bass brought 'art' into film credits which, before his innovations with *Carmen Jones* and *The Man with the Golden Arm*, each employing adventurous graphics, had been nothing more than banal, processional lists done by lettering artists. For *Around the World in Eighty Days* and *West Side Story* Bass made the credits into animated or live-action features in their own right.

For blue-chip America, Bass assembled an impressive range of logotypes whose crisp, clean lines say more attractive things about the corporations than mere facts ever can. He did the bell for 'Ma Bell' (AT&T); for the Aluminum Corporation of America he produced a clean logo with a novel typeface which had curves like those of an extruded aluminium beer can; he produced a scientific, optical and oriental look for Minolta, curlicues for Celanese and Lawry's, and the blobby W for Warner Communications. But it has been for airlines that his work has achieved its most singular handwriting: Continental, United and Frontier all have Saul Bass colour schemes and logos to unite them in appearances of freshness, efficiency and credibility. When asked what he'd do with a free year, Bass replied 'create projects with terrible deadlines'. His *curriculum vitae* looked like the Fortune 500 and the Academy Awards of 1963; he was a very professional designer.

Bibliography *Saul Bass* exhibition catalogue, Design Museum, London, 2004

1

1: Saul Bass, titles for *The Man With the Golden Arm*, 1955 and *Vertigo*, 1958, and corporate identity for United Airlines, 1974. The movie screen and an aircraft's rudder provide highly visible, but extremely restricted, scope for graphic creativity.

Bauhaus

The first director of the most influential art school ever, the architect Mies van der Rohe, said 'The Bauhaus was not a school, it was an idea.'

'Bauhaus' is an untranslatable word, coined by Walter Gropius, which combines the root of the German verb *bauen*, to build, with *Haus*, house. It is the name given to an art school founded by Gropius under the original title of the Staatliches Bauhaus Weimar, when he combined the Grossherzogliche Sächsische Kunstgewerbeschule and Grossherzogliche Sächsische Hochschule für Bildende Kunst.

Yet for all its influence and reputation, the Bauhaus is the most misunderstood of all 'schools' in modern art and design. There are two views about it. Tom Wolfe satirized its legacy in his book *From Bauhaus to Our House* (1981) when he deplored the prevalence of its influence on modern architecture, saying, 'Every child goes to school in a building that looks like a duplicating-machine replacement-parts wholesale distribution warehouse.'

On the other hand, Joseph Hudnut of Harvard University wrote of the Bauhaus masters in his introduction to *The New Architecture and the Bauhaus* (1936), 'In the clarity and truth of the intentions which guided them they transcend any similar enterprise.' More recently, the historian Andrew Saint called the Bauhaus a 'superhuman achievement'.

The psychology of the Bauhaus was founded in the reform movements in politics and art education that were a product of defeat in the First World War. The Treaty of Versailles had impoverished and humiliated Germany and there was a widespread feeling that a new start was

necessary. In 1919 German industrial production was less than half of what it had been six years before. Inflation was out of control and revolution was in the air. An Arbeitsrat for Kunst was set up, inspired by Soviet methods. The young architect Marcel Breuer said, 'It was very exciting. But to have such excitement you must be in a country that has just lost a war, where money has no value, where you do not know whether you will eat the next day.'

Walter Gropius's response was to create 'the crystal symbol of a new faith', but the first Bauhaus manifesto did not use a factory as a symbol, but instead used an Expressionist woodcut of a medieval cathedral. Both in the breach and observation, the Bauhaus sets the standard for modern architecture, art and design, yet its intellectual origins lay with the Arts and Crafts (as well as with the distinctly German traditions of Biedermeier and neo-classicism). Its early years, before Gropius moved the school to his purpose-designed building in Dessau, when it became known simply as the Bauhaus, were dominated by Expressionist art, thought and behaviour.

Under Gropius, the Bauhaus became an art school of immense creativity and influence. The curriculum was a broadly based foundation year, followed by craft specializations. Gropius injected a medieval flavour, calling staff 'masters' and 'journeymen'. His approach to design was to stress aesthetic fundamentals and strive for geometrically pure forms, but unlike the practitioners of the Arts and Crafts he did not disdain machines, in fact he actually encouraged their use to achieve economy. Before the Bauhaus, art teaching had been little more than organized sketching, painting and sculpting, but

Gropius's Bauhaus saw art education as no less than a training for life. With the same mentality that gave the world DIN industry standards, Gropius made art education systematic. The Vorkurs, or foundation course, was established in 1920 and led by Johannes Itten. Its proposition is now so familiar that it is hard to appreciate its revolutionary character. It proposed 'learning by doing', rather than by drawing plaster casts of antique statues.

What this meant in practice was that students would analyse old newspapers, feathers and string and learn from them. This training of the senses goes back to Jean-Jacques Rousseau, and through Johann Heinrich Pestalozzi's *ABC der Anschauung* (1803) became established in German education. This fed into Friedrich Froebel's Kindergarten movement. One of Walter Gropius's first architectural projects at the Bauhaus was a building that appeared to be made out of Froebel blocks.

For all its influence and reputation, the Bauhaus is the most misunderstood of all 'schools' in modern art and design

Gropius hired some of the greatest painters, graphic designers, thinkers and architects of his day, and a roll-call of his staff looks like an index to a comprehensive volume on twentieth-century art and design, including Wassily Kandinsky, Johannes Itten and Paul Klee The building itself was a remarkable monument in its own right, and a vindication of Gropius's educational philosophy: its entire fittings and decorations were produced by staff and students of the school.

Yet, despite its prestige and its reputation, the immediate achievements of the Bauhaus were slight, and throughout its entire 14-year life it had a mere 1250 students and only 35 full-time staff. Although it was at the Bauhaus that Marcel Breuer and Mies van der Rohe established some of the canons of modern furniture design in their experiments with tubular steel, very little of the art-into-industry process which Gropius promulgated

was actually achieved there, and most of the production of the school's workshops was, in fact, crafts based. Perhaps sensing the irony and futility of his mission, at least in Europe, Gropius resigned in 1928, leaving the direction of the school to the Swiss Marxist architect Hannes Meyer. Meyer's politics alienated the school from the local government, whose ruling Social Democrat party dismissed him to placate conservative opposition. Meyer was replaced by Mies van der Rohe, who moved the school into a disused telephone factory in Berlin until it closed under the Nazis in 1933. The Bauhaus belief that 'Dead styles have been destroyed; and we are returning to honesty of thought and feeling' was clearly unacceptable to the NSDAP.

In a sense, the greatest effect of the Bauhaus was in America, where Gropius realized some of his finest buildings, and where, as professor of architecture at Harvard University, his teaching influenced an entire generation of students with ideas that fascism had driven out of Europe. These included Eliot Noyes, whose vast corporate identity programmes for IBM and Mobil were the most complete expression of the Bauhaus aesthetic. Similarly, Mies van der Rohe and Laszlo Moholy-Nagy settled in Chicago, one establishing the New Bauhaus (now the Institute of Design), the other becoming a teacher at Illinois Institute of Technology. Herbert Bayer left the Bauhaus in 1928, briefly joining German *Vogue* in Berlin before joining the J.Walter Thompson advertising agency in New York, where he put his idiosyncratic photographic style to work for FMCG (fast-moving consumer goods) clients. Bayer then became Chairman

of Design at Walter Paepcke's Container Corporation of America, sponsor of the annual conferences at Aspen, Colorado, which made design a part of American popular culture. In 1966 he designed the corporate identity of the Atlantic Richfield Oil Company. It was not what the Bauhaus had originally meant by art and technology being a new unity, but it was important work.

But recently, with the failure of pseudo-Modern Movement housing policies and the rise in popularity of Post-Modernism, the achievements of the Bauhaus have come to be viewed with scepticism. In Milan, the avant-garde group Studio Alchymia ironically named two of its bizarre collections of furniture 'Bauhaus'. Journalists tend to use 'Bauhaus' as the label for a style while, in fact, the Bauhaus was an educational institution with a sophisticated pedagogic programme, whose main contribution to design has been its educational theory. As it flourished in the Twenties, that pedagogic programme was often expressed in metaphors which drew on cars and aeroplanes, and so the Bauhaus has come to stand for the machine culture in art.

Herbert Bayer, looking back on the Bauhaus, wrote in verse form: 'The Bauhaus existed for a short span of time but the potentials inherent in its principles have only begun to be realized, its sources of design remain forever full of changing possibilities…'

Bibliography Hans Maria Wingler *Bauhaus* MIT, Cambridge, Mass., 1969; Hans Maria Wingler *Kunstschul reform* 1900–1933 Gebrüder Mann, Berlin, 1977; Frank Whitford *The Bauhaus* Thames & Hudson, London, 1984; Klaus Herdeg *The Decorated Diagram* MIT, Cambridge, Mass., 1984

1: Walter Gropius' Bauhaus, Dessau, 1926. This was the single greatest monument to Modernism, a heroic symbol of enlightened social purpose. Closed by the Nazis in 1933, its memory was further traduced when Dessau became part of the German Democratic Republic in 1945. After years of neglect (and long after its masters had disappeared in a Modern diaspora) it was restored as a Scientific-Cultural Centre.

2: Herbert Bayer designed the cover of the catalogue of the Bauhaus' exhibition about itself, 1923.
3: Joost Schmidt, brochure for Verkehrsburo, Dessau, 1930. Machine romance was a disguised return to classical order.

Herbert Bayer 1900–65

Herbert Bayer was born at Haag, Austria. He was first employed as an architectural assistant, but became a student at the <u>Bauhaus</u> between 1921 and 1923 and was subsequently a teacher there. The Bauhaus graphic style is immediately identifiable. Depending on strictly observed structural grids and sans serif typefaces, it achieved a clarity that still looks fresh and takes the viewer on a rapid short-cut to an impression of what it is to be 'modern'. The Lufthansa corporate identity, as well as <u>BMW</u>'s, depend on assumptions made at the Bauhaus.

This revolution was the work of Herbert Bayer. He was committed to sans serif typefaces as a symbol of the longed-for breakaway from stultifying nineteenth-century culture: 'why repeat customs?' he scribbled on one of his radical designs. The infamous two-million Reichsmark banknotes of 1923 were designed by Bayer.

For Bayer, 'the typographic revolution was not an isolated event, but went hand-in-hand with a new social and political consciousness and consequently with the building of new cultural foundations.'

In 1925 Bayer started a course called 'Typography and Advertising Art'. In the same year his signature 'Universal' font appeared: using only a compass, a ruler and a T-square, Bayer reduced classical Roman letter forms to basic geometrical shapes. With typical Bauhaus thoroughness (not to say naivety), it was intended to be a complete writing system, to be used by typewriters and fountain pens as well as printing presses. Speaking of the abolition of serifs, Bayer asked why replicate in the machine age the strokes of a calligrapher's pen or a chisel? In 1974 the International Typeface Corporation redesigned Bayer's 'Universal' and called it 'Bauhaus'. Click on the fonts menu and you will very likely find it on your computer.

Bibliography *Herbert Bayer* exhibition catalogue, Bauhaus-Archiv, Berlin, 1983

BBPR

The letters in this abbreviation stand for Gianluigi Banfi (1910–45), Lodovico Barbiano di Belgioioso (born 1909), Enrico Peressutti (1908–76) and Ernesto Rogers (1909–69). Banfi died in a Nazi concentration camp.

All four graduated in 1932 and joined <u>CIAM</u> in 1935. Belgioioso wrote poetry and Rogers wrote books about architecture, including *Esperienze dell'architettura* (1958) and *L 'Utopia delta realtà* (1965). The architectural work of BBPR is the quintessence in building form of the Milanese design culture, especially the Torre Velasca (1958), a building in the centre of Milan which, while uncompromisingly modern in technique, purpose and appearance, has some traditional and historically minded elements. BBPR had a huge influence on Fifties taste, especially to be seen at the <u>Triennales</u>.

Bayer was committed to sans serif typefaces as a symbol of the longed-for breakaway from stultifying nineteenth-century culture

1: Herbert Bayer, cover of the How to Live? exhibition by the Deutscher Werkbund, 1927.
2: Herbert Bayer, Bauhaus typeface, 1974.

3: Belgioioso, Perresutti and Rogers' (BBPR) Torre Velasca, Milan, 1957, became a symbol of Italy's design capital.
4: Peter Behrens, AEG Turbine Hall, Berlin-Moabit, 1909. A vast industrial shed, dignified with ghosts of classical architecture, became part of Modernist propaganda.

Peter Behrens 1869–1940

The German architect Peter Behrens was the most outstanding industrial designer of the early twentieth century. He pioneered what is now called corporate identity (see chapter 1).

Born in Hamburg, he trained at the Karlsruhe and Düsseldorf Art Schools before joining the Munich Secession in 1893. There he mixed with the artistic radicals of his day. He moved from Munich to Darmstadt at the request of Prince Albert's grandson, Grand Duke Ernst Ludwig, who was building an artists' colony in Hesse's state capital. In Darmstadt, Behrens built his own house, in which he designed every component, from the structure down to the cutlery. From 1906 he was in charge of graphics and then factory building, workers' housing and industrial design for Emil Rathenau's huge AEG. As artistic adviser his brief was to transform the entire image of the sprawling company. It was like an industrial version of Richard Wagner's *Gesamtkunstwerk*: as one of the first architect-designers to be given such

scope by a large industrial concern, Behrens designed buildings, appliances and graphics, establishing a unified identity for the company, in a macrocosm of what he had done in Darmstadt. In 1907 he helped found the Deutsche Werkbund. His achievement in the design of every aspect of AEG was the most complete example of what it set out to achieve. Behrens' pupils included Walter Gropius, Mies van der Rohe and, very briefly, Le Corbusier. He was director of architecture at the Vienna Academy in 1932 and director of the department of architecture at the Prussian Academy in Berlin from 1936 until his death. Behrens summarized his views about design in *Kunst und Technik* (1910): 'We have become used to some modern forms of construction, but I do not believe that mathematical solutions will be visually satisfying. Otherwise it would mean a purely intellectual type of art, which is a contradiction in terms.'

Behrens was also a passionate contributor to the Werkbund journal, *Die Form*, where he wrote in 1922,

'We have no choice but to make our lives more simple, more practical, more organized and wide ranging. Only through industry have we any hope of fulfilling our aims.' Yet the intuitive side of design remained strong with him: commenting on something Rathenau had once said Behrens wrote, 'Don't think that even an engineer, when he buys a motor, takes it to bits in order to scrutinize it. Even he… buys from the external appearance. A motor ought to look like a birthday present.' (See also page 19.)

Bibliography Tilmann Buddensieg & Henning Rogge *Industriekultur: Peter Behrens and the AEG 1907–1914* MIT, Cambridge, Mass., 1984; Fritz Hoeber *Peter Behrens* Georg Muller & Eugen Rentsch, Munich, 1913; Alan Windsor *Peter Behrens – architect and designer* Architectural Press, London, 1981; Watson-Guptill, New York, 1982; *Peter Behrens und Nürnberg* exhibition catalogue, Germanisches National-Museum, Nuremberg, 1980

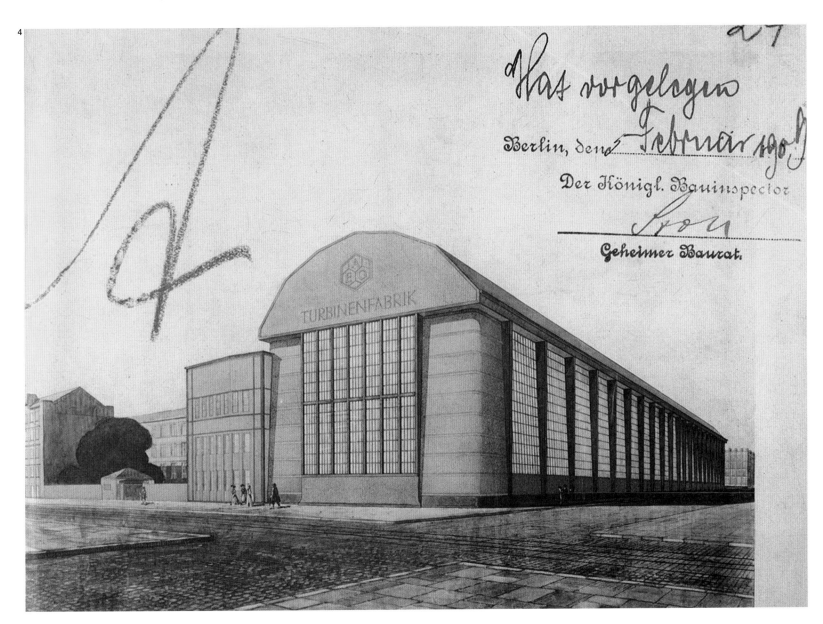

4

Norman Bel Geddes 1893–1958

Norman Bel Geddes once said that theatre was his 'fickle mistress', and throughout his riotous life, dramatic effect dominated his work.

As a theatre set designer, painter, illustrator, self-publicist, author, architect and sometime industrial designer, Norman Bel Geddes was always interested in the total effect. Among his projects were scales for the Toledo Scale Factory, an automobile for Graham Page, and radio cabinets for RCA, but his importance lies not in his completed projects (of which there were very, very few), but in his profoundly felt conviction that design was one of the great driving forces of the age. He became an influential prophet, predicting in his books *Horizons* (1934) and *Magic Motorways* (1940) everything from the freeway system to air conditioning. In the General Motors Futurama at the New York World's Fair of 1939 he put flesh on the bones of some of these visionary ideas.

Bel Geddes had met the German Expressionist architect Erich Mendelsshon in 1924, but although he was no doubt an inspiration, Bel Geddes' vision was very much his own. He employed the techniques of an impresario and was the first of the pioneer consultant designers to come to public notice when a profile of him appeared in *Fortune* magazine in 1930, even though he did not actually have a single finished project or implemented design to show to the journalist who interviewed him. The apocalyptic *Horizons* maintained the pace. In it Bel Geddes wrote, 'The few artists who have devoted themselves to industrial design have done so with condescension, regarding it as a surrender to Mammon… On the other hand, I was drawn to industry by the great opportunities it offered *creatively*.'

After the Second World War Bel Geddes continued to run an office and was briefly retained by IBM, but he had become disenchanted by not having enough ideas realized. He died in 1958.

Bibliography Norman Bel Geddes (edited by William Kelley) *Miracle in the Evening* Doubleday, New York, 1960; Jeffrey L. Meikle *Twentieth Century Limited Temple* University Press, Philadelphia, 1979

Bel Geddes was a theatre set designer, painter, illustrator, self-publicist, author, architect and sometime industrial designer

Mario Bellini born 1935

Mario Bellini was born in Milan and studied architecture there, graduating in 1959. He has collaborated continuously with Olivetti since 1963, working on their entire product range, but has also worked for Cassina, BrionVega, Yamaha, Ideal Standard, Marcatre, Artemide, Flos, FIAT, Lancia and Renault. Bellini's chief work for Olivetti has been the 'Programma' microcomputer (1965), the 'Logos' and 'Divisumma' calculators (1973), the 'Lexikon 83' typewriter (1976), the TES 40l text-editing system and the ET101 series of electronic typewriters.

Bellini was one of the most visible industrial designers of the Seventies and Eighties. He eschews philosophy, but that is not to say his designs do not have a metaphorical quality that raises them far above the day-to-day into the realms of art. His work had a strong sculptural presence and a hint of zoomorphic character: for the revolutionary ET101 electronic typewriter, Bellini claims to have derived his inspiration from a photograph of a shark torn from *National Geographic* magazine. He was among the first designers to realize (and then put into practice) the idea that when all machines are driven by essentially the same electronic circuitry, the old notion of 'form follows function' can have no real meaning. After the integration of solid-state circuitry into office equipment, the typewriter's appearance was determined solely by a mixture of tradition, aesthetics and ergonomics. During the last years of the typewriter, Bellini extended an understanding of this further than anyone,

1

2

so much so that his ET101 became for the few years remaining before computers usurped its bureaucratic and creative role, as much a stereotype for the electronic typewriter as was <u>Henry Dreyfuss</u>' Bell telephone for the telephone 40 or 50 years ago, and it is as widely imitated. With <u>Giorgio Giugiaro</u>, Bellini is the most practical of contemporary Italian designers, but may have sensed the end of classic <u>Modernism</u> by putting a limit on the value of practicality and allowing a sense of rhetoric: 'Ergonomics is nothing but a starting point: man is much more complex than an animal or a gadget that can be measured with a rule. He can be read and decoded through many other standards, such as culture, psychology, human relationships. Our needs cannot be reduced to the functional ones. Acting from this starting point I try to give things a value, a content beyond simple appearance…'

Bellini does not sketch the designs himself, but has his model-maker, <u>Giovanni Sacchi</u>, contrive them in wood and 'only after I touch it, feel it, look at it, can I really tell what I have . . . then I have an artist render it on paper'. A Yamaha cassette deck that was in production in 1974 is possibly the very first product to carry the legend 'designed by' followed by the designer's signature. In 1986 Bellini became editor of the Milanese magazine *Domus*.

Bibliography *Mario Bellini – designer* exhibition catalogue (ed. by Cara McCarty), Museum of Modern Art, New York, 1987

J.H. Belter 1804–63

Johan Heinrich Belter was born in Hanover, Germany, and emigrated to New York in 1833 after training as a cabinet-maker. He started up a cabinet-making business in Manhattan in 1844. Belter came from the same artisan tradition as his contemporary <u>Michael Thonet</u>, but his translation to the United States changed the course of his career mightily. He was perhaps as ingenious as Thonet, but the demands of American taste forced him into some strange creative manoeuvres. In 1847 he took out a patent for 'Machinery for Sawing Arabesque Chairs', and another in 1858 for the 'Improvement in the Method of Manufacturing Furniture'. This second patent was primarily concerned with the technique of manufacturing laminated furniture, whose industrial application Belter pioneered at the same time as Thonet.

Belter normally used seven laminations of wood, but disguised his technique with grotesque and exaggerated carvings, sometimes politely known as the Rococo Revival, but more nearly comparable to the furnishings familiar in New Orleans bordellos. Belter's furniture and his 'parlor sets' became so popular that 'Belter' became a generic term for a style of elaborately carved and upholstered furniture. When he died he left an estate of $83,218, and countless imitators (although his business fell into the hands of his brother-in-law, J. H. Springmeyer, and went bankrupt in 1867).

Walter Benjamin 1892–1940

Walter Benjamin was a member of the Marxist Frankfurt School of Sociologists. His contribution to design is a highly intelligent and influential essay, 'The Work of Art in an Age of Mechanical Reproduction', one of the first attempts to reconcile traditional aesthetics with the industrial world.

Bibliography Walter Benjamin *Das Kunstwerk im Zeitalten seinen technischen Reproduzierbarkeit* Suhrkamp Verlag, Frankfurt, 1968

1: Norman Bel Geddes, Emerson Patriot radio, circa 1940.
2: Mario Bellini's ET121 electronic typewriter for Olivetti was the final evolution of the conventional typewriter before the arrival of desk-top computers in the first half of the Eighties. A perfect miniature monument to the high-concept consumerism of the decade, its angular charcoal shape was inspired by a shark.
3: J. H. Belter, detail of laminated rosewood sofa, circa 1856.

Ward Bennett born 1917

Ward Bennett, an American sculptor and designer, studied in New York with Hans Hoffmann and in Paris with the Romanian avant-garde primitive Constantin Brancusi, who taught him that 'the important thing is not to be clever'. In 1938 he became an apprentice of Le Corbusier. These two great men influenced him profoundly.

After the Second World War he began to concentrate on interior design, and his notable works include a concrete beach house at Southampton, Long Island, a vacation house in Easthampton made entirely of telegraph poles, and his own eyrie perched on top of New York's Dakota apartment building. Bennett, who has, like an inspired scavenger, frequently used industrial waste as the basis of new products, once remarked: 'You can be sure Toscanini and Einstein had great houses. You have to be something first. The insecurity of being nobody – that's what starts people buying pseudo-Baroque and pseudo-Spanish.' But Bennett has also been an eclectic and as such has been an influence on the contemporary interest in mixing materials and styles. In the early Eighties Bennett became celebrated as the high priest of High-Tech, a man before his time.

Berliner Metallgewerbe

Berliner Metallgewerbe was a furniture manufacturer whose proprietor, Joseph Muller, put Mies van der Rohe's first chair design – the 'MR' – into production in 1928.

2

Harry Bertoia 1915–78

Harry Bertoia was born near Venice and emigrated to the United States in 1930, inspired, he said, by the American Dream. From Cass Technical College in Detroit he entered the new Cranbrook Academy, where he was a contemporary of Charles Eames. In 1942 he joined Eames in Santa Monica, California, where he helped develop his moulded plywood furniture which was exhibited at the Museum of Modern Art in 1946. In 1950 he went to the East Coast to work on his own furniture designs for Hans Knoll. Just as Eames used plywood, an industrial material, in his designs, so Bertoia's most famous chair used steel rods, worked into a grid. His education at Cranbrook left him very aware of sculptural concerns and he said of his chair, 'Like the body in Duchamp's "Nude Descending a Staircase", I wanted my chair to rotate, change with movement.' Later he devoted himself entirely to sculpture in a lonely rural community just outside the Knoll plant at East Greenville.

Bibliography Clement Meadmore *The Modern Chair – Classics in Production* Studio Vista, London, 1974; Van Nostrand Reinhold, New York, 1974

Just as Eames used plywood in his designs, so Bertoia's most famous chair used steel rods, worked into a grid

1

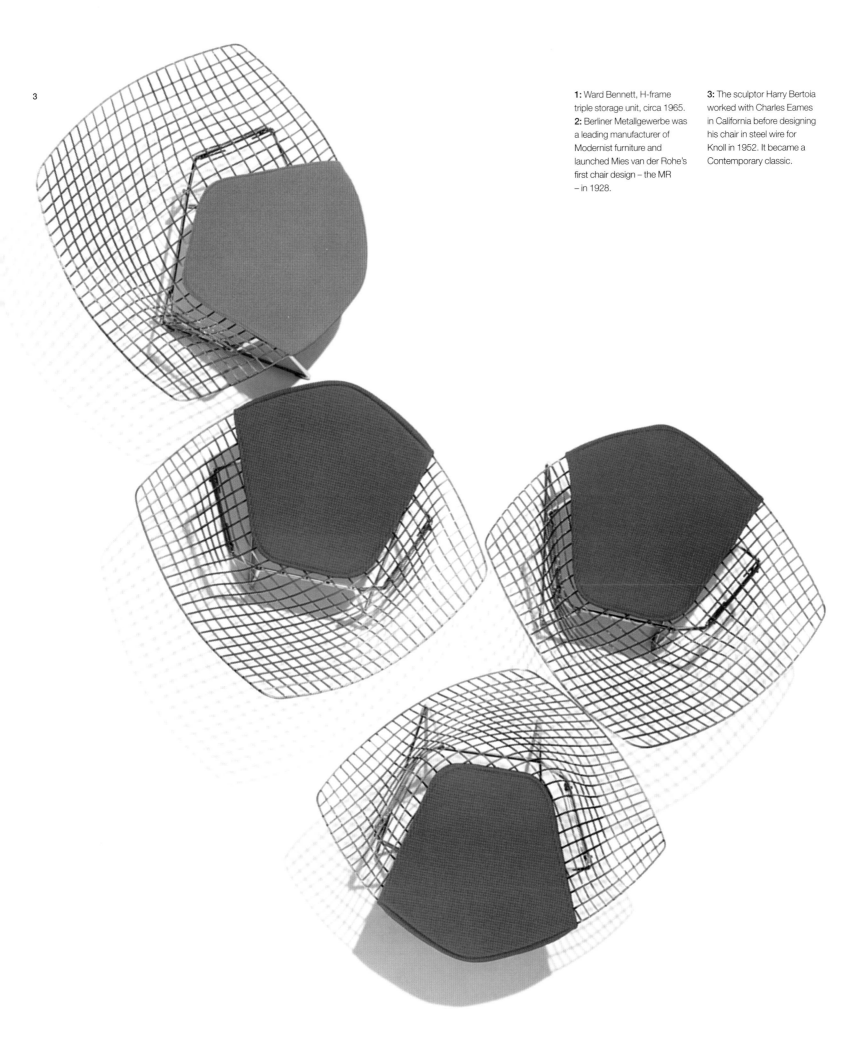

1: Ward Bennett, H-frame triple storage unit, circa 1965.
2: Berliner Metallgewerbe was a leading manufacturer of Modernist furniture and launched Mies van der Rohe's first chair design – the MR – in 1928.

3: The sculptor Harry Bertoia worked with Charles Eames in California before designing his chair in steel wire for Knoll in 1952. It became a Contemporary classic.

Nuccio Bertone 1914–97

Giuseppe 'Nuccio' Bertone was born in Turin, where his father had established a body shop. He joined the firm in 1934 and eventually became its manager, changing it from an artisan tin-bashing business to a studio full of inspired designers, making cars, some fantastic, some real, that were the envy of the world. After Pininfarina, Bertone is perhaps the most celebrated Torinese consultant car designer. Apprentices have included Giovanni Michelotti and Giorgio Giugiaro. Bertone's great designs, characterized by their quirky angularity, include: Alfa Romeo Giulietta Sprint (1954), Lamborghini Miura (1966), Ferrari Dino 308 (1973), British Leyland Innocenti Mini (1974).

Bertone's designs have a self-consciously avant-garde character. This has always attracted eager apprentices to work at the Bertone Style Centre, established in new premises at Caprie, just outside Turin. Since 1950 Bertone has produced almost 60 influential prototypes and 40 production cars, including the Lamborghini Bravo of 1974 and the Citroën BX of 1982.
Bibliography Angelo Titi Anselmi *La Carrozzeria italiana – cultura e progetto* Alfieri, Turin, 1978

Flaminio Bertoni 1903–64

Flaminio Bertoni, born in Masagno, near Como, is the least known genius of automobile design. He graduated from Varese technical school in 1918 and, citing inspriration from Leonardo and Michelangelo, was one of the sculptors who built the war memorial there in 1919. At the time he was working for Carrozzeria Macchi as a joiner. After various promotions and an influential trip to France in 1923, Bertoni established his own studio-workshop in 1929. Acknowledging, like Leonardo, no very important distinctions between fine art and industrial design, Bertoni exhibited paintings and sculptures in Milan and Rome. His painterly style had links with late Surrealism and, as a sculptor, he was clearly indebted to Medardo Rosso, but the crucial event of his life was taking himself to Paris to work for a sub-contractor to Citroën. On 27 April 1932 he was hired by André Citroën himself.

We know tantalizingly little of the design processes at Citroën during this fascinating period because most of the documentation in the Bureau des Etudes was destroyed by a German bomb in July 1940, but what seems clear is that in the course of a single night in 1934, Bertoni, using a sculptor's tools, designed the bodywork for the Traction Avant, the car that was Citroën's manifesto: 'On the road… the comfort of the home' said the advertisements. This was in the same year that Bertoni exhibited at 46eme Exposition des Beaux Arts in Asnieres. Next, Bertoni worked on the Toute Petite Voiture (TPV) project. Here he had another entirely novel conception: surviving sketches show a Bauhaus purity, unusually pure geometry, a strong formal sense, explicit industrial finishes, uncompromising clarity and a shocking minimalism. After the Second World War, the TPV went on sale as the Citroën 2cv. Its body was held together by a mere 16 bolts and it was known as a 'deckchair under an umbrella'. In the same year he designed this epochal car, Bertoni also exhibited with Giorgio di Chirico at Paris Salon d'Automne.

In 1938 Citroën's chief engineer, Pierre Boulanger, started a notebook which he inscribed VGD (for 'Voiture de Grand Diffusion'). He said to his team 'Study all the possibilities, even the impossible' and this was the brief for what eventually became the design of the greatest car of all time. But during the War, Bertoni designed magnetic

1

torpedoes and married the prima ballerina from La Scala. After the war, with the TPV in production, the Citroën team and Bertoni turned to the VGD.

Boulanger was killed in a testing crash in 1950, but not before he issued a statement saying the VGD was to be: 'The world's best, most beautiful, most comfortable and most advanced car, a masterpiece to show the world and the American car factories in particular that Citroën and France could develop the ultimate vehicle.'

The template of the VGD – front-wheel drive, long wheelbase, low centre of gravity with front track greater than the rear – was established by engineer Andre Lefebvre. And Bertoni did the rest, using a plastic roof because Lefebvre liked the new material. Bertoni used unique high level indicators and a single spoke steering wheel (also an idea of Lefebvre's) in a *tableau de bord* that was a radical mix of sculpted curves and minimalist instrumentation.

This car was the astonishing DS, revealed at the Turin Motor Show of 1955 seated on a pylon with the wheels removed so as not to compromise the public's perception of its astonishing form. When it appeared at the Paris

Salon two years later, Roland Barthes was transfixed. So too was the public which, using a phonic slip from Citroën DS to 'Déesse' christened the car 'The Goddess'. Bertoni's sketches hint at concepts by Le Corbusier, Ferdinand Porsche and Buckminster Fuller, but his synthesis of interests was given unique direction by his sculptural inspiration. The Citroën DS would be a sensation if launched today, more than 50 years after the original.

Then, in a career move confirming his Renaissance conception of himself, Bertoni became an architect and built a thousand low-cost homes in St Louis, returning to car design only with the very odd 1961 Citroën Ami 6 which, confirming a contrary personality, he declared to be his favourite. The sculptor who inspired Barthes to say 'cars are our cathedrals' died virtually unknown in 1964.

Robert Dudley Best 1892–1984

British engineer-designer of the 1930 Bestlite, the first Bauhaus-inspired native British product.

1: The Citroen Toute Petite Voiture or TPV (known everywhere as the Deux Chevaux) may have been aimed at French peasants, but was inspired by Bauhaus design principles.
2: The Bestlite was a rare example of commercially viable English Modernism.

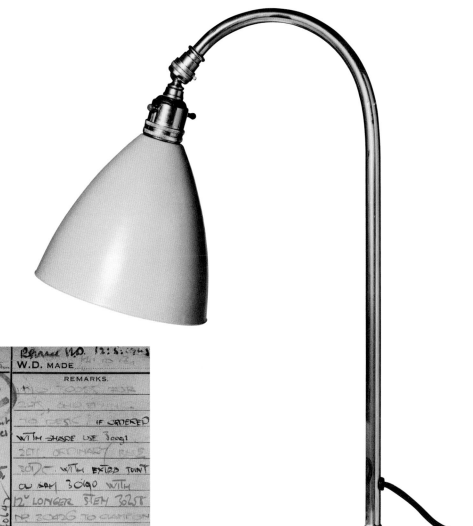

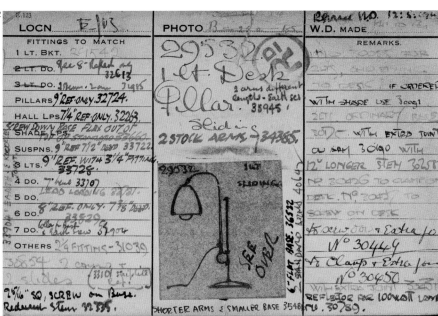

Alfonso Bialetti 1888–1970

Bialetti, trained in the French aluminium industry, made espresso an everyday reality ('*in casa un espresso come al bar*') with the creation of his 'Moka Express' in 1933. Inspired by old laundry systems, Bialetti's Moka Express had no moving parts and was virtually indestructible. It is estimated that 300 million have been made and that 90 per cent of Italian homes own at least one, making it a symbol of modern Italy at least as evocative as a Vespa or a Cinquecento. Bialetti's amiable advertising cliché, the *omino con i baffi* (moustachioed man), helps project an image of welcoming domesticity.

Marcel Bich 1914–94

Bich was the French industrialist who created the world's best-selling pen, the Bic Crystal. With partner Edouard Buffard, Bich formed a company making components for propelling pencils and fountain pens in 1945. He soon discovered Laszlo Biro's 1938 patent for a ball-point pen (the 'biro') and by 1950 early versions of the Crystal were in production. It was a masterpiece of anonymous design and clever marketing: Bich dropped the 'h' from his name so anglophones would not sound misogynistic and selling at a mere 29 cents in the United States, the Bic became the first disposable product. It was also among the first consumer products to be assiduously advertised on television.

Biedermeier

Biedermeier is a term used to describe petty-bourgeois German and Austrian furniture and interior design style in the period of late neo-classicism. It is a Teutonic equivalent of the Regency. The word derives from *bieder*, which means inoffensive, and Meier, a common German surname.

1

The Bic became the first disposable product. It was also among the first consumer products to be assiduously advertised on television

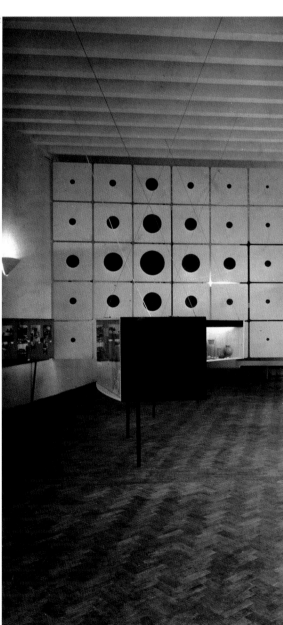

2

Max Bill 1908–1994

Max Bill is a Swiss architect who worked as a painter, designer and increasingly as a sculptor. His work was often identified with the austere minimalism of the Swiss Style, although his first influences came from the Bauhaus, where he was a student. From 1949 he promoted the *Gute Form* competitions for the Swiss Werkbund and from 1951 to 1956 he was director of the Hochschule für Gestaltung in Ulm, whose buildings he also designed. Bill's product designs include a wall clock for Junghans (1957) and some electrical fittings (1958). His contribution to modern design was less through his own creativity than through his continued international presence as a supporter of Bauhaus principles. To many designers educated in the Fifties, Bill was the complete hero.

Bibliography *Max Bill: Oeuvre 1928–1979* exhibition catalogue, Paris-Grenoble, 1969–70

Misha Black 1910–77

Misha Black founded the Design Research Unit (DRU) with Milner Gray in 1944. It was Britain's first design consultancy. Black was born in Russia and died in London, a 'radical beneath his subfusc suitings', according to Paul Reilly. His main area of interest was in exhibition design, often for the Ministry of Information. He was active in both the 'Britain Can Make It' (1946) and Festival of Britain (1951) exhibitions, but his chief contribution was as professor of Industrial Design at the Royal College of Art, where his commitment to the practicalities of industrial design did much to break down the barriers between design and engineering in education.

Bibliography John and Avril Blake *The Practical Idealists* Lund Humphries, London, 1969

John Blatchley born 1913

Blatchley was chief stylist at Rolls-Royce in Crewe. In 1950 he was given, with engineer Harry Vernden, the brief to design the 'Silent Sports Car'. This became the 1052 R-Type continental, with a distinctive fastback bizarrely influenced by Harley Earl's 1949 Chevrolet Fleetline. Blatchley's body was, with the modification of a notchback roof, later adapted for the 1955 Rolls-Royce Silver Cloud and Bentley S-type. Employing perfect neo-classical car design, with architectural proportions, Blatchley used razor-edge styling and set the headlamps into the body work.

1: Bialetti's Moka Express and Bic's disposable razors and pens describe two extremes of industrial possibility: one perfect and timeless, the other perfect and ephemeral.
2: Max Bill, Swiss Pavilion at the 6th Milan Triennale, 1936.
3: Max Bill, Junghans Model 32/0389 clock, 1957: unnegotiable aesthetic severity.
4: John Blatchley, Bentley S1 convertible, 1959: gentelmanly authority.

BMW

The company that became BMW (Bayerische Motoren Werke or Bavarian Motor Works) was founded by Karl Rapp in Munich in 1916 as the Bayerische Flugzeug Werke, manufacturing aero engines. At the time Munich had a lively art culture: the Russian painter Wassily Kandinsky had arrived to join the Blaue Reiter group in 1911. Naum Gabo and Alexei von Jawlensky were already there and the R. Piper Verlag was busy publishing influential art books by Wilhelm Worringer which made the case for abstract art.

But no work of any Munich art gallery ever managed what BMW's first motorbike achieved. BMW's chief designer Max Friz drew the R32 flat-twin, 8.5hp, shaft-drive as if it were a Bauhaus diagram. Based on a rigid grid, it was a disciplined masterpiece that made a coherent pattern out of separate elements. That it established an enduring architecture for BMW motor-raden is interesting proof of the German pedagogic theory of Hauptformen, concerning the enduring abstract essence of objects.

Five years after the epochal R32, BMW manufactured its first car when it took over the Fahrzeugfabrik of Eisenach, which was producing the Austin 7 (known as the Dixi) under licence. The BMW 328 of 1937 was the most celebrated sports car of the pre-Second World War era. BMW established a department of Kunsterliche Gestaltung in 1938, the first of its type in Europe. Its only significant projects before the War were 328s specially built for the Mille Miglia. Drawn by Wilhelm Meyerhuber with bodywork of Carrozzeria Touring of Milan, these cars were the sculptural source of the Jaguar XK120.

After the War BMW design briefly looked to America and Italy: Pininfarina made proposals for the 501, the first post-War saloon, and the most dramatic BMW of the decade, Albrecht von Goertz's 507 sportscar used the style of Harley Earl. Production versions of the 501 became known as 'Baroque Angels'. But the most distinctive products of the Wirtschaftswunder were the Kleinwagen, or bubble cars. In the Sixties Eberhard von Kuenheim rebuilt BMW on the basis of the 1961 'Neue Klasse', the first 'executive' car. Wilhelm Hofmeister established another enduring style language. Using conservative but refined engineering, and conservative but aggressive design (which made up in presence what it lacked in flair) BMW established a firm market position. Forceful, even aggressive, marketing enhanced the excellence of the actual products by making a BMW car seem to be more than just an agreeable and efficient machine, but the very token of crisp, youthful, worldly success. The design of the cars, under Paul Bracq, Claus Luthe and latterly the American Chris Bangle enforced this. A crease at the beltline, a questing snout, a kidney-shaped air-intake, the kink the C-pillar (or 'Hofmeiser-knick'), but most of all the satisfying appearance of looking as if they have been machined from a solid bullet of steel, characterize the appearance of all recent BMW cars. In the whole motor industry, BMW is one of the best instances of visual appeal contributing to commercial success.

Cini Boeri born 1924

Cini Boeri graduated in architecture from Milan Polytechnic in 1951. Her first job was as an apprentice to Marco Zanuso, in whose studio she worked until 1963. She has designed furniture for Arflex and Knoll, and lighting for Stilnovo and Arteluce. Her 'Strips' seating system won a Compasso d'Oro award in 1979.

1: BMW's logogram was inspired by an aircraft propellor (aero-engines were the source of the company's fortune).
2: The BMW 2002, 1968–71, a wheeled synecdoche of success and a perfect expression of BMW's design language.
3: Brigadier sofa, 1977, designed by Cini Boeri for Knoll.

4: Michel Boue with a small-scale clay model of the Renault 5, 1972. The Renault 5 was a French interpretation of Issigonis's Mini. Although based on the crude Renault 4L, or Quattrelle, the Cinq was a very sophisticated package and an influential pioneer of the hatchback format. No changes were made in the exterior metalwork of the car throughout its life and when an all-new successor came in 1984, it was only an evolution of Boue's original idea.

Rodolfo Bonetto born 1929

Rodolfo Bonetto's first job was in Pininfarina's car-design studio in Turin. He founded his own firm in 1958 and includes BrionVega, Driade, Borletti, Olivetti and FIAT among his clients. His 'Sfericlock' won a Compasso d'Oro award in 1964, while he was teaching at the Hochschule für Gestaltung in Ulm. With Veglia-Borletti, Bonetto has specialized in the design of instruments for cars, and this developed in 1977 into his completely redesigning the interior of the FIAT 131 Super Mirafiori, where he used single-piece plastic mouldings in a more sophisticated and satisfying way than ever before (or since).

Bibliography Anty Pansera & Alfonso Grassi *Atlante del design italiano* Fabbri, Milan, 1980

Borax

Borax is a contemptuous name given to a popular design style that appeared on certain American consumer products in the years either side of the Second World War. It is characterized by a markedly dysfunctional, expressive aesthetic which derived from a watered-down Art Deco and streamlining. It was most frequently used on cheap furniture, and other domestic objects.

Bibliography Edgar Kaufmann 'Borax, or the chromium-plated calf' *Architectural Review* London, August 1948, pp. 88–93

Michel Boué 1936–71

Michel Boué is identified with one phenomenally successful car design. His Renault 5 appeared in 1972 and became the best-selling French car ever, and the only successful one, ever, with only two doors. There was little radical about the mechanics: the 5 was based on the ancient, agricultural Renault 4, but Boué gave it a superbly packaged and elegant body. Just as the BMC Mini car created a type, so Boué's 5 advanced it, creating a market segment for the 'supermini' in which every manufacturer had to compete.

The 5 story is one of inspired management as much as of inspired design (where the two are not the same thing). Boué received a brief in 1967 to design a hatch-back car which would create new volume for Renault by appealing to market segments which disdained the Regie's previous products, namely young people and women. It took Boué just two days to sketch the 5 and it was accepted immediately: Renault's engineering chief, Yves Georges, has said: 'It was amazing. Normally the management of any major car company ask for changes and then for more changes, with styling advice coming from all sorts of different people. Most times this ends up damaging the look of a car. But that did not happen with the R5. It is a pure design. And that is why it looks good and has never needed a facelift. Leonardo da Vinci or Picasso would not have wanted people playing around with their work. A car designer… is no different.'

By 1984 Renault had sold 4.5 million R5s, but Boué did not live to see its introduction. He died at 35 of cancer of the spine in 1971.

3

Michel Boué's Renault 5 appeared in 1972 and became the best-selling French car ever with only two doors

4

4

Pierre Boulanger 1886–1950

A French automotive engineer, Pierre Boulanger worked for Michelin until the tyre company assumed responsibility for the debt-ridden car manufacturer <u>Citroën</u> in 1935, when he embarked on a programme which led to the creation of the highly influential 2CV, the Traction Avant, and ultimately the DS.

Paul Bracq born 1933

Born in Bordeaux, Bracq was trained as a painter, then joined the office of Philippe Charbonneaux in Paris. In 1957 he joined the Mercedes-Benz advanced design studio, working on the concept that became the 1963 'pagoda roof' 230SL. Back In France from 1967 to 1970 he worked at Brisson & Lotz, where his ideas fed into <u>Roger Tallon</u>'s TGV project. In 1970 he succeeded Wilhelm Hofmeister as Design Director of <u>BMW</u>. His body for the first generation BMW 5-series defined the expectations of middle-class automobile design for at least a generation. In 1974 he joined Peugeot.

Constanin Brancusi 1876–1957

Brancusi was a fine art 'primitive' sculptor, not a designer, but his superb, high-concept abstract forms are, like <u>Elbert Rutan</u>'s aircraft, frequently cited as a source of inspiration by designers themselves. And besides, one aspect of Brancusi's critical history was illuminating of the vexatious relationship between art, design and industry in the twentieth century. In 1926 the photographer Edward Steichen attempted to import one of Brancusi's brass sculptures of a *Bird in Space* into the United States. Under Paragraph 339 of the US Tariff Act of 1922, a 'manufacture of metal' was taxed at 40 per cent, while under Paragraph 1704 works of art were duty free. Brancusi hired the celebrity attorney Maurice J. Speiser (who had met Ezra Pound and Ernest Hemingway in Paris and was thus well-briefed on the lore of <u>Modernism</u>). Barncusi and Speiser won the case in the Third Division of the US Customs Court on 26 November 1928. The authorities had thought Brancusi's abstract work of art was the prototype of an airscrew.

The first generation BMW 5-series defined the expectations of middle-class automobile design for at least a generation

1

1

1: Paul Bracq, sketches for BMW M1, circa 1975. Although the 1974 BMW 5-series was all new, its design featured the aesthetic and practical principles of the 'neue klasse'.
2: Constantin Brancusi, Bird in Space (Yellow Bird), 1923–4. Brancusi's superbly elegant sculpture were a cross-over between art and product design. One example was taxed by US Customs as an industrial object.

2

Branding

Old-fashioned accountants used to describe the intangible value of a business as 'good-will'. This has been recently translated into 'brand values', that mixture of associations and expectations that successful products have. As technical differences between, say, toothpaste become less significant, the consumer's appreciation of the toothpaste's 'brand' as expressed by consistent advertising and attractive graphics grows. In, for example, the automobile industry, technical distinctions are also becoming less a matter of competitive advantage than imagery. The voodoo of 'branding' now dominates much discussion about design.

All long-lived businesses have a commitment to branding. AEG was one of the first to realize the importance of this metaphorical extension to manufacturing. The work of the Michelin brothers is another obvious example: product, architecture, graphics and advertising were construed as a whole. Since its appearance in 1898, Michelin's Bibendum symbol has represented a company committed not only to tyres, but to the finer things in life, including art and travel. Michelin was the first to realize a connection between the pleasures of motoring and of gastronomy, a link that continues today with the publication of incomparable guides and maps. 'Michelin' now means a leading hotel or restaurant as much as it means innovations in tyre technology.

At the headquarters of Audi at Ingolstadt, the chief designer gives you a business card that says 'Audi Brand Group'. The cars may be Volkswagens in drag, but their brand values distinguish them and justify higher prices. Brand values are all about association and expectation and you build them through having a strong identity, a heavy weight of advertising, consistency in PR… and, of course, a worthwhile product.

Curiously and satisfyingly, the historiography of the artist Picasso is one of the clearest examples of how branding works to combine imagery with media with money and with meaning. Born Pablo Diego Jose Francisco De Paula Juan Nepomuceno Maria de los Angeles Remedios Cipriano dela Santisima Trinidad Ruiz Picasso, he rapidly developed a brand strategy of his own. His first paintings are signed with the patronymic 'P. Ruiz'. He later adds his mother's maiden name to become 'P. Ruiz Picasso'. Then 'P. R. Picasso'. By 1902, the 'Picasso' brand was launched.

Initially, it was Picasso's fine product that created his reputation. Later his wealth became a source of fascination in itself. Financially independent by the age of 28, at the time of his death he had perhaps 500 of his own canvases. Today these might be worth several billion in whatever hard currency you care to mention. But Picasso always controlled the relationship between production and distribution. As John Berger said in *Success and Failure of Picasso* (1965) he knew 'the works would have to be sold tactfully, so as not to flood the market'. Or, in other words, he had a premium product strategy that would be the envy of Unilever. Quite intuitively, it seems, Picasso understood the voodoo of brand management. 'Actually, I wanted to

become a painter,' he once admitted. 'Now I have become Picasso.'

Every step of his career was handled with calculation and enterprise. Success would never have been achieved in his native Malaga, nor La Coruna, not even in Barcelona. Instead, Picasso saw that the emerging Paris art market with its new generation of private collectors was ripe for exploitation. First he did what the brand managers call 'benchmarking', assessing the market leaders. Thus, early Picassos had their similarities to Pissarro, Toulouse-Lautrec, Cezanne and Degas, market leaders in their day. But Picasso had a product development programme of his own. Fifty years before Detroit created the annual model change. Picasso excited demand with the invention of new styles. Collectors dutifully moved from his Blue Period to his Rose Period and then to Cubism. Just as Apple launches new products when there is still demand for the old, Picasso's fidgety creativity kept the market alive. The critic Georges Besson said he was as 'mercurial as a crowd'.

And long before anyone recognized the importance of what word-of-mouth does in getting obscure or advanced products to the tipping point of acceptabiity, Picasso had established networking. His brand values were continuously reinforced by his critics and his dealers. And Ambroise Vollard, Paul Durand-Ruel, Apollinaire and Gertrude Stein were fed a continuous diet of freebies. He formed a strategic alliance – just short of a merger – with Georges Braque, but did a buy-out when he needed more market share and Braque's sluggish performance was inhibiting growth. Even when collaborating on the Cubist product launch, Picasso's dealer Daniel-Henri Kahnweiler enforced the premium strategy by charging four times more for his pictures than for Braque's.

Picasso was no blurry mystic. Instead, he controlled his brand image with a very high-degree of self-consciousness. Brand extension was limited to graphics and ceramics (with a few theatrical joint-ventures) and he only ever allowed his picture to be taken by the leading photographers of the day: Robert Doisneau, Man Ray and Irving Penn among them. Seven long-suffering women enhanced his reputation for prodigality, confirming the saying that a bad reputation never did anyone any harm. PR was important too: *Guernica* became the most famous painting of the twentieth century because of the painter's adroit manipulation of the media. So effective was this communications policy that 20 years after his death, an international survey showed that spontaneous recognition of the Picasso brand was 84 per cent (rather higher than the US president of the day).

Despairing of his ex-partner's ruthless and inventive creativity, and perhaps a little jealous of his high profile and momentous m-cap, Georges Braque once said 'Picasso used to be a great painter. Now he is just a genius.' Today, for 'genius' read 'brand'.

Bibliography Bernd Kreuz *The Art of Branding* Hatje Cantz Verlag, Ostfildern-Ruit, 2003; Wally Olins *On Brand* Thames & Hudson, London, 2003

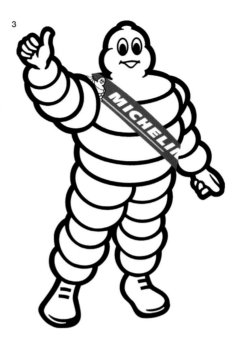

3: Monsieur Bibendum was inspired by a pile of tyres. Named after the latin poet Horace's imprecation *nunc est bibendum, nunc pede libero puisunda tellis* (now is the time to drink, to dance to a good beat), he was designed by Marius Rousillon (who branded himself as Mr O'Galop) in 1898.

4: Portrait of artist Pablo Picasso, September 11, 1956 in Cannes, France,

Marianne Brandt 1893–1993

Born in Germany, Marianne Brandt, with Wilhelm Wagenfeld, was the most famous product of the <u>Bauhaus</u> metalwork studio, run by <u>Laszlo Moholy-Nagy</u>. Although she was in no sense an industrial designer (because all her work was craft prototypes), Brandt's designs for domestic metalware laid the basis for a design aesthetic based on uncompromising geometric purity. A Brandt teapot reflects the inheritance of the Bauhaus in its ostentatious use of pure forms.

Bibliography Hans Maria Wingler *The Bauhaus* MIT, Cambridge, Mass., 1969

Andrea Branzi born 1939

A Florentine architect, Andrea Branzi was a member of <u>Archizoom</u> in the Sixties and went to Milan after the decline of interest in radical design. He worked with <u>Studio Alchymia</u> in 1979 and has contributed furniture designs to <u>Memphis</u>.

Bibliography Andrea Branzi *The Hot House* MIT, Cambridge, Mass., 1984

Braun

Braun was a small, family-run radio company based in Frankfurt when Artur Braun (born 1925) took it over in 1951. In the rebuilding programme after the First World War, the company had begun to diversify into household appliances and, with an interest in design shared with his brother Erwin, this presented Artur Braun with a wonderful opportunity to give form to Germany's 'economic miracle'. He hired <u>Fritz Eichler</u>, <u>Hans Gugelot</u> and <u>Otl Aicher</u>, who all came from the <u>Hochschule für Gestaltung</u> in Ulm, and later <u>Dieter Rams</u>, to achieve this.

Working on Braun's hi-fis, razors and kitchen machines, these designers quickly developed an image of visual sophistication, based on attention to detail and geometrical simplicity – a formal and stylized image which created a sensation when it was shown to the public at the 1955 Radio Show in Düsseldorf. While the Bauhaus masters had spoken of integrating art with industry and achieving rational, modern products, the fact was that virtually all <u>Bauhaus</u> production was crafts-based. Here, though, was a Frankfurt electrical company achieving the goal of rational, undecorated design. Braun became a synonym for '*Gute Form*' in Germany and for 'good design' in Britain.

However, Braun's excellence in design management did not lead to commercial success. Braun engineers spoke of the 'Rams surcharge', or the extra cost of design in the controlled, mystical austerity of mature Braun products. As a result Braun was taken over by the American Gillette concern in 1967 and since then there has been a progressive dilution of the company's standards and identity, although the influence of the Braun style continues to be profound and far-reaching, especially in Japan. Richard Moss, an American journalist, best summed up Braun's achievement. In an article in *Industrial Design* (November 1962) he wrote: 'All Braun products, from desk fan to kitchen mixer, belong unmistakably to the same family… Three general rules seem to govern every Braun design – a rule of order, a rule of harmony, and a rule of economy.'

Bibliography Wolfgang Schmittel *Design: Concept, Form, Realisation* ABC, Zürich, 1977; Inez Franksen et al. 'Design: Dieter Rams &' exhibition catalogue, IDZ-Berlin, 1982

1: Marianne Brandt.
2: Braun design was an expression of the new Germany of the Wirtschaftswunder when Bauhaus design principles were evidence of social democracy at work.

3: Carl Breer's Chrysler Airflow, 1935. A fascinating attempt by the adventurous Walter Chrysler to bring advanced design to the retarded American consumer. A result of Breer's experiments with aerodynamics, the Airflow was too advanced for the consumer's taste. A commercial disaster, production ceased after two years.

Carl Breer 1883–1970

Carl Breer was chief engineer at Chrysler when Walter Percy Chrysler decided to try to take the company from tenth largest US car manufacturer further up the Fortune 500. Chrysler had in mind a radical new car called the Airflow, innovative in many ways but most of all in its styling. Early models had marbled vinyl floor-covering, moulded roof panels, tubular steel seats and tripartite bumpers blended into a streamlined shape that was a decade ahead of its time. The American public hated it. Production ceased in 1937, just three years after it had begun. But the influence of Breer's Airflow was immense, and it donated forms to both Ford and General Motors and ideas to Ferdinand Porsche. (See also reference to aerodynamics in chapter 7.)

Bibliography Howard S. Irvin 'The History of the Airflow Car' *Scientific American* August 1977, pp. 98–106

Marcel Breuer 1902–81

Marcel Breuer was born in Pecs, Hungary, and trained at the Vienna Academy of Art. Like many architects and designers from the undeveloped east of Europe, Breuer was attracted by the new German art school, the Bauhaus, and became Walter Gropius's star pupil at Dessau.

Breuer's most celebrated designs, cantilever tubular steel chairs of 1925–28, emerged from studies made for furniture intended for the Bauhaus experimental house, a staff and student project. The story is that Breuer got the idea of using tubular steel from the handlebars of his bicycle (although it is more likely that the Junkers aircraft factory, adjacent to the Bauhaus, was more of an influence).

After the Bauhaus was closed by the Nazis, Breuer came to England, where he worked for Jack Pritchard's Isokon company, designing an elegant bent plywood chair, based on an earlier Bauhaus project, which went into production in 1936. Breuer briefly worked with the Maxwell Fry architectural practice and the pair built some celebrated houses in the International Style, but just as the Bauhaus had drawn him from the east, the allure of the United States drew Breuer from Britain. In 1937 Gropius invited him to join the teaching staff at Harvard University School of Architecture, where his pupils became the leading American architects and designers of the next generation: I.M. Pei, Paul Rudolph, Philip Johnson and Eliot Noyes. Once in the USA it was architecture rather than furniture design that occupied Breuer, but the latest version of his steel Bauhaus chair, known as the 'Cesca' after his daughter Francesca, became a classic produced by Knoll. In retrospect, Breuer's contribution to design was to invent aesthetic solutions to the problems of new materials.

Bibliography Marcel Breuer *Marcel Breuer 1921–1962* Gerd Hatje, Stuttgart, 1962; *Marcel Breuer* exhibition catalogue, Museum of Modern Art, New York, 1981

4: Marcel Breuer, B5 chair, 1926. Breuer's continuous experiments with cantilevered tubular steel led to that Modernist classic, the 'Bauhaus' chair. The B5 was manufactured first by Thonet Mobel of Berlin, then by Thonet.
5: Breuer's self-portrait

BrionVega

A manufacturer of hi-fis, radios and televisions, BrionVega was established in Milan by the Brion family in the mid-1940s. By commissioning some of Italy's outstanding designers to create his products, Ennio Brion has championed the highest standards in product design. BrionVega's most celebrated products have been a record-player in a Pop style by Achille Castiglioni in 1966, and the 'Doney 14' television of 1962, the 'Black 12' television of 1969 and a hinged radio of 1965, all by Richard Sapper and Marco Zanuso. BrionVega's house style produced technical purism with a high finish, and much of the effect of the company's products is created by the quality of their plastic shells. These appliances populated film sets during the later years of *la dolce vita*, a quick visual shorthand among movie stylists for 'sophisticated, modern', but the BrionVega company could not compete with ever more competitive Japanese imports. A fitting memorial to a lost age of industrial optimism is Carlo Scarpa's BrionVega tomb of 1970–2, a sombre, sculpted concrete four-square monument at San Vito d'Altivole, near Venice.

Vannevar Bush 1890–1974

Vannevar Bush was Professor of Radio at Massachusetts Institute of Technology and one of the architects of the Information Age. One of his PhD students was Frederick Terman, a founder of what became known as Silicon Valley. Bush was an influential advocate of atomic weapons, but is more positively remembered for an essay titled 'As We May Think' published in *Atlantic Monthly* in July 1945. In the Thirties he made an astonishing prediction of desk-top computers in his 'Memex' concept. He wrote: 'Consider a future desk for individual use, which is a sort of mechanized private file and library... It consists of a desk, and while it can presumably be operated from a distance, it is primarily a piece of furniture... on the top are slanting translucent screens, on which material can be projected for convenient reading. There is a keyboard, and sets of buttons and levers.' Although Bush was an emotional conservative, arguing against NASA's space programme, his fundamental belief that technology would not just record knowledge, but multiply it, shaped the modern world.

Bibliography G. Pascal Zachary *Endless Frontier: Vannevar Bush, Engineer of the American Century* MIT Press, Cambridge, Mass., 1999

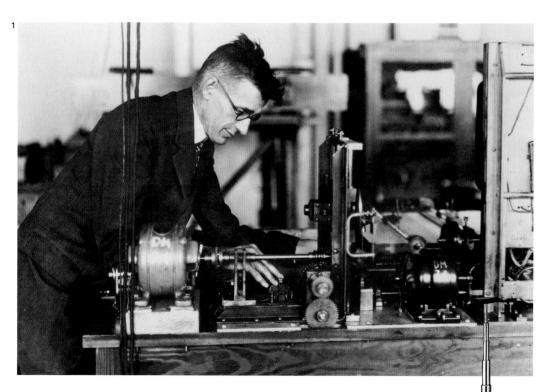

1

BrionVega's house style produced technical purism with a high finish

2

Wallace Merle Byam 1896–1962

Byam's imprecation: 'Go see what's over the next hill' was made easier for generations of Americans who realized their nomadic version of the national dream in one of his Airstream trailers. Caravans and transhumance were in Byam's DNA: his father had led a mule train to Baker, Oregon and before graduating in law from Stanford University in 1923 he worked as a shepherd and lived in a two-wheeled trailer. His first job was as a copywriter for the *Los Angeles Times*. A restless inventor, he published trailer designs in the widely read *Popular Mechanics*. He coined the term 'Airstream' in 1934 and in 1936 the first 'Clipper' caravan was manufactured by Airstream Trailers of Van Nuys, California. This was Californian aerospace territory and the aluminium 'Clipper' used lightweight aircraft monocoque construction as well as streamlining. It soon took its place in Americana. Byam said: 'I make good travel dreams come true.' For $1,200 he allowed American consumers access to a great collective myth.
Bibliography Richard Sexton *American Style – classic product design from Airstream to Zippo* Chronicle Books, San Francisco, 1987

1: Vannevar Bush at work, 1940s.
2: Richard Sapper's and Marco Zanuso's 1965 radio for BrionVega. A splendid example of period Italian style.
3: Wally Byam, an adman who became an intuitive designer.
4: The Airstream trailer: a capsule of the American Dream.

CAD-CAM

CAD-CAM stands for Computer Aided
Design–Computer Aided Manufacture. CAD uses
computers so that designs can be generated on a visual
display unit (VDU), rather than on paper. As designs can
be modified and visualized from any angle, it allows
enormous flexibility and speeds the development process,
particularly in the design of complex three-dimensional
shapes, such as car and aeroplane bodies. Furniture
designers, including Thomas Heatherwick, adapted
computer-modelling technologies in the early twenty-
first century to make complex techno-organic shapes.

1

Santiago Calatrava born 1951

A bridge designer from Valencia, Calatrava studied at the Escuela Tecnica Superior de Arquitectura and at the Erdgenossisches Technische Hochschule in Zurich. His PhD thesis was devoted to space frames and how they fold. Calatrava has a genius for spectacular shape-making. In the 1985 Bach de Roda bridge in Barcelona, or Dublin's 1998 James Joyce Bridge, this genius is made apparent. This powerful aesthetic completely transcends the disciplines of civil-engineering and gave the late twentieth century a defining aesthetic. Calatrava makes bridges into symbols, sculpture, product, diagrams.

In his work old distinctions between architecture, sculpture, engineering and design seem quaint.
Bibliography Alexander Tzonis and Rebeca Caso Donadei *Calatrava Bridges* Thames & Hudson, London, 2005

Pierre Cardin born 1922

Pierre Cardin worked as a young man in <u>Christian Dior</u>'s couture house when the 'New Look' was produced in 1947. The experience was fundamental to his development: inspired by the range of opportunities which Dior's success suggested was ready to be tapped, he opened his own house in 1953, and became the first couturier fully to exploit the mass-market opportunities of Paris fashion. In 1959 he produced the first line of *prêt-à-porter* clothes for women, quickly moving into licensing operations which covered menswear, bed linen, lingerie, perfumes and stockings. This also made him one of the first couturiers to turn his signature into an instantly recognizable logotype on all sorts of merchandise. In 1966 the Chambre Syndicale, the watchdog of French couture, forced him to resign because his activities were becoming so diversified that the very concept of couture was being undermined. Since then he has designed aeroplane interiors, theatres and restaurants.

Obsessed with ideas about space, technology and the environment, Cardin can infuriate or bore with his monomania, while his taste rises to the inspired or plunges to the catastrophic. The fastidious shudder with embarrassment.

2

1: Santiago Calatrava, Campo Volantin bridge over Bilbao's Nervion river, 1990–97. A boldly angled pipe arch supports 41 steel ribs carrying glass treads. Calatrava's formal intelligence rivals Brunel's.

2: Pierre Cardin created brand extension. He had never read John Updike's remarks that 'celebrity is a brand that eats the face.'

Matthew Carter born 1937

Matthew Carter is perhaps the most influential type-designer ever. In 1955 he worked at Enschede type foundry in Haarlem and at the Plantin-Moretus Museum in Antwerp, sorting out sixteenth-century punches. In the early Sixties he travelled to New York; this was a moment when American graphics were the best in the world and he connected enthusiastically with the energetic culture of Milton Glaser and Herb Lubalin. Back in England he designed sans serif faces for Heathrow Airport. In 1974 Carter designed Bell Centennial for AT&T's telephone directories, creating a new standard of clarity and legibility. Seven years later he established Bitstream in Cambridge, Massachusetts (home of Nicholas Negroponte's influential Media Lab), leaving an increasingly commercial concern to establish the more creative Carter & Cone in 1991.

In 1994 Microsoft commissioned Carter to design Verdana, the incalculably well-known computer typeface. Designed for use with pixels rather than ink, Verdana delivers exceptional clarity on plasma screens from studios in Notting Hill to corporate headquarters in Guangzhou.

Cassandre 1901–68

Cassandre was the pseudonym of Adolphe Jean-Marie Mouron, a French graphic designer and poster artist. He was born in the Ukraine of a Russian mother and a French father, and moved to Paris in 1915 to study at the Ecole des Beaux Arts and the Académie Julien. Between 1923 and 1936 he designed an astonishingly powerful range of posters for the Compagnie des Wagons-Lits and other clients. He reduced his motifs to silhouettes or to exaggerated pictograms, but always treated his subjects with elegance. Typography and imagery are synthesized in Cassandre's posters, as in Edward McKnight Kauffer's, to enhance the total effect. He also worked for the Deberny et Peignot type foundry.

[1] Verdana

ABCDEFGHIJKLMNOP
QRSTUVWXYZabcdefg
hijklmnopqrstuvwxyz1
234567890!@£$%^&
*()+[]{};:'"|,./\<>?~

Cassina born 1909

Cesare Cassina was born into a Milanese family that had traditions in the furniture industry going back to the eighteenth century. He trained as an upholsterer and set up his own business with his brother in 1927, on Milan's via Solferino. In 1935 it became Figli di Amedeo Cassina. Whereas before the Second World War Cassina made only customized furniture for particular clients, during Italy's post-War *ricostruzione* the firm pioneered a more progressive approach to design, hiring <u>Franco Albini</u>, <u>Gio Ponti</u>, <u>Vico Magistretti</u>, <u>Mario Bellini</u> and many other leading Italian furniture designers to contribute to its catalogue. But in the mid-Sixties the firm returned to its origins in reproduction furniture, with the 'Maestri' series of classics by <u>Le Corbusier</u>, <u>Gerrit Rietveld</u> and <u>Charles Rennie Mackintosh</u>. Cassina's reputation is nonetheless as one of Italy's most forward-thinking furniture companies.

Bibliography Pier Carlo Santini *Gli anni del design italiano – Ritratto di Cesare Cassina* Editrice Electa, Milan, 1981

1: Sinbad chair for Cassina, by Vico Magistretti, 1982. The designer was inspired by horse blankets found in a London shop and slung an imitation of them over a metal frame.

2: Achille Castiglioni's 'Mezzadro' stool, manufactured by Zanotta since 1957, employs a tractor seat as a ready-made. In his Milan studio Castiglioni kept a bizarre collection of junk and ephemera which inspired his often surreal designs.

Achille Castiglioni 1918–2002

Achille Castiglioni is one of three Milanese brothers who were all designers. Achille's interest in design was first inspired by his elder brothers, Pier Giacomo and Livio, who designed a dramatic plastic-cased radio receiver for Phonolain in 1938 with the help of Caccia Dominioni. Achille read architecture at Milan Polytechnic, graduating in 1944, and was one of the founders of the Associazione per il Disegno Industrial in 1956. He designed furniture, lighting and appliances, and his products won <u>Compasso d'Oro</u> awards in 1955, 1960, 1962, 1964, 1967, 1979 and 1984. Six of his pieces are in the permanent collection of New York's <u>Museum of Modern Art</u>. Among his best-known pieces are a kneeling stool for <u>Zanotta</u> and his 'Arco' light for <u>Flos</u>. After the Second World War, Achille Castiglioni was one of the most prolific of all Italian designers, and he evolved a unique philosophy which derives from the 'ready-made' concept of Marcel Duchamp, like his chair inspired by a tractor seat. His clients included <u>BrionVega</u>, <u>Flos</u>, <u>Gavina</u>, <u>Knoll</u>, <u>Kartell</u>, <u>Zanotta</u>, B&B, Ideal Standard, Siemens and Lancia, and he contributed to design magazines and the Italian national press. His philosophy of design was that it is an 'attitude arising out of critical habit… an art insofar as it invents a function and translates it into a form'. Wit was the central element in his designs; sometimes incongruous materials, such as found objects, are bound together in pursuit of functional elegance. His 'Arco' lamp for Flos uses a marble base weighing about 100 pounds to support a thin arc of pressed aluminium and a light spun-aluminium reflector; his 'Toio' lamp for the same company uses a car headlamp.

In his ingenuity with materials, his sense of joy, his imaginative use of industrial components and techniques, Achille Castiglioni was the absolute definition of what a great industrial designer should be – he has a sense of humour!

Bibliography Anty Pansera & Alfonso Grassi *Atlante del design italiano* Fabbri, Milan, 1980

Central School of Arts and Crafts

London's Central School of Art and Design was founded as the Central School of Arts and Crafts in 1896 with the brief of displaying design, encouraging manufacturers and, in particular, educating the public about the material environment in general. Its first director was W.R. Lethaby, under whom its first courses were very much crafts-based. In 1946 it established Britain's first course in industrial design. Its distinguished pupils have included David Carter and Tom Karen. It remains one of Britain's leading industrial design schools.

Bibliography *Central to Design – Central to Industry* Central School of Art and Design, London, 1983

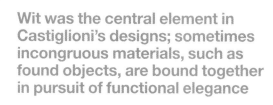

Wit was the central element in Castiglioni's designs; sometimes incongruous materials, such as found objects, are bound together in pursuit of functional elegance

Gabrielle Chanel 1883–1971

'Coco' Chanel's career as a couturier began during the First World War in fashionable Deauville, on the Normandy coast. Her first essay in style was to assemble an outfit composed of a man's sweater pulled over her pleated skirt, tied at the waist by an artfully careless handkerchief. This daring assemblage won her a reputation for chic. The Duke of Westminster helped her start a Paris boutique, and while cruising the Mediterranean in the Duke's yacht Chanel developed a suntan and, practically single-handed, turned *bronzage*, hitherto considered the mark of a peasant labourer, into an international status symbol. Her style was established in the Twenties: a neat, tailored suit, matching silk shirt and two-toned shoes. Chanel's boutique closed during the Second World War but reopened in 1954, and such was the classic nature of her style that it sold virtually the same lines as it had during the Thirties. Her achievement was to introduce simplicity into women's clothes and her designs were adaptable for the ready-to-wear market. Today her house is run by Karl Lagerfeld. Luxury, Chanel once explained, is not the opposite of poverty, it is the opposite of vulgarity.

Colin Chapman 1928–83

Colin Chapman was a British automotive designer who pioneered the successful use of lightweight structures, aerodynamics and other aerospace techniques in the design of racing and road cars.

The Lotus company was set up in Hornsey, North London, in 1952, and was originally run from Chapman's garage. Chapman produced a series of highly competitive sports and racing cars throughout the Fifties, then, with the 'Elite' in 1959, Lotus made a passenger car available to the public. The Elite was a sensation, and with its lightweight aerodynamic shape and highly efficient, small-volume engine predicted by 20 years the general concerns of the automotive industry.

But it was with racing cars that Colin Chapman applied his aeronautical experience most thoroughly. The Formula 1 Lotus 25 of 1962 was the first car in which Chapman used an aircraft-style stressed monocoque, and its successor, the Lotus 33, became one of the most successful racing cars of all time. Throughout the Sixties and Seventies Chapman pursued the technical limits of racing car design, experimenting using wedge shapes, 'ground effect' and advanced materials. He was so successful that only Ferrari has won more Grands Prix.

Chapman's road cars were admired for their elegance of conception but were often let down by reliability and finish. Nevertheless, the Mark 26 or 'Elan' of 1963 and the 'Europa' of 1966, both using fibreglass bodies elegantly designed by Chapman's associate John Frayling, created new standards in the performance of light cars. After the Sixties Lotus' performances were mixed. Chapman ran the company in a headstrong way and frequently over-extended himself and his associates. There were a number of radical innovations in racing car design, but the production cars were affected by the oil crisis. Chapman had Giorgetto Giugiaro design the body for the Lotus 'Esprit' of 1976, but an association with John De Lorean brought the hitherto unimpeachable company into some disrepute, and Chapman's premature death from a heart attack was blamed on tensions arising out of the De Lorean scandal.

3: 'Coco' Chanel was accused of 'miserablisme de luxe' by Paul Poiret, but her own belief was that luxury is not the opposite of poverty, but the opposite of vulgarity.

4: Colin Chapman's Lotus 49, 1967. Chapman brought aesthetic economy and intuitive genius to the design of racing cars. 'Simplify and add lightness' was his belief.

Pierre Chareau 1883–1950

Born in Bordeaux, Pierre Chareau dallied between painting, music, decorating, furniture design and architecture. In 1930 he was one of the founders of the Union des Artistes Modernes. He emigrated in 1939 to the United States. Chareau made some exceptional and eccentric designs for furniture in wood and metal, some of them for the Compagnie Parisienne d'ameublement, which can loosely be described as <u>Art Deco</u>. These were always exclusive rather than popular. Chareau also designed remarkable houses for the Parisian doctor Dalsace and the American painter Robert Motherwell. The former, with walls of glass – the Maison de Verre, is one of the great, if impractical, romantic monuments of <u>Modernism</u>.
Bibliography René Herbst *Pierre Chareau* Editions du Salon des Arts Ménagers, Paris, 1954

Chartered Society of Designers (CSD)

The Society of Industrial Artists and Designers was founded by <u>Milner Gray</u> and others in 1930. Its first members came from the worlds of graphic and exhibition design and it was the first professional society of its kind in the world, and is still the largest. It was granted a Royal Charter in 1976, and changed its name to the Chartered Society of Designers in 1986.

Chermayeff & Geismar

Ivan Chermayeff, born 1932, the son of the Russian émigré architect of the <u>International Style</u>, Serge Chermayeff (1900–96), and Thomas Geismar (born 1931) opened a graphic design office with Robert Brownjohn in 1957. They were given the job of designing a corporate identity for the Chase Manhattan Bank, and then <u>Eliot Noyes</u> commissioned them in 1964 to do the graphics for Mobil. Their solution to this task was very simple: the 'o' in the name was made red, both to symbolize the wheel and to give the logotype a special character which reflected the circular, mushroom-like motifs which Noyes used throughout the filling stations. They were fiercely proud of their elegant, unpretentious simplicity, and Tom Geismar once said, 'We get clients who don't want to pay a lot to find answers to easy questions.'

The Chartered Society of Designers was the first professional society of its kind in the world and is still the largest

1: Pierre Chareau's (and Bernard Bijvoet's) Maison de Verre, 31 rue Saint-Guillaume, Paris 7eme, 1931. A Modernist shrine, Chareau's and Bijvoet's audacious glass house nicely combines Modernist austerity with French luxury.

Fede Cheti 1905–78

Fede Cheti established her own textile firm in 1930 and caught the attention of Gio Ponti with her exhibits at the Monza Biennale of 1930 and the Milan Triennale of 1933. She printed chintz, silk and velvet with strong, though subtle, motifs derived from nature that expressed the mood of Surrealism then fashionable in Italy. Her upholstery fabrics, sold from her Milanese showroom, were particularly popular in the Fifties.

Chiavari

Chiavari is, with Brianza, one of the homes of traditional furniture manufacture in Italy. A fishing village near Genoa, its ship-building traditions were passed on into furniture workshops. The modern industry of Chiavari was founded in the early nineteenth century by Gaetano Descalzi, known as 'il Camponino'. He started production by imitating a chair brought from Paris, refining the traditional design and perfecting a new technique of weaving the seat done by the fishermen's wives, as well as rounding off wooden details. His objective was to make these chairs, known as 'Camponino' chairs, lighter and lighter. Gio Ponti adopted this element of the traditional Chiavari chair in his 'Superleggera' design of the Fifties, which Cassina manufactured.
Bibliography G. Brignardello *G. G Descalzi* 1870

Walter Percy Chrysler 1875–1938

Born in Kansas, Walter Percy Chrysler's first job was as a sweeper in the Union Pacific Railroad. When promoted to machinist's apprentice he forged his own tools out of scraps of metal. From there he worked his way through the American railway industry and became superintendent of motive power at the Chicago Great Western Railroad in 1908. In the same year he bought his first car, a Locomobile. His work as a railroad engineer attracted the attention of the founders of General Motors and in 1912 Chrysler was made manager of the Buick plant. By 1916 he had become first vice-president of General Motors in charge of operations. He resigned in 1919 and, after flirting in management jobs with some other manufacturers, formed the Chrysler Corporation in 1925.

Walter P. Chrysler's reputation is as a builder of soundly engineered cars, ones which often employed advanced design principles: his company was responsible for the Airflow, one of the most radical and influential cars of the Thirties.

2: Chermayeff & Geismar, corporate identity for Mobil 1964. This superbly clean and authoritative signage contrasts nicely with the suggestive imagery of the 'portrait' of Churchill for a television series called *The Forgotten Years*.

3: Chrysler was always the most technologically daring, if not the most successful, of the American automobile manufacturers.

CIAM

The Congrès Internationaux d'Architecture Moderne was an international organization formed to bring together all the architects and spokesmen of Modernism in a campaigning body which would give public relations force to the architectural monument which they had already created at the Deutsche Werkbund's exhibition at Weissenhof in 1927.

Its first meeting was held in 1928 at the château of La Sarraz, outside Lausanne in Switzerland. Organized by Sigfried Giedion, the delegates included Josef Frank, Le Corbusier and Mart Stam. The meeting was a symbol of the unity of purpose which the Modern Movement architects and designers felt was expressed in the International Style. A series of conferences followed – Frankfurt in 1929, Brussels in 1930 and Athens in 1933 – where the major items of Modern Movement policy were debated and established.

Bibliography Jacques Gubler *Nationalisme et Internationalisme dans l'architecture moderne de la Suisse* L'Age d'Homme, Lausanne, 1975

Citroën

The French car manufacturer Citroën was founded by André Citroën as an arms factory at the beginning of the First World War. Citroën's father was a Jew whose original name was Limoenmann, but he changed it to a phonic near-miss of the French word for 'lemon' in order to escape the anti-semitic prejudice which was rife in France well into the early years of the twentieth century. Citroën's reputation as a firm of car manufacturers has rested upon a richly deserved reputation for ingenuity. Citroën was a great showman and had his name in lights on the Eiffel Tower. He also was a counsel of perfection in a usually parsimonious industry. He said 'Des l'instant ou une idée est bonne, le prix n'a pas di'importance.' ('From the moment an idea is worthwhile, price doesn't matter.') This stirring principle resulted in bankruptcy and a takeover by Michelin in 1934.

When the demand for arms declined after 1918, Citroën set up a car factory in order to take advantage of the gear-cutting machines he had to hand for his munitions. His first designer was Jules Saloman, and their Type A of 1919 was Europe's first mass-produced car. With disc wheels, fitted hood, electric lights and on-board starter it raised the standard of automotive engineering overnight; on the day it was announced a vast number of orders was received. But the first Citroën to become a classic was the Type C, a primitive design made interesting by its simple but adventurous chassis and suspension: with a flexible frame, no shock absorbers and no bump-stops. This 5CV established Citroën's reputation as a mass-market manufacturer. It was followed by the Traction Avant (front-wheel drive) of 1934,

engineered by André Lefebvre (the first Frenchman to wear a nylon shirt), and Pierre Boulanger's 2CV of 1939. The 2CV was conceived as basic transportation that could carry 50kg of luggage at 50km/h, which Boulanger saw as a rival to the Volkswagen, although ironically its use of simple materials and geometric forms betrays the influence of Bauhaus thought in France. André Citroën himself over invested in retooling for the Traction Avant and died broke after his major creditor, Michelin, had taken over the company.

The Traction Avant was introduced as the 7A. It was a car whose appearance and engineering were so advanced that 20 years after its introduction it was still ahead of its rivals in both respects. By using front-wheel drive, Citroën was able to produce a car which had a wheel at each corner, allowing a free use of passenger space, and the immensely long wheelbase which this system afforded gave passengers greatly enhanced comfort. Citroën's policy when launching new cars was for them to be radically new designs, and to produce and mature them over an extended period. Thus, the successor to the Traction Avant did not go on sale until 1957, but was to be the now-legendary DS19.

The DS19 first appeared at the Turin Motor Show of 1955, where it was displayed without wheels on a pylon, so that the startling shape drawn by Flaminio Bertoni could be better admired. It was the most advanced popular car of all time, the vehicle celebrated by Roland Barthes in a rhapsodic essay. DS is an abbreviation of *voiture de grande diffusion*, but because of the way the letters sound in French the car became known as the *Déesse*, or 'Goddess'. It featured a unique

1

1

Citroën's policy when launching new cars was for them to be radically new designs

oleo-pneumatic suspension system, and its full-width body, large glass area, plastic roof and almost total lack of ornament made the DS, like the 7A, 20 years ahead of its time.

Citroën products became tokens of educated, design-conscious taste; despite or because of this the company rarely made a profit. The last eccentric Citroën was the SM, a curiosity with a leaky Maserati engine created under the design leadership of Robert Opron, a man who fetishized fared-in headlamps. In 1975 it was taken over by the ultra-conservative Peugeot Group, PSA, and design direction wavered. An Englishman called Trevor Fiore, appointed chief designer in 1979, achieved very little and, to the horror of the purists, the Citroën BX of 1982 used styling consultancy provided by Bertone. The Citroen XM that followed was, according to English critic Jonathan Meades, 'the last Gothic car'. A period of exceptional drabness followed, with Citroën being scarcely more than re-branded assemblages from Peugeot's corporate parts bin. Such creative direction as there was could only be seen as a pitiably deliberate attempt to ape the ingenuity and inventiveness of the past, or, at least, the expression of it. By 2006 some new directions had been discovered: the C6 limousine was a genuinely imposing car of real visual character. But any new product by Citroën is severely tested by comparison with a backlist of cars that are among the greatest monuments to the Machine Age.

Bibliography Jacques Borge & Nicolas Viasnoff *L'Album de la DS* Editions EPA, Paris, 1983; *Modelfall Citroën-Produktgestaltung und Werbung* exhibition catalogue, Kunstgewerbemuseum, Zürich, 1967

Clarice Cliff 1899–1972

Clarice Cliff trained at Burslem School of Art in the British potteries area. She worked for the local manufacturer A. J. Wilkinson, for whom she designed her 'Bizarre' service, now a collector's piece for those interested in Art Deco. Cliff also painted patterns designed by painters Laura Knight and Graham Sutherland onto domestic ceramics manufactured by Royal Staffordshire Pottery. She was typical of the small-scale designer-entrepreneurs of the Thirties, producing exclusive work that ultimately had a popular influence and a high price at contemporary auctions.

Bibliography Martin Battersby *The Decorative Thirties* Studlo Vista, London, 1971; Clarkson Potter, New York, 1971

Cliff was typical of the small-scale designer-entrepreneurs of the Thirties, producing exclusive work that ultimately had a popular influence and a high price at contemporary auctions

1: Boulanger's and Bertoni's Citroën DS, 1957.
2: Citroën's Type A, 1919, was Europe's first mass-produced car.
3: Clarice Cliff, 'House and Bridge' teapot for Stamford, 1931–33.

Wells Coates 1895–1958

Wells Wintemute Coates was, perhaps, the outstanding English architect of the International Style, as well as being a product designer of considerable originality.

He was born in Tokyo, the son of a professor of comparative religion, and left Japan when he was 18 to attend Canada's McGill University. After the First World War he worked as a journalist and as a lumberjack in Canada, then arrived in London in 1929 and designed some elegant, moderne shops whose sparseness reminded some critics that he had, after all, been educated in the Orient. He founded the Modern Architecture Research Group (MARS) in 1933, having the previous year set up the Isokon company with Jack Pritchard, for whom he designed the Lawn Road flats. This building was the first essay in England of the International Style. Another of his major buildings was Embassy Court in Brighton, with some photo-mural decorations by Edward McKnight Kauffer. In 1932 Coates designed a radio set for Eric Kirkham Cole (1901–65), who founded the Ekco company in 1921. It was the first authentic expression in Britain of modern design applied to a domestic appliance.

A polymath, and an enthusiastic driver of Lancia cars, Coates researched a PhD thesis at London University on the gas flow in diesel engines. He also designed the most daring of the studio interiors for the BBC's new Broadcasting House. Coates was a skilled Japanese cook and an impassioned conversationalist on all aspects of art and science. In his work he expressed his sense of the drama of the modern age and, as the London Times obituarist remarked, 'For him modern design was not a fashion but a cause demanding unquestioning devotion.'

Bibliography Sherban Cantacuzino *Wells Coates* Gordon Fraser, London, 1978

Luigi Colani born 1928

Luigi 'Lutz' Colani was educated in Paris and Berlin. He produces fantastic 'organic' designs for cars and other consumer products that have frequently been published in popular magazines, but his implemented designs have been few. One of his clients is Rosenthal, for whom his 'Drop' porcelain service of 1971 won a Gute Industrieform prize at the Hanover Fair. Concepts of Colani's that seemed fantastical were especially influential in Japan where his bizarre formal sense, partly ergonomic, partly science-fiction, soon became part of the repertoire of camera design. He is a cult figure among students who easily identify with his counter-culture character. 'Germans are cubic' he said, 'you can put them on a shelf. I am a ball'.

Bibliography *Luigi Colani* exhibition catalogue, Design Museum, London 2007

1

Colani's 'Drop' porcelain service of 1971 won a Gute Industrieform prize at the Hanover Fair

2

3

Henry Cole 1808–82

In 1846 Henry Cole became a member of the Society of Arts, and in the same year the Society awarded him a medal, under his pseudonym of Felix Summerley, for a tea service design of astonishing simplicity. The following year the Society was given a royal charter and became the <u>Royal Society of Arts</u>; Cole joined the council and worked on the plans that led to the <u>Great Exhibition</u> in 1851.

Cole was the central figure in the establishment of design in Britain, founding the *Journal of Design* in 1849. Institutions he created and reforms he proposed helped build what has become the <u>Victoria and Albert Museum</u>, and his idea for an 'Albert University' as a memorial to his mentor, Prince Albert, eventually found form in the <u>Royal College of Art</u>. He also invented the adhesive postage stamp. He was made a KCB in 1875.

Britain's first art schools, called the Schools of Design, were founded as a consequence of the Parliamentary Select Committee's Report on Arts and Manufactures of 1836. The idea was to establish in all Britain's manufacturing cities institutions half way between museums and schools to teach industrial artisans by example, in order to raise taste. Many manufacturers, however, expressed disappointment at the ability of the graduates, who seemed to have been more highly skilled in painting and sculpture than in industrial techniques. Under Henry Cole's direction 90 art schools with 16,000 students had been established by 1864. This was the basis for Britain's entire system of art education, still the most extensive in the world.

Bibliography Elizabeth Bonython *King Cole* H.M.S.O., London, n.d.; *Victoria and Albert Museum*, H.M.S.O., London, n.d.; Quentin Bell *The Schools of Design* Routledge & Kegan Paul, London, 1963

Colefax and Fowler

Colefax and Fowler is a firm of interior decorators founded in London in 1935 by Sybil Colefax, a widowed society figure and a close acquaintance of another decorator, <u>Syrie Maugham</u>. John Fowler joined her firm in 1938. Colefax had the right connections and Fowler, through his assiduous studies at the <u>Victoria and Albert Museum</u> and elsewhere, the right knowledge to start the most enduring of all firms of decorators. Their style was influenced by Fowler's particular taste for 'pleasing decay', which he nurtured by doing oil paintings in the manner of the Italian architectural *capriccios* of the eighteenth century. The result has been described as 'unpretentious grandeur', although the clients were often the owners of the grandest country houses (as well as the National Trust). The Colefax and Fowler style is the *locus classicus* of that understated, faded gentility which suggests 'Englishness'. John Fowler died in 1977, but the firm still operates from the premises in London's Brook Street, which it acquired in the mid-Fifties.

Gino Colombini born 1915

As technical director of <u>Kartell</u> since the foundation of this specialized injection-moulding company in 1949, Gino Colombini became responsible for masterpiece buckets and was the first to have his name attached to such a banal object on display in New York's <u>Museum of Modern Art</u>. Through Kartell, Colombini was responsible for bringing genuine technical and aesthetic quality to objects made of plastics, whether in the design of a colander, a bucket or a chair. He won <u>Compasso d'Oro</u> awards in 1955, 1957, 1959 and 1960, for a range of small domestic products. His achievements in giving aesthetic quality to ordinary things is a perfect example of the culture of the Italian *ricostruzione*, indeed, of *Italina cultur*, where art was never completely separated from life.

1: Wells Coates was an English champion of Modernism, a fine example of 'le style est l'homme'. Embassy Court, Brighton, 1935, brought the International Style to the South Coast.
2: Ekco AD65 radio, 1934.

3: Luigi Colani, 'Drop' porcelain service for Rosenthal, 1971.
4: Gino Colombini used Kartell's sophisticated injection moulding technology to translate ordinary domestic items, including these vegetable baskets, into useful objects with genuine aesthetic merit.

4
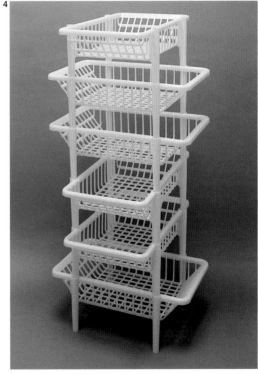

Joe Colombo 1930–71

Joe Cesare Colombo, an Italian designer who became a cult figure among design cognoscenti during the Sixties, died of a heart attack in the 'arms' of his lover in 1971 and was immediately turned into a hero of modern design. His great achievement was to see that Pop and technology could work together.

Colombo studied painting at the Brera in Milan and architecture at Milan Polytechnic, and while still a student in his early twenties erected his first building. He experimented with avant-garde painting and sculpture until 1962, when he set up his own architectural office in Milan. As his interest was mainly in interior design, he was led to thinking about the design of furniture and fittings. He soon designed his 'Elda' chair and lights for O-Luce.

All Colombo's designs have a very strong formal value. Nevertheless, he denied that his work had simply a visual character, even speaking in favour of 'anti-design'. As was required of leading Italian intellectuals of the day, he was explicitly anti-capitalist – at least in matters of personal presentation, if not in matters of personal banking. This theory about furniture and products was modishly followed by self-styled Italian radicals for a while in the late Sixties and Seventies, and proposed that the purpose and meaning of a chair or any product should be considered as more important than its appearance. Although he linked himself with this 'radical' posture, with the perspective of time, Colombo's work, excellent as it was, seems only to be an evanescent, if perhaps perfect, expression of Sixties taste.

Colombo was known for experimental, even audacious, interiors. Always using plastic and fibreglass, always shiny and in combative colours, these projects often had a cinematic character. Ken Adams' sets for James Bond films may have been inspirations for Colombo as certainly as Colombo was an inspiration for the home of poet Luna Schlosser in Woody Allen's 1973 movie, *Sleeper*. Yet, despite the obvious and transient glitz, Colombo followed a version of functionalism: he designed a glass to be held by the thumb alone so the fingers could be free for that obligatory Italian cigarette.

A passionate avatar of technology as the art of the later twentieth century, Colombo called furniture 'equipment', and said: 'In the past, space was static, but our century has a fourth dimension: time. Now this must be introduced into space to make it dynamic.' Accordingly, more than one Milanese apartment designed by Colombo had a decorator's demonstration of the space-time continuum: pendant lights whizzing hither and yon on tracks. Colombo began to suggest new ways of living in what became known as Total Living Units, with everything integrated into a plastic module. His old friend Alessandro Mendini said 'In Italy in the Sixties he was considered a bit crazy, but today he is taken more seriously.'

Bibliography *The New Domestic Landscape* exhibition catalogue, Museum of Modern Art, New York, 1972; Anty Pansera & Alfonso Grassi *Atlante del design Italiano* Fabri, Milan, 1981; *Joe Colombo – inventing the future* Vitra Design Museum, Weil am Rhein, 2006.

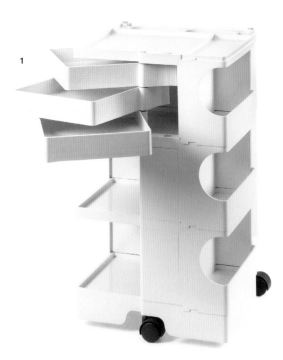

1

Colombo followed functionalism: he designed a glass to be held by the thumb alone so the fingers could be free for that obligatory Italian cigarette

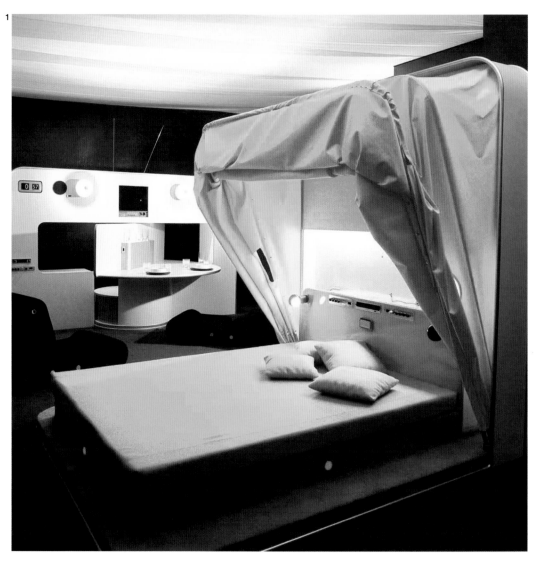

1

Compasso d'Oro

Compasso d'Oro is the name of a series of design awards established by the Italian stores <u>La Rinascente</u>. First offered as a one-off in 1954, the awards were so popular that they became annual events from 1956. Like the awards offered by the British <u>Council of Industrial Design</u>, the aim was to isolate those qualities that made products both attractive and a commercial success.

Constructivism

Constructivism is a term which covers a loose federation of meanings, and eludes precise definition. In Russia Constructivism was the art of the years immediately following the Revolution of 1917, although 'art' is itself a misnomer because the Constructivists wanted to do away with fine art. They believed that art should take on the quality of the machine, and that industry could transform life. The most important 'artistic' expressions in the post-Revolutionary years were architecture, town planning, agitprop (posters and propaganda) and <u>industrial design</u>. In the Soviet Union, Constructivism is at least easy to define historically because it has precise limits: the heroic age of experimentation that started with the Revolution ended with the introduction of the New Economic Policy in 1921. For a brief moment, avant-garde art was totally identified with popular needs.

In the rest of Europe Constructivism is less susceptible to definition. The Dutch <u>De Stijl</u> group of architects and painters, the middle years of the <u>Bauhaus</u> in Germany, and <u>Laszlo Moholy-Nagy</u> in England are all examples. If it means anything at all here, it means a form of artistic expression that relies not on the traditional materials of oil and canvas and marble but on 'modern' ones – say, plastics and steel and film. It is concerned not with the traditional aims of art (to delight and to exalt), but with the unemotional advancement of social purpose.

Despite its Utopian democratic intentions, Constructivism was nonetheless a rarefied phenomenon, much the same in its exclusivity as any other 'movement' in the fine arts. There was actually little Constructivist design, but the dramatic, austere graphics and paintings of Kasimir Malevich and El Lissitsky have been frequently imitated in the mass-market.

Bibliography Stephen Bann *The Tradition of Constructivism* Thames & Hudson, London, 1974

1: Joe Colombo experimented with an entire kitchen on castors in 1963. The year after, he productionized the idea into a storage trolley that was a mobile office. His 'Cabriolet' bed for Sormani, 1970, continued this way of thinking. In the decade of happenings and art installations, Colombo extended the concept of furniture design to the making of miniature environments.

2: El Lissitsky, Proun 19D, circa 1922. 'Proun' was a coinage turning Constructivist art into a mechanistic commodity.

2

Contemporary

The term 'Contemporary' came to be used in Britain in the years immediately after the Second World War to describe an expressive, sculptural style in furniture and interior design that began to replace the more austere forms of the Modern Movement.

Contemporary designs were inspired by the Surrealist forms of the sculptors Alexander Calder and Hans Arp, and made possible by new materials and techniques such as steel rod and moulded plastics. Jean Prouvé's architecture and furniture, intended to be so industrially pure when designed in the Fifties, now appear to be perfect exemplars of Contemporary: elegant, non threatening curves and a taste for decorative effects.

The new style was made public at the Festival of Britain. Inspired by technical drawings of the structure of the atom, Lucienne Day, for example, designed abstract textile patterns that struck the young Terence Conran as 'not quite a crime, but not worthy of the recognition they have received'. There was a taste for experimentation and variety and the new fabrics, as well as Ernest Race's 'Springbok' and 'Antelope' chairs, soon became widespread (especially in the new towns of the Fifties, Harlow and Stevenage). Although Contemporary started out as an exclusive style with encouragement from the Council of Industrial Design, it soon became exaggerated and debased so that boomerang coffee tables and coat racks made out of black enamelled steel rods with coloured plastic balls were widely sold.

British Contemporary was an expression of an international style. It synthesized features that had appeared in Italy, Scandinavia and the United States. The style itself, somewhat modified in accordance with national preferences, appeared throughout the world. It was a mass style, encouraged by mass taste, driven by popular rather than by establishment values, and emphasizing fantasy rather than function in interior design. (See also Ercol and G-Plan.)

Bibliography Cara Greenberg *Mid-Century Modern: Furniture of the Fifties*, Harmony, New York, 1984

Hans Coray 1907–91

Hans Coray's aluminium 'Landi' chair was the sensation of the 1939 Schweizerischen Landesausstellung (Swiss National Exhibition). It originated in an approach made to a metal plate processor by Hans Fischli, architect of the exhibition. Coray's subsequent design used drop-forging to mould the seat and the latest heat-treatment processes to make it durable. It is light, strong and ingenious, and has been in continuous production for almost 50 years. It was the chief influence on the British designer Rodney Kinsman, in the design of his own 'OMK' stacking chair.

1

Council of Industrial Design (CoID)

A Council for Art and Industry was established in London under the auspices of the Board of Trade in 1934. This was the basis for the Council of Industrial Design, founded in 1944. The Council was set up to encourage manufacturers to use designers and to raise the level of popular taste. To these ends it organized an exhibition called 'Britain Can Make It' at the Victoria and Albert Museum in 1946, and the Council acquired a public face when the Design Centre was opened in the Council's Haymarket premises in central London in 1956. Gordon Russell was director from 1947 to 1960, when it became the Design Council under his successor, Paul Reilly.

The Council of Industrial Design was set up to encourage manufacturers to use designers and to raise the level of popular taste

2

Cranbrook Academy

The Cranbrook Academy was an educational community, founded in the early Twenties by George C. Booth, a British-born newspaper publisher, on his estate 20 miles outside Detroit. Part of Booth's motivation was to create a balance to the increasingly commercial and mercantile character of American design. Cranbrook was a re-invention of a cherished American ideal: a dedicated, Utopian community. In 1923 Booth met Eliel Saarinen, a Finnish Arts and Crafts designer teaching at the University of Michigan, who had come to the United States as a consequence of taking part in the 1922 architectural competition to design a new building for the *Chicago Tribune*. Astonishingly, Saarinen had made his skyscraper designs while living in a forest outside Helsinki. That degree of independent vision helped him to become both the leading creative force behind the Cranbrook Academy and the architect of its buildings.

Cranbrook's influence on American design was in inverse relation to its degree of isolation in the Mid-West, and its teachers and graduates included Eero Saarinen, Niels Diffrient, Charles Eames, Florence Knoll, Jack Lenor Larsen and David Rowland. It has been compared to the Bauhaus in its influence, but if the Bauhaus was Germanic in spirit, then Cranbrook was Anglo-Saxon and Nordic. Eliel Saarinen described its philosophy in a speech in 1931: '[Cranbrook] is not an art school in the ordinary meaning. It is a working place for creative art: creative art cannot be taught by others. Each one has to be his own teacher. But [contact] with other artists and discussions with them provide sources for inspiration.'

George Booth died in 1949 and Eliel Saarinen (who had anyway become preoccupied elsewhere) died the year after. Without the presence of its two creators, Cranbrook lost its novelty and its special significance.
Bibliography *Design in America: the Cranbrook Vision 1925-1950* exhibition catalogue, Detroit Institute of Arts/Metropolitan Museum, New York, 1984

Walter Crane 1845–1915

Walter Crane was a painter, illustrator and wallpaper and textile designer of no particular distinction, but was an administrator and polemicist of some influence. Awed by William Morris, he became the chief spokesman for the Arts and Crafts movement in his roles as president of the Arts and Crafts Exhibition Society and Master of the Art Workers' Guild. He published a book, *The Claims of Decorative Art*, in 1892, and he was principle of the Royal College of Art in 1898.

Crane's illustrations helped popularize the Arts and Crafts.
Bibliography Elizabeth Aslin *The Aesthetic Movement* Paul Elek, London, 1969; Praeger, New York, 1969; Isobel Spencer *Walter Crane* Studio Vista, London, 1975; Macmillan, New York, 1976

3

1: Powell and Moya's Skylon was the most striking architectural feature of the taste-making Festival of Britain, 1951. Although temporary, it predicted the style of Fifties modernismo.

2: Hans Coray, 'Landi' chair, 1939.
3: Walter Crane, Frog Prince and Maiden, 1874.

Danese

Bruno Danese founded his company in Milan in 1957. It specializes in what the French call '*le petit design*' – small, exquisite objects in metal and ceramic, and glasses, bowls and vases. Danese's production is characterized by elegance and quality. From the beginning he used Enzo Mari and Bruno Munari who, since 1964, have been joined by Angelo Mangiarotti.

1

Jean Daninos 1906–2001

Jean Daninos created France's last great luxury cars. His 3,000 Facel-Vegas that appeared in the ten years after 1954 were legitimate successors to the glorious Delages, Delahayes and Bugattis of the period before the Second World War. Daninos studied at Paris' Ecole des Arts et Metiers and joined Andre Citroën in 1928, working on the coupé version of the Traction Avant (which Citroën himself feared might undermine the company's mainstay). Daninos then went to Morane-Saulnier, where he specialized in advanced electric welding techniques in the fabrication of fighter wings. In 1939 he established his own concern, Forges et Ateliers de Construction d'Eure et Loire, to specialize in metal bashing for the automobile and aircraft industries; 'Facel' was its acronym. In the United States during the Second World War he designed the Panelectric Cuberator fridge. Returning to France, Facel made its money from sub-contracts for hub-caps and radiator grilles as well as its own-brand kitchen sinks. Coachwork for Simca, Bentley and Ford France helped establish the design language, much influenced by Pininfarina, which culminated in his masterpiece, the Facel-Vega HK-500. With its razor edges, large glass house, elegantly assertive snout, evocative jewellery and confident surfacing, it was a design of great elegance and purity, but also of power and authority. The writer Albert Camus was killed in a Facel-Vega driven by his publisher, Michel Gallimard. Other celebrities who found in Daninos' Facel-Vega a car of appropriate glamour and cachet included Francois Truffaut and Ringo Starr.

2

Corradino d'Ascanio 1891–1981

The Italian aviation pioneer Corradino d'Ascanio studied mechanical engineering at Turin Polytechnic and became technical director of Società d'Aviazione Pomilio. Soon after the First World War he left the Pomilio company to found a firm of his own with Veniero d'Annunzio, the son of the poet Gabriele. In 1926, under the patronage of Pietro Trojani, he set up another company dedicated to realizing Leonardo da Vinci's concept of a helicopter. His first model appeared at Pescara in 1926, but was a failure because its rotor blades were rigidly attached to its mast. However, in 1930 he achieved his goal and produced a helicopter that established records for height and duration of flight.

The Italian establishment not being interested in the military potential of the helicopter, d'Ascanio joined the Genoese engineering firm of Piaggio in 1934, for whom he designed a range of aircraft components, which included variable pitch propellers. He persuaded Piaggio to work on helicopters in 1939, but it was on a completely new project that he made the greatest impact. At the end of the War, Enrico Piaggio asked him to collaborate on a radical two-wheeled motor vehicle aimed at the mass-market. D'Ascanio had had little experience with the design of ground transportation, but he took up the challenge as a task in pure engineering. The result was the Vespa motor scooter of 1946, a consumer product designed mainly on aeronautical principles. Not only was its shape streamlined, but its construction in drawn steel was based on aircraft monocoque principles. Eighteen thousand Vespas were produced during its first year of production. It was followed by the 'Ape' car of 1946, a three-wheeled light truck, using scooter components, and by the unsuccessful Vespa 400 car of 1955.

The PD.3 and PD.4 helicopters by d'Ascanio first flew in 1949–52. His last design was for an agricultural helicopter in 1961. D'Ascanio's work demonstrates the influence of Futurism on Italian engineering and, in turn, demonstrates the influence that engineering had on popular culture. The Vespa, inspired by d'Annunzio's poetry and the thrill of flight, became a symbol of mobility and affluence for the Italian generation of the *ricostruzione*.
Bibliography 'Veicoli, 1909–1947' *Rassegna* VI, 18/2, June 1984

Robin Day born 1915

Robin Day studied at a local art school in High Wycombe, then at the Royal College of Art. He came to international attention when a storage unit he designed won first prize in the Museum of Modern Art's 'International Competition for Low Cost Furniture Design' in 1948. Very much inspired by Charles Eames, in 1949 he started working for the furniture manufacturer Hille. He produced for them a variety of chair designs in plastic and plywood culminating in his 'Polypropylene' chair of 1962, one of the great successes in modern chair design which can be compared to pieces by Michael Thonet, Marcel Breuer and David Rowland. Day's wife Lucienne (born 1917) became his partner in 1948. She has achieved success as a fabric designer, working for Heal's and Edinburgh Weavers (see also Contemporary).
Bibliography Hille: *75 Years of British Furniture* exhibition catalogue, Victoria and Albert Museum, London, 1981; Fiona MacCarthy *British Design since 1880* Lund Humphries, London, 1982

3

1: Euzo Mari, 'Timor' table calendar, 1967.
2: Facel-Vega HK500, France's last great luxury car.
3: Robin Day, 'Polypropylene' chair, 1962.

Michele de Lucchi born 1952

Michele de Lucchi studied first at Padua and then at Florence, where he got a degree in architecture in 1975. While at Florence he experimented with avant-garde art and film, and even held a seminar on 'Culturally Impossible Architecture' in the Monselice quarries, just outside Padua. Between 1975 and 1977 he was a teaching assistant at Florence University's faculty of architecture, but moved to Milan in 1978. Here he contributed to Studio Alchymia and later to Memphis, for whom he has created some of their most memorable pieces. In 1979 he became a consultant to the office furniture manufacturer Olivetti Synthesis in Massa, and in 1984 to Olivetti SpA in Ivrea. De Lucchi has designed, with Ettore Sottsass, Olivetti '45CR' and 'Icarus' office furniture, as well as more than 50 Fiorucci shops. His aesthetic is influenced by his philosophy – to render domestic appliances and furniture less hostile and alienating by making them look more like toys. This work for Olivetti continued through the Nineties, although as Italian manufacturing industry declined, de Lucchi has become increasingly more interested in more abstract projects. Of his collaboration on Memphis, the authors of this book say: 'Do you actually know anybody who's got a piece of Memphis in their living rooms? Or who would want to?'

Bibliography Fiorella Bulegato and Sergio Polano *Michele de Lucchi – from here to there to beyond* Electa, Milan, 2004

De Pas, D'Urbino, Lomazzi

The De Pas, D'Urbino, Lomazzi team was founded in Milan in 1966, in the middle of the decade in which their work is forever located. They are best known for a Pop-inspired inflatable 'Blow' chair of 1967 and their 'Joe' chair of 1970, which is in the shape of a stuffed baseball glove. These were succeeded by less memorable designs for other Italian manufacturers.

> Michele de Lucchi's aesthetic is influenced by his philosophy – to render domestic appliances and furniture less hostile

De Stijl

'De Stijl' is Dutch for 'the Style' and is the name of a group of artists and architects who gathered around the (largely theoretical) architect Theo van Doesburg. He founded the group in Leyden in 1917 and published the magazine *De Stijl*, which ran from 1917 to 1928.

De Stijl was one of the European expressions of Constructivism. Van Doesburg believed that modern life required a revolutionary, new art for which he coined the term 'Neo-Plasticism'. De Stijl intended to radicalize the public into an appreciation of this art, but it was not an easy job. With his requirement that Neo-Plastic art should reject any form of overt representation, and that it should be restricted to flat planes of colour (either the primaries, or white, black and grey) orchestrated with straight lines, van Doesburg, ironically, took the 'new art' a long way from the taste of the public, which seemed to prefer the old sort.

1

2

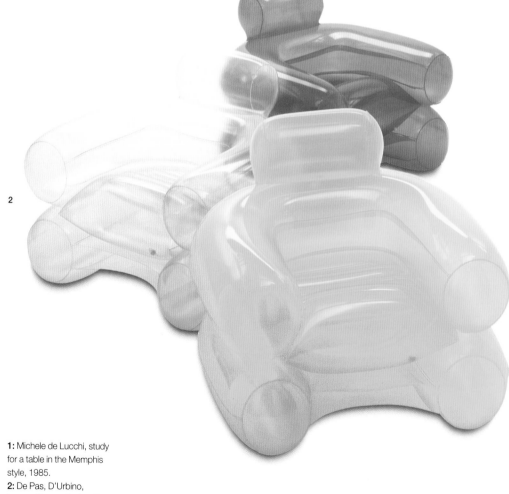

1: Michele de Lucchi, study for a table in the Memphis style, 1985.
2: De Pas, D'Urbino, Lomazzi began their series of inflatable chairs in 1967.
3: Theo van Doesburg, poster for 'De Styl', 1917.
4: Fortunato Depero, Campari packaging, circa 1930. Futurism becomes popular culture.

De Stijl reached its poetic peak in the paintings of Piet Mondrian (1872–1944). Mondrian's status and authority (to say nothing of his ambition to reform human mentality through his art) made De Stijl one of the most influential of the oddball radical groups which flourished in the early twentieth century, and as a result, many of the aesthetic assumptions of the Modern Movement can be traced back to Theo van Doesburg's aesthetic theories. Similarly, Mondrian's inspired pattern-making has been a consistent stimulus (and source) for graphic designers. The architect and furniture designer Gerrit Rietveld became a member of the group in 1918.

Bibliography H.L.C. Jaffe *De Stijl 1917–1931–the Dutch Contribution to Modern Art* Meulenhoff, Amsterdam, 1956; Joost Baljeu, *Theo van Doesburg* Studio Vista, London, 1974; Macmillan, New York, 1974

Paolo Deganello born 1940

Paolo Deganello was, with Andrea Branzi one of the founders of the Archizoom group of radical designers who came together in Florence in 1966. When Archizoom petered out, Deganello founded the Colletivo Technici Progettisti to continue his campaign for furniture design that appeals to the imagination. His 'Torso' lounge chair of 1982 for Cassina rivalled the collections of Memphis in perversity, but was also a serious re-working of furniture ideas and forms from the Fifties.

Fortunato Depero 1892–1960

Artist, eccentric and graphic designer, and of a generation younger than the founders of Futurism, Depero wrote *Ricostruzione futurista dell'universo* in 1915 (with the painter Giacomo Balla). Its ambitious scope was no less than to re-design the universe, but in the years immediately following its publication circumstances demanded that Depero temporarily limit himself to stage design. Depero built his own 'House of Futurist Art' in Rovereto in 1919 and represented the Futurists at the great Paris Expo of 1925. He then developed what he called 'Promotional Architecture', a type of building design that prophetically blurred distinctions between advertising and corporate identity. A proposal for a 'Padiglione di Libro', or book pavilion, for the Bestetti Tuminelli and Treves publishing house, for example, was composed out of giant typograpghical elements. In 1928 Depero, always in trouble with authorities, left for New York where he designed covers for *Vogue* and the *New Yorker* magazines. In 1930 a long association with Campari began: the distinctive conical glass bitters miniature, still in production today, is Depero's. He also produced graphics and advertising for the company. He lived quietly in a cottage in New Milford, Connecticut, before returning to Italy to die.

Bibliography Fortunato Depero *Fortunato Depero nelle opera e nella vita* Trento, 1940 (Translated as So I Think, So I Paint).

3

4

Elsie de Wolfe 1865–1950

Elsie de Wolfe, a professional interior designer, invented the term 'good taste' in her book, *The House in Good Taste* of 1915. Although she ushered into American homes a form of brightness with her motto 'plenty of optimism and white paint', her devotion to antiques produced an inertia in upper-class taste in America. American art historian Russell Lynes characterized her global achievement as 'defeatism in high places'.
Bibliography Penny Sparke *Elsie de Wolfe* Acanthus Press, New York, 2005

Design Management

Design management is the process, now studied at an academic level, in which design activities in commercial bodies are rationalized and organized. It includes the study of the relationship of design to other management functions, but is also being extended to mean how designers can be more effectively used in business.

Donald Deskey 1894–1989

Donald Deskey was, with Raymond Loewy and Henry Dreyfuss, one of the pioneer consultant designers in the United States. He was also one of the most outstanding figures in Art Deco in the Thirties. His career as a designer began in 1920 with a job in a Chicago advertising agency, and he was very much influenced by his visit to the Paris exhibition of 1925. Like many of his contemporaries, Deskey was responsible for only a few realized products, but he did design the interior of Radio City Music Hall in New York's Rockefeller Center, and a number of other interiors and pieces of furniture. His work was characterized by experimentation with new materials, such as aluminium, cork and linoleum.
Bibliography Carol Herselle Krinsky *Rockefeller Center* Oxford University Press, New York, 1978; David A. Hanks *Donald Deskey* E.P. Dutton, New York, 1985

1: Donald Deskey, 1932, Radio City Music Hall, First Mezzanine Lounge with a mural depicting a map of the world by Witold Gordon.
2: Exhibits from the 1914 Deutsche Werkbund exhibition in Cologne, by Henry van de Velde and Theodor Müller.
3: The Christian Dior collection, 1957.

Deutsche Werkbund

The Deutsche Werkbund was an association founded for educational and propaganda purposes, intended to unite business, arts, crafts and industry. It was loosely modelled on the English guilds that sprang up in the second half of the nineteenth century, but was more practical. It was founded in 1907, but, as Reyner Banham has said, its 'golden legend' depends on what happened in a few months around 1914. This was when the Werkbund held its first major exhibition, an enormous festival of German art and industry for which Walter Gropius designed exhibition buildings.

The year 1914 also saw a public debate between Hermann Muthesius and Henry van de Velde over whether the Werkbund should promote standardization and machine-manufacture of products, or free and independent artistic expression. Muthesius prevailed, and his views had a profound influence on the Modern Movement.

During the peaceful Weimar years, to use Banham's words, 'the sense of involvement in the manifest destiny of the German Volk persisted… in… the emphasis on standardization,' a sentiment which can trace its origins far back into German culture, and even to the Prussian military ideal which, in 1911, Muthesius had said was an example to German industry. The Werkbund's exhibition of housing at Weissenhof in 1927, the Weissenhof Siedlung, organized by Mies van der Rohe, was a vindication of Muthesius' beliefs.

The Werkbund was dissolved in 1934 (see Hermann Gretsch), but revived again in 1947.

Bibliography Joan Campbell *The German Werkbund – the politics of reform in the applied arts* Princeton University Press, Princeton, New Jersey and Guildford, 1980

Niels Diffrient born 1928

Niels Diffrient was born at Star, Mississippi and graduated from the Cranbrook Academy. He worked with Eero Saarinen for five years and with Henry Dreyfuss for twenty-five. In 1955 he designed a sewing machine with Marco Zanuso. With Dreyfuss, Diffrient designed Lockheed, Learjet and Hughes aircraft interiors, as well as instruments, X-ray and diagnostic equipment for Litton Industries and Honeywell. Diffrient has a profound concern for ergonomics and left his partnership with Dreyfuss to develop office furniture for Knoll and seating for Sunar. Although, or perhaps because, he was responsible for so many aircraft interiors, Diffrient is acutely aware of the shortcomings of most popular seating, and now runs his own consultancy in Ridgefield, Connecticut, intent on bringing rational planning into chair design.

Christian Dior 1905–58

Christian Dior's 'New Look' of 1947 captured the post-Second World War mood and established him as the master of international fashion. European and American women shared a keen appetite for the style and enthusiastically accepted what he offered: a wasp waist with a slim bodice and bouffant skirt, accompanied by stiletto heel shoes which usually emphasized the exaggeratedly feminine shape. Dior studied traditional tailoring techniques and researched historical costume; he was modest and self-effacing, in spite of his influence. Each year he introduced new lines which were immediately pirated by international ready-to-wear merchants: the 'H' line of 1954, the 'Y' line of 1955 and the famous 'A' line of 1956 being the best known. The house of Dior was run for a brief time by his protégé Yves St Laurent, who was succeeded by Marc Bohan.

3

Christian Dior's 'New Look' of 1947 captured the post-Second World War mood and established him as the master of international fashion

Walt Disney 1901–66

Walter Elias Disney's best-known creation, Mickey Mouse, was called by the Russian film director, Eisenstein, 'America's most original contribution to culture'. Born in Chicago, Disney first set up a cartoon company called Laugh-o-Gram at Kansas City, Missouri, then moved to Hollywood. He conceived the animated beast that made him famous on a journey to New York and introduced him to the world in 1928. He opened Disneyland in 1955 in Anaheim, California, to provide 'a nice clean place to take the kids'. Before he died, Disney had created a leisure empire that incorporated all-American cultural fantasies into a sugar-glazed system for making money.

Disney was stubbornly unintellectual. According to the writer Russell Davies, this was probably because 'he shared with most self-made men a dislike of the thought that he might in some ways be a product of forces outside the range of his own initiative'.

His one-time animator, Art Babbit, said of Disney that he had 'the innate bad taste of the American public', and the writer Ray Bradbury said, 'He is the faucet through which the American Dream runs… Well… maybe he is. Dreams are always in bad taste. It's part of what they're for.'

Disney made the cartoon into a popular medium, and the great success of his features added a new element to the repertoire of graphic designers working in mass communication.

Nana Ditzel born 1923

Nana Ditzel studied at the Kunsthandvaerkskolen (Crafts school) in Copenhagen and opened her first design office in partnership with her first husband, Jorgen Ditzel (1921–61), in 1946. With their combination of natural materials and simple, elegant forms, her interesting designs for jewellery, textiles, tableware and furniture epitomized what was meant by Danish design. Since 1954 she has worked for Georg Jensen and from 1970 onwards in London. Her woven textile collection is remarkably successful.

2

1: Walt Disney and Mickey Mouse, circa 1928.
2: Nana Ditzel, hanging wicker chair for Wengler, Copenhagan, 1959.
3: *Domus* – the Milanese architecture and design magazine founded by Gio Ponti in 1927.

Jay Doblin 1920–89

Jay Doblin studied at Brooklyn's Pratt Institute and worked as a designer both in government service and in private practice (for Raymond Loewy) before becoming the director of the Illinois Institute of Technology, one of America's premier design schools, from 1949 to 1959. He has also been a design consultant to General Motors, Shell and Coca-Cola. In 1966 he was one of the founders of the Unimark consultancy, which specialized in corporate identity, and became a significant figure in the American design and educational establishment. His book *One Hundred Great Product Designs* was the inspiration of this… and a hundred others.

Bibliography Jay Doblin *One Hundred Great Product Designs* Van Nostrand Reinhold, New York, 1970

Domus

Domus is a Milanese architecture and design magazine founded by Gio Ponti in 1927. It has consistently projected progressive Italian architecture and design to the rest of the world. Under the editorship of the communist Ernesto Rogers, *Domus* argued the importance of prefabrication and other architectural solutions to social problems. However, Ponti then restored himself to the editorship and returned *Domus* to its glossy presentation of *la dolce vita*. In 1979 Alessandro Mendini became editor. Mendini's role in Studio Alchymia made him briefly, a central figure in the Milanese avant-garde. But in the late Eighties and Nieties, *Domus* became dull, repetitive and its cutting edge became blunt. It was shaded by new design titles and new media.

Gillo Dorfles born 1910

Gillo Dorfles trained as a painter, was a founder of Concrete Art and became the influential professor of aesthetics at Bologna University, with special interests in semantics, semiology and anthropology. His central role in the formation of Milanese design after the Second World War is a testament to the eclecticism and the taste for intellectual analysis that has made Milan the centre of Italy's industrial renaissance. He was a key figure in the organization of the Compasso d'Oro awards and in the Milan Triennale. He was the first Italian to write a book on industrial design, and his titles include: *Nuovo riti, nuovo miti, Simbolo comunicazione consumo, Introduzione al disegno industriale, Le oscillazione del gusto* and *Dal significato alle scelte*. His book on kitsch is the major study of the topic.

Bibliography Gillo Dorfles *Kitsch: the world of bad taste* Universe Books, New York, Thames & Hudson, London, 1969

Domus **consistently projected progressive Italian architecture and design to the rest of the world**

3

Donald Wills Douglas 1892–1981

Douglas was one of the great aircraft designers of America, a romantic engineer whose solutions to aeronautical problems were so visually original and had such an impact on culture that his influence extends into the area of design.

Douglas was born in Brooklyn in 1892 and was educated at the US Navy Academy in Annapolis. In 1912 he went to study at the Massachusetts Institute of Technology and between 1915 and 1916 was chief engineer at the Glenn L. Martin Company. After a brief period as chief civilian engineer to the US Signal Corps, he founded the Douglas Company in 1920. The Douglas Cloudster was the first aircraft to carry a payload greater than its own weight, and following this technical success Douglas and his colleagues made a series of innovations which helped make popular civil aviation possible, culminating in the celebrated DC-3 series of civil transports. DC stood for Douglas Commercial and this plane (known in its military guise as the C-47 and the Dakota) made mass air travel a commercial reality.

It became the most successful aircraft of all time, celebrated for its technical virtuosity and its clean, streamlined, platonic beauty by Le Corbusier and Walter Dorwin Teague, who illustrated it in their books, *Aircraft and Design This Day*. The DC-3 was followed by a series of larger piston-engined transports, and by jet transports such as the DC-8 and DC-9.

In 1967 Douglas' company merged to become the McDonnell-Douglas Corporation of St Louis, Missouri. Pressure led to corners being cut in the design of the DC-10, the last Douglas airliner, and its spectacular accidents at Paris in 1974 and Chicago in 1979 brought the revered Douglas name into books about product liability legislation. In 1996 the rump of Donald Wills Douglas' company was taken over by Boeing, effectively disappearing soon after (although the MD-80 was briefly and unsuccessfully re-branded as the Boeing 717).

Bibliography John B. Rae *Climb to Greatness* MIT, Cambridge, Mass., 1968

1: Margaret Bourke-White's magnificent photograph of a Douglas DC-4 crossing lower Manhattan, 1939. Le Corbusier said 'l'avion accuse', meaning the superlative functional form of aircraft mocked the crassness and excess of most design and architecture.

2: Christopher Dresser, electroplated nickel silver teapot with ebony handle, for James Dixon & Sons, Sheffield, circa 1881.

Christopher Dresser 1834–1904

Christopher Dresser was a botanical draughtsman who became one of the very first industrial designers, an avatar of the ultimate form of democratic art. His Art Furniture Alliance of 1880 may have been the very first firm of interior designers – less democratic, perhaps, but significant nonetheless.

He was one of those exhausting, over-active, over-confident, prodigal Victorians. At one end of the Victorian era there was William Hazlitt saying that 'the great requisite for the prosperous management of ordinary business' was 'the want of imagination'. A century of technological innovation and giddyingly wider horizons brought a vivid change of opinion about these humdrum matters. At the other end of the Victorian era was Christopher Dresser, positively fizzing with intellect and ideas.

He was born in Glasgow, but came to London when he was just 13 to enrol in the new Government School of Design, one of a number of mid-century initiatives to improve public taste and enhance manufacturing by instruction in art. Dresser made his speciality the systematic study of plant forms with a view to applying their principles to industrial products. In 1855 he was awarded a patent for 'nature printing' and at 25 he was a lecturer on 'art botany'. Given a chair the year after, he also received an honorary doctorate from a German university. In 1857–8 Dresser published a series of 11 articles in the influential *Art Journal* and was elected a member of the Linnaean Society in 1861. Before an influential trip to Japan in 1876, he was a consultant to more than fifty leading Victorian manufacturers, including Wedgwood, Minton and Coalbrookdale.

His experience of Japan is especially interesting. After the last medieval shogun ceded power to the new Emperor Meiji in 1867, Japan was anxious to modernize itself. Dresser travelled there as a member of an official delegation. Leaving Liverpool, he passed through the Philadelphia Exhibition (where he met the jeweller Louis Tiffany) onto San Francisco, then Yokohama. The Emperor offered him factory tours in exchange for advice about trade opportunities and a deal was struck. Dresser had brought 2,000 British products to Japan (a glass vase is still on display in the Tokyo National Museum), but he brought back a cache of 800 *objets d'art* which he gave to the Victoria and Albert Museum. Eventually, he published *Japan – its Architecture, Art and Art Manufactures* (1882), but the real treasure he repatriated was not so much lacquer boxes as a belief in the quintessential principle of design. As he put it, the Japanese attached as much value to a pair of well-designed chopsticks as the Victorians did to Landseer.

It was this principle, as well as the pleasing formal austerity he found in Japan, which joined botany as an inspiration. By the time he was back in England, Dresser began working on the astonishing series of out-of-time geometrical teapots and toast-racks which seem to predict the Bauhaus designs of Marianne Brandt or of Wilhelm Wagenfeld. These form the basis of his revived reputation. 'Revived' because after his death in 1904, Dresser fell into obscurity. Strange to say for so entrepreneurial an individual, he left his business affairs in a mess.

Our current interest in Dresser is attributable to what can be called the Pevsner Effect. The great German-Jewish art-historian first noted Dresser in his influential *Pioneers of the Modern Movement* in 1936 and soon took him up as a cause. In the same year Pevsner joined the staff of the *Architectural Review*. With the industry of an emigré, Pevsner decided to establish his credentials as an authority on the true story of English modernism. Beginning cautiously with 'Carpets' and 'Electrical Fittings', he published an article, based on conversations with the old man's daughters, on Christopher Dresser in 1937. At the same time, he was visiting the elderly and grumpy architect C. F. A. Voysey. Pevsner decided to fit these two glorious late-Victorian eccentrics into his deterministic and somewhat skewed history of modernism.

Pevsner's promotion of Christopher Dresser as a herald of modernism was a version of the *post hoc ergo propter hoc* fallacy. Christopher Dresser was submitted to his system. Yes, he possessed a powerful and original insight into the significance of design: he believed that industrial production was superior to craft because with a commitment to volume, it is absolutely essential to get the original idea right. Dresser even believed in branding: many of his pieces ostentatiously carry his signature, something Alessi paid tribute to when they issued a series of reproductions in the early1990s. But as Dresser's later glass and ceramics show in their crawling, verminous, disfigured forms and nauseating colourways, his taste was essentially Victorian. Despite his intellectual originality, he was unable to escape the suffocating excess of the age. While Edison worked on his light bulbs, Dresser was still designing tin candlesticks.

Dresser became a buyer for Tiffany of New York, designed carpets and was a manager of the Art Furnishers' Alliance.

Bibliography *Christopher Dresser 1834–1904* exhibition catalogue, Camden Arts Centre, London, 1979; *Christopher Dresser* exhibition catalogue, Victoria and Albert Museum, London, 2004

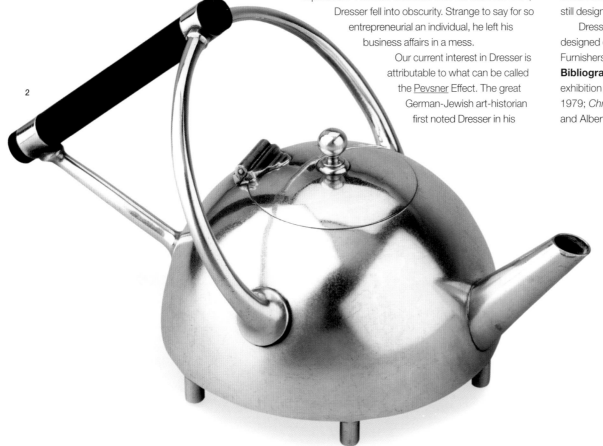

2

Henry Dreyfuss 1903–72

Dreyfuss was a contemporary and rival of <u>Raymond Loewy</u>, <u>Walter Dorwin Teague</u> and <u>Norman Bel Geddes.</u> He was born into a family which dealt in prop and costume hire, and on leaving college at 16 was drawn to the theatre, where he met Norman Bel Geddes and worked with him on several hit shows. During the Twenties many stage designers and advertising draughtsmen were drawn from the box office and the billboard to the bigger theatre of American industry, which at that time seemed to offer almost unlimited opportunities for ambitious young designers. Dreyfuss was such a man. He set up his own office in 1929 and his first essay in industrial design was a re-working of a

traditional storage jar, which he modified on space-saving, functional lines. Of the first generation of American designers Dreyfuss was the most proficient 'exponent of cleanliness', according to the journal *American Artist*. Although his crack train for the New York Central Railroad, 'The Twentieth Century Limited', became for many people the very symbol of American design in its most luxurious and expressive years, Dreyfuss generally avoided stylish extravagance. His commitment to <u>Functionalism</u> expressed itself both in a refusal to do pure and simple facelifts of inadequate products, and in his interest in what came to be called in America 'human engineering', or anthropometrics.

His masterly survey of the concerns of the industrial designer, *Designing for People* (1955), began a tradition of concern with this science which is still maintained in the office he left behind.

Dreyfuss' major clients included Bell (for whom his 1933 telephone design virtually defined a shape which has not been improved in 50 years), RCA television, Hoover vacuum cleaners, Goodyear tyres, Ansco cameras, John Deere agricultural equipment and some plane interiors for Lockheed.

Dreyfuss and his wife committed suicide in 1972.
Bibliography Henry Dreyfuss *Designing for People* Simon & Schuster, New York, 1955

1

1

Of the first generation of American designers Dreyfuss was the most proficient 'exponent of cleanliness', according to the journal *American Artist*

1

James Dyson born 1947

James Dyson was born in Norwich and is well known for his uncompromising attitude to pet hair. Dyson describes himself as an 'inventor, engineer and artist', joining a long tradition of English eccentrics uniting these fields, although he is distinguished in being very much more commercially successful than most of his predecessors, especially Heath Robinson. Dyson's first invention was the 1974 Ballbarrow, an ingenious water-filled combo wheel-barrow and garden roller, but it is his astonishing commitment to perfecting household cleaning that has made him famous. His work is characterized by commitment, perfectionism, ingenuity and meticulous, painstaking research and development.

Irritated by the inefficiency of even the best conventional vacuum cleaners, in 1978 Dyson began to rethink the entire concept and then to engineer his thinking. Becoming convinced, almost obsessed, by the principle of cyclonic force, Dyson based his technology on the generation of 150,000gs of centrifugal force which remove pet hair, dust and dirt from the airflow.

His work is characterized by commitment, perfectionism, ingenuity and meticulous, painstaking research

More than 5,000 prototypes of Dyson's bagless vacuum cleaner were made before a patent was granted for the 'Dual Cyclone' in 1983. The product design – strident colours and expressive, even mannered, technology – alienated some customers, but gave indisputably emphatic form to Dyson's innovation. A rare example of a successful British manufacturer (with 20 per cent of the US market), Dyson controversially shifted production to Asia in 2003. His Malmesbury, Wiltshire, headquarters now concentrates on research and development.

Bibliography James Dyson *Against the Odds*, Texere Publishing, New York, 1997

1: Of all American design consultants, Henry Dreyfuss was most concerned with ergonomics. Here Dreyfuss is on the left with Bell Systems engineer, William H. Martin in this 1949 double portrait. Dreyfuss' ergonomic research continued into the seventies with the tragic Polaroid camera, although his firm was also capable of drama and romance: the New York Central Systems 20th Century Limited, 1939.
2: A development model of a Dyson bagless vacuum cleaner.

2

Charles Eames 1907–78

Charles Eames was born in St Louis, Missouri, and laboured in a steel mill before becoming a technical draughtsman. He won a scholarship to Washington University's School of Architecture, but did not finish the course and set himself up as an architect and industrial designer (without very much work in hand). He came to prominence when, with Eero Saarinen, he won the 'Organic Design in Home Furnishings' competition at New York's Museum of Modern Art in 1940. In 1946 he was the first designer of any nationality to have a one-man show at the museum, with furniture that combined bent plywood with steel rods. These designs used the moulded plywood technique first seen in the 'organic' chairs, somewhat refined after he made splints for the US Navy in 1942. Eames's designs were all manufactured by Herman Miller of Zeeland, Michigan. Eames's most famous design, the culmination of all his efforts and Herman Miller's most celebrated product, was a rosewood and leather lounge chair and ottoman which was first made in 1955 for the film director Billy Wilder: it became an international symbol of architectural style and, like Marcel Breuer's 'Bauhaus' chair, was widely imitated but never equalled. In 1958 Eames designed the 'Aluminum' chair and at about the same time his tandem seating, using similar constructional principles, was installed at Washington's Dulles and Chicago's O'Hare airports.

The public relations efforts of Herman Miller, together with Eames's decision to become more involved with exhibition design and education (in partnership with his wife, Ray), made him into a more formidable and celebrated spokesman for American design than his relatively modest portfolio of mass-produced products would suggest. Some exaggerated claims have been made for Eames and his work, but he is nevertheless a genuinely important and influential figure.

After 1959, when he produced a multi-screen presentation for the US exhibition in Moscow, Eames became progressively more concerned with experimental film, and his *Powers of Ten*, a short about the house he and Ray designed for themselves in Santa Monica, became a cult movie. Before his death, that house (which he had assembled in 1949 out of stock, mass-produced components) became a shrine for student designers all over the world.

In an interview with *Interiors* magazine Eames offered an insight into his philosophy: 'I visited a good toy store this morning… It was sick-making. I longed for the desert even though quite a few of the things in other times would have been treasures… Affluence offers the kind of freedom I am deeply suspicious of. It offers freedom from restraint, and virtually it is impossible to do something without restraints… when somebody is on the ball he eliminates choices and establishes limits for himself… We have to rediscover limitations.' Terence Conran recalls: 'The Eameses had the wit, style and ingenuity I so desperately wanted to emulate, but found so difficult to achieve with the limitations on raw materials and the restricted home market. Interestingly, however, I discovered when looking at Eames' prototypes in the Vitra Museum Archive that his workshop models were as dog rough as mine. I realized the difference was Herbert Matter's glamorous photographs. Still, Charles and Ray Eames were innovators with originality, charm and an inclusive view of life. They were the most influential designers of them all.'

Bibliography *Connections: the work of Charles and Ray Eames* exhibition catalogue, Frederick S. Wright Gallery, University of California, Los Angeles, 1976–7; Ralph Caplan *The Design of Herman Miller* Whitney Library of Design, New York, 1976; M. & J. Neuhart & Ray Eames, *Eames Design*, Thames & Hudson, 1989; E. Demetrios *An Eames Primer*, Thames & Hudson, 2002

1

Harley Earl 1893–1969

Harley Earl was born in Hollywood into a family of coach builders. With increasing numbers of orders for customized car bodies coming in from the first generation of film stars, his family set up the Earl Automobile Works in 1908. In 1914 Earl went to Stanford University, while the family firm kept the cash-flow moving by making chariots for epic movies. On being bought out by a local Cadillac dealership in 1919, the company was given over entirely to customized car bodies. At this time Harley Earl developed the now standard technique of using clay models to design car bodies, which gave considerable scope for sculptural expression and enabled car design to become more and more free.

In the early years of the motor industry, as it struggled merely to satisfy the demand from the first generation of car buyers, appearance had not been considered an important factor in an automobile's showroom performance. But in the early Twenties the chairman of General Motors, Alfred P. Sloan, aware of greater manufacturing capacity, started to suspect that looks might have a beneficial effect on sales performance, and in 1925 invited Earl to Detroit. On 1 January 1928, General Motors' Art and Color section came into existence, under Earl's leadership. His first success for the company was the La Salle of 1927; his first 'dream' car was the 1937 Buick Y Job, and there followed a series of more or less original shapes and motifs. In the year of the Y Job Earl became vice-president of the newly formed Styling Division and his commercial successes with Cadillacs, Chevrolets, Pontiacs, Oldsmobiles and Buicks brought him, by the time of his retirement in 1959, to a position of influence unequalled by any motor designer before or since. However, the inventor of two-tone paint, chromium plating, the tail fin, and designs derived from the shape of jet planes and rockets, never won a design award.

'I like baseball and *love* automobiles,' Earl once said. And by the time he died he had been responsible for the appearance of 50 million of them, and for producing a model of automotive design that was emulated by every other American car manufacturer.

Bibliography Stephen Bayley *Harley Earl and The Dream Machine* Weidenfeld & Nicolson, London, 1983; Knopf, New York, 1983

Tom Eckersley 1914–96

Tom Eckersley was born in Lancashire and studied at Salford College of Art, moving to London in 1934 where he became, along with Abram Games, one of the last masters of drawing in poster design. Before the Second World War, Eckersley worked for those great British mixed-economy patrons, London Transport, Shell-Mex, the BBC and the Post Office. Eckersley's style involves simple, two-dimensional image-making; the messages are simple and the image nicely matches the text. He flourished in the London media world of the late Forties and Fifties when the scene was much enlivened by inspired émigrés including Germano Facetti. The degree of artifice in Eckersley's work is slight. From 1957 to 1977 Eckersley was head of graphic design at the London College of Printing, and was an influential teacher of more than two generations of British graphic designers.

Bibliography Tom Eckersley *Poster Design* Studio Publications, London, 1954

Fritz Eichler born 1911

Fritz Eichler studied art history and drama before working as a theatre designer from 1945. In 1954 he met Artur Braun at just the time when the new image for his company was being prepared for its launch at the 1955 Radio Show in Düsseldorf. Eichler coordinated the company's design policies and first suggested that Artur and Erwin Braun commission designs from teachers at the Hochschule für Gestaltung in Ulm.

Earl's commercial successes with Cadillacs, Chevrolets, Pontiacs, Oldsmobiles and Buicks brought him to a position of influence unequalled by any motor designer before or since

1: Chair and ottoman, 1955; Eames' now classic lounge chair and ottoman were inspired by the leather armchairs of English gentlemen's clubs. 'The' Eames chair is the most complete expression of mid-century Modern. Its clean lines and thoughtful construction contrast violently with the flatulent bravura excess of Harley Earl's Cadillac Eldorado Brougham of 1959. One an example of all that can be achieved by applied intelligence, the other an example of what can be achieved by tickling cupidity. **2:** Tom Eckersley, invitation to the London College of Printing's 18th Annual Dinner, 1967.

Karl Elsener 1860–1918

Designer of the Swiss Army pen knife. See also Bernard Rudofsky.

Erco

The German firm Erco is one of the leading international suppliers of high-quality architectural lighting. It was founded in 1934 by Arnold Reininghaus, Paul Buschhaus and Karl Reeber as Reininghaus & Co., but is now known as Erco Leuchten GmbH.

Erco's fortune was made in the years of reconstruction after the Second World War, when demand from new home builders during the 'economic miracle' helped many medium-sized manufacturers to flourish. Although Erco has always stressed the priority of technical characteristics in its product development, the company started to use designers to help in creating the corporate character as long ago as the late Fifties: Terence Conran, Ettore Sottsass, Roger Tallon and Emilio Ambasz all have products in the current Erco range. The company's logogram was designed by Otl Aicher, and he also designed a complete sign system for the firm which was marketed in 1976. Since 1963 Erco has been run by Klaus-Jurgen Maack.

The company's policy has been to promote a modern, elegant image for lighting and hence to attract a market that would appreciate such qualities.

Ercol

Ercol was founded in 1920 in High Wycombe by Lucian Ercolani, an Italian who came to England at the age of seven in 1895. His business specialized in the traditional Windsor chair and in simple, solid elm furniture. Ercol became one of the best-known British furniture companies in the Fifties, producing work in the Contemporary style. Ercol remains a family owned company manufacturing fine furniture in its new modern factory in Princes Risborough.

1

2

3: Virgil Exner's De Soto Adventurer, 1954. Exner brought (a modest amount of) restraint to car design during what Tom Wolfe called America's 'Bourbon Louis romp'.

4: Trademark bold striped patterns on a Vuokko Eskolin-Nurmesniemi cushion.

1: The Swiss Army Pen Knife.
2: Ercol, 'Butterfly' chair, beech and elm laminate, 1958. Danish design comes to English suburbia.

Ergonomics

Ergonomics is an interdisciplinary science, established during the Second World War, concerned with the relationship of man to machine in the fullest sense. Its main subject is the machine in human work.

In particular, ergonomists study the most comfortable and efficient methods of designing controls and dials, according to the performance of the human hand, eye and brain. Where the hand is concerned an important element is the different types of grip which, in fact, number only four. The first two, the power grip and the precision grip, are the most important because they are the only two which involve fingers and thumb in opposable action. The other two are subsidiary: the hook grip, as used when holding the handle of a suitcase, and the scissors grip, as when holding a cigar. With the eye, ergonomists examine the layout of instruments to find the best way of arranging them so that the operator can work the machine efficiently — any kind of machine is relevant, whether a supersonic jet, a domestic food-mixer, or a hi-fi.

Bibliography Ray Crozier *Manufactured Pleasures* Manchester University Press, 1994

Exner's 1957 production Chryslers radicalized Detroit with their bold compound curved windscreens and dramatic tailfins

Vuokko Eskolin-Nurmesniemi born 1930

The textile designer Vuokko Eskolin was born in Helsinki and worked for Marimekko before setting up her own firm in 1964. She is married to Antii Nurmesniemi, a furniture designer, and is known for bold striped patterns printed on fine, robust cottons.

4

Virgil Exner 1909–73

Virgil Exner worked first in advertising, drawing trucks, then became an office junior in the General Motors Styling Studio under Harley Earl. He joined Raymond Loewy in 1938 where many suspect he did the creative work on what became the successful 1947 Studebaker Starlight ('First by far with Post-War Car' the ads said). Despite, or because of, this, Loewy fired him so Exner joined The Chrysler Corporation in 1949 and donated to the ailing US automobile company some of the glitter, glare and ideas of Harley Earl's Detroit Byzantium. Exner created an Advanced Styling Group, working closely with Luigi Segre of Turin's Carrozzeria Ghia, a collaboration unique at the time which produced remarkable concept cars in the Chrysler d'Elegance, Dodge Firearrow and De Soto Adventurer. Exner's 1957 production Chryslers radicalized Detroit with their bold compound curved windscreens and dramatic tailfins (which Exner insisted played a role in stability). Exner called this longer and lower style the 'Forward Look' (although the Corporation perhaps more accurately called it 'The Million Dollar Look'). In 1957 Chrysler ads had the copyline 'Suddenly, it's 1960!'. When it was actually 1960 Exner again reproportioned the American automobile and introduced the radically 'compact' Valiant, an American first. Management was, quite wrongly, unconvinced, and Exner left Chrysler to become a consultant.

3

Germano Facetti 1928–2006

Facetti was one of a generation of influential Italians – mostly restaurateurs and graphic designers – who shaped British taste in the middle of the last century. Born in Milan, he was transported to the Mauthausen concentration camp, an experience that, entirely understandably, left an enduring impression. Back in Milan during the *riocostruzione*, he worked with the communists buildings schools and became archivist of the city's leading architectural practice, BBPR. At the time Ernesto Rogers was editor of *Domus* and inspired Facetti with his conviction 'to educate in aesthetic judgement, in technical skills and ethical attitudes. All three directed to the same purpose – building a society.'

With his English wife he came to London in 1950, working as a labourer and a designer of eclectic products including sandals and a chair. He studied typography at the Central School, became art director of Aldus Books and was a member of a group that colonized the Café Torino in Soho. Facetti ate raw coffee beans by the handful and was a participant in the influential 'This is Tomorrow' exhibition at the Whitechapel Gallery in 1956 which launched Pop Art in Britain.

Briefly in Paris, he got to know Alain Resnais and Agnes Varda, helped found the Snark International picture agency, but returned to London in 1960 to work at Penguin Books. Here he acted as an entrepreneurial art director, bringing in young designers, including Alan Fletcher, to recast Penguin's stodgy identity in what became the most consistently excellent campaign of publishing graphics ever. He designed many of the covers himself, briefing himself to provide 'a visual frame of reference… as an additional service to the reader'.

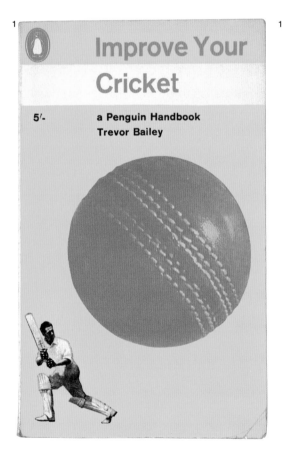

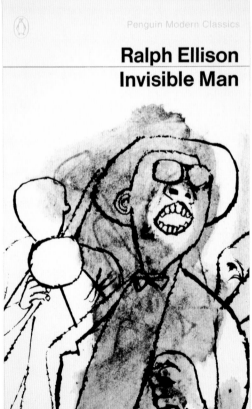

He wanted to use images for the 'construction of a sequence of understanding which leads beyond the text'. The Penguin Classics with their distinctive black grounds, handsome spare typography and thoughtful picture research were particularly impressive. Under Facetti's influence, John Gower's *Confessio Amantis* (five shillings) suddenly looked refreshingly modern and surprisingly desirable. A headstrong character, much given to throwing books to emphasize points in his argument, Facetti was continuously at odds with conservative management and left Penguin in 1972, returning to Milan where he designed travel guides for *L'Espresso*. His engagingly eccentric archive is in the Museo della Resistenza, Turin. His achievement was, through disciplined graphics, distinguished illustration and clever picture selection, to make Penguin a brand that meant intelligence, quality and good taste.

Jorge Ferrari-Hardoy 1914–77

The Hardoy chair is an example of how a vernacular or Anonymous design can gain fashionable acceptance. First patents for a sling chair go back to 1877 when a British civil engineer called Joseph Fenby registered a design of wood and canvas. Put into production in the United States in 1895 by the Gold Medal Furniture Company of Racine, Wisconsin, Fenby's chair was pictured with <u>Henry Ford</u>, Thomas Edison and Harvey Firestone, an early example of how celebrity endorsement can enhance the consumer's perception of a product. In 1940 Argentinian architect Jorge Ferrari-Hardoy, who had worked with <u>Le Corbusier</u> in Paris, working with two colleagues, re-designed the Fenby using leather and metal. With this they won an Argentinian design competition, and were noticed by John McAndrew of New York's <u>Museum of Modern Art</u>. McAndrew persuaded modern furniture entrepreneur Clifford Pascoes to build 1,500 of them. This in turn was noticed by <u>Hans Knoll</u> who acquired the rights in 1945 and turned the Hardoy into a contemporary classic, featuring in <u>Contemporary</u> photo shots in the Fifties and Sixties almost as often as the classics of <u>Charles Eames</u>.
Bibliography Jay Doblin *One Hundred Great Product Designs* Van Nostrand Reinhold, New York, 1970

1: Germano Facetti's graphics helped confirm Penguin Books as one of the most successful Modernist projects of them all.
2: Ferrari-Hardoy's 1940 chair was an inspired reworking of a utilitarian British design of the nineteenth century.

FIAT

FIAT stands for 'Fabbrica Italiana Automobili Torino'.
It is Europe's leading vehicle manufacturer and the
largest industrial undertaking in Italy. From its inception
FIAT has taken a positive attitude to design: its Lingotto
factory outside Turin was heavily influenced by the
Futurists: Giovanni Agnelli, the founder, asked his
architect, Matte-Trusco, to build a race track on the
roof. Since 1928 FIAT has employed the brilliant
designer Dante Giacosa as its chief engineer. Under
him FIAT has also employed Ghia, Pininfarina and
Giorgio Giugiaro as consultant designers, and has
produced some of the best-designed cars to come
from any of the large international companies. In
particular the original 500 of the Thirties, the Nuova 500
(see page 44), the 127 of the Seventies and the Uno of
the Eighties have led the field in small-car design.

**FIAT is Europe's leading vehicle
manufacturer and the largest
industrial undertaking in Italy**

Leonardo Fioravanti

Leonardo Fioravanti was born in 1938 and joined Pininfarina in 1964 after studying mechanical engineering at Milan Polytechnic. His graduate project was for a six-seater aerodynamic car, an idea ahead of its time. He became head of Research and Design at Pininfarina's Cambiano headquarters.

Fioravanti has created shapes for cars that have been universally celebrated for their beauty and voluptuous elegance. His designs include the experimental BMC 1800 of 1967 (which became the Citroën CX and drew on ideas which he had developed while a student), the Ferrari Daytona of 1968, the Ferrari Mondial of 1980 and the Peugeot 205 of 1983. Among the most remarkable cars which Fioravanti has designed is the CNR (Consiglio Nazionale delle Ricerche) experimental vehicle for aerodynamic research.
Bibliography Vittorio Gregotti *Carrozzeria italiana – cultura e progetto* Alfieri, Turin, 1979

Elio Fiorucci born 1935

Elio Fiorucci was closely identified with and created the direction for the explosion of fashionable interest in Milan as a design capital of the Eighties. He was trained as a shoemaker, setting up his first clothes shop in Milan's Galleria Passarella in 1967 with the aim of bringing the King's Road to Italy. It was designed by Ettore Sottsass. Since then Fiorucci shops have become synonymous with Pop, Punk and every passing brazen fashion, including what author Eve Babitz called 'junky chic'. Nevertheless, Fiorucci symbolized the avant-garde end of mass-consumed Pop and was a huge stylistic influence on youth.
Bibliography Eve Babitz *Fiorucci – the Book* Harlin Quist, New York, 1980

Richard Fischer born 1935

Richard Fischer is of the same generation of German designers as Dieter Rams – too young to have participated in the Second World War, but old enough to be imbued with the German tradition in engineering. He first studied mechanical engineering, then went to Ulm to read product design at the Hochschule für Gestaltung. Working for Braun in Frankfurt from 1960 to 1968, he designed a distinguished series of electric razors. In 1968 he went freelance; perhaps his most successful design has been the ingenious Minox '35EL' camera of 1972, a marvel of precision engineering, but also a marvel of careful and harmonious design which takes the values of Ulm into the Eighties. Since 1972 Fischer has been professor of product design at the Hochschule für Gestaltung in Offenbach.

Richard Fischer is of the same generation of German designers as Dieter Rams – too young to have participated in the Second World War, but old enough to be imbued with the German tradition in engineering

1: FIAT, Italian institution and often an inspired patron of democratic design, became too complacently dependent on its home market and almost succumbed to Japanese competition in the early twenty-first century.
2: Aero-engine assembly at Lingotto. Before the Second World War FIAT's nationalism occasionally became confused with Mussolini's fascism.
3: FIAT 1100 Special Saloon, first shown in Turin, 1960: the clean, modern lines of la dolce vita.

4: Citroên CX GTi, by Leonardo Fioravanti.
5: Richard Fischer, Minox 35EL compact camera, 1972. The end of an era: one of the last great film camera designs.

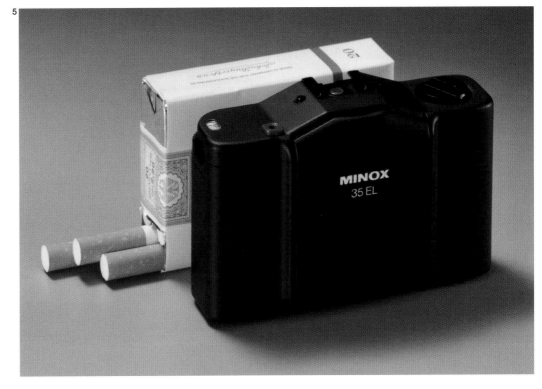

Alan Fletcher 1931–2006

Alan Fletcher was Britain's best graphic designer of the twentieth century. He was trained at the Royal College of Art in London and at Yale University's School of Architecture and Design, where he was taught by Paul Rand and Josef Albers. His career began in New York in the mid-Fifties, with jobs for the Container Corporation of America, for Fortune magazine and for IBM, working for Saul Bass and the magazine designer Leo Lionni. Back in London in 1959 he formed Fletcher, Forbes & Gill, a firm which did for graphics what Mary Quant did for clothes; that is, gave it stylish mass appeal. Fletcher, Forbes and Gill's proposition was to combine the disciplines of Swiss typography with the flair of American advertising. In 1972 Fletcher, Forbes & Gill became three-fifths of the design group Pentagram.

Fletcher had a creative genius and a great talent for lateral thought, always being inclined to avoid the obvious. His basic proposition was not how to do a job, but why. With the answer established, creative directions followed. Major graphic projects at Pentagram included an enduring corporate identity for Reuters. Fletcher left Pentagram in 1992, to work on his own account for clients including Novartis and Phaidon Press. Fletcher's interest was in visual ambiguity and visual puns. He was a witty illustrator and an avid collector of curios. He said: 'Function is fine, but solving the problem is not the problem. The problem is adding value, investing solutions with visual surprise and above all with wit. To misquote: "A smile is worth a thousand pictures."'

Bibliography Alan Fletcher *The Art of Looking Sideways* Phaidon Press, London, 2001; Alan Fletcher *Picturing and Poeting*, Phaidon Press, London, 2006

Flos

Flos was founded in 1960 at Merano in northern Italy, and was intended to pursue research into the use and value of lighting in the home. Its factory moved to Brescia in 1963. Flos is most often associated with the designs of Achille Castiglioni, the Milanese architect who has best sensed the possibilities which playing with light offers the designer. Since the Castiglioni-designed shop and showroom opened on the Corso Monforte Flos has become an established part of the Milanese design community. A great deal of its reputation has come from Castiglioni's restless inventiveness in lighting design. Flos has acquired Arteluce and has associated companies in Germany, France, Switzerland and the United Kingdom.

Paul Follot 1877–1941

The decorator Paul Follot's first interior designs were Art Nouveau. He matured then into the Frenchified Modernist mode of Art Deco, a style whose exclusiveness he can make some claim to have invented. In 1923 Follot became design director of the Bon Marché store and exhibited regularly at the Parisian 'Salon des artistes décorateurs', producing interior designs for the Paris exhibition of 1925, the *annus mirabilis* of Art Deco. His market demanded extravagant materials, fine craftsmanship and the symbolism of luxury. These are what he produced.

Bibliography *Les Années 25* exhibition catalogue, Musée des Arts Décoratifs, Paris, 1966

1: Alan Fletcher's graphics combined Swiss discipline with American flair.
2: Achille Castiglioni's 'Arco' light for Flos is typical of the designer's whimsical conceits: an immensely heavy lump of marble anchors a light spun aluminium reflector. This 1962 design became almost a standard feature in many metropolitan Italian restaurants in the Sixties and Seventies.
3: Henry Ford said he had to invent the 'gasoline buggy' to escape the mind-numbing boredom of life on the far. This is the genius of the automobile. The picture was taken in 1896.

PAVITT'S PRODUCE
PURVEYORS OF QUALITY FRESH FRUIT & VEGETABLES

UNITS C1-C3
FRUIT & VEG MARKET
NEW COVENT
GARDEN MARKET
NINE ELMS LANE
LONDON SW8 5JJ
T 020 7720 5252
F 020 7720 5326

V&A

Henry Ford 1863–1947

It is unjust that Henry Ford's two pronouncements, about colour and the nature of history, should have become so famous. Ford was not anti-intellectual: he was a friend to Thomas Alva Edison, the inventor, and, when he founded his own museum at Greenfield Village, near Detroit, he said that 'an object can be read like a book… if only you know how'. Nor was he contemptuous of the customer: his perfection of series production on assembly lines opened up greater choice to the ordinary customer than ever before. Ford's achievement was an influence on Walter Gropius and he was also well acquainted with Gordon Russell and Ferdinand Porsche.

Henry Ford was born in Springwells township, Michigan, of Irish Protestant stock. It was a remote, rural community and he was struck early in life by the nature of labour there: 'My earliest recollection was that, considering the results, there was too much work on the place.' He started work as a machinist's apprentice and by 1893 had become chief engineer of the Edison Illuminating Company, supplying electric light to urban Detroit. He resigned in 1899 and established the Ford Motor Company in 1903. Success was phenomenally rapid. Between 1908 and 1927, 16 million Ford Model Ts were produced, and in 1919 it cost Ford $106 million to buy out the minority stock holders. In 1913 he perfected the moving production line, and in 1932 he launched his second most celebrated car, the V8. His son, Edsel, was president of the company from 1919 until he died in 1943. Henry Ford then resumed that role himself until his own death, when his grandson Henry Ford II took over.

Henry Ford's main contribution to design was to translate the methods and ideals of standardization, both aesthetic and practical, into the manufacture of consumer products. Fordism was the name given to this rationalization of the industrial process by the introduction of the moving assembly line in 1913. In this he was influenced by Taylorism – Frederick Winslow Taylor's *The Principles of Scientific Management* proposed that efficient industrial production should entail men working as an analogue of the machine. Ford took the idea a step further and actually replaced men with machines. In fact, the assembly line was not so much an invention of Ford's as the culmination of a tradition of American industrial experiments. However, his system revolutionized the structure of the work process and, in turn, the way industrial products were conceived and designed. Fordism became for architects like Walter Gropius an exemplar of what rational industrial society could achieve, and in Europe it became Gropius's ambition to apply Ford's techniques to the construction and design of dwellings (with similar influence, but less happy results).

It was in response to Henry Ford's achievements in creating the popular car that Alfred P. Sloan organized General Motors and hired Harley Earl to give his vehicles style, so that they might be differentiated in the marketplace from the utilitarian products of Ford. Despite Ford's toughness, he had a strong streak of sentimentality. He named the Fairlane after his grandmother's birthplace and the Edsel after his son.

In 1903 the first Ford cars were imported privately into Britain; the Model T arrived in 1909; and separate production began at Dagenham in 1931. With the introduction of the post-War Consul, Zephyr and Zodiac range in 1950, Ford brought a revolution in styling to the British market: these were the first cars to introduce the glitter of America to a country just emerging from rationing. In 1962 Ford of Britain produced the Cortina, an extraordinarily successful car, which was drawn by Roy Brown. Brown was a Canadian designer who had been responsible for the disastrous Edsel of 1958. In exile in Dagenham, however, he produced the car that was Britain's Model T. It was a typical Ford product – conservatively engineered, but shrewdly marketed. The name itself was an astute choice, responding to the changing taste of a British public discovering the delights of skiing in the Alps. Whereas Ford's previous range had names taken from the classical world, and the Cortina's rivals had the tweedy associations of the university towns, Oxford and Cambridge, after which they were named, the Cortina and its stable-mate the Capri were called after smart but accessible Italian resorts.

Ford's other main European operation was in Germany, where it first imported cars from America in 1907. In 1926 Ford started to produce cars in Germany, having incorporated a factory in 1925 in Berlin. A plant followed in Cologne in 1931, and Henry Ford himself got on well with the leaders of the Nazi regime.

In 1967 Ford of Britain joined with Ford-Werke to become Ford of Europe. The Ford Cortina continued in production until 1982, making it perhaps the most commercially significant British vehicle ever. A period of advance and retrenchment followed for Ford. The ambitious Sierra, which succeeded the Cortina, was not initially a popular success. More conservative designs followed, although by the time Ford began to explore more adventurous designs in the early twenty-first century its whole commercial position had been undermined by a vast restructuring of the market that saw Ford's traditional middle ground disappear. J. Mays (Chief Creative Officer in 2004) was criticized for spending more time on image-building concepts and commercially irrelevant projects, including the unsuccessful 1999 Thunderbird revival, while letting Ford's main product lines deteriorate into mediocrity, or what French critics called '*presentation triste*'.

Bibliography Henry Ford *My Life and Work* Doubleday, New York, 1923; Heinemann, London, 1924. Judith A. Merkle *Management and Ideology* University of California Press, Berkeley and London, 1980; *The Car Programme: 52 Weeks to Job One or How they designed the Ford Sierra* exhibition catalogue, The Boilerhouse Project, Victoria and Albert Museum, London, 1982

3

FIRST · CAR

Piero Fornasetti 1913–88

Piero Fornasetti is one of the great independents of Italian design, a man whose work continuously crossed boundaries. He is best known for decoration, often Surreal in inspiration, applied to his furniture and ceramics. Not part of the chic circle that dictates fashions in injection-moulding from the smart salons of central Milan, he comes from a background in the theatre and Surrealist painting. He has said that his greatest fortune was to know the works of the painters Carlo Carrà and Ardengo Soffici, and the Italian school of the nineteenth century, as they have influenced his own idiosyncratic style.

After being expelled from the Liceo Artistico he studied at the Accademia di Belle Arte di Brera and came to notice at a competition sponsored by the Cassa di Risparmio. At the Fifth Milan Triennale, Fornasetti met the architect Gio Ponti, and the two men worked together on interior designs and *trompe l'oeil* furniture for which Fornasetti designed surface patterns. Fornasetti began to establish a personal character with decorative designs for a set of dinner plates which he called 'Temae Variazioni'.

Considered an eccentric throughout the Fifties, Sixties and Seventies, now that decoration is being reconsidered, Fornasetti's strange and complex pattern-making is accessible to contemporary taste via computer graphics. One of his favourite concepts was '*egocentrismo*'.

Today, Barnaba Fornasetti still continues his father's work, reviving popular pieces and collaborating with other designers such as Nigel Coates.

Bibliography *Mobile e oggetti anni '50 di Piero Fornasetti* exhibition leaflet, Mercanteinfiera, Parma, 1983

144

Mariano Fortuny 1871–1949

Mariano Fortuny y Madrazo was born in Granada, Spain, but was brought up in Rome and Paris, and moved to Venice in 1889. He dabbled in music and stage design, and at the beginning of the century developed his own patent theatrical lights, which were eventually manufactured under an arrangement with AEG. He was a subtle and distinguished photographer, but is best known as a fashion designer. Fortuny began this aspect of his career by experimenting in 1907 with processes to print and pleat silk, and opened a factory to manufacture it in 1919. From 1907 he also took to producing fashion designs, combining his printed silks with his own versions of classical Greek designs. These dresses became de rigueur for a certain species of fashionable, artistic lady during the Twenties. He also enjoyed some success as an interior designer and was famous for cushions and curtains.

Bibliography Silvio Fusco et al. *Immagini e materiali del laboratorio Fortuny* Marsilio Editori, Venice, 1978

Kaj Franck 1911–89

Having trained at Helsinki's Institute of Industrial Art, Kaj Franck worked as an independent designer of lighting, furniture and textiles until 1946, when he joined the Arabia ceramic factory as its art director. He retired in 1978. Franck was one of the most influential and imitated designers of everyday ceramics, and one of the creators of the image of Scandinavian Modern. He injected 'artistic' qualities into Arabia's mass-produced utility wares and his 'Ruska' and 'Kilta' ranges are witnesses of his dedication to quality in the everyday. Franck won a Compasso d'Oro award in 1957.

1: Piero Fornasetti's playful designs turned surrealism into decoration.
2: Josef Frank, 'Primavera' printed textile pattern, 1930s.
3: Max Friz established an architecture for BMW motorbikes that lasted 80 years.

Josef Frank 1885–1967

The Austrian designer Josef Frank was the main contributing force to the concept dubbed 'Swedish grace' by the English writer P. Morton Shand, to describe a refined, bourgeois, <u>moderne</u> style that dominated Swedish taste between the wars.

Frank studied at the Viennese Institute of Technology. He worked in interior design in Germany and became a professor at the Kunstgewerbeschule (school of applied art) in Vienna in 1919. Here he knew and worked with <u>Peter Behrens</u> and <u>Josef Hoffmann</u>, ran his own interior design firm called Haus und Garten, and designed some bentwood furniture for <u>Thonet</u>.

Although Frank had been firmly entrenched in the <u>Modern Movement</u> he changed direction when he was introduced to Sweden by his Swedish-born wife. He began what was to become a life-long association with that country when he first worked for Estrid Ericson's Svenskt Tenn store in 1932, and settled in Stockholm in 1934. Apart from 1941–6, when he was professor of architecture at the New School for Social Research in New York, he lived there for the rest of his life.

In Sweden he was able to develop an individual style of interior design, which respected the principles of the Modern Movement, but which was also genuinely responsive to popular taste. He had already expressed reservations about too thoroughgoing an interpretation of <u>Functionalism</u> in a book, *Architektur als Symbol*, in 1931. In it he quoted Goethe in claiming that architecture was not just about building structures, but about creating sentiment, and he scorned the austere aestheticism of, say, <u>Mies van der Rohe</u>, only permitting tubular steel chairs in the garden.

Frank designed furniture, wallpaper, fabrics and lamps. His fabrics used bright, floral patterns, reflecting his conviction that 'a plain surface is tiring; the more pattern the more peaceful the effect'. His furniture expressed (and delivered) comfort, and his lamps, often employing brass, possess what his friend Eva von Zweigbergk called a 'refined neutrality'. Frank wanted his chairs to be complementary to the human body, so that any comfortable chair would necessarily have a complicated shape, and he thought that 'those who choose chairs with square seats harbour totalitarian thoughts in some corner of their hearts'. He considered orderliness to be deathly.

Today Frank's work has high social status not only in Sweden where it is is much sought after.
Bibliography *Josef Frank* exhibition catalogue, National Museum, Stockholm, 1968

Max Friz 1883–1966

Friz was the designer of the 1923 <u>BMW</u> R/32 motorbike, a flat-twin masterpiece that was like a <u>Bauhaus</u> diagram and established the architecture of the large motorbike.

2

Frank's fabrics used bright, floral patterns, reflecting his conviction that 'a plain surface is tiring; the more pattern the more peaceful the effect'

3

Adrian Frutiger born 1928

Born near Interlaken, Switzerland, Frutiger served an apprenticeship as a compositor before studying at the Kunstgewerbeschule (school of applied art) in Zürich where he specialized in drawing letter-forms. He then became a typographer himself. In 1952 he joined the Fonderie Deberny-Peignot in Paris, and it was while working there that he developed the 'Univers' typeface in 1954. 'Univers' is a sophisticated and much used family of founts in seven different weights, each one capable of being used with the next.

The popularity of 'Univers' helped establish the 'Swiss style' of typography that became shorthand for 'modern' during the later Fifties and Sixties. In 1960 he joined with Bruno Pfaffli (born 1935) to form the Atelier Frutiger & Pfaffli in Paris.

Bibliography Philip B. Meggs *A History of Graphic Design* Allen Lane, London, 1983

Maxwell Fry 1899–1987

The English architect E. Maxwell Fry was born in Wallasey, Cheshire, and studied at Liverpool School of Architecture. From Sir Charles Reilly and Patrick Abercrombie, professors of architecture and town planning respectively, he received a disciplined, classical training. However, Fry became disenchanted with the traditional architectural styles, which he felt to be irrelevant to the twentieth century, and, after a short period working in New York and in a London town planning office, he joined the group surrounding Wells Coates and Jack Pritchard. In 1931 he was one of the founders of the Modern Architecture Research Group (MARS), a dedicated group of professionals determined to introduce modern architecture into Britain.

Throughout the decade before the Second World War, Fry built more or less distinguished houses and flats in and around London in the International Style, but perhaps his greatest influence on British taste was not the buildings themselves but his achievement in luring Walter Gropius and Marcel Breuer to England after the Nazis created an atmosphere unsympathetic to their work and ideals in Germany. Fry was also concerned with functional interior planning and with his wife, Jane Drew, he designed fitted kitchens that made early use of modern materials and electrical appliances. They exhibited a compact kitchen at the Victoria and Albert Museum's 'Britain Can Make It' exhibition of 1946.

1

univers

39

Univers

45	46	47	48	49
Univers	*Univers*	Univers	*Univers*	Univers

53	54	55	56	57	58	59
Univers	*Univers*	Univers	*Univers*	Univers	*Univers*	Univers

63	64	65	66	67	68
Univers	*Univers*	Univers	*Univers*	**Univers**	***Univers***

73	74	75	76
Univers	***Univers***	**Univers**	***Univers***

83	84	85	86
Univers	***Univers***	**Univers**	***Univers***

2

1: Adrian Frutiger, 'Univers' typeface, 1954, made the Swiss Style international.
2: Maxwell Fry was one of a small group of architects who introduced Modernism to England. The Sun House, Frognal Way, Hampstead, 1935.

Roger Fry 1866–1934

Roger Fry studied at Cambridge, and then studied dilettantism. He was a so-so painter and art critic of, among other publications, *The Burlington Magazine*. His main contribution to design was to found the Omega workshop in 1913.

Fuller was an idealist who viewed the world as a single entity, without national boundaries, and who was committed to the idea that design should serve the needs of man, not of industry

Buckminster Fuller 1895–1983

Richard Buckminster Fuller was one of the most ardent and prolix supporters of high technology. Although his actual material creations were relatively few, the apocalyptic, prophetic character of his writings and thought have in recent years made him the darling of High-Tech architects and of all designers who are concerned with the earth's resources.

Fuller was born at Milton, Massachusetts. He never had any formal architectural training; in fact he never had much formal training of any sort. Traditional building techniques came to antagonize him, and in 1927 he created the concept of a 'Dymaxion' house – a name he coined by combining 'dynamic' with 'maximum'. It was not to use bricks and mortar, timber and lath, but was to be a tensile, domed structure where the fabric would be used as a grid to supply the services man needed for survival. A 'Dymaxion' car followed in 1932. Ironically, when

the house was tested in 1940 in Wichita, it in fact proved expensive and ill-suited to either mass-production or to housing. The car was equally ill-considered. However, his Geodesic dome, an extension of the principle, was used as the US Pavilion at Expo '67 in Montreal, and much influenced those interested in alternative technology.

Fuller's books are his best memorial: *Nine Chains to the Moon* (1938), *No More Second Hand God* (1963) and *Operating Manual for Spaceship Earth* (1969). Fuller was called 'the first poet of technology'. He was an idealist who viewed the world as a single entity, without national boundaries, and who was committed to the idea that design should serve the needs of man, not of industry.

Bibliography Joachim Krausse and Claude Lichtenstein (editors) *Your Private Sky – the art of design science* Lars Muller, Baden, 1999

3: Buckminster Fuller's Dymaxion car – 'Reshape environment; don't try to reshape man' – was shown at the 1934 Chicago World's Fair, and eventually sold to conductor, Leopold Stokowski. A bold concept, it was curiously overweight and never commercialized: Fuller's rhetoric was always more influential than his designs.

Functionalism

Functionalism is often confused with the <u>Modern Movement</u>, although it is in fact 200 years older, having been a philosophy before it was a movement in architecture and design. At its most simple, Functionalism proposes that the beauty and value of an object or an edifice depends on its fitness for its purpose. This view is even older than eighteenth-century Rationalism: in his *Memorabilia* Xenophon makes the philosopher Socrates say that a dung basket is superior to a golden shield if the one is better made than the other.

This point of view was somewhat modified by <u>Walter Gropius</u> and others, who wholly identified Functionalism with the form and spirit of the machine. However, as <u>Reyner Banham</u> pointed out in his book, *Theory and Design in the First Machine Age*, there was not much that was necessarily 'functional' about sitting on a metal chair, with a bare globe in a white room. Because the Functionalists' understanding of form was determined by the construction and materials of the object rather than by its purpose, it was an introverted philosophy of design which made no reference to the use to which an object was to be put. The American architect Louis Sullivan, who said 'form ever follows function', took his inspiration from biological growth, not from any abstract principle. Not surprisingly he is Norman Foster's hero.

Bibliography E.R. de Zurko *Origins of Functionalist Theory* Columbia University Press, New York, 1957

1: Louis Sullivan and Dankmar Aaler, Wainwright Building, St Louis, 1891. Sullivan's functionalism was influenced by ideas of organic growth.
2: Umberto Boccioni, The City Rises, 1910. Futurist art was concerned with the dynamism of cities and the beauty of machines.

3: Front cover of the first publication of *Zang Tumb Tumb* – a sound poem written in 1914 by Italian Futurist Filippo Tommaso Marinetti.
4: Marinetti, Futurism's mad genius, in 1910.

Futurism

The Italian Futurist Movement was the first group of artists and writers to celebrate the seductive power of the machine. The leading spirit was the poet Filippo Marinetti, a friend of d'Annunzio, the unseen legislator of Fascism. Marinetti's acoustic poem *The Raid on Adrianople* celebrated the first use of aircraft in military action. He also wrote *La Cucina*

Futurista, whose recipes cited gasoline as a useful ingredient. As well as being inspired by the dynamism of the 'mass' environment, some of the Futurists aimed to contribute to it. Sant'Elia, the architect, was, however, killed in the First World War before his projects for cities could be realized (he anticipated an environment dictated by modes of

transport). In the Thirties Giacomo Balla and others applied their vision to ceramics and interiors.

Bibliography Raffaele Carrieri *Futurism* Edizioni del Milione, Milan, 1961; Marianne W. Martin *Futurist Art and Theory* 1909–1915 Oxford University Press, London, 1968; *Futurism* exhibition catalogue, Beinecke Rare Book and Manuscript Library, Yale University, 1983

2

The Italian Futurist Movement was the first group of artists and writers to celebrate the seductive power of the machine

3

4

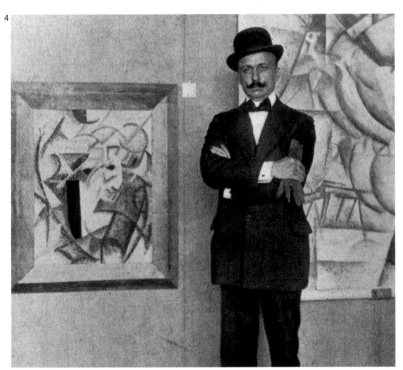

g

Emile Gallé 1846–1904

The glass-maker Emile Gallé was educated as a mineralogist and worked at the Meisenthal glassworks before travelling to England in 1871, where he studied the oriental glass in the South Kensington collections. The first important exhibition of his work was in 1884 at the Union Centrale des Art Décoratifs in Paris. By 1890 he was running a factory providing for the tastes of the new consuming class who, rejecting High Victorian bourgeois cut glass, favoured instead the sensuous, colourful shapes of Art Nouveau (to which glass lent itself so readily). Between his death in 1904 and its closure at the beginning of the First World War, Gallé's factory continued to turn out designs that were essays in expressive form and colour. His achievement was to introduce artistic freedom into glassware and to popularize Art Nouveau.

Bibliography Jean-Claude Groussard & Francis Roussel *Nancy Architecture* 1900 exhibition catalogue, Secrétariat de l'Etat à la Culture, Nancy, 1976

1: Emile Gallé, engraved and decorated glass vase, circa 1900.
2: Abram Games was the last master of the drawn lithograph. Army recruiting poster, 1940s. Games created the corporate identity of the 1951 Festival of Britain.
3: Gatto, Paolini, Teodoro's epochal 'Sacco', 1969.

PRINTED FOR H.M.STATIONERY OFFICE BY CHROMOWORKS LTD, LONDON. 51–2080.

Abram Games 1914–96

The British graphic designer Abram Games was the last master of the drawn lithograph before photography almost completely dominated poster design. Like Lewitt & Him and Henri Henrion, Games was one of several Jewish graphic designers who gave the British profession its strength at the mid-century (although, unlike the others, Games was not an émigré). In the late Thirties he designed posters for Shell, BP and the War Office; the latter were masterful expressions of his philosophy 'maximum meaning, minimum means'. It was his wartime work, however, doing propaganda for the Ministry of Information, which secured his reputation. In 1951 he was put in charge of graphics for the Festival of Britain, whose logogram he designed, and throughout the following decade he made a most distinguished contribution to the quality of British street life with his colourful and visually witty posters for British European Airways, the *Financial Times* and El Al. He was a guest speaker at the 1959 Aspen conference and published his book *Over My Shoulder* in 1960.

Gatti, Paolini, Teodoro

Piero Gatti (born 1940), Cesare Paolini (born 1937) and Franco Teodoro (born 1939) formed their design group in Turin in 1965, almost a twin to the Milanese De Pas, D'Urbino and Lomazzi. They were influenced by current theories of 'radical design' and became famous for the 'Sacco' chair of 1969, produced by Zanotta out of polystyrene balls.

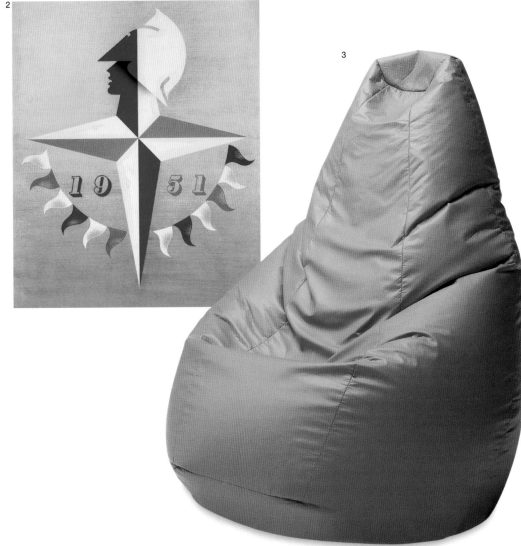

Antoni Gaudí I Cornet 1852–1926

Gaudí was a Spanish Catalan architect who designed no mass-produced consumer products, but who has nonetheless had a remarkable influence on twentieth-century taste.

He was trained in Barcelona during the time when the Gothic Revival was popular amongst leading architects and, in particular, was influenced by Viollet-le-Duc, the great French architectural thinker. A religious man, Gaudí's first commissions were for church furniture and metalwork, but an invitation to design cast-iron street lamps for Barcelona in 1879 involved him in civic architecture. Some major houses followed: Casa Vicens (1883–5) and the Palacio Guell (1885–90), where he also designed the furniture. Gaudí's style evolved into a highly personal mixture of Gothic and Moorish, with a large element of his own invention. Although he was an unclassifiable genius, Gaudí's free play in design and his willingness to subjugate all rules (including those of construction) to the god of expression made him an important influence on much of the avant-garde art and design of the twentieth century.

Evelyn Waugh made some typically acute and two-edged remarks about Gaudí's designs in a book about his travels: 'I could easily have employed a happy fortnight at Barcelona tracking down further examples of Gaudísm. He designed many things besides houses, I believe, making it his special province to conceive designs for tables and chairs and other objects of common utility which would render them unfit for their ostensible purposes.'

Gaudí was a pioneer of the architectural model as a means of expression, but despite the rationality of the model-maker's technique he was an eccentric at heart: it was said that he conducted the building workers on the church of La Sagrada Familia (which remains uncompleted today) with a conductor's baton. When his body was found after he had been run over and killed by a tram, his shabby clothes led his discoverers to believe that he was a vagrant, not Spain's greatest architect.

Bibliography George Collins *Antoni Gaudí* Mayflower, London, 1960; Gijs van Hensbergen *Gaudí* HarperCollins, London 2001

Gaudí's free play in design and his willingness to subjugate all rules (including those of construction) to the god of expression made him an important influence on much of the avant-garde art and design of the twentieth century

1

2

72156 GENERAL MOTORS BUILDING, DETROIT, MICH.

Dino Gavina

Dino Gavina was born in 1932 and founded an Italian furniture manufacturing company which was absorbed by Knoll in 1968. It was Gavina who made Marcel Breuer into a celebrated furniture designer, acquiring the rights to his tubular steel designs and shrewdly marketing them with names instead of Germanic numbers. This acquisition brought Breuer's 'Cesca', 'Wassily' and 'Laccio' chairs and tables into the Knoll catalogue. (At the same time and in the same deal, Knoll also acquired the rights to the furniture of Cini Boeri and Tobia Scarpa, which Gavina also manufactured.)

3

General Motors

In founding the General Motors Corporation Alfred P. Sloan did for industrial production what Karl Marx had done for political economy: he imposed a whole, new structure upon something that was hitherto indeterminate.

The world's largest industrial undertaking began in 1908 when William C. Durant founded the General Motors Company. Through take-overs, deals, bids, counter-bids, exchanges of stock and other financial machinations, Sloan created a corporation in 1919 that represented the greater part of American vehicle manufacturing interests. Sloan himself wrote, 'No two men better understood the opportunity presented by the automobile... than Mr Durant and Mr Ford.'

One of Sloan's greater *coups* was in recognizing that appearance would sell cars, and in hiring Harley Earl to mastermind their design. From 1925 to 1959 the story of General Motors is really the story of Harley Earl, and from then to his retirement in 1978 it is that of Bill Mitchell.

In the early Eighties the once impregnable General Motors felt an icy economic wind, and as if to underline America's industrial decline, an extraordinary announcement was made in February 1984. Cadillac, the division that hired Harley Earl to give style to America's master product, entered into a $606 million contract with Pininfarina to buy bodies designed and manufactured in Turin for a new Cadillac product to be launched in 1986. Part of the crisis following Ralph Nader's attack on General was a progressive dilution of the market profile of its most famous products. Cadillac was beginning to lose the identity which Earl and Bill Mitchell had created for it, but now the torch had to be handed to Italians because America had become conscious of 'designer' labels: the generation that bought Armani jeans might now buy a Pininfarina Cadillac.

It was not enough to save General Motors. Lazy, unimaginative management failed entirely to understand the threat of the Japanese at one end of the market and of Germans at the other. The attempt to by a European 'trophy brand' in SAAB was mis-managed too. The company that so completely understood mid-century American consumer psychology had by about 2000 completely lost any insights into market tastes or preferences. Within a few years General Motors was technically bankrupt.

Bibliography Alfred P. Sloan *My Years at General Motors* Doubleday, New York, 1963; Stephen Bayley *Harley Earl and The Dream Machine* Weidenfeld & Nicolson, London, 1983; Knopf, New York, 1983

Ghia

Giacinto Ghia (1887–1944) was born in Turin and learnt production techniques in the workshops of Diatto. Although from a simple background, Ghia soon specialized in luxury sporting cars. Mario Boana continued the tradition when he took over after Ghia's death. Designs coming from Ghia's shop have included the Volkswagen Karmann-Ghia (1961), the de Tomaso Mangusta (l966) and the Maserati Ghibli (1968). In 1972, in order to acquire the advantages of an Italian coach-building concern, Ghia was taken over by Ford, which half-heartedly used the Torinese shop as an experimental station to complement the work done at its own design centres at Dunton and Soho in England and Merkenich in Germany, but the historic facility fell into desuetude.

4

1: Antonio Gaudí, La Casa Mila (also known as La Pedrera), Barcelona, 1906–10.
2: The General Motors Building, Detroit. Albert Kahn's vast monument to industrial capitalism on Grand Boulevard was an expression of corporate ambitions.

3: Gavina's commercialized version of Marcel Breuer's 'Wassily' chair.
4: Alfred P. Sloan in 1929.

Dante Giacosa 1905–96

Dante Giacosa was one of the great designers of the high Machine Age. His series of neat, generally small, cars for FIAT combined a clear and economical engineering logic with great humane charm. Italians, it is often said, do not separate art from life. That was Giacosa's attitude to his automobile projects. As a result, some technologically uncompromised vehicle designs became some of the great symbols by which Italy in the twentieth century will be remembered.

Giacosa was born in Rome and joined FIAT in 1928, after responding to a newspaper advertisement offering a position in the drawing office. He first worked on military vehicles, then designed liquid-cooled aero engines, but was soon to make his name as the greatest of all Italian auto-engineers.

Giacosa transferred to FIAT's car division at Lingotto in 1929. As Capo Gruppo nell'Ufficio Technico his brief was to develop a well-engineered, sophisticated, but simple small car, an Italian equivalent to Boulanger's Citroën 2CV and Porsche's Volkswagen. This began as Progetto Zero which was launched as the 500A in 1936, a car which became known by the affectionate name of 'Topolino' ('Little Mouse'). It was the greatest advance in small car design since the launch of the Austin 7 in 1922, and became the best-selling import in the United States in 1938–9. The 500B introduced in 1948 was a substantial modification and came to be identified world-wide with post-War Italian design, like the Vespa and the Olivetti typewriter. The 500C followed in 1959, and when the line was abandoned (after selling 3.7 million vehicles) in 1955, it was to make way for another Giacosa design, the Nuova 500. Giacosa was also responsible for the conception and execution of the FIAT 124, 128 and 130.

Bibliography Dante Giacosa *I miei quaranti anni alla FIAT* Automobilia, Turin, 1979

> Dante Giacosa was one of the great designers of the high Machine Age

1: Dante Giacosa with 'Zero A', the 1934 prototype of the FIAT Cinquecento, 820m above sea level on the Andrate Pass, near Turin.

Sigfried Giedion 1888–1968

Sigfried Giedion was a Swiss art-historian whose influence on modern thought equals that of Nikolaus Pevsner and, later, Reyner Banham.

Giedion studied under Heinrich Wölfflin, who had himself been a pupil of Jakob Burckhardt. He was adept at establishing categories in art history and laying out new areas for research – in fact, his doctoral thesis of 1922 coined the term 'Romantic Classicism'. His second book, *Building in France – Building in Iron – Building in Concrete*, used Laszlo Moholy-Nagy as typographer and was published in 1928. In the same year he was appointed secretary of CIAM, and for more than 12 years Giedion, although a historian, devoted himself to the practical matter of promoting modern architecture. In 1938, via Walter Gropius, he was invited to deliver the Charles Eliot Norton lectures at Harvard and these were published in 1941 as *Space, Time and Architecture*. Seven years later his greatest book, *Mechanization Takes Command*, appeared. This was a magnificent work, a fitting contribution to the tradition of all-embracing cultural history established by Burckhardt, whose scriptural presence can be perceived on every page. *Mechanization Takes Command* puts forward the case for technological determinism, arguing that the character of the modern world and its artefacts is continuously moderated by scientific progress. With its analyses of the Yale lock, the Colt revolver (see page 23), the Pullman car, and air-conditioning, this study made the history of art into the history of things. The book emphasized the anonymous, technical aspects of history, instead of the creative individual, and thus reversed the approach of conventional art history.

Bibliography Sigfried Giedion *Bauen in Frankreich* Leipzig and Berlin, 1928; Sigfried Giedion Space, *Time and Architecture* Harvard University Press, Cambridge, Mass., 1941; Oxford University Press, London, 1941; Sigfried Giedion *Mechanization Takes Command: a contribution to anonymous history* Oxford University Press, New York, 1948; *Hommage à Giedion* Birkhauser, Basle & Stuttgart, 1972

2: The 'Gill Sans' typeface, 1928. Gill was a reclusive craftsman-stonecarver, ruralist, eccentric animal lover, graphic artist and mystic. This typeface of uncompromised clarity was designed for the Monotype Corporation became a token of English Modernism when it was adopted by the LNER railway company in 1929.

Eric Gill 1882–1940

Eric Gill was a fantastically prolific engraver, type-designer, sculptor, stone-carver and writer. He produced architectural carvings for Westminster Cathedral and the BBC's Broadcasting House, but he is best remembered for the design of the 'Gill Sans' typeface for the Monotype Corporation. This 'grotesque' (square-cut, sans serif) face became, for many people, the symbol of <u>Modernism</u> in England.

Gill was possessed by a social ideal loosely modelled on the early Christian communities. He also had a mystical approach to the handicrafts, and David Kindersley, a stone-cutting apprentice in Gill's last workshop at Piggotts in Buckinghamshire, recalled that he was taught an 'all-pervading truth in the making of simple objects'. Gill's ideas about life and work, with their romantic anti-capitalism and exaltation of worthy toil, have been crucially influential not only on the recent Crafts Revival, but also on an entire generation of students (including Terence Conran) that was exposed to his or his disciples' teaching.

Gill's professional life began with an apprenticeship to the minor Gothic Revival architect, W. H. Caröe. At the same time he was a student at <u>Lethaby</u>'s <u>Central School</u> <u>of Art and Crafts</u> in London, where he studied lettering under Edward Johnston. He dallied with the Arts and Crafts, but had dissociated himself from it by 1909. Instead, he found what he was looking for in the Church and became a Catholic in 1913. Religion and socialism went hand in hand for Gill, and he set up workshops in Ditchling in Sussex and Capel-y-ffin in Wales, where he taught students much like a medieval master with his apprentices. He left behind a portfolio of ideas which were not merely eccentric but which prefigure recent left-wing thinking about the structure of the economy. Gill knew that the problem was not just that working men should have access to more of the wealth, but that the means of producing the wealth should be changed.

A sensational biography by Fiona MacCarthy revealed that Gill's piety and dignity at work had its counterpoint in exceptionally colourful sexual tastes while at play.

Bibliography Brian Keeble *A Holy Tradition of Working: passages from the writings of Eric Gill* Golganooza Press, Ipswich, 1983; Fiona MacCarthy *Eric Gill* Faber, London, 1989

2

2

Ernest Gimson 1864–1919

The furniture designer and craftsman Ernest Gimson moved with the Barnsley Brothers to the Cotswolds in 1895 and, life imitating art, set up a workshop like that of William Morris at Daneway House in 1902. Gimson is best known for his architecture and furniture designs, which were firmly entrenched in British rural traditions and which were loyal to the Arts and Crafts ideals of natural materials and simple forms.

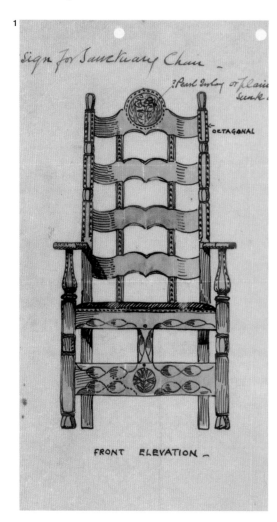

The Girard Foundation at Girard's home in Santa Fe, New Mexico, maintains an international collection of toys and 'objects of whimsy' from all over the world

Alexander Girard 1907–93

Alexander Girard, American architect and interior designer, came to fame in 1949 when he created the influential 'For Modern Living' exhibition on modern design at the Detroit Institute of Arts. In 1951 he was, with Eero Saarinen, a colour consultant to General Motors, and from 1952 was working for Herman Miller as a designer of furniture, fabrics, showrooms and shops. He introduced colour and pattern into Herman Miller's previously austere range of merchandise. He has run architectural offices in Florence, New York and Detroit and established the Girard Foundation at his home in Santa Fe, New Mexico, where he maintains an international collection of toys and 'objects of whimsy' from all over the world.

Girard won an Architectural League Silver Medal for design and craftsmanship for his 1960 interior design for the Fonda del Sol restaurant in New York's Time-Life Building; the design was colourful and exuberant, using collage techniques and evoking South American folklore, but at the same time was highly disciplined and controlled. His most celebrated commission was to redesign the entire appearance of the Texan airline, Braniff International. Taking his brief as being 'to destroy the monotony', in 1965 Girard created for Braniff a corporate identity which had every plane in the fleet a different colour: 'This idea was to make a plane like a racing car – with the fuselage painted a solid colour clearly expressing its shape. Incidentally, it couldn't be a simpler or cheaper method of achieving identity.'

Bibliography Alexander Girard *The Magic of a People* Viking, New York, 1968

Ernesto Gismondi born 1931

Ernesto Gismondi became professor of rocket technology at Milan Polytechnic, but is better known as founder and owner of the furniture manufacturer Artemide. Gismondi, at the pinnacle of the city's design *famiglia*, gave practical support to the radical group Memphis, but he maintained the Machiavellian position of representing the Milanese establishment while funding the Milanese avant-garde which is struggling to undermine it.

1: Ernest Gimson, design for the Sanctuary chair in pen and ink wash, circa 1905–25.
2: Alexander Girard, La Fonda del Sol, restaurant, Time-Life Building, New York, 1960. Girard's collages reflected his enthusiasm for Latin-American culture and predicted theme restaurants of the future.

3: Giorgetto Giugiaro's 'Marille' pasta for Voiello, 1983. Designed as an inspired promotion rather than a viable new pasta form, Giugiaro claimed to have applied thermo and hydro-dynamic theory to the creation of a new pasta shape. His 1974 drawing of the Volkswagen Golf was more influential, creating a new standard of excellence in the design of small cars.

W.H. Gispen 1890–1963

A Dutch furniture designer, W.H. Gispen studied at the Academie van Beeldende Kunst in Rotterdam. In 1916 he founded a Werkstätte für Kunstgewerbegegenstande aus Metall (workshop for applied art forms in metal). He began producing lights in 1929 and chairs in 1930; with his countryman Mart Stam (who is credited for producing the first cantilevered chair), Gispen was among the first Modern Movement designers to make furniture in metal.

Bibliography Otakar Macel & Jan van Geest *Stühleaus Stahl* Walther Köing, Cologne, 1980

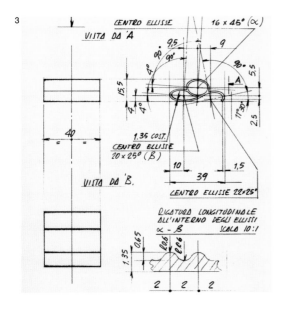

Giorgetto Giugiaro born in 1938

Giorgio Giugiaro studied at Belli Arte in Turin, and at 17 went to work for FIAT, the local firm. At 21 he joined Nuccio Bertone and in 1965 became chief executive of the design centre of Ghia. He set up his own firm, ItalDesign, in 1968.

Giugiaro is one of the most imitated and innovative of all consultant product designers: his work combines style with a sympathy for technology that is rare in Italian design. While still with Bertone he designed the Alfa Romeo Giulia GT, a car widely considered to be one of the understated classics of all time. At ItalDesign Giugiaro's esoteric influence was huge before he became known as a cult figure. ItalDesign worked on the Alfa Romeo Alfasud (1971), on the Volkswagen Golf (1974) and on the FIAT Panda (1980). The oil crisis of 1973 stimulated a change in Giugiaro's views about design. Having established a particular mode of stylish sporting car, he changed to a more practical, more functional one. He even began to practise a form of obsolescence, saying: 'I contributed to making the long, low, sleek car fashionable, and now it is time to change. I have to eat, you know.' Since the firm has become recognized as *the* leading Italian car design consultancy, more and more effort has gone into producing speculative dream cars, unveiled to the industry of the world at every year's Turin Motor Show. Of these, the Medusa of 1980 and the Capsula of 1983 have, with their respective concerns for aerodynamics and modularity, predicted the preoccupations of the major manufacturers.

Giugiaro designs sewing-machines for Necchi, cameras for Nikon, watches for Seiko, crash-helmets for Shoiei and furniture for Tecno. While his car designs all share a crisp, razor-edged elegance, Giugiaro's product designs can be recognized by a deliberately 'technical' aesthetic.

In all his designs Giugiaro does more than offer his clients dramatic and persuasive renderings of projects-to-be. For instance, with the FIAT Panda the first stage of the presentation included two full-scale models, four alternative solutions for the sides, a buck of the passenger compartment and a comprehensive comparative study putting the Panda-to-be alongside its competitors. When these proposals were approved, ItalDesign was requested to start production studies, build a master model and design provisional tooling and engineer pre-production prototypes. Within a year ItalDesign had produced 20 rolling chassis.

Giugiaro has continued to work for FIAT, but has also lent a dignity they might otherwise lack to the emerging vehicle manufacturers of Korea.

Bibliography Giorgetto *Giugiaro: Nascita del progetto* exhibition catalogue, Tecno, Milan, 1983

Giugiaro's esoteric influence was huge before he became known as a cult figure

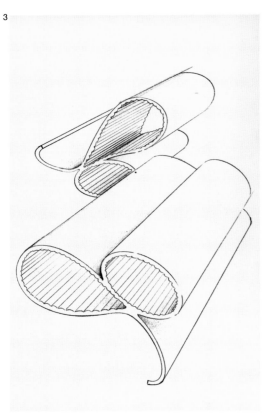

Milton Glaser born 1929

Milton Glaser is the most celebrated living American graphic designer. He was born in New York and studied at Manhattan's High School of Music and Art until 1946, and at the Cooper Union until 1951. In 1952–3 he won a Fulbright scholarship which took him to Italy where he studied at Bologna and learnt print-making techniques from the artist Giorgio Morandi. On his return to the United States he founded the Push Pin Studio (with colleagues Seymour Chwast and Ed Sorel). In 1968 Glaser began an important association with Clay Felker, a publisher, designing the influential *New York* magazine, a resuscitated version of a Sunday supplement from an admired, but defunct, newspaper. *New York* not only established new standards in graphic design but was also a specialist category in the publishing market. It was widely imitated.

The popular and critical success enjoyed by *New York*, at least until it was taken over by Rupert Murdoch in 1977, gave Glaser terrific puissance in the field of magazine design. In 1973 he redesigned *Paris Match*, the French weekly news magazine, and *Village Voice; L 'Europeo, Le Jardin des modes, New West, L'Express* and *Esquire* soon followed.

In 1974 Glaser began to undertake major supergraphics for architectural interiors: a fresco for the New Federal Office Building in Indianapolis and the restaurants in New York's World Trade Center. In the same year he designed the whole interior and fittings for the Childcraft store in New York and in 1980 was commissioned to create an entire graphic character for the Grand Union supermarket chain – everything from label and package design to the corporate identity, shop-fittings and interiors.

Milton Glaser has expanded the role of the graphic designer and openly sees himself as an artist: 'I feel a great personal identification with Piero della Francesca,' he has remarked. He is, however, less reverent about art in his posters: to advertise Ettore Sottsass's 'Valentine' typewriter for Olivetti, Glaser used a detail from a Piero di Cosimo painting, declaring that 'the whole visual history of the world is my resource'. The most striking thing about Glaser's work seen as a whole is the diversity of styles which he has employed, in order, he says, to obviate boredom: 'Anything I did long enough to master was no longer useful to me.' If there is any feature that unites his work in this diversity it is the frequent use of tight, nervy typography together with a taste for images, as in his famous Bob Dylan poster, which can be read in two ways – a technique derived from Surrealism.

Glaser has said that being born Jewish in New York has helped him to assume his huge range of reference: it is much the same to him whether he is commissioned to design all the jackets for the Signet Shakespeare or the poster for a Stevie Wonder concert. Let's abandon the word 'art' he once said, and let's just call it 'work'.

Bibliography Peter Mayer *Graphic Design: Milton Glaser* Overlook Press, New York, 1972

G-Plan

G-Plan is a furniture range launched in 1953 by Donald Gomme's (born 1916) family firm in High Wycombe. Inspired in part by wartime Utility, G-Plan became popular in Britain in the Fifties and Sixties with its moderately priced and subtly suburbanized versions of the modern style, known as Contemporary. G-Plan's profile in the home market was greatly ehanced by the adroit advertising campaigns of J. Walter Thompson.

Albrecht Goertz 1913–2006

Count Albrecht Goertz was born in Brunkensen, Germany, but emigrated to the United States in 1936. He opened a custom body shop in California, but his design career proper began when Raymond Loewy found him at the wheel of one of his cars in a New York parking garage in 1945. He was self-taught, but also learnt from Carl Otto and Norman Bel Geddes, as well as the ineffable Loewy.

In 1953 he set up his own studio and won the job to design the 1955 BMW 507 sports car after an introduction by Max Hoffmann, the American BMW importer. The 507 clearly shows American influence, especially of Harley Earl. Goertz also joined the team that created the Porsche 911, the Toyota 2000 GT and the Datsun 240Z.

The most striking thing about Glaser's work seen as a whole is the diversity of styles which he has employed, in order, he says, to obviate boredom

1

Kenneth Grange born 1929

Kenneth Grange is Britain's leading 'name' product designer. He received his most important training as a technical illustrator while doing national service in the Royal Engineers. He then worked as an assistant in various minor architectural and design offices until setting up his own consultancy, Kenneth Grange Design, in 1971. Then, with Fletcher, Forbes & Gill and an architect called Theo Crosby, he founded the design consultancy Pentagram in 1971.

Grange belongs to the generation of writers, fashion designers, painters and film-makers who created the distinctive flavour of British cultural life after the Second World War, when, despite the practical constraints, there was an air of simple optimism. He was one of the first British designers to recognize the significance of the rational style emerging from Germany in the post-War years, and cheerfully admits to the influence which Braun has had on his own attitudes to design. More than any other designer in Britain, Grange has enjoyed the thrill of seeing his visions come into being in the everyday world: the 'Venner' parking meter, Kodak 'Instamatic', the Kenwood mixers, the Parker '25' pen, and a cosmetic job on British Rail's 125 train.

Bibliography *Kenneth Grange at the Boilerhouse* exhibition catalogue, The Boilerhouse Project, Victoria and Albert Museum, London, 1983

Michael Graves born in 1934

Michael Graves became the Princeton spokesman for Post-Modernism. He studied architecture at Harvard, and has taught architecture at Princeton since 1962. He first came to public notice in the Seventies, when journalists began to write about the 'New York Five', in whose number he was counted. A gifted draughtsman, until 1982 Graves's only substantial contribution to the history of architecture and design was a series of exquisitely coloured drawings, sold in galleries on New York's 57th Street, a dressing table called 'Plaza' for Memphis, a table and chair for the American manufacturer Sunar, and a coffee service for Alessi.

Graves's first realized architectural project has been the Public Services Building in Portland, Oregon, completed in 1982. His infamous *bollitore* for Alessi (with a tweety bird on the spout, a whistle like an Amtrak train and a handle too to hot hold) was for many people a superlative demonstration of the look-at-me absurdities of Post-Modernism. He now works for Target stores.

Bibliography Charles Jencks *Kings of Infinite Space* Academy Editions, London, 1983

Eileen Gray 1878–1976

Eileen Gray was an Irish designer who translated the German Functionalist style of tubular steel furniture into a form of French chic. With great style, taste and humour she understood elegance better than any other Modernist. She was born at Enniscorthy, County Wexford, Ireland, into a family that was part Scots–Irish nobility, part *plein air* amateur painters. In 1898 she began to study drawing at London's Slade School and took a personal interest in lacquer-work. This assumed greater importance in her creative life when she moved to Paris in 1902 and started a dedicated study of this oriental craft with Sugawara, a Japanese lacquer master who was enjoying celebrity at the time among artistic circles in the French capital.

Her first jobs included lacquer screens and tables, and she began to get noticed in magazines such as *Vogue*, which published an article about her in 1917, but already she was tending toward a different sort of design, personal but more restrained. It was Eileen Gray's achievement to see in the architecture of Gropius and Le Corbusier a new style for the twentieth century, which its proprietors' revolutionary zeal had disguised as functional purposefulness. In 1924 she began dabbling in architecture. With Jean Badovici, the editor of *L'Architecture vivante*, she designed in the mid-Twenties a house called E-1027 at Roquebrune in the south of France. For all her chic and lack of revolutionary fervour, this house was, at the time it was built, as aggressively modern a statement about the new architecture as anything built by Gerrit Rietveld in Holland or Le Corbusier in France. It was from this house that Le Corbusier swam to his death in 1965.

She also designed the 'Transat' chair in leather, wood and lacquer, as well as a tubular steel side table, numerous chests of drawers, and some striking lacquered screens.

Bibliography Stewart Johnson *Eileen Gray: designer 1879–1976* Debrett, London, 1979

1: Milton Glaser's 'I Love New York' device, 1977, has been copied the world over. Bob Dylan, 1967, a music icon becomes a graphic one.

2: Eileen Gray built her own house, Modernistically called E-1027, at Roquebrune on the Riviera, 1926–9. A showcase of her furniture and textiles, it became a key image in the promotion of Modernism. From the balcony here Le Corbusier swam to his death in 1965.

Milner Gray 1899–1997

The English graphic designer Milner Gray was trained in the days when the calling was more usually known as 'commercial artist'. In 1930 he helped found the society of industrial artists, SIA, that became SIAD, one of the world's first professional organizations for designers. During the Second World War he worked with his partner Misha Black, doing propaganda exhibitions for the Ministry of Information. It was during the War that he established the principles and ambitions of DRU, the design consultancy he was to set up in 1944. The final aim was to present a service so complete that it could undertake any design case which might confront the State, Municipal Authorities, Industry or Commerce. Milner Gray has lectured and written extensively on exhibition and packaging design.

Bibliography John and Avril Blake *The Practical Idealists* Lund Humphries, London, 1969

Great Exhibition of the Industry of All Nations

Queen Victoria's husband, Prince Albert of Saxe-Coburg Gotha, and Henry Cole, an official at the Public Record Office who had dabbled in ceramic design for Minton's, shared a missionary zeal about design in industry. Having unsuccessfully tried to revivify the (Royal) Society of Arts through a series of exhibitions of industrial design, they decided to organize a better one themselves. Their planning began in 1848; it was originally for a national exhibition, but Cole and Prince Albert decided it should also embrace foreign products. Cole used his colleagues, who helped him with his short-lived *Journal of Design*. The exhibition took place in London's Hyde Park in 1851, in a huge glass structure by Joseph Paxton, a greenhouse designer. Its contents were the applied arts and machinery; the emphasis was on the commercial impact of applied decoration and the excitement of mass-production.

This excitement was felt nowhere more strongly than by the organizers: Prince Albert claimed, 'Man is approaching a more complete fulfilment of that great and sacred mission he has to perform in this world.'

Although the exhibition was a popular triumph, its results shocked its organizers, demonstrating to the officials what they had already known since the 1836 Select Committee *Report on Arts and Manufactures*: that Britain was far behind its continental rivals in matters of design. Cole regarded this as a vindication of his idea and, with renewed zeal, used the Great Exhibition and the surplus of its exhibits and profits to create the series of institutions which eventually became the Victoria and Albert Museum.

Bibliography Jeffrey A. Auerbach *The Great Exhibition of 1851 – a nation on display* Yale University Press, New Haven and London, 1999

The Great Exhibition took place in London's Hyde Park in 1851, in a huge glass structure by Joseph Paxton

1

Horatio Greenough 1805–52

Horatio Greenough was an obscure and mediocre American sculptor who assumed more prominence in the twentieth century than in his own on account of thoughts contained in his book, *The Travels, Observations and Experiences of a Yankee Stonecutter*.

After studying at Harvard he travelled around Italy in pursuit of his vocation as sculptor. Although his appreciation that architecture had a moral character predates <u>John Ruskin</u>'s, Greenough did not share the Englishman's tastes: he admired the Greeks and was impatient with the Gothic. When in 1843 there was a public commotion about Greenough's semi-nude statue of George Washington, he began to question American taste. Although his observations all fall within the cultural tradition of the Greek Revival, Greenough's vision was admirably clear: he was, essentially, a machine romantic and admired machines for their elegance and simplicity, being amongst the first ever to do so. His book was published under the pseudonym of Horace Bender, in the year of his death. Some writers have seen in it the basis for the twentieth-century ideology of <u>Functionalism</u>.
Bibliography E. R. de Zurko *Origins of Functionalist Theory* Columbia University Press, New York, 1957

Eugene Gregorie 1908–2002

Eugene Turenne 'Bob' Gregorie, a yacht designer by training, joined the <u>Ford</u> Motor Company in 1931. In 1935 he became head of the styling department, after Edsel Ford had been impressed by the success of his Model 40, advertised on account of its elegant appearance as 'The Car without a Price Class'. The Thunderbird was produced under his supervision. Gregorie's work for Ford is said to have influenced André <u>Citroën</u> in his design of the Traction Avant of 1936.

Hermann Gretsch 1895–1950

After the dissolution of the <u>Deutsche Werkbund</u> in the early years of Nazism, Hermann Gretsch headed its successor, Der Bund Deutscher Entwurfer (the association of German designers). His Model 1382 tableware, which he designed for the Arzberg Porzellanfabrik in 1931, was a realization of the standards in mass-produced consumer design that the Werkbund had been promoting for two decades. Gretsch was, with <u>Wilhelm Wagenfeld</u>, one of the few designers who worked prolifically and successfully throughout the Nazi regime.

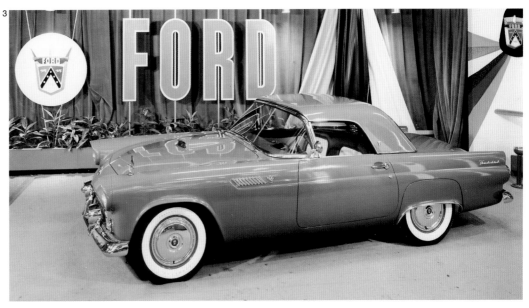

3

2

1: The Great Exhibition, 1851. The awesome impression made by machines contrasted with the suffocating fussiness of the decorative arts and inspired a revolution in design theory.
2: Horatio Greenough's statue of George Washington once exalted the DC public, but is now safely in the Smithsonian Institution. Greenough was a mediocre artist, but an influential thinker whose ideas predicted 'Functionalism'.

3: The Thunderbird, 1955, was Ford's response to Harley Earl's Corvette sportscar for General Motors. A classic of US popular culture, its successor inspired The Beach Boys to sing 'We'll have fun, fun, fun 'til daddy takes the T-bird away'. An artful retro revival by J Mays in 1999 was a commercial failure.

Walter Gropius 1883–1969

When Walter Gropius arrived at Harvard he put an end
to the Beaux-Arts tradition of architectural education
and changed the face of American design, forever.
He was, indeed, one of the most influential figures
of the twentieth century, a man idolized by three
generations of students from the Bauhaus in Germany
to Harvard University School of Architecture in the
United States, and eventually satirized by Tom Wolfe
as austere and unworldly.

Gropius was born in Berlin into a family of architects
whose experience of building went back to at least the
beginning of the nineteenth century. Prussian military
culture may have had an influence on his own creative
development: his Bauherren were eventually to discipline
architecture and design as if they were a conquering
army, defeating the stultified culture of the past with
their weapons of geometry, iron, glass and concrete.

He studied architecture in Berlin and Munich, and
worked as an assistant to Peter Behrens. Here he learnt
Behrens's credo that 'we have no alternative but to make
life more simple, less complicated'. Accordingly, when
he established his own office, in partnership with Adolf
Meyer, in 1910, the world was astonished by a series of
remarkable buildings – such as the Fagus factory at
Alfeld in 1911 and the Deutsche Werkbund exhibition
building of 1914 – which, despite their smallness and
remoteness, became some of the most published and
familiar of all modern buildings.

· During service as an air observer in the First World
War Gropius was granted leave to discuss with the
Grand Duke of Saxe-Weimar the possibility of his taking
over the Saxon Academy of Arts and Crafts from the
Belgian Henry van de Velde (who had recommended
him). This was the beginning of the Bauhaus, whose
influence in the world of art and design can be compared
with the influence of the theory of relativity in physics. But
curiously, while the Bauhaus advocated the pursuit of 'truth'
through modern building, it had no formal architecture
department until 1927. When conservative local
politicians, as well as representatives of craft groups and
trade unions, felt threatened by the Bauhaus, Gropius
handed over the directorship to Hannes Meyer in 1928.
This left him free to resume his own architectural practice:
his largest project was *Existenzminimum* housing at
Siemensstadt, outside Berlin. His life in Weimar and Dessau
was colourfully described by his ex-wife, Alma Mahler
Werfel, in a memoir, *And the Bridge Was Love* (1957).
Mahler soon left Gropius for playwright Franz Werfel.

Gropius was a complex individual, by no means as
geometric as his buildings, although his Bauhaus
colleagues were always struck by his austerity: the painter
Paul Klee called him 'the Silver Prince'. The comic novelist
Evelyn Waugh satirized him as the 'mad' Dr Otto Silenus
in his breakthrough novel *Decline and Fall* (1927). 'The
problem of architecture,' Waugh makes Silenus/Gropius
say, 'is the problem of all art – the elimination of the
human element…The only perfect building must be the
factory, because it is built to house machines, not men.'
Waugh's parody was surprisingly prescient for 1927.

1

Group of Ten

Gropius left Germany in 1933 because he felt his ideas would never gain official recognition under the Nazis and went to England, where he formed a partnership with the English architect <u>Maxwell Fry</u>. In 1937 he took up an appointment as a professor of architecture at Harvard and founded The Architects' Collaborative (TAC) in 1945. The title of this architectural practice emphasized Gropius' belief in the importance of teamwork, which had been one of the fundamental principles of Bauhaus education.

Gropius thought that all building should be defined in terms of its (supposed) function, and that the different architectural elements that were inevitably created by this rule should be arranged into a pleasing compositional effect. While <u>Le Corbusier</u>'s intention was to make his buildings into elegantly simple sculptural forms (with complex and subtle interior spaces), and <u>Mies van der Rohe</u> aimed at perfection of detail and discretion of shape, Gropius sought to create a dynamic interpretation of forms and spaces. When he taught at Harvard he embodied his principles of functional subdivision in the curriculum.

Even without his architecture, and despite a somewhat narrow interpretation of <u>Functionalism</u>, Gropius would be remembered as the most persuasive and sophisticated of all the theoreticians, educators and critics who struggled to accommodate civilized, humane values into a mechanized world. The great influences on his thought were <u>William Morris</u>, from whom he took the ideal of the unity of art and life, and <u>Henry Ford</u>, from whom he took the concept of standardization of machine-made products.

Bibliography Walter Gropius *Idee und Aufbau des Staatlichen Bauhauses* 1923; *Internationale Architektur* 1925; *Bauhaus Bauten* 1933; *The New Architecture and the Bauhaus* New York, 1936; *Bauhaus 1919–1928* 1939 (with Use Frank and Herbert Bayer); Sigfried Giedion *Walter Gropius* London, 1954; Hans Maria Wingler *Bauhaus* MIT, Cambridge, Mass., 1969; James Marston Fitch & Ise Gropius *Walter Gropius — buildings, plans, projects 1906–1969* exhibition catalogue, International Exhibitions Foundation, 1972–4; Klaus Herdeg *The Decorated Diagram — Harvard architecture and the failure of the Bauhaus legacy* MIT, Cambridge, Mass., 1983; *Modernism*, exhibition catalogue, Vctoria and Albert Museum, London, 2006

The Group of Ten is a group of textile designers founded in Stockholm in 1970. Their motivation was to replace the client/designer relationship with one where they were able to oversee the entire process from concept through to sales. The first collection, with one design from each of the ten designers, appeared in 1972. Its Stockholm showroom opened the following year. Now reduced to six, it aims to make collections of textiles and wallpapers of a lasting rather than a fashionable nature.

1: Walter Gropius' study in the first Bauhaus building, Weimar, 1923.

2: Sweden's Group of Ten was a collaborative specializing in fabrics with bold colours and strong designs.

Gruppo Strum

Gruppo Strum was a late starter among the Italian radical design groups that briefly flourished in the later Sixties. It was motivated by naive ideas about the political possibilities of architecture. In 1972 Gruppo Strum reached its greatest prominence with an exhibition, 'Mediatory City', at the Museum of Modern Art's 'New Domestic Landscape' exhibition in New York. Then its leaders sank back into the comfortable obscurity of provincial Italian academic life.

1: Luvelle Guild, Electrolux model XXX (30) vacuum cleaner, with its 'meet me on the moon next Tuesday' styling, 1937. An energetic self-promoter, Guild wrote more than 200 books and pamphlets.
2: The Kodak Carousel first appeared in 1962. In the days before Powerpoint, this exemplar of systematic design was the most familiar technology in lecture rooms and business pitches.

3: Hector Guimard, gates of the Castel Beranger, Paris, 1894–98. These 'logements de standing' at 14 rue Fontaine, in the 16eme, are masterpieces of Art Nouveau.
4: Stig Lindberg for Gustavsberg in *Form* 10/1955, featuring products selected by MoMA for 'good design'.

Hans Gugelot 1920–65

The Dutch–Swiss architect and designer Hans Gugelot was head of the product design department at the Hochschule für Gestaltung in Ulm from 1955 until his death.

Gugelot was born in Indonesia and studied at the Eidgenossischen Technische Hochschule (federal technical college) in Zürich and worked with Max Bill from 1948 to 1950 when he designed his first furniture for the Horgen-Glarus stores. He met Erwin Braun in 1954, the same year that he started teaching at the Hochschule für Gestaltung, and was to produce several designs for him.

Gugelot was one of the great influences on the forms adopted by the post-Second World War Western manufacturing industry (and those imitated elsewhere). With his pupil and later colleague Dieter Rams, he was the most ardent and austere exponent of the Functionalist style, which became associated with German design of that period. He persuaded himself and his clients that his own preference for muted greys, right angles and the complete eradication of decorative detail produced the inevitably correct and timeless appearance of machines. The 'Phonosuper' record player of 1950, designed with Dieter Rams, known in Germany as the 'Schneewittchens Sarg' (Snow White's Coffin), was the perfect expression of this style. Gugelot was consultant to the Hamburg U-bahn (1959–62) and was also responsible for the design of the Kodak 'Carousel' side projector (1962), a machine whose timelessness supports the validity of his taste. However, the electro-mechanical hearts of the machines he designed had been replaced by solid state circuitry, making the attitude to design that he had championed on the basis of 'logic' no more than another preferred style.

Bibliography Alison and Peter Smithson 'Concealment and Display: Meditations on Braun' *Architectural Design* vol. 36, July, 1966, pp. 362–3; *System-Design Bahnbrecher: Hans Gugelot 1920–1965* exhibition catalogue, Die Neue Sammlung, Munich, 1984

Lurelle Guild 1898–1986

Like Norman Bel Geddes and Henry Dreyfuss, Lurelle van Arsdale Guild was a pioneer American consultant designer who had his training in the theatre. By 1920 he was selling cover artwork to *House & Garden* and the *Ladies' Home Journal*, and he soon found that the advertisers for whom he designed layouts actually wanted him to design their products too. As a result he produced a range of spun-aluminium kitchenware and other small objects in the fashionable streamlined style, and also some textured linoleum. Guild had two great skills. First, to interpret futuristic themes from popular culture and apply them to industrial products. Thus, an Elecrolux vacuum cleaner that looks like a flying saucer. Second, self-promotion. This latter was a fundamental part of any pioneer New York designer's portfolio. Throughout his career magazine ads ran showing Guild with a strapline 'Tomorrow's products are designed by this genius.'

2

1

Hector Guimard 1867–1942

Hector Guimard is best known for his contributions to the vocabulary of Art Nouveau, and for making street furniture into works of art. His fantastical Castel Béranger flats in Paris of 1894–8 announced the characteristics of his style: ostentatious applied architectural ornament and cast-iron stairways and balconies with sinuous, asymmetric, tendril-like forms, as if derived from over-cooked vegetables, or slides of spermatozoa. Guimard also designed the Métro entrances, where wrought iron is worked into organic curves, topped by electric globes looking as if they are the buds of the plant. Guimard's combination of structure with decorative form was typical of the attempts by Art Nouveau designers to replace nineteenth-century historicism with stylistic novelty.

Bibliography *Hector Guimard* exhibition catalogue, Museum of Modern Art, New York, 1970

Gustavsberg

Gustavsberg is a small town 15 miles outside Stockholm which, since 1825, has given its name to Sweden's leading ceramics factory. The first products to appear were earthenware, following current German technical practice, but printed patterns began to appear around 1830 under the influence of England.

In the late nineteenth century the predominant style of domestic ceramics was Nordic National Romantic, an overbearing decorative manner heavy with folklore and light on art. But a great structural change overcame the company in the 1890s with the appointment of the painter Gunnar Wennerberg as artist-in-residence. Wennerberg's much more refined designs were first seen at the 1897 Art and Industry exhibition in Stockholm: he chose as motifs freshly observed paintings of wild flowers, in effect offering the Swedish consumer a version of the principles of Art Nouveau.

Wennerberg's appointment created a precedent that Gustavsberg readily augmented by a series of further distinguished appointments: Wilhelm Kåge joined the company in 1917 and promptly designed a working man's service (as if in direct response to Gregor Paulsson's appeal for 'more beautiful everyday things'). This 'Praktika' service was a direct response to the international Modern Movement, although the majority of his work manifested more obviously decorative qualities. Stig Lindberg joined in 1937 and in 1949 he succeeded Kåge as artistic director of the company. Under Lindberg's direction Gustavsberg produced the first acceptable oven-to-table earthenware, which did much to characterize 'Swedish Modern' to consumers throughout the world.

Lindberg hired other artists to work for Gustavsberg, Karin Bjorquist and Lisa Larson joining during the Fifties. A set of stoneware pots with 'hare's fur' glaze designed by Berndt Friberg became famous, populating the room dividers that so often featured in magazine articles about Scandinavian Design.

In 1937 Gustavsberg had passed from the private control of the Odelberg family into that of the Swedish Cooperative Society, and its commercial interests broadened into sanitary ware and plastics. Gustavsberg now uses its new plastics expertise to manufacture intelligent tools for the disabled, and in employing the Stockholm human factors consultancy, Ergonomi Design, continues the inspired tradition it began nearly 100 years ago with the job it gave to the academic painter Gunnar Wennerberg.

Bibliography *Gustavsberg 150 ar* exhibition catalogue, Nationalmuseum, Stockholm, 1975

3

4

Habitat

The Habitat chain of stores brought design to the public's notice in Britain. The first store opened in London's Fulham Road in 1964, a furnishing shop to meet the needs of the new Pop culture. The founder was Terence Conran (born 1931), who has remained its head and guiding force ever since. Conran trained as a textile designer at London's Central School of Art and Design, and when he left set up a studio with the sculptor and print-maker Eduardo Paolozzi, making modern metal furniture and designing fabrics and ceramics. Conran had opened his own bistro, the Soup Kitchen, in 1954, the same year that his consultancy, the Conran Design Group (now Conran & Partners), was founded. Two years later he designed the Bazaar boutique for his friend Mary Quant, but despite these local successes he was consistently frustrated by the conservative buyers in the big department stores who refused to consider stocking his bright, modern flat-pack furniture called Summa.

The first Habitat was a response to this, and its impact was immediate: it was the first shop to offer a complete range of stylish and sensible goods at reasonable prices. It was not only merchandise that Habitat offered for sale, but a whole way of life (or, at least, the vision of it): furniture, cookware, glass, crockery, cutlery, rugs, tiles, fabrics and lights, stacked floor-to-ceiling as if in a warehouse. In some quarters Habitat won itself a reputation for being a sort of commercialization of the Bauhaus, but the merchandise is very much more eclectic: on its opening, the first store stocked not only Braun appliances, but also French professional cookware and Polish enamel. As one store has evolved into an international chain, Habitat is necessarily less the expression of one man's taste and more the product of sophisticated, professional retailing, but it still has a fundamental philosophy. Terence Conran expressed it in a 1967 interview with *House & Garden*: 'I am not interested in "pure" design, which designers do for other designers… I am interested in selling good design to the mass market.' The validity of Conran's interpretation of the modern shop has been proved by Habitat's growth; there are now branches in France, Belgium, Iceland, the United States and Japan. In 1981 Habitat took over Mothercare, a major retailer of clothes and equipment for mothers and children, and in 1983 the company acquired Heal's, bringing a phenomenon that was a child of the Sixties directly into the established tradition of British furniture design and manufacture.

IKEA acquired Habitat in 1989. Tom Dixon became Design Director in 1998. Of this Terence Conran says: 'I don't think this has led them in the right direction. Sadly.'

Bibliography Barty Phillips *Conran and the Habitat Story* Weidenfeld & Nicolson, London, 1984; Terence Conran *Q&A* HarperCollins, London, 2000

Edward Hald 1883–1980

A Swedish glass and ceramics designer, Edward Niels Tove Hald once studied painting under Henri Matisse. With the help of the Svenska Sljödföreningen he worked at Rörstrand and then at the Orrefors glassworks, where he started as designer in 1917, rising to become managing director from 1933 to 1944. With Simon Gate, Hald was one of the founders of Modernism in Sweden, designing simple, decorative forms that were made by the company's craftsmen. His son Arthur was artistic director of Gustavsberg until 1981.

Both father and son contributed fine-art talents to the applied arts, designing ceramics and glass characterized by the application of light, often figurative decoration, which caused 'Swedish Modern' to be perceived as being more humanistic than the style emerging from Germany at the same period.

Bibliography *Edward Hald – Malare, Konstindustripionjar* exhibition catalogue, Nationalmuseum, Stockholm, 1983

2

1: In 1964 Habitat brought Bauhaus values to the English high street.
2: Edward Hald, 'Hald' brandy glass for Orrefors, 1935.

Harley-Davidson

Since a management buy-out in 1981, the tiny Harley-Davidson is now a more valuable company than General Motors, its success a result of consistently ingenious product development as well as an example of consumer psychology and its role in design. Like Wilbur and Orville Wright, the Davidson brothers and their friend William Harley were among America's pioneering bicyclists. While the Wrights applied their enthusiasms for amateur engineering to flight, the Davidsons started attaching small engines to triangulated frames to make motorbikes. Their firm was founded in Milwaukee, beer capital of the United States, in 1902.

The first Harley-Davidson was sold to the police in 1907 and military contracts soon followed. Harleys only began to acquire their attractive outlaw reputation after the Second World War when a bunch of disaffected ex-Servicemen (mostly familiar with the 80,000 or so US Military Model U 74 cubic inches vee twins manufactured during the War) gathered in the small Californian town of Hollister to misbehave with Milwaukee beer and Milwaukee bikes. When this event was recorded in a classic of photo-journalism by *Life* magazine, motor-bikes were established as a symbol of rebellion. This was later confirmed by Marlon Brando in *The Wild One* (although he actually used a Triumph Speed Twin) and by the establishment of the Hell's Angels at Fontana, near San Bernardino, an event mythologised by Hunter S. Thompson.

A touching redneck patriotism required the Angels to use Harleys, the sole native American motor-bike manufacturer since Indian went bust in 1953. At first Harleys could not compete with the more worldly Japanese and Italian competition – despite superbly dissipated styling in the style of the American Dream by consultant Brooks Stevens working with Willie G. Davidson. The company was sold to the AMF Corporation in 1969 and would not have survived for long thereafter without a significant revolution in consumer tastes. A group of ad executives in Chicago started using Harleys on weekends and they became known as the Rolex Rangers. Someone made the happy coinage Attila the Stockbroker to describe this middle-class affair with bad boy bikes.

The 'Captain America' Harley-Davidson featured in *Easy Rider* was based on the 1200cc 1962 Model FL, bought from the Los Angeles Police Department and customized with heavy chrome, extended 45-degree front forks and ape-hanger handlebars by Peter Fonda. But the quintessential Harley-Davidson, the one that taps into the consumer's deep wells of nostalgia, is the 1965 Electra-Glide, an evolution of the 1949 Hydra-Glide, now with an electric starter. The evocative language is powerfully appealing: engines are Panheads or Shovelheads, suspensions Hardtails or Softails. In a way that is typically American, Harley-Davidson turned simple matters of specification – namely cylinder heads or springs – into intoxicatingly desirable consumables.

Bibliography *Motorbikes* exhibition catalogue The Solomon R. Guggenheim Museum, New York, 1998

Josef Hartwig 1880–1955

Hartwig was, between 1922 and 1924, a designer of a chess set that was a perfect example of Bauhaus principles: unambiguous materials, forms which can be clearly read and geometrical exposition of purpose. Hartwig was a product of the Bauhaus's wood-carving workshop. He explained, 'The new chess pieces are made out of simple stereometric bodies – the cube and the sphere. Singly or in combination, their shape indicates how the piece moves on the board, and their volume indicates its value.'

Bibliography *Donation Dora Hartwig* exhibition catalogue, Bauhaus-Archiv, 2006–7

Ambrose Heal 1872–1959

Ambrose Heal's family had been involved in furniture since his great-grandfather, also Ambrose Heal, had established a London furniture business in 1810. After an education at Marlborough and apprenticeship to a cabinet-maker in Warwick, Heal joined the family firm in 1893. His cousin, Cecil Brewer (an architect who was to design the new Heal's store just before the First World War, in which he was killed), had introduced him to W.R. Lethaby, C.F.A. Voysey and the Arts and Crafts Exhibition Society, where Heal began showing his furniture designs in 1896. The great achievement of Heal's early career was to get his simple designs into the stores. Tottenham Court Road, where the family store had moved in 1840, was a centre for the manufacture of reproduction furniture, for which the public had a keen appetite, and Heal's own salesmen asked him how on earth they were expected to sell 'prison furniture', so stark did his designs seem in contrast to the vulgar and gross ornamentation of the popular 'Queen Anne' cabinets. The turning-point in Heal's search for recognition amongst the London furniture trade came when C.R. Ashbee's foreman joined the company rather than move with the respected Guild of Handicrafts from London to Chipping Campden.

Ambrose Heal became chairman of the business in 1913, helped to found the Design and Industries Association (DIA) in 1915 and was knighted in 1933.

As a craftsman-designer Heal was influenced both by the ethics and idealism of William Morris, and also by the standards of craftsmanship of the great English furniture designers of the eighteenth century: the quality of the wood itself and a respect for the tools and the materials (learnt at the bench) were fundamental to his own work as a cabinet-maker, winning him a silver medal at the Paris Exhibition of 1900. His influence extended far: as chairman of Heal's he expanded the business to include a comprehensive range of household merchandise, while continuing the tradition of bed-making which had been the foundation of the firm. Antique furniture, textiles and studio pottery were added to the stock, and when the Tottenham Court Road building was enlarged in 1929, a gallery for exhibitions was added. During the Fifties Heal's introduced a discriminating English public to Scandinavian design, and at the same time fabrics designed by Lucienne Day and others. In 1983 Heal & Son was taken over by Habitat Mothercare and radically modernized. By the time it was taken over again, it had lost all status and direction. A deadly reputation for worthiness attaches to the name.

Bibliography Susanna Goodden *At the Sign of the Four Poster – A History of Heal's* Lund Humphries, London, 1983

1
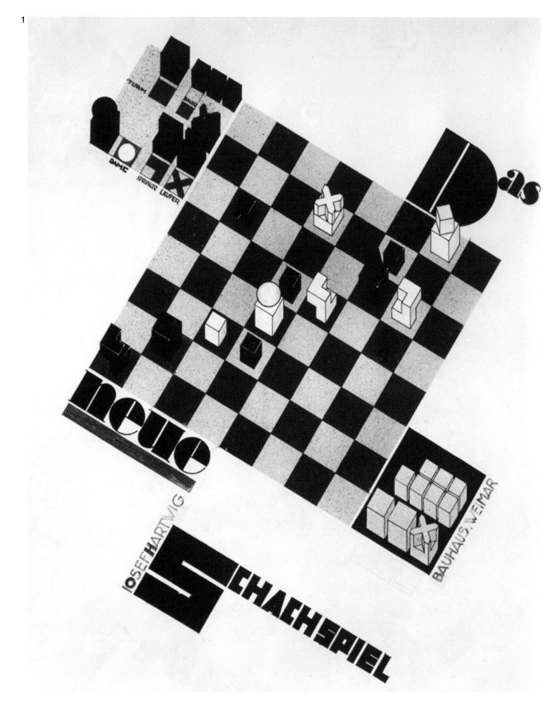

2

Thomas Heatherwick born 1970

In the sense that his work indefinably involves architecture, sculpture and product (while avoiding mass-production) the prodigally talented Heatherwick is the leading representative of British design in the early twenty-first century. Inheriting a passion for free invention, he studied at Manchester Polytechnic and The Royal College of Art, and then set up Thomas Heatherwick Studio in London in 1994. He has designed major public monuments in Manchester, a curling bridge in London's Paddington Basin, a buddist Temple in Japan, a gazebo for Terence Conran, a handbag for Longchamp, and the same company's flagship New York store, which opened in 2006.

1: Sales brochure for Josef Hartwig's Bauhaus chess-set, developed between1922–24.
2: Ambrose Heal, two-tier, circular-topped occasional table in oak, plywood and bakelite, 1932.
3: Thomas Heatherwick, Longchamp store, New York, 2006.
4: The B of the Bang, Manchester, UK, 2005.
5: Thomas Heatherwick's Rolling Bridge, 2004, over Paddington Basin in London, UK. Rather than a conventional swing bridge mechanism, the Rolling Bridge curls up until its two ends touch.

Rather than a conventional swing bridge mechanism, the Rolling Bridge curls up until its two ends touch

Jean Heiberg 1884–1976

Jean Heiberg was a Norwegian painter who studied in Munich and in Paris, latterly under Matisse, and became the designer of arguably the first 'modern' telephone, and certainly the most familiar one to British eyes.

About 1930 the Swedish Ericsson company was developing a new technology for telephones, replacing cranks with dials, and the search went out for a designer to provide them with a new, marketable shape. Initially the job was given to a company engineer of Oslo's Elektrisk Bureau, an Ericsson subsidiary, called Johan Christian Bjerknes. His brief was to develop a machine that would have universal appeal, as Ericsson considered that its market was no less than the entire world. Bjerknes decided to use Bakelite, but then discovered that he needed help with the design, Norway's leading artist of the day, Alf Rolfson, was too busy with a hospital mural so the job was given to Jean Heiberg, who had just returned from the ateliers of Paris to take up a post as professor in Oslo's National Academy of Fine Art. Production of Heiberg's design, which still retains elements of the neo-classical stylobate which dominated his first plaster drafts, went into production in 1932 as the 'DBH1001'. By 1937 there were six presses in England alone, stamping out the Norwegian painter's designs.

Piet Hein 1905–96

The Danish mathematician, cartoonist and designer Piet Hein became a popular figure in the Sixties when his mathematically determined 'super-ellipse' was applied both to urban roundabouts and to a table manufactured by Bruno Mathsson from 1964. A 1966 *Life* magazine profile called him a 'poet with a slide rule'.

Bibliography *Design: the problem comes first* exhibition catalogue, Danish Design Council, Copenhagen, 1982–3

Poul Henningsen 1895–1967

The Dane Poul Henningsen became famous for the 'PH' lamp he designed in 1925, which is still manufactured by the Copenhagen factory of Louis Poulsen.

Henningsen was an articulate spokesman for the integration of artists into manufacturing industry, and condemned the pretentious solipsism of painters locked in their studios. He was a significant contributor to 'Scandinavian Modern' design, and the long-lived 'PH' lamp is a symbol of that achievement.

With Kaare Klint in the later Twenties Henningsen edited the journal *Kritisk Revy*. This architectural magazine was Denmark's most influential publication as far as increasing popular awareness of standards in design is concerned, Henningsen using it to harangue both manufacturers and artists to become more responsive to the twentieth century. He once wrote: 'Throw away your artists' berets and bow ties and get into overalls. Down with artistic pretentiousness! Simply make things which are fit for use: that is enough to keep you busy and you will sell vast quantities and make lots of money.'

Bibliography *Design: the problem comes first* exhibition catalogue, Danish Design Council, Copenhagen, 1982–3

1: Jean Heiberg, Ericsson DBH1001 telephone, 1932. A modern classic inspired by classical sculpture.
2: Poul Henningsen, PH5 pendant light, 1958. Designed for Copenhagen's Louis Poulson, the PH5 was one of a series intended to provide soft, diffused light for Danish 'contemporary' interiors.

3: A Henrion poster for Britain's Second World War Ministry of Information. Henrion was one of a group of continental designers who began to vitalize London graphics in the Thirties.
4: Rene Herbst, Sandows nickel-plated tubular steel chair, 1928.

Henri Kay Frederick Henrion 1914–2000

Henri Henrion studied textiles in Paris and went to Palestine in 1936 to work as a poster artist. He came to England during the Second World War and was a consultant designer to the Exhibitions Division of the Ministry of Information, for whom he designed many distinguished propaganda posters which mixed the concepts of <u>Surrealism</u> with those of commercial art.

Henrion settled in London and became a major figure in both national and international design bodies, while simultaneously developing his graphic design practice.

He began to find that his work was extending beyond commercial art, and in the Fifties began to offer his clients – who included Blue Circle Cement, BEA and KLM – a total design package which integrated all aspects of a company's visual character. Henrion can thus be seen as a pioneer of corporate identity. He also designed the Country Pavillion at the 1951 Festival of Britain.

Bibliography H.K.F. Henrion & Alan Parkin *Design Coordination and Corporate Image* Studio Vista, London, 1968

René Herbst 1891–1982

A Parisian, Rene Herbst was one of the founders of the Union des Artistes Modernes in 1930, and his designs, mostly formal exercises in new materials, are characteristic examples of French modernism. A nickel-plated tubular steel chair he designed in 1930–2 and manufactured in his own Etablissements, has become a modern classic, and since 1979 has been reproduced by Ecart International.

Bibliography René Herbst *25 annees UAM* Edition du Salon des Arts Ménagers, Paris, 1956

3

4

Henrion was a major figure in both national and international design bodies, while simultaneously developing his graphic design practice

Erik Herlow born 1913

Head of the department of industrial design at the Royal Academy of Denmark, and consultant to the Royal Copenhagen porcelain factory, Erik Herlow, has been instrumental amongst those who have been responsible for getting Danish design recognized throughout the world.

Herlow's clients in the consultant design practice he opened in 1945 include Georg Jensen and Dansk Aluminium. His designs are mostly in steel, a medium to which he has brought the sophisticated, sculptural forms that have also dominated other areas of Danish design. Herlow's achievement in promoting Danish work was such that when Cyra McFadden published her satire about Californian lifestyle, *The Serial*, in 1976, she only had to mention 'Dansk stainless' to evoke a whole concept of modern taste.

David Hicks born 1929

David Hicks' career as an interior decorator began during the austere post-Second World War years in Britain. By the late Fifties he had established a distinctive personal style: a Hicks interior would often use uncompromising contrasts of colour with pinks and oranges juxtaposed. With his crisp clarity of detailing and his flair in the arrangement of objects, Hicks' style became the quintessence of chic for London town houses. For country houses he evolved a style which re-interpreted eighteenth-century design in terms of strong colours and geometric patterns. Modern elements such as light fittings would often be used in traditional rooms. Hicks' own house, Britwell Salome, was the perfect expression of this simplified grand style in that it combined old and new ('the mix'), and featured precious groupings of objects that the decorator christened 'tablescapes'.

Bibliography David Hicks *On Living – With Taste* Leslie Frewin, London 1968

High-Tech

Like Post-Modernism, High-Tech was a style label invented by journalists. It therefore had more influence on newspapers and magazines than it did on real life.

The basis of the style was the idea that utilitarian products, originally designed for use in factories and laboratories, could provide the raw material for interior design. As a result, objects like surgeons' trolleys, metal shelving and rubber flooring suddenly invaded some homes.

Bibliography Joan Kron & Suzanne Slesin *High-Tech – the industrial style and source book for the home* Clarkson Potter, New York, 1978

2: Oliver Hill, Holthanger, Portnall Drive, Wentworth, Surrey, UK, 1935. The influential photographers Dell & Wainwright were energetic missionaries of English Modernism.
3: Josef Hoffmann, fruit bowl, circa 1904.

1: David Hicks' own living room, London, 1973. Walls of lacquered Coca-Cola, painting by Ellsworth Kelly. 'Tablescape' by Hicks.

Oliver Hill 1887–1968

Oliver Hill contributed brilliantly to that stylized vision of architecture as entertainment which was the <u>moderne</u> world of Britain in the Thirties. However, as Sir James Richards saw him, he was little more than a skilled eclectic, 'a man of taste rather than conviction who liked to try his hand at every style in turn'. He did not discriminate between historicism and modernism as either furniture designer or as architect, but would build in any style that suited his purposes.

Hill was educated at Uppingham, and before joining the architectural practice of William Flockhart was apprenticed to a firm of builders. After exhibiting a drawing of a country house at the Royal Academy in 1930 Hill became a frequent exhibitor there and many commissions followed.

Hill's major works included the decoration of the Midland Hotel, Morecambe, where <u>Eric Gill</u> was among the artists commissioned to work on the interior, and a house called Holtshanger at Wentworth in Surrey (1933–5). He was a member of the Council for Art and Industry (1933-8) and designed the exhibition of 'British Industrial Art' which was held at Dorland Hall in 1933.

Bibliography *The Thirties* exhibition catalogue, Hayward Gallery, London, 1979; David Dean *The Thirties: recalling the English architectural scene* Trefoil, London, 1983

Hochschule für Gestaltung

The Hochschule für Gestaltung (College for Design) in Ulm has often been called the new <u>Bauhaus</u>. In purpose, form and practice it was inspired by and imitated its legendary pre-Second World War predecessor.

The Hochschule was founded after the war by Grete and Inge Scholl, whose family had been persecuted by the Nazis, with the Swiss architect-sculptor <u>Max Bill</u> as its first director and designer of its buildings. He was succeeded by the Argentinian theoretician <u>Tomas Maldonado</u>. The purpose of the Hochschule was to revive the ideals of cooperative endeavour which had been <u>Gropius</u>'s inspiration (if not his practice) and its aim was to humanize a mechanistic civilization as well as to make the process of design a systematic one. The curriculum at Ulm included a great deal of contextual study, including psychology, games theory, <u>semiotics</u> and anthropology. Every effort was made to move away from design as a purely *formal* exercise.

Perhaps paradoxically, the most famous products to emerge from the Hochschule seem to modern eyes to be highly formal, stylized symbols of that very mechanized civilization which the school's fathers were trying to ameliorate. The school's spirit was the influence behind the work of <u>Hans Gugelot</u> and <u>Dieter Rams</u> and, therefore, was the inspiration for the design of <u>Braun</u> electrical products.

The Hochschule was closed down in 1968 by local authorities, who thought its policies were too avant-garde.

Josef Hoffmann 1870–1956

The Austrian architect Josef Hoffmann was born in Pirnitz, Moravia, and studied under <u>Otto Wagner</u>. In 1899 he was one of the founders of a Viennese group of architects and designers who styled themselves the 'Secession' in order to identify their avant-garde and anti-establishment motivation. Hoffmann wrote in the Viennese journal *Das Interieur* that the purpose of all architects and designers should be to break away from the historicist stranglehold of the museums and to create a new style.

In 1903, with Kolo Moser and Fritz Waerndorfer, he founded the <u>Wiener Werkstätte</u> (Viennese workshop), which executed some of his metalware designs. One of Hoffmann's direct sources of inspiration for the Werkstätte was <u>C. R. Ashbee</u>'s Guild of Handicrafts. He was to design for the Werkstätte for nearly 30 years, but all of his greatest work was done before the First World War, his masterpiece being the Palais Stoclet in Brussels, which was completed in 1911.

Hoffmann's achievement was to create a style of interior and furniture design that, under the influence of the British Arts and Crafts, as well as the simple peasant architecture he had seen on his Prix de Rome trip to Italy in 1895, was more minimal and elegant than anything created heretofore. His style is characterized by grid patterns, a sort of rectilinear <u>Art Nouveau</u>. He wrote in the Werkstätte's manifesto: 'An incredible disaster has come upon us – mass production and thoughtless imitations of bygone styles. This sickening influence infiltrates the entire arts and craft production of the world… our workshop… should become a centre of gravity surrounded by the happy noise of handicraft production and welcomed by everybody who truly believes in <u>Ruskin</u> and <u>Morris</u>.' Hoffmann and his contemporary <u>Adolf Loos</u> made fine British thoughts into fine Viennese furniture and decorative objects. They and their contemporaries waited avidly for copies of *The Studio* to arrive in their Viennese coffee houses, and designed furniture, tea-sets, fruit-bowls and many small domestic objects from its inspiration. However, as the historian Edward F. Sekler has pointed out, 'Hoffmann was incompletely informed about British architecture and design, but what he knew was sufficient to provide him with guiding principles and to activate his imagination towards the invention of forms that were unmistakably his own.'

Hoffmann's designs have recently enjoyed a sort of bastardized revival, as the inspiration for some New York designers of <u>Post-Modernism</u>.

Bibliography *Josef Hoffmann* exhibition catalogue, Fischer Fine Art, London, 1977

3

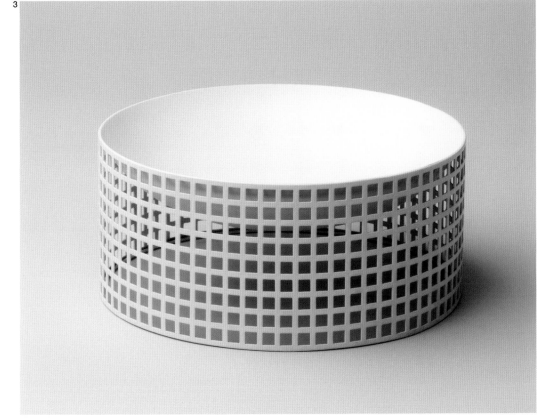

Wilhelm Hofmeister 1912–78

A designer and body engineer, born in Stadthagen, Hofmeister studied at the Wagenbauschule in Hamburg before joining <u>BMW</u> in 1939. In 1952 he became head of Body Engineering, in 1962 Chief Designer. He was the author of a number of signature BMW features including the 'Hofmeister-knick' (the reverse bend in a car's C-pillar, first seen on the influential 1961 BMW 'Neue Klasse' 1500. The same car established BMW's architecture – a prominent beltline, large glass-house and distinctive face that lasted for 40 years.

Hans Hollein born 1934

An Austrian architect, Hollein graduated from the University of California in 1960 and has been consistently involved with architectural experiments designed to reverse the supposed domination of the <u>Modern Movement</u>. He became a professor at the Staatlichen Kunstakademie, Düsseldorf in 1967, and designed the new museum in Mönchengladbach (1981). Hollein has been associated with <u>Memphis</u>, the avant-garde Italian design group, and his frequent use of historical reference in his drawings and designs has identified him with <u>Post-Modernism</u>.

Knud Holscher born 1930

The Danish architect Knud Holscher worked early in his career with <u>Arne Jacobsen</u>, but is best known for his partnership with the English designer Alan Tye. They have designed architectural ironmongery for Modric and the 'Meridian One' ceramic bathroom fittings for Adamsez. Each is characterized by quality of execution and an elegant minimalism.

1: Hans Hollein, Städtisches Museum, Mönchengladbach, designed 1972–3, finished 1981. In 1969 Hollein proposed a radical mobile office, a miniature environment that predicted the mobile communications of the future.

Honda

The Honda Motor Cycle Company was founded by Soichiro Honda in Hamamatsu, Japan, in 1948. Honda's idea was to use army surplus engines and harness them to bicycles. The eventual result was the Honda '50' (known as the C-100 Super Cub in Japan), which, since its introduction in 1958, has become the world's most popular motorcycle. Honda cleverly exploited European standards of design and by 1983 had diversified into power appliances and motor cars to such an extent that motorbikes accounted for only 29 per cent of the firm's business.

The head of Honda's Research and Development Department is Shinya Iwakura, who trained as a fine artist. Honda was the last of the Japanese automotive companies to start producing passenger cars (in 1964) and Iwakura says, 'The fact that Honda was such a new company meant that there were no old influences to overcome. We could establish our own independent ideas.' Under Iwakura, Honda, like <u>Sony</u>, has designed sophisticated products which employ technology transfer and symbolism (as well as advanced engineering) to achieve an effect which is highly seductive to the consumer mentality.

2

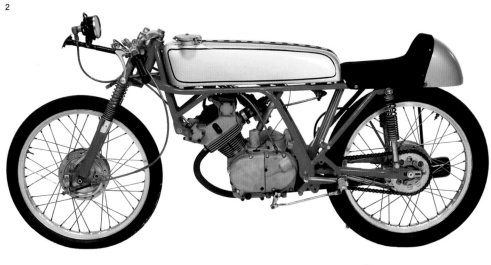

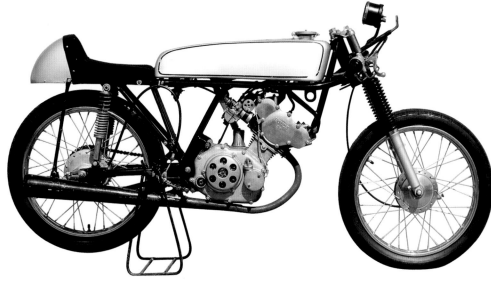

House & Garden

House & Garden is an interior design magazine, created by <u>Condé Nast</u> in 1915 after taking over the original title and amalgamating it with *American Homes and Gardens*. With this publication Nast took architecture and interior design to a level of popular chic similar to that achieved in fashion, manners and style by his other magazines, *Vogue* and *Vanity Fair.*

Elbert Hubbard 1856–1915

Elbert Hubbard was an American disciple of <u>William Morris</u>, whom he met in London in 1890. His Roycroft Press was established at East Aurora, New York, in imitation of Morris' Kelmscott. His Roycrofters Corporation grew out of this. Hubbard managed a uniquely American reconciliation of Morris' medievalizing utopian socialism with American capitalism. His work ethic tract *Message to Garcia* was routinely cited, by <u>Harley Earl</u>, for example, as uniquely inspirational. Hubbard had a philosophy both mystical and practical, profitable and poetical. He wrote, 'I believe in sunshine, fresh air, spinach, apple sauce, laughter, buttermilk, babies, bombazine and chiffon.'

His famous 'Credo' includes:

'I believe <u>John Ruskin</u>, <u>William Morris</u>, Henry Thoreau, Walt Whitman and Leo Tolstoy to be Prophets of God who should rank in mental reach and spiritual insight with Elijah, Hosea, Ezekiel and Isaiah.'

'I believe we should remember the Week-day and keep it holy.'

Elbert Hubbard died when the SS Lusitania was torpedoed in the Irish sea by Unterseeboot-22. His nephew, L. Ron Hubbard, founded Scientology.

Hubbard managed a uniquely American reconciliation of Morris' medievalizing utopian socialism with American capitalism

2: Honda CR1110 racing motorbike, 1962. Designed for the new 50cc formula, the Honda weighed 134lbs, cost less than $1,000 and produced 8.5hp at 13,500 rpm.

3: The Roycroft settlement and shop was founded by Elbert Hubbard, William Morris' inspirational US disciple.

IBM

In the world of office automation and data processing, there used to be a trope that said 'IBM isn't the competition; it's the *environment*.' This remarkable state of affairs came about not only through technical excellence, but also through a commitment to design management that was unique in American industry. IBM was one of the first American corporations to appreciate every aspect of design, from products through graphics to buildings. And through the work of Eliot Noyes in the Fifties and Sixties, IBM created an international stereotype for the appearance of modern office machines, indeed of modern corporations. IBM became known as 'Big Blue' because that was the colour Noyes painted a mainframe. Up to about 1984 when Apple introduced its radical, intuitive Mac, IBM defined the culture of information technology. But a corporation that once innovated became sclerotic and slow. IBM managers failed to anticipate or even appreciate changing consumer behaviour. In 2004 IBM sold its last consumer manufacturing unit to Chinese business interests, choosing to concentrate on the abstractions of consultancy. This was a striking metaphor: although IBM was an electronics business, its culture was firmly based in all the mechanical assumptions of the outgoing Machine Age.

Bibliography Thomas J. Watson, Jnr. *Father Son & Co – my life at IBM and beyond*, Bantam, New York, 1990

IKEA

IKEA is one of those four letter words that always gets a response. Modestly priced unpretentious furniture enrages people (especially if they have just failed to assemble it). The letters represent the initials of the founder, Ingvar Kamprad and the E and the A stand for Elmtaryd, Agunnaryd, respectively the farm and village in harsh southern Sweden where the business was established in 1943 when Kamprad was 17 years old.

Kamprad is a wily peasant carpenter whose natural frugality was enhanced by access to the world's first popular design movement. The Swedes believed in 'More Beautiful Everyday Things'. It's a democratic country with a democratic culture and a part of this is the gently didactic catalogue.

This masterpiece of consumer persuasion, an essential part of the IKEA belief-system, first appeared in 1951. The notorious self-assembly furniture followed in 1956, bringing as many economies in production and storage costs for the manufacturer as it did frustrations to the ham-fisted consumer. From the beginning, IKEA was sensible, undemonstrative, useful, affordable stuff.

Next in IKEA's revolution was a self-service warehouse in Stockholm in 1965. Soon after, IKEA's world conquest began. Switzerland, Germany and Singapore in the Seventies; France, Saudi Arabia and the United States in the following decade. Significantly, Britain was (in 1987) among the last developed countries to have an IKEA. Only Italy – with a vigorous domestic furniture industry of its own – succumbed to IKEA later than Britain.

1

1: One of the 'before and after' transformations that was a calling card of American consultant designers in their boom years. The 1948 typewriter was the last machine produced by IBM before Eliot Noyes said to Thomas Watson, Jnr. 'you would prefer neatness.'

The 'Selectric' of 1961 had a moving 'golfball' type head and a stationary carriage. Noyes created an entirely new look appropriate to the new technology, but also paid careful attention to the ergonomics: keys were angled to suit the attitude of the typist's fingers.

Industrial design

IKEA's belief that 'Most of the time, beautifully designed home furnishings are created for a small part of the population – the few who can afford them' does not sit well in a culture like Britain's where snobbery is an art form. Acceptance of modern design in Britain was for years frustrated by the sheer weight of history, the vast stock of stuff to be passed-on.

Instead, IKEA was aimed at new types of consumer: young professionals, the first generation of graduates from new universities, nurses, teachers. Its success is based on satisfying people who deserved and wanted decent furniture, but never inherited the money to pay for it. IKEA speaks about intelligent economy and making the most of contemporary possibilities. It is an ordinary thing done surprisingly well… and at extraordinary prices.

An American journalist, musing on the threat of a homogenised universal utopia built from wobbly shelves and synthetic foam, said IKEA was a socialist plot. The shopping experience can suggest the hardships of communist bread queues, rather than a life of luxury. But when IKEA opened in Moscow, the descendents of the first socialist paradise saw all that clean, modern, uncynical furniture as symbols of the brighter, more optimistic post-Communist world they had been yearning for.

It's a lot to attribute political principles to a sofa-bed, but IKEA is the essence of democratic design, or – at least – of democratic retailing. Of course, it is not perfect. Among the unfussy delights are some eyesores. But then who eats the entire contents of a supermarket?

The term 'industrial design' came into use in Britain in the Thirties, but not into general use until after the Second World War. In the United States the expression was known a little earlier. Characteristically, it was Norman Bel Geddes who claimed, in 1927, to be the first 'industrial designer', but Joseph Sinel, who set up a studio in 1919, has priority. Until the Thirties the term 'industrial art' was in more general use, as in Britain's first professional association of designers, the Society for Industrial Artists (now the SIAD), which was founded in 1930. Of this, Milner Gray recalled: 'It is noteworthy that only one of the signatories of the original Memorandum… listed himself as a "designer" and none as an "industrial designer"'; but in 1944 the Board of Trade in Britain established a Council of Industrial Design.

These English terms, 'industrial design' and the more familiar ellipsis 'design', have become international currency. No other language has a viable synonym, and the Italian *Migliorini* dictionary of 1963 included the term under its *Parole Nuove* (new words) section, even though the English word derives from the *disegno* described by Vasari and other Renaissance writers.

The first generation of industrial designers was anxious to map out the limits of its territory. Henry Dreyfuss, Walter Dorwin Teague and Harold van Doren all made some extravagant claims about the degree of 'science' involved in their design studios. Certainly, each of these pioneers had a primitive understanding that their work should pay attention to ergonomics, to efficient function and to cost-effectiveness, but with the perspective of history we can see that they were really most concerned to blend aesthetics with morals in order to create a 'style' all of their own. Although styling, which is often held to be inferior to industrial design, was reviled as meretricious, it is merely an approach to industrial design which uses visual tricks and effects in order to stimulate sales. Therefore, any industrial designer at work in a commercial economy has to devote himself, at least to an extent, to styling.

2: IKEA Museum in Ämhult in Sweden, 2004; the conclusion of the Swedish 'House Beautiful' experiment.

Institute of Design, Chicago

The Institute of Design in Chicago was founded in 1937 by Laszlo Moholy-Nagy after his 'New Bauhaus', also in the city, failed. In 1940 it was absorbed, with the Armour Institute of Technology, into the Illinois Institute of Technology. The original curriculum included not only design, but also contextual studies such as literature and psychology. Like the original Bauhaus before it, very little real designing for industry went on there and some of the Institute's most famous students were to become craftsmen.

International Style

The International Style was a name invented by Philip Johnson for an exhibition he arranged at New York's Museum of Modern Art in 1932. The exhibition took its name from Walter Gropius's book, *Internationale Architektur*, of 1925.

The first buildings of note were French, Dutch and German, designed by Le Corbusier, J.J.P. Oud and Gropius. These architects did not at first refer to their efforts as 'the International Style', but after Johnson's exhibition the label tended to stick. The name refers to the supposed international validity of the Modern Movement, but, as Johnson's own later career demonstrated, the International Style was just a fashion and its claims to timelessness or permanence proved to be false.

Bibliography Henry-Russell Hitchcock & Philip Johnson *The International Style* W. W. Norton, New York, 1966

Isokon

Isokon was a company established by Jack Pritchard in the early Thirties to manufacture in laminated plywood the furniture designs of Marcel Breuer and Wells Coates.

1: Le Corbusier's Villa Savoie – or Les Heures Claires – at Poissy, outside Paris, 1928. This is a perfect expression of the International Style and a demonstration of Le Corbusier's 'five principles'.

2: The 1930's best selling Penguin Donkey bookcase by Isokon. It was named the Donkey because it had four legs and two panniers. The spaces between the side compartments were just the right size to house Penguin's distinctive orange-covered paperback books.

Alec Issigonis 1906–88

Born in Smyrna, Turkey, Alec Issigonis became one of the few British automotive engineers to achieve international celebrity. He was educated at Battersea Polytechnic before working as a draughtsman with Rootes Motors in Coventry. He then joined Morris Motors in Oxford and became its chief engineer. In 1961 he was made chief engineer and technical director of the British Motor Corporation.

Issigonis is famous for the conception and execution of three cars: the Morris Minor of 1948, the Morris Mini of 1959 and the Morris 1100 of 1962. Each was pioneering in its own way, but the Mini was undoubtedly the most important. It cost £448 and was the first car to become classless, and it symbolized the aspirations of an entire generation. It also created an international demand for sophisticated, small, front-wheel-drive cars which Michel Boué's Renault 5 and Giorgio Giugiaro's Volkswagen Golf also satisfied, perhaps more efficiently.

But Issigonis' Mini was perhaps the single most influential car of all time. Designed from the inside out, it was uncompromised – and, indeed, uncomfortable – although its designer argued that there were ergonomic plus health and safety advantages in a modicum of pain. Its packaging was, nonetheless, a work of mechanical genius. Nothing so small had ever before been so commodious. Issigonis would tolerate no fripperies: original models had sliding windows and door pulls of plastic rope. Long before cup-holders, Issigonis created surprising amounts of storage space.

Like many other great designers, Issigonis bludgeoned his concept through BMC's management. It was not until 1976, a full 17 years after its launch, that the manufacturer realized it was making each Mini at a loss. It was on examining the complicated Mini that Ford decided to commit to the simple, but cost-effective, Cortina.

When in 2000 BMW re-launched the (somewhat Retro) Mini, it was technologically very different to the 1959 original, but paid strict homage to the place Issigonis' design had in the national imagination.

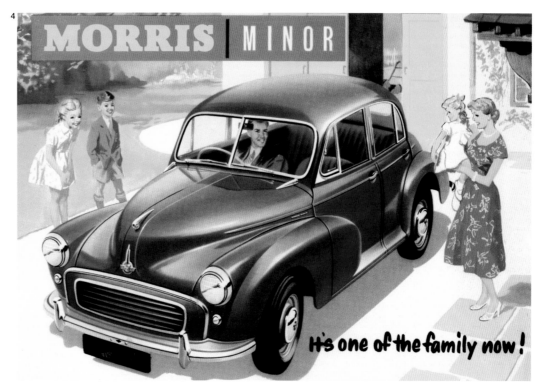

It's one of the family now!

3: Morris Mini Minor, 1959; The Mini is the most successful British car of all time; it influenced European car production for at least two decades. The BMC Mini became one of the symbols of an entire generation.
4: Morris Minor, 1949; The Morris Minor appeared in 1948. Its unitary construction and torsion bar suspension made the Morris Minor Britain's first modern car.
5: Alec Issigonis.

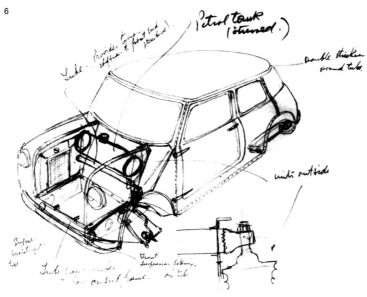

6: Drawing for Morris Mini Minor; Issigonis' design for the Mini was emphatically unstyled. Its appearance was dictated almost entirely by the engineering and the passenger space (although it did also owe something to BMC's own Austin A35). The Mini was perhaps the most radical departure from conventional design ever to appear. Its tiny ten-inch wheels, transverse engine, front-wheel drive, rubber suspension, uniquely functional interior bins and original window slides all introduced advanced design to the general public.

Johannes Itten 1888–1967

Johannes Itten was a Swiss pedagogue, mystic and designer who developed the Foundation course, or Vorkurs, at the Bauhaus, after being introduced to Walter Gropius by Alma Mahler, Gropius' adventurous wife. Itten was a disciple of the bogus pseudo-Iranian religion Mazdaznan and when he left the Bauhaus he studied oriental philosophy. However, his influence on art education has been profound. He insisted that students should 'learn by doing', and this stipulation has affected all subsequent art education.

Itten left the Bauhaus in 1923 after a disagreement over policy with Gropius. He founded his own school in Berlin in 1926, and later became director of the art schools in Zürich and Krefeld.

Bibliography Johannes Itten *Mein Vorkurs am Bauhaus: Gestaltung und Formlehre* Ravensburg, 1963

Jonathan Ive born 1967

Jonathan Ive is the only twenty-first century product designer whose stature can be compared to Dieter Rams, Eliot Noyes and other giants of the Machine Age. He was born in London and studied art and design at Newcastle Polytechnic before joining a consultancy called Tangerine. One of its clients was Apple Computer, then at an undistinguished phase of its corporate existence. In 1992 Ive went to work at Apple headquarters in Cupertino, California (where the terrestrial address includes 'Infinite Loop', a nice reference to the dreamy culture that so distinguishes colourful Apple in a grey-beige business environment). Ive worked in obscurity until 1997 when his iMac appeared. The influence of California car culture with its customizing workshops may, perhaps, be seen in this breakthrough machine: transparent polycarbonate and

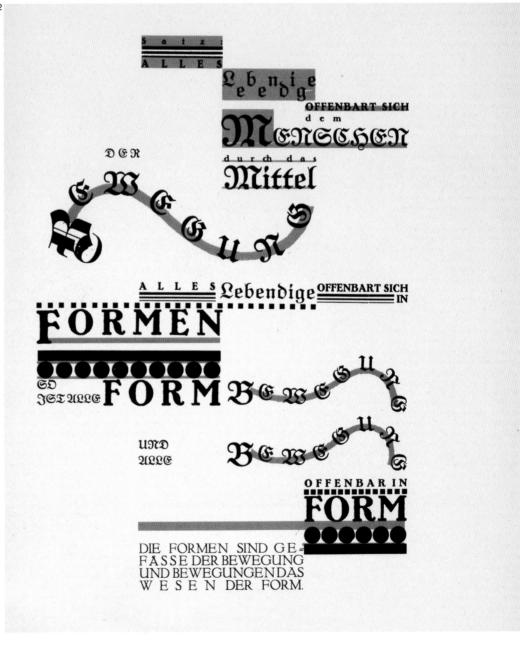

1: Johannes Itten, the Swiss teacher and adept of Mazdaznan, a cult devoted to Sun worship and macrobiotic diet, who revolutionised design education at the Bahaus.
2: Design for a newspaper by Itten and Friedl Dicker. The idiosyncrasies are typical of Itten and led to a dispute with Walter Gropius who wanted to concentrate on rational architecture and design rather than free expression.

3: Jonathan Ive's iMac, Cube and iPod for Apple Computer. The iPod is a superlative example of design principles surviving into the dematerialised information age. With extraordinary attention to detail and specification of fine materials, Jonathan Ive transcended and then beautifully extended the language of high density data storage and signal compression to make a product, already technically impressive, almost erotically desirable as well.

bubblegum colours did for computers what Sottsass had earlier done for typewriters. Retail packaging was superb too: the whole drab routine of buying and using a computer was turned into a sensuous, hip, communitarian experience. Ive's aesthetic is gorgeous, combining great purity with tactility. Together with the possible influence of pearlescent hot-rods, there is an evident influence of Zen-like thought patterns. Ive says he has a 'fanatical care beyond the obvious stuff'. He meditates on his designs, on colour and form, with results that eventually excite the consumer's cupidity, even his amatory responses: Steve Jobs, Apple's idealistic founder, says you know that a design is good when you want to lick it. Other Ive designs millions of consumers have wanted to lick include the Cube and the epochal iPod. Ive is a rare example of that paradigm of the designer: creating new demand and new expectations. Ive is aware of and energetically exploits the potential of new materials: new moulding technologies which bind polymer to metal allow formal opportunities which did not exist in the Eighties. The iPod is, for example, made from twin-shot plastic with no fasteners. Because it has no battery door, Ive was able to create a design that is 'dense, completely sealed'.

3

3

Ive's transparent polycarbonate and bubblegum colours did for computers what Sottsass had earlier done for typewriters

3

j

Arne Jacobsen 1902–71

Arne Jacobsen designed both chairs and buildings. He trained as a mason, studied architecture in Copenhagen, graduating from the Royal Academy of Fine Arts in 1927, but only came to prominence in the Fifties. It was Arne Jacobsen's achievement to turn the austerity of <u>Functionalism</u> into refinement and elegance, as was characteristic of <u>Danish design</u>. As a contemporary wrote, 'A distinctive feature of Arne Jacobsen's work is the care with which every detail is designed to support the whole. He saw a building as a physical setting for the life to be lived there, and he considered furniture and fittings, floor and wall materials, lighting and window details to be just as important as the building's general design and outward appearance.' Jacobsen designed three important chairs for Fritz Hansen: a stacking chair in 1952 and the 'Egg' and the 'Swan', both of which first appeared in his SAS Hotel in Copenhagen of 1958. Like all his work, they combine sculptural elegance with technical sophistication, modern ergonomics with traditional craft skills.

Bibliography M. Eidelberg (ed.) *What Modern Was: Design 1935-1965*, exhibition catalogue IBM Gallery of Science and Art, New York, 1991

Paul Jaray 1889–1974

Paul Jaray was a Swiss engineer who pioneered the study of aerodynamics as applied to motor vehicles. His career began as an engineer in the Zeppelin airship works, where he helped refine the airship into a tear-drop-shaped tube with the aid of mathematical models. In 1922 he won a patent for an aerodynamic car, using many of the principles he had established as sound on the Zeppelin. Jaray's vocabulary of form – which included faired-in headlights, wraparound windscreens, flush door handles – was eventually to pass into the language of car design, although not before he and his solicitors had tried to sue almost all his imitators. Jaray's ideas about the shape of cars were a profound influence on Ferdinand <u>Porsche</u> and his <u>Volkswagen</u> project engineers.

Bibliography Ralf J.F. Kieselbach *Stromlinienautos in Deutschland-Aerodynamik im PKW-Bau 1900 bis 1945* Kohlhammer, Stuttgart, 1982

1

1

Jeep

Since its appearance at the beginning of the Second World War, the Jeep has been admired as a masterpiece of utilitarian form and proportion. It arose from a government pecification issued to 135 US vehicle manufacturers in 1941.

It was designed by Army Captain Robert G. Howie, in co-operation with Colonel Arthur W.S. Hetherington, the co-founder of a company intended to manufacture four-wheel-drive utility vehicles. The prototype was delivered after only 75 days and appeared at Fort Benning, Georgia. Production was taken over by Willys-Overland and Ford. More than 600,000 were built during the War.

After the War, a domesticated version was launched as the CJ, or Civlilian Jeep. Even more consumerized versions, known as Jeepsters, were designed by Brooks Stevens. The source of its name is controversial. There is a general belief that it derives from a phonic contraction of the Army usage, 'General Purpose' vehicle, or 'Gee Pee', although DaimlerChrysler, now owners of the brand, say the original's codename was Government Pygmy Willys. The name Jeep became a registered trademark in 1950.

Georg Jensen 1866–1935

Georg Jensen was a Danish silversmith who evolved an elegant, simple style for tableware. He opened his Copenhagen workshop in the early years of the twentieth century, inspired by the British Arts and Crafts movement. At first Jensen's style was highly decorative, but gradually became more simplified. Most of the leading Danish silversmiths, including Kay Bojesen and Erik Herlow have done work for his company.

Jakob Jensen born in 1926

Jakob Jensen was chief designer of Bang & Olufsen, the Danish audio manufacturer whose elegant rosewood and satin steel products were the last words in consumerist chic before Japanese technology overtook Danish taste. Jensen studied at Copenhagen's Kunsthandvaerkskolen (applied arts school) and then worked with Sigvard Bernadotte before going to the United States and working at the University of Illinois from 1959 to 1961. Although his achievement is very much that of styling, Jensen has been responsible for some technical innovations, including the tangential pick-up arm, which was introduced on the 'Beogram 4000' in 1972. He was succeeded by his protégé, Englishman David Lewis.

1: Arne Jacobsen's 'Egg' chair, 1958, was designed for the lobby of Copenhagen's SAS Hotel.
2: Henning Koppel, sterling silver pitchers 1052 for Georg Jensen, 1956.
3: Søren Georg Jensen, sterling silver coffee pot 1064 for Georg Jensen, 1957.

Betty Joel 1894–1985

For a short period during the Twenties and Thirties, Betty Joel was one of the outstanding designer-decorators in London working in the <u>Modern</u> style. But the shortness of her career underlines how evanescent the influence of the Modern Movement was on British design.

In 1921 Joel set up a furniture workshop on Hayling Island, with a showroom on London's Sloane Street. She used the skills available at the nearby Portsmouth Dockyards to have yacht fitters make her furniture. At first this was an austere version of the Arts and Crafts, but it later turned into an exuberant form of <u>Modernism</u>. This transformation did not come about through a commitment to the socialist aims of <u>Walter Gropius</u>, but purely for stylistic expression. There was very little that was austere in her designs: although she favoured simple,

uncluttered, curved forms (which she felt to be 'feminine'), her flamboyant use of luxury woods and decorative veneers led to criticism from the then hard-line *Architectural Review*, although it also brought commissions to design interiors for the Savoy Group hotels, as well as for Winston Churchill and Lord Mountbatten. She went into retirement in 1937 after her divorce.

Bibliography David Joel *The Adventure of British Furniture* Benn, London, 1953

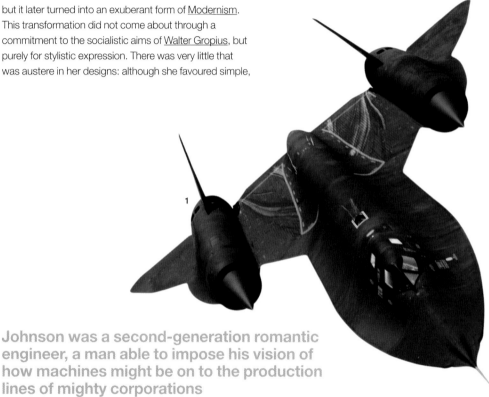

Johnson was a second-generation romantic engineer, a man able to impose his vision of how machines might be on to the production lines of mighty corporations

1

Clarence L. Johnson 1910–90

'Kelly' Johnson studied aerodynamics and structures at the University of Michigan, joining Lockheed as a tool designer in 1933. He became chief engineer in 1938. At Lockheed Johnson's secret research and development centre, a continuous source of aeronautical amazement for half a century, became known as 'the Skunk Works'.

Johnson was a second-generation romantic engineer, a man able to impose his vision of how machines might be on to the production lines of mighty corporations. His first remarkable design was for the Lockheed P-38 pursuit plane of 1941, a remarkable creation with dramatic twin-tail booms which influenced <u>Harley Earl</u> to introduce decorative tail fins on to his line of <u>General Motors</u> cars. The P-38 proved that even within the strict rules of military aerodynamics there was enough room for personal expression. At Lockheed's 'Skunk Works' in Burbank, California, Johnson's team brought science fiction to reality with the P-80 'Shooting Star', America's first jet fighter, which was designed and built in just 143 days during 1943. He was appointed Lockheed's chief designer in 1952 and was responsible for the overall layout and, no doubt, the appearance of the U-2 spy plane, the C-130 ('Hercules') transport and the 'Jetstar' liaison aircraft. As vice-president of advanced development from 1958, Johnson was responsible for the SR-71 'Blackbird', the most technologically advanced aircraft in the world. Kelly Johnson became a senior vice-president of Lockheed in 1969.

Johnson has been given every civilian award available to an American citizen and in 1983 Lockheed re-named its Rye Canyon facility as the Kelly Johnson Research Center. Perhaps his greatest achievement transcends his actual products and his designs and lies in his ability to integrate theoretical insights with solid, hard-won practical skills. He deplores specialization and was proud that he had a very high proportion of non-graduates working for him. And, inherited from his Swedish parents was the motto: 'Be quick, be quiet, be on time.'

Although none of Johnson's aircraft designs is a 'consumer' product in the strictest sense, they are widely admired by designers and architects as symbols of high technology allied to imagination. A plane like the SR-71, although at the summit of modern technology, is also a powerful expression of a will-to-form. Because his dramatic shapes have fascinated designers, Johnson could claim to be one of the important hidden influences on modern taste.

He became an Honorary Royal Designer for Industry in 1984.

Bibliography Ben Rich and Leo Janos *Skunk Works*, Little Brown, New York, 1996

Philip Johnson 1906–2003

Philip Cortelyou Johnson, an American socialite who became an architect and a creator of styles, was born into a wealthy family in Cleveland. As his family became even wealthier he did not need to graduate from Harvard's architecture school until he was 36. Walter Gropius was among his teachers, but Johnson had already made his name with an exhibition he organized at New York's Museum of Modern Art with the architectural historian Henry-Russell Hitchcock in 1932. This was the first major American exhibition on the International Style, a movement that it introduced to American art-lovers looking for a new fashion. He returned to the Museum of Modern Art as director of the architecture and design department from 1946 to 1954, when he left to concentrate on architecture.

Johnson has remained an influential figure in American taste. A right-wing anarchist, he recently said, 'What good does it do to believe in good things?' Although he continued to work in Park Avenue's Seagram Building, a Mies van der Rohe tower block on which he was the job architect, Johnson soon tired of the purity of the European Modernism he had introduced to America and began, on his own admission, to work like an architectural whore and design anything for anyone who paid him. In 1961, at a speech in London, Johnson said 'You cannot not know history,' and this opened up a whole vista of more-or-less witty historicism which would have been antithetical to his hero, Le Corbusier.

In 1975 Johnson was approached by AT&T Corporation to design their corporate headquarters in New York. Johnson produced a monumental tower block with a Chippendale open pediment about a thousand storeys off the ground. It was one of the first expressions of Post-Modernism in architecture. Johnson said of himself that he wanted to be remembered as the man who introduced the glass box and 50 years later... broke it.
Bibliography Charles Jencks *The Language of Post-Modern Architecture* Academy Editions, London, 4th edn 1984

2

3

1: Clarence 'Kelly' Johnson with a Lockheed U2 spyplane, circa 1960. Johnson was the resident genius of Lockheed's legendary and secretive 'Skunkworks' in Burbank, California. His astonishing SR-71 'Blackbird' took aerodynamics and aesthetics to the outer limits of possibility. Everything on the aircraft, from rivets and fluids, up through materials and powerplants, had to be invented from scratch.

2: Philip Johnson, with a model of his Manhattan AT&T building, 1978–84. The Chippendale pediment is typical of Post-Modernism's meretricious gestures.

3: Johnson's garden pavilion in the suburban designer encvlave of New Canaan, Connecticut. 'Minimalism' Johnson said 'is easy to copy'.

Edward Johnston 1872–1944

Edward Johnston had intended to become a doctor, but poor health prevented him and he became a calligrapher instead, carrying on <u>Eric Gill</u>'s principles of simplifying lettering. In 1899 he was invited to teach writing at the <u>Central School of Arts and Crafts</u> by W. R. Lethaby. He published two books, *Writing and Illuminating, and Lettering* (1906) and *Manuscript and Inscription Letters* (1909), which were important contributions to the revival of calligraphy in the twentieth century. Although much of Johnston's work was handicraft, he became famous for a commission given him in 1916 by <u>Frank Pick</u> to design a sans serif typeface for London Transport, which is still in use today. He became Rector of the Central School of Arts and Crafts and encouraged artists and designers to act as visiting teachers.

Owen Jones 1809–74

A Welsh architect, Owen Jones formed part of the circle around <u>Henry Cole</u> and was, therefore, in a position to influence modern taste. His great work was *The Grammar of Ornament* (1856), in which he illustrated architectural decoration he had seen on his tours of the Middle East and Spain. *The Grammar* was not just another book of architectural details, but was a polemical tract (and, incidentally, an early monument to the skills of the colour lithographer). Jones assembled all the ornaments he could, not so that designers might copy them, but so that they might be inspired by their underlying principles, such as made, say, Jacobean linenfold and Greek meander, each successful in its way. The book was prefaced by 37 propositions about design in which Jones attacked historicism and slavish fidelity to the past, and encouraged designers to create new, rational, formalized patterns, long before <u>William Morris</u> had the same idea. Proposition 37, for example, says, 'The principles discoverable in the works of the past belong to us; not so the results. It is taking the end

for the means.' Jones had a profound influence on <u>Christopher Dresser</u>.

Bibliography Nikolaus Pevsner *Some Architectural Writers of the Nineteenth Century* Oxford University Press, Oxford and New York, 1973

1: Edward Johnston's signage programme for London Transport after 1916 remains one of the most complete of its kind, establishing a uniform standard of graphic excellence for a sprawling, muddled network.

2: Finn Juhl, teak and leather chairs manufactured by Niels Vodder, Copenhagen, 1951.

1

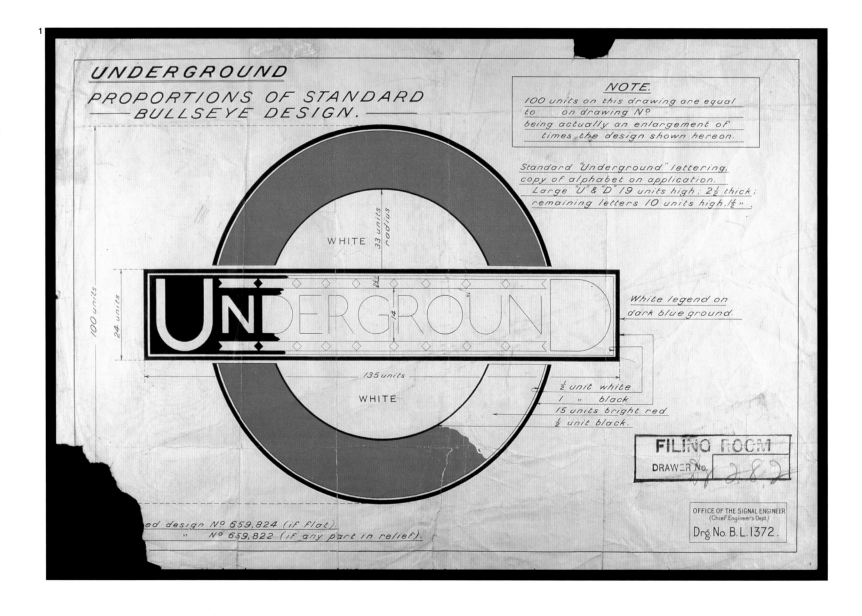

Journal of Design and Manufactures

The *Journal of Design and Manufactures* was founded by <u>Henry Cole</u> in 1849. Earlier than the <u>Great Exhibition</u> and the <u>Victoria and Albert Museum</u>, it was the first vehicle to bring his ideas to the British nation. It was short-lived, but succeeded in communicating to a wide audience many of the central ideas about design reform and the relation of art to industry in those years.

Jugendstil

Jugendstil, literally 'Youth Style', is the term used in the German-speaking and Scandinavian countries for <u>Art Nouveau</u>.

Finn Juhl 1912–89

A designer of eloquently sculptural chairs, Finn Juhl studied architecture under <u>Kaare Klint</u>. With <u>Erik Herlow</u>, <u>Arne Jacobsen</u> and <u>Hans Wegner</u>, Juhl was one of the individuals who made Danish design into a phenomenon in international taste. By showing in his designs from the late Forties and Fifties – including the 'Chief Chair', first shown at the Cabinetmakers' Guild Exhibition of 1949 – the influence of primitive African sculpture, he was influential in moving Danish designers away from their indigenous craft traditions towards a more expressive, even modern, aesthetic. Production versions of the Chief were made by Niels Vodder.
Bibliography M. Eidelberg (ed.) *What Modern Was: Design 1935-1965*, exhibition catalogue IBM Gallery of Science and Art, New York, 1991

Juhl was one of the individuals who made Danish design into a phenomenon in international taste

2

Vladimir Kagan born 1927

Vladimir Kagan was born in Worms, Germany, came to the United States in 1938 and opened his first shop on East 65th Street in 1949. A year later he was established eight blocks away on the more fashionable 57th Street. Here he produced interiors and furniture for the Manhattan aristocracy of the day, including Gary Cooper, Xavier Cugat and Marilyn Monroe, latterly Andy Warhol and Robert Mapplethorpe. His style is a cheerfully vulgarized Modernism, which he describes as 'romantic, organic, sculptural, curvaceous, architectural'. The 'Moon' sofa of 1949, or 'Omnibus' armchair of 1969 are typical: assertive shapes, with big, confident profiles, presented in bright colours. Kagan's designs have a strong formal sense and make the more polite Modernism of Knoll and Herman Miller look epicene in comparison. Indubitably twentieth century, Kagan's furniture is also assertively American: brashly consumerized and stylishly packaged.

Bibliography Vladimir Kagan *Autobiography* Pointed Leaf Press, New York, 2004

Kagan's style is a cheerfully vulgarized Modernism, which he describes as 'romantic, organic, sculptural, curvaceous, architectural'

Wilhelm Kåge 1889–1960

Wilhelm Kåge's name is inseparable from that of his employer, the Swedish ceramics manufacturer Gustavsberg. He trained as a painter, but like Gunnar Wennerberg and Jean Heiberg found the appeal of industry irresistible. Kåge once remarked, 'From the old, provincial handicrafts to the modern industrial worker's taste there are no pathways.' During his 43 years at Gustavsberg he was responsible for many formal and practical innovations: oven-to-table ware, stacking china and attractive services designed for low-income families, known as 'KG' in the Gustavsberg catalogue. For the Stockholm Exhibition of 1930 he experimented with Functionalism, producing an abstract dinner service called the 'Pyro' service. It was intended for volume production and was designed to be rational: it was stackable, dishes could double as lids, there was no applied decoration apart from some simple banding, and there were no inaccessible recesses. It was a commercial failure, but a great critical success. As a result of that failure he introduced a softer and less stylized version called 'Praktika', which remained in production for 30 years.

In the later Thirties Kåge continued with his restless inventiveness; his 'Set of Soft Forms' appeared just before the New York World's Fair of 1939 and gave rise to the expression 'Swedish Modern'. It was to establish the aesthetic standards of the Fifties. Kåge left Gustavsberg to return to painting in 1949.

Bibliography Nils Palmgren *Wilhelm Kåge* Nordisk Rotogravyr, Stockholm, 1953

1

2

Wunibald Kamm 1893–1966

With <u>Paul Jaray</u>, Kamm is one of the great automotive engineers. His name is not well known, but his theories about aerodynamics have had a pervasive effect on our assumptions about how cars should be designed.

Kamm was born in Basle and graduated from Stuttgart's technical college in 1922. His first job was also in Stuttgart, working for Daimler-Benz. He went on to become head of the Forschungsintitut für Kraftfahrwesen und Fahrzeugmotoren Stuttgart (FKFS, or Research Institute for Motor Transport and Motor Vehicle Engines), where he had the opportunity to develop theories outlined in an undergraduate thesis on aerodynamics. In fact, he was the first engineer to make aerodynamics an exact science rather than an empirical one, and as part of this process he developed the first commercial wind tunnel. Kamm promulgated the so-called 'K-Heck', or Kamm tail, a device where a car's bodywork is dramatically truncated just to the rear of the passenger area, as his research indicated that this enhanced a vehicle's aerodynamic effectiveness by improving the behaviour of 'boundary layer' air.

In 1935 Kamm set up the automobile department in Munich's Deutsches Museum. For ten years after 1945 he worked at the Stevens Institute of Technology at Hoboken, New Jersey, returning to Germany in 1955 to head the Department of Mechanical Engineering at Frankfurt's Battelle Institut.

Bibliography Ralf J.F. *Kieselbach Stromlinienautos in Deutschland-Aerodynamik im PKW-Bau 1900 bis 1945* Kohlhammer, Stuttgart, 1982

Kartell

Kartell is a Milanese furniture manufacturer, founded in 1949. It specializes in high-quality plastic injection mouldings, and in the early Fifties was innovative in producing plastic objects designed by <u>Gino Colombini</u>. His aesthetic was aggressively modern and his use of plastics not imitative of other materials. Since then Kartell has made furniture to the designs of <u>Joe Colombo</u> and <u>Marco Zanuso</u>.

1: Vladimir Kagan's interior for Marilyn Monroe, 1950s.
2: Wilhelm Kåge's poster for Stockholm's influential 'Home' exhibition, 1917. Kåge evokes the calm domesticity and concern for nature felt, at the time, to be essential elements of Swedish national identity.
3: Kartell Spring brochure, 1956, and the Ero/S chair by Philippe Starck for Kartell.
4: Ron Arad, 'Bookworm' for Kartell, 1994.

Edward McKnight Kauffer 1890–1954

Edward McKnight Kauffer was born in Great Falls, Montana, and, after a series of dead-end jobs, arrived at the Art Institute of Chicago and then went to study in Munich and Paris. On his way back to the United States on the outbreak of the First World War he stopped in London and decided to stay.

Unusually for a designer, he had keen intellectual interests, read Dante and Kierkegaard and was a friend of the poet T. S. Eliot. His first commission came in 1915 from London Underground to design a poster; so successful was this and subsequent posters that he gave up painting in 1920. Kauffer's reputation continued to rise in the early Twenties and in 1926 he was given an exhibition at Oxford's Ashmolean Museum, a rare honour

for a 'commercial artist'. He developed a technique he called the photo-mural, used in Wells Coates' Embassy Court and elsewhere. In 1937 he had a retrospective show at New York's Museum of Modern Art.

Kauffer's poster technique was one of dramatic stylization, rather comparable to Henri Gaudier-Brzeska's sculpture or Wyndham Lewis' illustrations. It suited posters very well, but worked less happily when contained by the edges of a page. He returned to the United States in 1941. John Betjeman said 'There was never so good a poster designer.'

Bibliography Mark Haworth-Booth *Edward McKnight Kauffer – a designer and his public* Victoria and Albert Museum, London, 2005

Frederick Kiesler 1892–1965

Frederick Kiesler was born in Vienna and studied there at the Technische Hochschule and at the Akademie der Bildenden Kunst. He worked on a slum clearance project with Adolf Loos. In the early Twenties he began to work on stage design, providing the *mise-en-scène* for the first production of Karel Capek's R.U.R. (1922), using motion pictures instead of painted backdrops. For the 1925 Paris Exposition Internationale des Arts Décoratifs Kiesler designed a sensational 'floating city'. He moved to the United States in 1926 and wrote an influential book about shop design in 1930. From 1933 to 1957 Kiesler was Scenic Director in the Design Laboratory of New York's Columbia University's School of Architecture.

Bibliography F. Kiesler *Contemporary Art Applied to the Store and its Display* Pitman, London, 1930

McKnight Kauffer was given an exhibition at Oxford's Ashmolean Museum, a rare honour for a 'commercial artist'

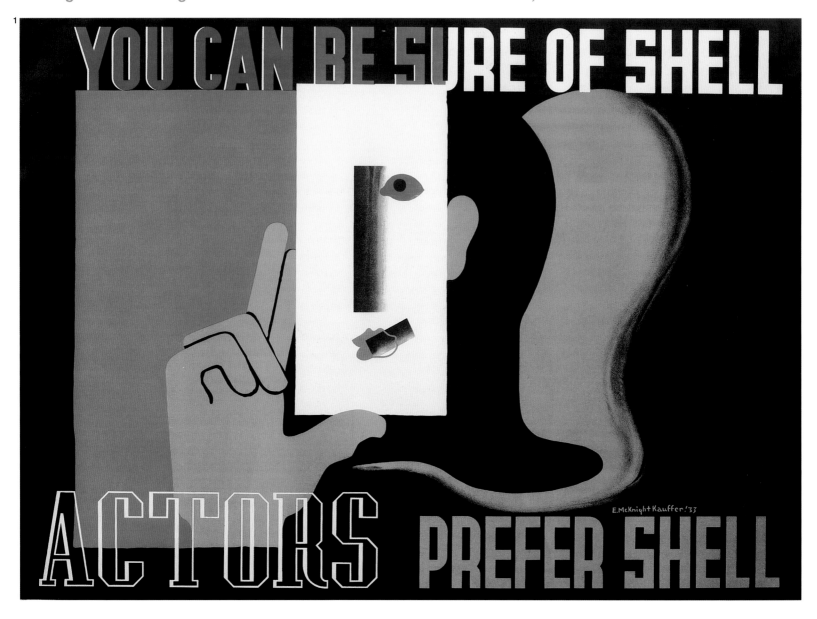

1

Kitsch

The word Kitsch is derived from the German *'verkitschen etwas'*, which means to knock something off. Its meaning is complex and subtle, but can broadly be said to imply the deliberate confrontation of accepted standards in design and manners. In an essay of 1939 'Kitsch and the avant-garde', Clement Greenberg, the veteran American critic of modern art, gave one of the best explanations of Kitsch, saying that it was an attitude to art and design which preyed on mature cultures, raiding them for tricks and effects, in order to achieve a facile and superficial result which betrays the consumer because it is undemanding and ultimately unsatisfying.

The term was first current in the German-speaking countries, particularly in Vienna, around the turn of the century, and as early as 1909 Gustav Pazaurek had opened a 'Museum of Bad Taste' in Stuttgart's Industrial Museum. The word was enshrined in the title of a book of 1924 by Fritz Karpfen, but the key work is an anthology of essays edited by Gillo Dorfles in 1969.

Since Post-Modernism became fashionable it has become acceptable in some quarters to celebrate Kitsch as the popularist expression of a taste which is opposite to that of the Modern Movement. The veteran American critic, James Marston Fitch, described thus, disapprovingly, the work of Michael Graves, a leader of Post-Modernism. Some people see Kitsch as a means of re-establishing expression and symbolism as parts of the designer's concern. But as the critic Peter Dormer has explained, 'Kitsch relies on duping the purchaser… It does not need and will not survive more than a first glance in order to deliver all it has to offer.'

Bibliography Clement Greenberg *Art and Culture* Beacon Press, Boston, 1961; Gillo Dorfles *Kitsch* Thames & Hudson, London, 1969; Gustav Pazaurek *Guter und schlechter Geschmack im Kunstgewerbe* Deutsche Verlags-Anstalt, Stuttgart & Berlin, 1912; *Taste* exhibition catalogue, The Boilerhouse Project, Victoria and Albert Museum, London, 1983; Celeste Olalquiaga *The Artificial Kingdom – a treasury of the kitsch experience* Bloomsbury, London, 1998

Poul Kjaerholm 1929–80

Poul Kjaerholm studied at Copenhagen's Kunsthandvaerkskolen (applied arts school) and then became a furniture designer. His speciality is a pure and elegant form of minimalism, using striking combinations of stainless steel with cane and African goat skin, so that the variety and contrast of textures is a complement to the austerity of the form. The icon of his career is a *chaise-longue* manufactured by E. Kold Christensen, which has been described as 'a diagram of relaxation'. Other important designs of his include a marble coffee table.

2

Kaare Klint 1888–1954

Perhaps more than any other individual, Kaare Klint can claim to have been responsible for the Danish tradition in modern furniture. Although Klint did not identify himself with Functionalism and regarded the Bauhaus curriculum as unhelpfully narrow, his early studies in design were concerned with standardization, modular construction and with actual need, rather than being self-conscious essays in style. He was amongst the first furniture designers to study anthropometrics seriously. He regarded the famous English cabinet-makers of the eighteenth century as models of excellence but was also attracted by the simplicity of below stairs furniture in English stately homes. Furthermore, he expanded the vocabulary of Danish design by making it possible for furniture manufacturers to use unvarnished woods, undyed leathers and plain fabrics. Klint's principal designs date from the Thirties when he reworked the safari chair and the deck chair, two classics of anonymous design and of functional seating. His demountable Safari Chair in stained ash with leather and brass was designed in 1933 and made by the cabinet-makers Rud. Rasmussen.

Bibliography Erik Zahle *Scandinavian Domestic Design* Methuen, London, 1963; C.&P. Fiell *Scandinavian Design* Taschen, Cologne, 2002

1: E. McKnight Kauffer, poster for Shell petroleum, 1933. During the Thirties Shell was a great patron of designers. In 1932 it combined its publicity efforts with BP under Jack Beddington who commissioned poet John Betjeman to write some of the Shell Guides to the counties of England. Shell became a private sector equivalent of Frank Pick's London Transport.

2: Tord Boontje 'The Other Side', ceramic, 2006 and 'Midsummer light', 2004. Kitsch is the corpse that is left when anger leaves art.

3: Poul Kjaereholm, 'Hammond' chair, 1965. The strength of the tempered steel frame allowed Kjaereholm to achieve an astonishing spareness.

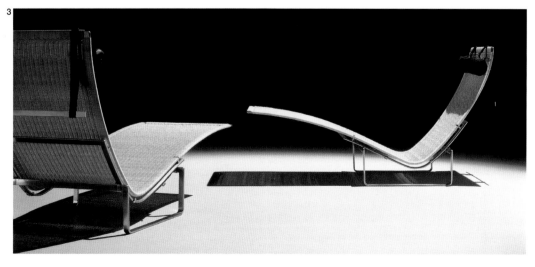

Hans Knoll 1914–55

Hans Knoll was born in Stuttgart, the son of a cabinet-maker. He was educated in Switzerland and in England, where he first attempted to set up a business, but the British market was slow to accept modern furniture design. Moreover, a cousin, Willi Knoll, had already established a business in Britain, based on a new system of springing chairs that he had devised. Parker-Knoll was the partnership he formed with Tom Parker; it specialized in well-sprung chintz and plush, tailored for middle-class British taste.

Hans Knoll went instead to America, in 1937, and established the Hans G. Knoll Furniture Company in New York. With his second wife, Florence Schust, who had studied at the Cranbrook Academy and was a friend of Eero Saarinen's, he established Knoll Associates in 1946. Hans Knoll's idea was to promote designers by name and to pay them royalties on furniture sold from his 'collection', and thus he reached a unique accommodation between European design and American business practice. The moment was absolutely

right: from its shop on Madison Avenue Knoll Associates was able to supply corporate America with the modern furniture which was to dominate US building for the 25 years after the Second World War. As merchant and manufacturer Hans Knoll introduced Danish furniture into America and made Marcel Breuer and Mies van der Rohe famous: Isamu Noguchi compared the achievement to that of the Bauhaus itself. Knoll is the only company allowed by Breuer's family to manufacture his furniture.

Hans Knoll was killed in a car crash in Havana, Cuba, in 1955, but Florence Knoll carried on running the company and attempted to sustain high design standards by working with other leading designers through the following decades.

Although continuously maintaining a high critical reputation, Knoll Associates was never wholly successful in financial terms. In 1968 it was taken over by Art Metal, and in 1977 was sold to General Felt.

Bibliography Eric Larrabee & Massimo Vignelli *Knoll Design* Abrams, New York, 1981

Mogens Koch 1898–1992

The Danish furniture designer Mogens Koch is best known for two timeless classics. First, the composite bookcase of 1928, put into production by Rud. Rasmussen in 1932: thin section, solid wood, unapologetic grid, no concessions to decoration, but decorative nonetheless in its purity and economy. Second, the 'MK' self-stabilizing chair of 1932 in beech and canvas, a refinement of the 'campaign' or 'director's' chair. Like his mentor, Kaare Klint, Koch helped revive other traditional chair forms in natural materials, and he was an important influence on the development of Danish design.

1

KNOLL ASSOCIATES, INC.   FURNITURE AND TEXTILES   575 MADISON AVENUE, NEW YORK 22

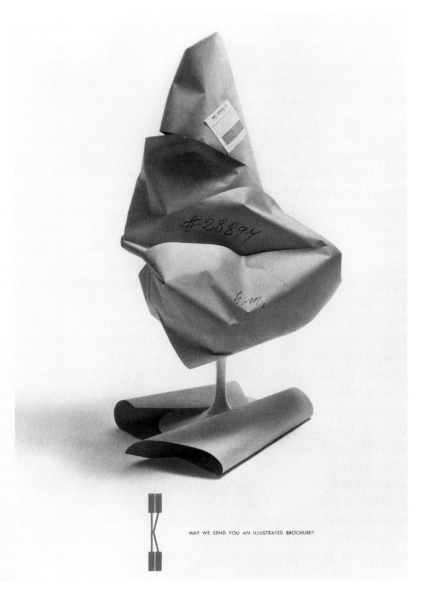

#28894

MAY WE SEND YOU AN ILLUSTRATED BROCHURE?

Pierre Koenig 1925–2004

Pierre Koenig was an architect rather than an industrial designer, but his greatest buildings used industrial components and became exquisite symbols of the American Dream: a world made perfect through consumerism, style and design. He was born in San Francisco and studied at the University of Utah School of Engineering. He was soon noticed by John Entenza, the idealist publisher of *Arts and Architecture* magazine. Entenza had acquired a plot of land where he commissioned a series of 36 'Case Study Houses': these were experiments in affordable construction and design excellence and became vastly influential on post-Second World War taste. So far from being austerely Existenzminimum, the California version of industrial architecture was deliriously sumptuous, especially in Koenig's interpretation.

Among the other architects and designers commissioned by Entenza were <u>Charles Eames</u> and his wife Ray, Richard Neutra and Craig Ellwood. Koenig built two Case Study Houses, Numbers 21 and 22 in 1959 and 1960. The architectural assumptions are generally based on <u>Mies van der Rohe</u>'s geometry and the expressive use of structural steel (in audacious cantilevers), but Koenig turned a limited repertory into high style. In the Hampton's on New York's Long Island, Norman Jaffe enjoyed a similar reputation for consumerizing Modernism, but his buildings are ragstone romantic rather than ravishing synopses of industrial possibilities.

Case Study House 21 was the Bailey House in the Hollywood Hills. Case Study House 22 was the Stahl House, also high in the Hollywood Hills above Sunset Boulevard. Each entered the international consciousness through frequent use in magazine shoots and film sets. Norman Foster said the 'heroic' Stahl House captured 'the whole spirit of late twentieth-century architecture'.
Bibliography *Blueprints for Modern Living*, exhibition catalogue, Museum of Contemporary Art, Los Angeles, 1989; James Steel and David Jenkins, *Pierre Koenig*, Phaidon, London,1998; Gloria Koenig *Koenig LA – Stories of LA's Most Memorable Buildings* Balcons Press, Los Angeles, 2000

1: An advertisement for Knoll's 'Tulip' chair by Eero Saarinen, circa 1957.
2: Pierre Koenig in Los Angeles, like Norman Jaffe on Long Island, turned Modernism into a stylish, luxurious and dramatically beautiful confection. The Stahl House in the Hollywood Hills was finished in 1960 and, illustrated in countless architecture journals, became a symbol of what it was to be modern. Its influence has been further enhanced by appearance in the movies: it features in Robert de Niro's film *Heat*.

Erwin Komenda 1904–66

Erwin Komenda was a body engineer who worked for Ferdinand Porsche and was responsible for the physical appearance of the original Volkswagen and also the series of Porsche cars that began with the Type 356 of 1949 and ended with the Type 901 of 1963. (The Type 901 has been marketed, for copyright reasons, as the Type 911.)

Komenda joined Porsche's Stuttgart office from Daimler-Benz where he had been chief designer for body development. His first assignment at Porsche was the body design for the astonishing Auto-Union racing car. Komenda's body design for the Volkswagen was a perfect consolidation of the ideas around at the time. It combined advanced aerodynamic qualities together with a sophisticated integrated appearance. There is no welded seam on the Volkswagen which has to be covered by leading, all the body panels fitting together organically. Although Komenda's interpretation of aerodynamics betrays the fashions of Thirties streamlining, he would never have accepted that styling had any part to play in car body design; he would, instead, have seen it as a question of engineering responsibility. In all its essentials the Volkswagen body which Komenda designed remained in production in Europe for more than 50 years.

Bibliography Ferry Porsche & John Bentley *We At Porsche* Haynes, Yeovil, 1976; Doubleday, New York, 1976; Karl E. Ludvigsen *Porsche – Excellence Was Expected* E. P. Dutton, New York, 1977

The Volkswagen body which Komenda designed remained in production in Europe for more than 50 years

1: Henning Koppel, silver fish dish, 1954. The polite formalism of Danish Modern was often inspired by Nature.
2: Erwin Kommenda drew the body for the ur-Volkswagen and the magnificent Porsche 356 of 1948. Its 1131cc engine produced 35hp.

Kosta

Swedish glassworks, founded in Smaland in 1742. In 1976 it was renamed Korta Buda, following an earlier merger with a neighbouring glassworks. Kosta designers, including Monica Backström and Bertil Vallien, have a near mystical relationship with Nature, expressed in their evolutionary organic forms.

Henning Koppel 1918–81

Koppel was a Danish designer of silverware and glass, which was often sculptural and attenuated in form. After 1945 he worked mostly for Georg Jensen in Copenhagen, but also became a freelance designer for Orrefors in 1971. Koppel's treatment of his medium is characterized by a strong sense of organic form, but without recourse to literal representation. Thus, a platter he designed for Jensen in 1954 suggests that it should hold a fish, but does not actually imitate one. Koppel's designs, whether in silver, glass or stainless steel, evoke the refined yet democratic mood of the Scandinavian interior of the Fifties.

Bibliography David Revere McFadden *Scandinavian Modern Design 1880–1980* Abrams, New York, 1982

Friso Kramer born 1922

The Dutch furniture designer Friso Kramer studied electrical engineering in Amsterdam and only became directly involved with the creative side of design when in 1962 he founded Total Design.

Yrjo Kukkapuro born 1933

Yrjo Kukkapuro was born in rural Finland and studied industrial design in Helsinki. He opened his own practice in 1959, producing designs almost exclusively for the Haimi Oy company. His 'Karuselli 412' chair of 1965 was one of the classics of the Sixties. The design employs a steel reinforced glass-fibre shell, thinly padded with leather; the shape of the shell is sufficiently organic for only slight upholstery to be necessary, while the cradle, which allows swivelling and rocking, means that the sitter can change his posture without shifting his body. Aesthetically, it achieves an imposing functionality. Kukkapuro became principal of Helsinki's school of applied arts.

Shiro Kuramata 1934–91

Shiro Kuramata was born in Tokyo and studied woodworking before joining the Teikokukizai furniture factory. He then worked in the interior design departments of San-Ai and other major Japanese department stores before founding the Kuramata Design Office in 1965.

Kuramata, influenced by the brainy nihilism of Marcel Duchamp, specialized in a highly refined furniture design that blends Western Modernism with the traditional Japanese taste for austerity. An admirer and contemporary of Dan Flavin and Donald Judd, Kuramata's work is contemporary evidence of the traditional Japanese refusal to distinguish between 'fine' and 'applied' art. Interiors he has designed for the fashion designer Issey Miyake and the Seibu store helped establish Japan as a leader in design during the Seventies and Eighties. He has also designed furniture for Ishimaru and Aoshima, although his most publicized pieces have been show pieces of 'Furniture in Irregular Forms' for Fujiko (1970), including the often copied 'S' shape cupboard, and a glass armchair for the Mhoya Glass Shop (1976). In 1981 he was quick to join the radical Italian group Memphis and considered Ettore Sottsass his 'maestro'. The influential minimalist architect, John Pawson, discovered Kuramata on the pages of *Domus* in 1968 and travelled to Tokyo to study with him in the Seventies.

Bibliography *Shiro Kuramata* exhibition catalogue Hara Museum of Contemporary Art, Tokyo, 1996

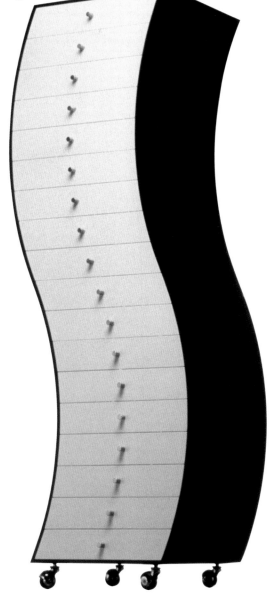

3

3: Shiro Kuramata, chest of drawers, 1970s. Kuramata was one of the most pleasingly idiosyncratic of independent Japanese designers. His furniture acknowledges both Western and Oriental influences, but has a quirkiness all his own.

4

4: Yrjo Kukkapuro, 'Karuselli 412' chair, 1965, manufactured by Haimi Oy. It is an elegant reduction of painstakingly developed structural ideas, a nice mixture of modern materials and a more old-fashioned formalism.

Karl Lagerfeld born 1939

The fashion designer Karl Lagerfeld was born in Germany, went to live in France when he was 14, but feels most at home in Italy. His internationalism is reflected in his work: for the past 20 years he has been chief designer for the French retail fashion firm Chloé, but since 1965 has also been designing clothes, shoes, furs and fragrances for Fendi, an Italian company. In 1983 Lagerfeld became chief designer for the house of Chanel and his sophisticated, glamorous clothes are very much in the Chanel tradition, but more aggressive and innovative (as one might expect of so enigmatic and philosophical a man). An early patron of Memphis, Lagerfeld is self-consciously at the apex of the European fashion world.

René Lalique 1860–1945

René Lalique was a glass-maker and jeweller whose style has become identified with Art Nouveau. Jewellery came first: reacting against the formalism of High Victorian or Empire design, Lalique produced jewellery where the semi-precious stones were often actually subordinated to their settings, and these settings usually had the favourite Art Nouveau motifs of wilting vegetables and lissom naked women. His glassware was equally typical of Art Nouveau, and he also designed car mascots. He established small factories at Combes-la-Ville in 1909 and at Wingen-sur-Moder in 1921.

1

Lambretta

With Corradino d'Ascanio's more famous Vespa, the Lambretta was one of Italy's most popular motor scooters. This type of vehicle was one of the first popular, deliberately designed products to emerge from Italian industry. Ettore Sottsass, looking back fondly at the post-Second World War years of *ricostruzione*, mused that the scooter seemed the very symbol of the new Italian industrial democracy.

The Lambretta, which was much more utilitarian than the Vespa, appeared in 1947. In its first phase its structure was visible and it lacked the curved body-shell which it soon gained, in imitation of the Vespa. It was designed by Cesare Pallavicino and Pierluigi Torre and was manufactured by Innocenti.

Bibliography Centrokappa (ed.) *Il Design italiano deglianni '50* Editoriale Domus, Milan, 1980

Allen Lane 1902–70

Allen Lane was the founder of Penguin Books.

As the managing director of the publishing house Bodley Head, Lane found the absence of cheap reading material at Exeter station an irritation on his frequent visits to and from star author, Agatha Christie. Lane imposed a new series of books priced the same as a pack of ten cigarettes. Bodley Head found the idea ludicrous, so Lane left and created Penguin Books. These paperbacks revolutionized the behaviour of British commuters and became a huge canvas for Britain's and Europe's best typographers and graphic designers. Lane was much influenced by Albatross reprints which, in turn, has been inspired by Taunitz Verlag of Leipzig, which began publishing in 1842.

Bibliography Phil Baines *Penguin by Design: a cover story 1935–2005* Allen Lane, London 2005

Anatole Lapine born 1930

Anatole Lapine was born in Latvia, but emigrated to the United States where he described his education – in Nathaniel West's phrase – as the University of Hard Knocks. He joined General Motors' design staff under Harley Earl, but moved to Germany in 1965 to work for the General's German subsidiary, Adam Opel. His brief at Opel was to revitalize the character of the marque and much of Opel's improved performance during the Sixties and Seventies can be directly attributed to the clean, aggressive lines that Lapine bestowed on their cars. In 1969 Lapine left Opel for Porsche, where he became head of the studio at the company's research centre at Weissach, outside Stuttgart. Lapine's brief was to maintain the Porsche character while moving the company ahead to a broader and more widely competitive market position. He was responsible for the design of the Porsche 928.

1: Karl Lagerfeld, 1984.
2: René Lalique, 'Dragonfly Woman' corsage ornament, circa 1897.
3: Lambretta motor scooter, 1957.

The Lambretta was one of the first popular, deliberately designed products to emerge from Italian industry

Jack Lenor Larsen born 1927

An American textile designer, Jack Lenor Larsen has specialized in using power looms and man-made fibres, while also developing ethnic resist-dying techniques for luxurious mass consumption. Larsen trained at Cranbrook Academy and opened his own studio in New York in 1952. His first major commission was the draperies in Park Avenue's Lever House, a glass-walled skyscraper by Skidmore, Owings and Merrill which has become a landmark of the Modern Movement in the USA: when it opened its contents must, as Paul Goldberger has remarked, 'have seemed like a dazzling vision of a new world'. Since that dazzling vision in 1952 Larsen has woven upholstery fabrics for airlines (including Pan-Am and Braniff) and made an upholstery fabrics collection for Cassina (1981), but his speciality is large-scale architectural works. His later major commissions include quilted silk banners for the Sears Bank in Chicago's Sears Tower (1974).

Larsen buys from all over the world and has run workshops in Africa, Haiti and Vietnam. An obsessive collector of textiles, he says, 'We started out as revolutionaries only wanting to make brave new designs for a contemporary society. Today our mission is to maintain the great tradition for luxurious quality as a buffer against mass-production.'

Bibliography Jack Lenor Larsen & Mildred Constantine *The Art Fabric* New York, 1981

Carl Larson 1853–1919

Larson was a painter and illustrator, but through continuous repetitions in his art, the house he decorated at Sundborn both directed and projected the evolution of Swedish furniture and interior design. The scrubbed wooden floors, the textiles by his wife, Karin Bergoo, a faint whiff of paedophile eroticism notwithstanding, all spoke of the – sometimes mawkish – Swedish vision of the idealized home: sensibly plain, but emotionally comfortable, suffused with often entirely imaginary sunlight. Larson's aesthetic was influenced both by the communitarian ways he discovered while living in the artists' colony at Grez-sur-Loing outside Paris as well as by the Japanese graphic idiom he picked-up while teaching at Goteborg Academy. He wrote his autobiography in 1917, but it was not published until 12 years after his death in 1931. 'Flowers and children,' he said, 'I ought never to paint anything else.'

Bernard Leach 1887–1979

Bernard Leach, Britain's most celebrated craft potter was born in Hong Kong and studied early Chinese and Korean art. His oriental background was fundamental to his later work, and in 1909 he went to study in Japan. On returning to England in 1920 he set up a pottery in the artists' colony at St Ives, Cornwall. Leach was responsible for establishing the pot, rather along the Japanese example, as a work of art. This celebration of individual artisanship ran parallel with other people's, ultimately worthier, attempts in Britain to establish genuinely higher standards in the day-to-day. Leach's works always had a down-to-earth quality.

All too aware that those who are nowadays attracted to the handicrafts are self-conscious rather than innocent, Leach was a hero of the Crafts Revival in Britain, the cultural phenomenon, also apparent in the United States and Scandinavia, which has united a number of different traditions of thought. At its core is the view that a return to some mythical ideal of pre-industrial production is the sole method of redressing the social and economic failings of the modern age, but the more positive aspects of the Revival include a concentration by its exponents on quality and individuality.

The agent in Britain of the Crafts Revival has been the Crafts Advisory Committee, established in 1971, which became the Crafts Council in 1975. The Council has advanced the cause of the artist-craftsman; but, under increasing pressure to broaden the Council's terms of reference to include artisan crafts, the director, Victor Margrie, announced his resignation to return to potting at the beginning of 1984.

In Britain artist-craftsmen work in a number of traditional media, while in the USA new aesthetic ideas have been applied to the materials of glass, wood and iron.

Bibliography Bernard Leach *A Potter's Book* Faber & Faber, London, 1940; Transatlantic Arts, Levittown, New York, 1965; Howard Becker 'Arts and Crafts' *American Journal of Sociology* January 1978, pp. 862–88

1: Bernard Leach, Yanagi, Hamada and Soto (the teamaster) at Toyama, circa 1960.
2: Le Corbusier chose his pseudonym as a 'nom d'artiste', rather as a 'nom de guerre' in the battle against the past.
3: The Unite d'Habitation, Marseilles, 1946–52, was Le Corbusier's masterpiece: a complete concrete city on stilts in a park. The 337 apartment structure is now officially an historical monument.

4: The Court of Justice Building, Chandigarh, Punjab, India, 1956.
5: 'Grand Confort' armchair, 1928. This design used the tubular steel fashionable at the time, but Le Corbusier complemented it with luxurious over-stuffed leather, a sly hint at French tradition. The shape of the frame was inspired by Thonet bentwood. Since 1965 the 'Grand Confort' has been manufactured by Cassina.

Le Corbusier 1887–1965

Le Corbusier was the *nom d'artiste* chosen by the Swiss architect Charles-Edouard Jeanneret. It means nothing, but suggests a meaning that combines the bird 'raven' with the architectural feature 'corbel'. What is perhaps more significant is Jeanneret's choice of the definite article: his *nom d'artiste* was like a *nom de guerre*. He was out to fight a battle.

Jeanneret was born in the Swiss watch-making town of La Chaux-de-Fonds in 1887. It had been burnt down in the eighteenth century and reconstructed on a grid pattern, and it is certainly possible that the severe geometry of his home town had an effect on the young man's creative imagination.

Jeanneret was to become the most inspired and original and inventive of all modern architects. The dimensions of his thought qualify him for the description of genius and the range and quality of his formal inventions qualify him for the description of great artist.

In La Chaux-de-Fonds he was apprenticed to an architect called Charles L'Eplattenier and then travelled to Germany, where he worked in <u>Peter Behrens</u>' office. He first came to international prominence at the 1925 Paris Exhibition, where he built the Pavilion de L'Esprit Nouveau and furnished it with <u>Thonet</u> bentwood chairs and fitted furniture which he designed himself. In 1927 he began an association with <u>Charlotte Perriand</u>, producing a distinguished and elegant set of furniture designs (which are now reproduced by <u>Cassina</u>). In each piece traditional luxury and aggressive modernity vie for dominance. All their chair designs were exhibited at the Paris 'Salon d'Automne' of 1929: a *chaise-longue*, the 'siège *grand confort*' and the 'basculant' chair. As designers Jeanneret and Perriand were at their strongest working together; after they separated in the late Thirties Le Corbusier designed no more significant furniture and Charlotte Perriand never really designed anything very much at all, preferring to take an interest in folk art rather than machine production.

Besides the furniture and the architecture, Le Corbusier's ideas were highly influential. He was in love with machines and with beauty; he was passionately concerned with social purpose and with healthy living; he was an architect and propagandist whose every thought was suffused by optimism. His vision was of a world where modern technology allied with a sense of beauty could create an ideal and socially beneficial environment. A one-time employee of the Voisin aircraft company and an enthusiast for fast cars, he understood and sympathized with the beauty often inherent in fine machines. His most famous dictum ('Good design is intelligence made visible') is usually quoted without the context. In full, it is: 'The aeroplane is the product of close selection. The lesson of the aeroplane lies in the logic which governed the statement of the problem and its realization. The problem of the house has not been stated. Nevertheless, there do exist standards for the dwelling-house. Machinery contains in itself the factor of economy, which makes the selection. The house is a machine for living in… As to beauty, that is always present when you have proportion.'

Le Corbusier made it possible, in theory, at least, for the world to appreciate the beauty of well-made ordinary things, introduced new systems of construction and new, cleaner, brighter, better, ways of living, but his ideas have subsequently often been badly misinterpreted and misapplied.

Le Corbusier swam to his death in 1965, from the pier of <u>Eileen Gray</u>'s house, E-1027, at Roquebrune.

Bibliography Renato de Fusco *Le Corbusier, Designer Furniture, 1929* Barron's, Woodbury, 1977; *Le Corbusier L'Art decorative d'aujourd'hui* Collection 'L'Esprit Nouveau', Paris, 1925; Stanislaus von Moos *Le Corbusier: Elemente eine Synthesis* Hüber, Zürich, 1968; Peter Serenyi (editor) *Le Corbusier in Perspective* Prentice-Hall, Englewood Cliffs, New Jersey, 1975

Le Courbusier was an architect and propagandist whose every thought was suffused by optimism

Hans Ledwinka 1878–1967

Ledwinka's Tatra cars were, first, evidence of Western technology becoming accepted in Eastern Europe, but second and rather more interestingly, the very best of them were superb examples of the Modernist spirit, combining high technology with high style. Hans Ledinka was born in 1878 in Klosterneuberg 15 years before the first automobile arrived in Bohemia. He joined the Nesseldorfer Wagenbau-Fabriks-Gesellschaft in 1897 and contributed to the design of its first powered goods vehicle the following year. In 1916 Ledwinka became chief designer of the Austrian firm Steyr, returning to Moravia and Nesseldorfer in 1921. At this time Czechoslovakian car production was about 3,000 units a year. Ledwinka's first design was the T11, a revolutionary concept: a flat twin engine was cooled by a flywheel which doubled as a fan. The engine and gearbox were in a monoblock and there was independent suspension. The business was re-branded Zavody Tatra in 1927. The first distinctive rear-engined prototype Tatra was shown in 1931 and two years later, Ledwinka was a rival to Ferdinand Porsche in the competition for the NSDAP Kampf durch Freude project which became known as the Volkswagen. The six-passenger, three-litre air-cooled V-8, aerodynamic, rear-engined Tatra 77 appeared in 1934, the first production car of this format. It was sold in England by Airstream Ltd of Davies Street in Mayfair. The T87 came in 1936, the definitive Tatra: a radical, smooth aerodynamic package compromised only by the lack of curved glass. Contemporary accounts describe travelling in great comfort, the engine noise isolated at the rear, the only sound being the rush of air. The T97 of 1937 was frustrated by the Germans as it was technically superior to Porsche's Volkswagen. In 1945 Ledwinka was imprisoned for six years and died in Munich in 1967. Tatra was nationalized by the Communists in 1946.

Bibliography V. Kresina (ed) *Sedmdesat let vyroby automobilu Tatrai* Koprivicne, privately published, 1967; R.J.F. Kieselbach *Stromlinien Autos in Europa und USA*, Kohlhammer, Stuttgart, 1982; *Czech Functionalism* exhibition catalogue, Architectural Association, London, 1987

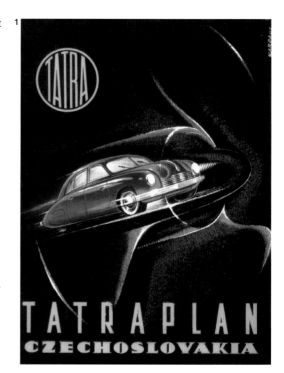

1

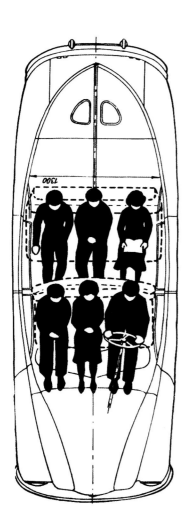

1

1

The six-passenger, three-litre air-cooled V-8, aerodynamic, rear-engined Tatra 77 appeared in 1934, the first production car of this format

Patrick Le Quement born 1945

Patrick Le Quement's tenure as Chef du Design at Renault in Paris was a fascinating case study of the compromises advanced design had to make in the mass market. Pascal said 'L'homme est capable de deux sortes d'esprit, qu l'on peut appeler l'esprit geometrique et l'esprit de finesse. Le premier deduit avec methode les multiples consequences d'un principe unique, le second embrasse d'une vue mille details.' (Man is capable of two kinds of spirit, geometry and finesse. The first methodically deduces the many consequences of a single principle, while the second embraces a thousand details.) You find a neat definition of this in Le Quement's adventurous, but sometimes ruinous, car design.

Le Quement was born in Birmingham and studied in the local art school under <u>Bauhaus</u> émigré, Naum Slutzky. He worked at <u>Ford</u> (where he drew the last version of the ineffable Cortina), then <u>Volkswagen</u> before joining Renault in 1987. Immediately, he started exploring new formats shown as concept cars, culminating in the 1996 launch of the revolutionary Scenic, a compact multi-purpose vehicle which established an entirely new category of vehicle. His latest interiors are characterized not just by ingenious use of volume, but by the mass of detail that is a modern car's control system being subordinated to an intelligent arrangement without any loss of ergonomic function or visual clarity.

In car exteriors, Le Quement was among the first designers to reject the cold German formalism that had for so long dominated the middle market in favour of sensualism and expression. The results of this audacity were mixed. Both the Avantime and Vel Satis, the former an intergalactic day van, the latter a brave confrontation of the me-too cynicism of the sector, were commercial failures. Yet their extraordinary aesthetics, a combination of explicit geometry, deliberate asymmetry and imbalance, and a refusal to conform, helped build a new image for Renault, or 'l'epannouissement de la langue aesthetique'. Le Quement said that a 'design statement that brings immediate returns, but doesn't build the brand is a mistake'. And he added that biggest risk in business is to take no risk at all.

In the *Cahiers d'Art* of 1929 modernist sculptor <u>Constantin Brancusi</u> wrote that theories are meaningless, only actions count. Le Quement calls design 'the locomotive of seduction'. In driving that locomotive he made false moves, but proved to the world that as things get flatter and technological distinctions between car manufacturers are diminishing, boredom will not be an option.

1: Hans Ledwinka's Tatra was one of the most advanced car designs of the Thirties, but political and economic circumstances thwarted its development.

2: The Nepta concept car, 2006; Twingo, 1991. Patrick Le Quement of Renault was the most imaginative designer at work in the mainstream car industry in the late twentieth and early twenty-first centuries. While others just designed shapes, Le Quement thought in terms of entire new formats.

David Lewis born 1939

David Lewis was born in London, studied at the Central School, but left for Copenhagen in the mid-Sixties where he worked with Bang & Olufsen designers Jacob Jensen and Henning Moldenhawer. He later opened his own studio in Copenhagen, becoming Bang & Olufsen's chief designer in 1980. Inspired by the idea of cleaning up technological mess, Lewis' work is characterized by a mixture of formal elegance, sculptural assertiveness and, almost paradoxical, reticence. Polished aluminium, for example, is used to fine formal effect, but at the same time takes its colour from its surroundings.

Liberty

Liberty is a store in London founded by Arthur Lasenby Liberty (1843–1917). Liberty himself was born in Nottingham, the son of a lace manufacturer, and moved to London in 1862 to take up a post as manager of Farmer & Rogers' Oriental Warehouse in Regent Street. The store was a magnet for many of the artists of the day, and between his appointment and its closure in 1874, Liberty added Frederick Leighton, Edward Burne-Jones, Dante Gabriel Rossetti, William Morris and James McNeill Whistler to his list of friends and acquaintances. In the year after the Oriental Warehouse closed, Liberty set up his own business near its old premises. Here he experimented with his own peculiar brand of mercantile philanthropy, being a supporter of the early closing movement and taking a passionate interest in the welfare of his employees.

Liberty was one of the first merchants to understand and exploit popular taste. He had realized that oriental merchandise appealed to more than just a narrow circle of artists, and when on his own he manufactured fabrics that had a fineness of quality and a subtlety of pattern and colour that had been hitherto unknown in home-produced goods, but which were present in those he had been selling previously. A trip to Japan in 1888–9 reinforced his oriental expertise. As the retail expression of Arts and Crafts, Liberty educated a pre-Modern public in taste. The store has recently expanded and contracted and is now back to its original site. It still has an admirably quirky approach to the selection of merchandise.

Lincoln Continental

The Kennedy era introduced new autonomy and confidence to an American car industry hitherto reliant on the symbolism of rocket ships. Chevrolet introduced the aesthetically and technically advanced Chevrolet Corvair (whose most famous accident gave rise to Ralph Nader and consumerism) while Ford's Lincoln Division introduced the '61 Continental. This car was a complete original, but shares some significant characteristics with famous passenger Jackie Kennedy's pillbox hat (designed by Oleg Cassini, brother of the journalist who coined the expression 'Jet Set'). Considered as a formal composition, the Lincoln disguises its enormous size through exquisite proportions and bravely undecorated surfaces, the designers letting metal express itself in bold horizontals. A brightwork highlight runs uninterrupted along the fenderline, but emphasizes sculptural confidence rather than advertising a taste for glitz. The '61 pioneered curved sideglass with its dramatic tumblehome. In summer 1961 the Continental was given the award for 'overall excellence' by the US Industrial Design Institute. President Kennedy used one on his last journey. Originally painted dark blue, it was painted black after his murder. The designers of the '61 Continental were Eugene Bordinat, Don De LaRossa, Elwood P. Engle, Gayle L. Halderman, John Najjar, Robert M. Thomas and George Walker.

Liberty was one of the first merchants to understand and exploit popular taste

1: David Lewis, 'BeoLab 4000' speakers, first designed in 1997 with a colour range introduced in 2005.
2: Tudor House, the frontage of Liberty, London, UK, 1924.
3: The 1964 Lincoln convertible, perhaps the greatest ever American car.

Stig Lindberg 1916–82

The ceramic designer Stig Lindberg was educated at technical school in Stockholm, and studied under Wilhelm Kåge in Paris before joining Gustavsberg in 1937. He spent two periods, interrupted by the important lectureship in ceramics at Stockholm's Konstfackskolan (applied arts school) and a brief time in Italy, as Gustavsberg's artistic director, from 1949 to 1957 and then from 1970 to 1977.

His first full service was called 'LB' and appeared in 1945; 'Servus' followed in 1950 and a range of flameproof cooking utensils called 'Terma', which summarize Lindberg, Gustavsberg and, indeed, the entire Swedish domestic design ideal, were first seen at the H55 exhibition at Halsingborg in 1955.

Lindberg also designed textiles for Stockholm's leading department store, the Nordiska Kompaniet.
Bibliography Dag Widman & Berndt Klyvare *Stig Lindberg* Raben & Sjogren, Stockholm, 1962

Lippincott & Margulies

J. Gordon Lippincott (1909–98) was trained as an engineer and surveyed bridges for the Saw Mill River Parkway. With Walter Margulies (1914–86) he founded Lippincott & Margulies in 1946. The firm worked on a development of Preston Thomas Tucker's ill-fated car project in 1948 (which came to an end the following year when the Securities and Exchange Commission indicted Tucker 31 counts of fraud). Lippincott & Margulies now turned to corporate identity, a term they coined. In the age when globalization was business orthodoxy, they changed the way the consumer perceives large corporations. Clients include Eastern Airlines, Borg-Warner, Esso, Chrysler, American Express, Chemical Bank, Uniroyal and Xerox. Gordon Lippincott had strong views about obsolescence. He once said: 'Industrial designers today have become commercial artists rearranging a lot of spinach to come up with a new model. If we eliminate yearly models, we put a premium on better design.'

Ludwig Lobmeyr 1829–1917

Ludwig Lobmeyr was founder of the traditional Viennese glassmakers, employed to make, for example, 36 crystal chandeliers for the Hall of Mirrors in the Schloss Herrenchiemsee. Under Lobmeyr's successor, Stefan Rath, the firm flirted with Modernism and used designs by Josef Hoffmann, Adolf Loos and other associates of the Wiener Werkstätte.

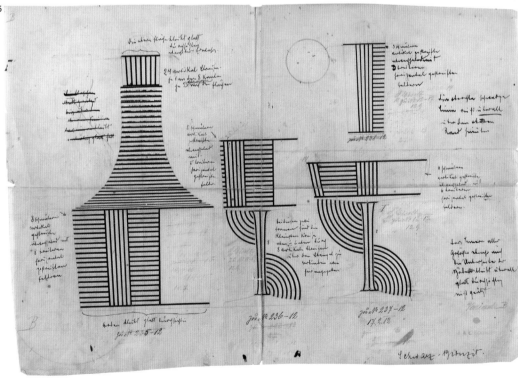

4: Stig Lindberg, Gnurgla ceramics, 1954.

5: The decorative excess of Lobmeyr's traditional glass production (this picture shows an electric crystal chandelier from 1883) was blown away by Josef Hoffmann's 'Serie B' sketch designs of 1912. In production from 1914, 'Serie B' took the aesthetics of the Wiener Werkstätte to the marketplace.

Raymond Loewy 1893–1986

Loewy was born in Paris but went to New York in 1919 as a demobbed captain in the French Army with artistic ambitions. Much of Loewy's career has passed into the region of myth, partly through the popularity of his autobiography *Never Leave Well Enough Alone* (1951).

Loewy was part of the generation of designers who created the consultant design profession in New York during the 1920s. His hallmark was the transformation of Hupmobile cars, Gestetner duplicators, Coca-Cola dispensers and Coldspot fridges into objects that became familiar icons of consumer journalism during the mid-century.

Like his pioneer contemporaries, Norman Bel Geddes, Walter Dorwin Teague, Henry Dreyfuss and Harold van Doren, Loewy's reputation is based on his pre-Second World War work, although he did design some notable products after the War, among them the Studebaker car and the Lucky Strike cigarette pack. Loewy's relationship with Studebaker began in 1933 when company president Paul Hoffmann hired him as a consultant (having realised there was no designer in-house). Loewy's 1947 Studebaker Starliner introduced a European lightness-of touch to an American market that was still using pre-War designs. By the late Forties the Starliner represented 40 per cent of Studebaker sales, but its innovations in styling were more successfully exploited in the marketplace by the famous '49 Ford.

Loewy's career was punctuated by periods of embarrassing self-parody. At the Paris Salon de l'Automobile 1960, Loewy showed the Loraymo, on which he eliminated the bumper. Bruno Sacco said 'I could not bring myself to believe that someone had seriously gone about designing a car like that,' although he later admitted that the 1963 Studebaker Avanti (designed in secret at Loewy's Palm Springs home by his unacknowledged colleague, Tom Kellogg) was a 'work of art'.

By 1978, although he ran a small office in London and a larger one in Paris, known as the Compagnie de l'Esthétique Industrielle, Loewy no longer did business in his own country though he did design the shopping centre west of Paris at Bures Orsay in 1972.

Although Loewy's flair for style and for publicity did much to bring the design of objects before the public eye,

and although his client list looks like a portion of the Fortune 500, his name has always been associated with styling, in the pejorative sense that Europeans used to condemn the commercialization of design and designing in America. Nonetheless, Loewy was responsible for many of the symbols and images which characterize, for the later twentieth century, modern America in its 'bourbon Louis romp', as Tom Wolfe described it. At some time during the Forties or Fifties an average American could have spent his entire day surrounded by products fashioned by Loewy (as his publicists were quick to explain): a Schick razor, Pepsodent toothpaste tube packaging, the Studebaker car, the Lucky Strike cigarette pack, a Coca-Cola dispenser and, at the end of the day, a tin of Carling Black Label beer. For Kennedy, Loewy also designed the colour scheme for 'Air Force One', the President's personal Boeing 707, and began the association with NASA that led to him making proposals, very largely unimplemented, for habitability systems in the Skylab series of spaceships.

Loewy once remarked of his career: 'I found it difficult to reconcile success with humility. I tried it at first, but it meant avoiding the very essence of my career – a total exhilaration and the ecstasy of creativity.' Loewy established the template which celebrity designers have ever since imitated. An inch deep and a mile wide, he created a coruscating personal lifestyle that was something for his clients to emulate (especially if they paid him a fee to help do so). His vanity was over-weening and he suffered from what would today be recognized by the American Psychiatric Association as 'narcissistic personality disorder' which is defined as a 'pervasive pattern of grandiosity, need for admiration and lack of empathy'. Loewy hired a publicist to get him onto the cover of *Life* magazine, duly achieved on 31 October 1949 with the headline 'He Streamlines the Sales Curve'. He wore correspondents' shoes and described his favourite dish as his 'famous Scallops St Tropez'.

Bibliography Raymond Loewy *Never Leave Well Enough Alone* Simon & Schuster, New York, 1951; Angela Schoenberger (ed.) *Raymond Loewy – pioneer of industrial design* exhibition catalogue, IDZ-Berlin, 1990

2

1: Raymond Loewy, the genius, huckster, booster of US consultant design. Loewy's products were rarely ever as successful as his propaganda, but he struck wonderfully persuasive poses. He was his own greatest design. Once described as 'an inch deep and a mile wide.'

2: With a model Studebaker, 1948. The first Silversides coach appeared in 1940. After Camel, Lucky Strike was the second modern American cigarette brand. Loewy redesigned its pack in 1941. Rita is sitting in a Ferrari-Hardoy chair: in the Fifties, Luckies were symbols of style.

Adolf Loos 1870–1938

Adolf Loos was the romantic radical of the Viennese Enlightenment. On reading Loos' numerous polemical, wide-ranging texts it is impossible not to recall that he came from the rich culture of Vienna, the city that produced Freud.

Loos was born in Brno, was in America from 1893 to 1896, and then returned to Vienna to work in the offices of Otto Wagner. He built some remarkable houses and shops, but his greatest influence came from his writings on design in *Die Zeit* and *Das Kunstblatt*. His most celebrated article was called *Ornament und Verbrecheri* (Ornament and Crime), appearing in 1908. In 1912 it was published by the Berlin review *Der Sturm* and the following year Le Corbusier published it in his own journal, *L 'Esprit nouveau*. The gist of the text was that ornament represents cultural degeneracy, and that modern, civilized society is represented by undecorated form: 'Ornamentation is wasted effort and therefore a waste of health. It has always been so. But today it means a waste of material as well, and the two things together mean a waste of capital.'

Instead of the aromatic vapours of high, decadent art, Loos offered in his architecture and his pamphlets the promise of a systematic evaluation of life. To him architecture was not merely the work of the building trade, but was the tangible expression of a society's culture.

Loos also published his own journal, *Das Andere* (The Outsider), in which he advanced his ideas, including one that the British gentleman was the model of taste. Loos execrated ornament in architecture and design in the same way that Freud excluded from his vision of the soul all those devices that had been used to disguise its essential primitivism.

Loos designed a set of glasses for the Viennese firm Lobmeyr, which is still in production, and other pieces of applied art, mostly intended for the interiors of his buildings. (See also pages 29–31.)

Bibliography Benedetto Gravagnuolo *Adolf Loos* Idea Books Edizioni, Milan, 1982; Adolf Loos *Spoken into the Void* MIT, Cambridge, Mass., 1982

Herb Lubalin 1918–82

The typographer Herb Lubalin was born in New York and graduated from the Cooper Union in 1939. He worked as an art director for Sudler & Hennessey before founding Herb Lubalin, Inc., in 1964, which became Lubalin, Peckolick Associates, Inc. in 1980. After 1973 Lubalin edited his own Journal, *U&LC* (for 'upper and lower case'), an international journal of typographies.

Lubalin worked in advertising, posters, packaging, editorial design and typeface design, but his very distinctive personal style is most of all concerned with typography. He made it his business to break the rules, jamming words together on the page, playing graphic tricks with letter-forms, using words to become images in themselves. When he was invited to design a logo for the magazine *Mother & Child* in 1967, he inserted the ampersand and the word 'child' into the 'o' of mother, thus creating not only a symbolic image of maternal protection, but also a tight and clever graphic form. Lubalin created the 'Davida' and 'Lincoln Gothic' typefaces during the Sixties.

3

Claus Luthe

Claus Luthe was the designer of the NSU Ro80, a car not so commercially successful as the Citroën DS, but one at least as beautiful and as technically advanced. The 1967 Ro80 had the world's first twin-rotor Wankel rotary engine. It also had advanced aerodynamics, front-wheel drive and a semi-automatic transmission with the vacuum clutch operated via a touch-sensitive switch in the top of the gear-lever. Unfortunately, NSU never managed effective seals for the rotor tips and warranty claims bankrupted the company.

Still, the body – whose concept went back to 1961 – remained to be enjoyed. Sharing some assumptions with Luthe's earlier NSU Prinz, itself a take on the 1960 Chevrolet Corvair, an elegant, smooth wedge with a very large glasshouse riding on a long wheelbase and wide track, Luthe's Ro80 used the compact rotary engine to advantage by enjoying a radically low nose. Badging and jewellery were restrained. Plans to have a stainless roof had to be abandoned for practical reasons.

Luthe later designed the original Polo and moved to BMW, where he was responsible for the second generation 7-series of 1986, the 8-series coupe, the 1990 3-series and the 1994 7-series. In 1992 he murdered his alcoholic son.

4: Adolf Loos, Moller House, Vienna, 1928. Loos' own diktat about 'ornament and crime' (forged in the hothouse atmosphere of turn-of-the-century Vienna) was not universally understood, at least not by all The Moller House's Owners.

3: Avant Garde – the typeface created by Lubalin was designed as a logo for a new magazine of the same name in the mid Sixties.

Charles Rennie Mackintosh 1868–1928

Charles Rennie Mackintosh entered Glasgow School of Art in 1885. He qualified in 1889 and joined the architectural firm of Honeyman & Keppie. As a young man Mackintosh came into contact with the work of Aubrey Beardsley, the Dutch Symbolist artist Jan van Toorop and the English architect C. F. A. Voysey through reading *The Studio*. Inspired by them, he produced some novel furniture and decoration, and designs that won a competition for a new Glasgow School of Art. This work was noticed and published by *The Studio*'s editor, Gleeson White, suddenly giving his ideas prominence and authority, and on the basis of *The Studio*'s articles alone, Mackintosh was invited to exhibit in Vienna at the 1900 Secession exhibition. His success in the Austrian capital made him suddenly a leading figure of an international group of architects and designers so that, with precious little of a backlist, he was thrust into equal status and inspired Josef Hoffmann and Koloman Moser. The first stage of the Glasgow School of Art was built between 1897 and 1899. It was his first (and, indeed, only) opportunity to design a total environment from the building down to the ashtrays. In the same year as he completed the Glasgow School of Art designs Mackintosh designed the first of the tearooms he was to be commissioned to do by Catherine Cranston, a Glasgow tearoom tycoon. His other major works followed over the next ten years: Hill House, just outside Glasgow, for the publisher Walter Blackie in 1902, further tearooms for Miss Cranston and the interior for a house in Northampton belonging to the model railway magnate J. Bassett-Lowke (who later commissioned Peter Behrens to design an entire dwelling). At the time he was the most influential Modernist architect in the UK.

Mackintosh's furniture is characterized by the use of strikingly emphatic rectilinear patterns, inspired by Japanese design. He often used painted wood, but lightened the severity of his forms with stylized motifs, loosely derived from Celtic ornament. Although he was contemporary with the Arts and Crafts movement, Mackintosh's work was much more concerned with visual effect than with either quality of execution or with 'truth to materials'.

Little more was heard of Mackintosh after his work for Bassett-Lowke. He retired to Port Vendres on the Basque coast and painted watercolours, returning to Britain to die in 1928. Some of Mackintosh's furniture designs are now reproduced by Cassina.

Bibliography Robert MacLeod *Charles Rennie Mackintosh*, Architect and Artist Collins, London, 1983

Mackintosh's work was much more concerned with visual effect than with either quality of execution or with 'truth to materials'

1

1

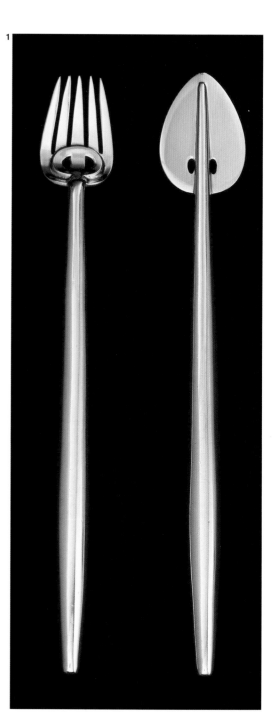

A.H. Mackmurdo 1851–1942

Arthur Heygate Mackmurdo was a friend of <u>John Ruskin</u> and <u>William Morris</u> and founded the Century Guild in 1882, an Arts and Crafts club. Mackmurdo is mainly famous today because the title page he designed in 1883 for his book, *Wren's City Churches*, was singled out by <u>Nikolaus Pevsner</u> as a pioneering work of modern design. Mackmurdo worked primarily as an architect, but some furniture designs, although Arts and Crafts in origin, approach the expressiveness of Continental <u>Art Nouveau</u>.

Vico Magistretti born 1920

The Italian furniture designer Vico Magistretti was born in Milan in 1920 and studied architecture at the Polytechnic there, graduating in 1945. Like many of his contemporaries, he turned from architecture to design in the years of Italy's *ricostruzione* after the Second World War. In 1962 he became the first Italian designer to produce a plastic chair, called 'Selene'. It was chic rather than cheap. His work for <u>Artemide</u> and <u>Cassina</u> from the Sixties on has included simple wooden chairs and padded sofas, as well as the curious 'Sindbad' chair of 1982 which was derived from a horse blanket. His most famous chair was 'Carimate' of 1959, made by Cassina; its bright red frame, light but sturdy structure, and rush seat was vaguely derived from the vernacular Chiavari type. It was one of Habitat's best-sellers and populated the terrazzo dining rooms of Sixties London *trattorie* which helped introduce the dining classes to Italian *modernismo*. Commuting between Milan and London, Magistretti was an influential teacher at the <u>Royal College of Art</u>.
Bibliography *Vico Magistretti* exhibition catalogue, Palazzo Ducale, Genoa, 2003

Louis Majorelle 1859–1926

Louis Majorelle, a native of Nancy and the son of a manufacturer of reproduction eighteenth-century furniture, was one of the chief beneficiaries of the <u>Art Nouveau</u> style and the most flamboyant representative of what has become known as the 'School of Nancy'. He mechanized his workshop so that he could turn out masses of highly decorated furniture at prices the middle classes could afford. His factory was burnt down in 1916; by the time it was possible to rebuild it, Art Nouveau had declined in popularity in favour of the next fashion, <u>Art Deco</u>. Majorelle quickly accommodated himself to that style.

2

3

MACKMURDO — MAJORELLE

207

DESIGN | BAYLEY | CONRAN

1: Charles Rennie Mackintosh chair, circa 1900. Fish knife and fork, circa 1900. Although his work was craft-based rather than industrial, Mackintosh was one of Nikolaus Pevsner's 'pioneers of modern design', a link between Britain and the Continent.

2: A. H. Mackmurdo, title page of Wren's City Churches, 1883. Another of Pevsner's citations: a 'pioneer' of Art Nouveau.
3: Vico Magistretti, 'setene' chair, 1962.

Tomas Maldonado born 1922

The Argentinian design theoretician Tomas Maldonado was born in Buenos Aires and studied at the Beaux-Arts there. By 1951 he was editing a journal called *Nueva Vision*. This brought him into contact with the Swiss sculptor and designer Max Bill, who invited him to join the new Hochschule für Gestaltung in Ulm. From 1954 to 1967 Maldonado's cerebral presence dominated the thinking at the Hochschule: his interest lay in systematizing design, both in terms of the process of making, and in terms of the process of analysing, or 'reading', designed objects. Because he thought the automobile was a symbol of 'Detroit Machiavellismus', car design was never taught at the Hochschule. His own design work, however, is pretty desiccated: some medical apparatus in 1962, an interior for a Prisunic store at Le Mans in 1972, and consultancy work for La Rinascente. He now lives in Milan and is a professor of design at the University of Bologna with an academic appointment that, magnificently, unites interior design with *filosofia*.

Robert Mallet-Stevens 1886–1945

Robert Mallet-Stevens was an architect who turned the Modern Movement into a chic style for wealthy Parisians. He was the first president of the Union des Artistes Modernes.
Bibliography Yvonne Brunhammer *Le Style 1925* Baschet et Cie., Paris, 1975

Carl Malmsten 1888–1972

Carl Malmsten achieved fame with a commission to provide furniture for the new Stockholm Town Hall (1916–23) and became an influential teacher and spokesman for the crafts. He disliked twentieth-century styles and, with Gunnar Asplund, campaigned to revive interest in vernacular furniture types. They developed a neo-classical style that became very popular in Sweden in the Twenties.

1: Robert Mallet-Stevens, Villa Cavroix, Croix, France, 1931–32.
2: Angelo Mangiarotti, carafe for Cleto Munari, 1981.
3: Marimekko, 'Jäävvoret' fabric by Fujiwa Ishimoto, 1983.

Angelo Mangiarotti born 1921

Angelo Mangiarotti was born in Milan and graduated from the Polytechnic there in 1948. In 1953–4 he was a visiting professor at the Illinois Institute of Technology's Institute of Design and ran his own office in Ohio. He returned to Italy in 1955. He has designed a clock called 'Secticon' (1962) for the Swiss manufacturer, Portescap. This clock was strongly sculptural and Mangiarotti tends to specialize in emphatic forms, including marble objects for <u>Knoll</u> and silverware for Cleto Munari.

Enzo Mari born 1932

Enzo Mari studied at the Accademia di Belle Arte di Brera in Milan between 1952 and 1956. Being interested in <u>semiology</u>, he is among the more intellectual of his generation of Italian designers, and has written on design, analysing it as a linguistic system. His aesthetic approach to the practice of design is, however, highly formalist, and he has designed strongly sculptural office products, storage jars and containers in melamine and polypropylene for <u>Danese</u>. His book *Funzione della ricerca estetica* was published in 1970.

Marimekko

Marimekko (which means 'Mary's little dress') is a Helsinki fabric store founded by <u>Armi Ratia</u>. In 1951 Ratia joined an oil cloth company called Printex. Her first job, it is said, was to leave the oil out. The next thing she did was to ask some designer friends to come up with patterns that could be used on the cloth. In the grisaille austerity of the post-Second World War years the colourful, monumental shapes caused a sensation and Marimekko became a cult. The colours and patterns of Marimekko combine subtle adaptations of the Finnish rustic tradition with a very fresh and uninhibited sort of <u>Modernism</u> (some of which comes from its Japanese designers). The designs were sold by Design Research and Crate and Barrel in the USA and <u>Habitat</u> in the UK. Since 1968 Marimekko has licensed its products worldwide.

2

3

The colours and patterns of Marimekko combine subtle adaptations of the Finnish rustic tradition with a very fresh and uninhibited sort of Modernism

Javier Mariscal born 1950

The playful Spanish designer Javier Mariscal studied at the Escuela de Grafismo Elisava in Barcelona. Known as a cartoonist and textile designer, his 'Hilton' drinks trolley was a part of the first <u>Memphis</u> collection in 1981. An energetic and funny designer, Mariscal was responsible for the graphics of the 1992 Barcelona Olympics, a symbol and driver of Spain's rehabilitation.

MARS

The Modern Architecture Research Group was founded in London in 1933 by a group of architects at the Architectural Association as an English response to <u>CIAM</u>. Its members, who included <u>Wells Coates</u> and the historian Sir John Summerson, were leaders of the British <u>Modern Movement</u>.

Enid Marx 1902–91

Enid Marx, a British fabric and book jacket designer, studied at the <u>Central School of Art and Design</u> and the <u>Royal College of Art</u> before setting up her own studio to design and print textiles. On the basis of the reputation established in doing this <u>Gordon Russell</u> invited her to join the wartime <u>Utility</u> Furniture Design Panel for whom she designed fabrics. The limitations of the brief – four colours, two types of yarn, frequent repeats – suited her style and imagination perfectly, as she was well known for fabrics with minimal pattern and restricted colour. Her designs were used as seating fabrics for London Transport and thus became very well known, a civilizing influence on the barbarity of commuting. Marx also desined the fine dust-jacket for the most famous English translation of Proust. Her students included Terence Conran.

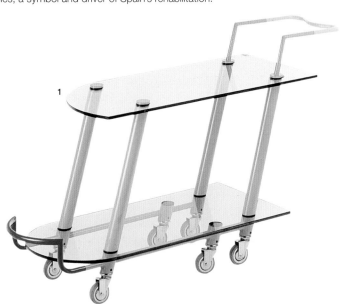

Bruno Mathsson 1907–88

Bruno Mathsson was born at Varnamo in Sweden where his father had a furniture factory. He became a furniture designer at just the moment when the Swedes were becoming conscious of their national design, and he was able to combine his training as a cabinet-maker with his family's expertise and an attitude to his products that pleased the consumer by using natural materials in a sophisticated and graceful way. His most famous design for a chair, the 'Pernilla', with a laminated beech frame and hemp webbing, has become known as the Bruno Mathsson chair. It was designed for Dux Mobel in 1934 and is still in production today. Mathsson collaborated on furniture design with Piet Hein and ran the family business Mathsson Mobler from the small town of Varnamo.
Bibliography C. & P. Fiell *Scandinavian Design* Taschen, Cologne, 2002

Herbert Matter 1907–84

Herbert Matter was born in Engelberg, Switzerland, and studied at the Ecole des Beaux-Arts in Paris from 1923 to 1925, a pupil of Amedée Ozenfant and Fernand Léger. At the Beaux-Arts Matter began to take photographs, got to know Cassandre and Le Corbusier, and after graduating worked on *Vogue* before returning to Switzerland to do travel posters for the Swiss Tourist Office. Matter's style was photo-montage, employing dramatic contrasts of scale and integrated colour with monochrome photography. Like Laszlo Moholy-Nagy he took the medium of the photograph beyond mere photo-chemical recording and created with it a vivid new form of graphic communication.

In 1939 Matter went to the United States, set up his own graphics studio, working for Condé Nast and others, becoming professor of photography and graphic design at Yale University in 1952. Here his pupils included Alan Fletcher. His best-known work there was to design the original Knoll logotype and fashion Knoll's entire graphic character over a 14-year period. An admired member of America's graphics intelligentsia, Matter designed the logo of the New Haven Railway in 1955. In a 1977 retrospective at Yale, Paul Rand wrote a laudatory poem including the line 'His work of '32 could have been done in '72.'

Syrie Maugham 1879–1955

Syrie Maugham, the wife for 12 years of writer Somerset Maugham, was one of the most famous interior designers of her day. Her firm, Syrie Ltd, was established in the early Twenties and designed rooms in a traditional idiom with the occasional flash of daring. By the end of that decade she had discovered the possibilities of the monochromatic paint schemes with which her name is principally associated: following the success of her own all-white drawing room, she bleached, pickled and painted old French furniture and whitened or silvered picture frames for more than a decade. Her interiors achieved a spare elegance.

1: 'Hilton' trolley for Memphis, 1981.
2: Enid Marx' 1942 fabrics for the wartime Utility Furniture Design Panel were limited by technical and financial restrictions to a small range of colours, but nonetheless achieved a pleasing effect. And had a very long life with London Transport.

3: 'The' Bruno Mathsson chair, 'Pernilla' for Dux Mobel, 1934.
4: Syrie Maugham, London drawing room with mirrored screen, circa 1933. Evelyn Waugh satirised Maugham's frivolous stylizing in his great comic novels of the Thirties.

Ingo Maurer born 1932

The German lighting designer was born in Reichenau, home of a fabled medieval monastic foundation. Maurer trained as a typographer in Germany and Switzerland, spending the three years after 1960 in the United States. Ingo Maurer gmbh is now based in Munich, producing lighting that is technologically pure, but artistically whimsical, innovative, sculptural and brilliant.

1: Ingo Maurer, 'Bulb' light, 1966.
2: Volkswagen's 'new' Beetle was derived from J. Mays's 'concept one' show car of 1994.

J Mays born 1955

J Carroll Mays (the initial is a cheerfully mysterious idiosyncrasy) was born in Maysville, Oklahoma. His interest in expressive geometry was inspired, he says, from a boyhood spent ploughing fields. Mays studied under Strother McMinn at Pasadena's Art College Center and was hired by Volkswagen-Audi on graduation in 1980, his new employers being impressed by a joint project he showed with the Jet Propulsion Laboratory. Moving to Germany, he was an influence in the Audi design department at Ingolstadt under Hartmut Warkuss. For Audi and its parent Volkswagen Mays helped define the clean lines and confident surfaces of the Volkswagen Passat and Audi TT. But his most significant design was rather different. The project called Concept One appeared at the Detroit Auto Show in 1994. Based entirely on circles, this was a re-drawing of the original Volkswagen Beetle, but a re-drawing that Mays insisted was not naïve copyism, but a finessed reinterpretation, an idea he later called 'Retrofuturism'. For Concept One Mays needed (and had) a deep understanding of heritage design cues (in fact, based on close scrutiny of the Disney movies *The Love Bug* and *Herbie Rides Again*). This resulted in a brilliant confection that rolled up its sleeves and rummaged deep in the consumer's id. After going on sale in the US in 1998, the new Beetle helped restore Volkswagen's commercial credibility.

Mays moved to Ford in 1997, excited at the huge portfolio of brands ripe for reinterpretation that Ford assembled into its ill-starred Premier Automotive Group. But his high-concept revival of Eugene T. Gregorie's classic 1955 Thunderbird in 1999 was not a commercial success and subsequent show cars, which included a version of George Walker's 1949 Ford, did not go into production. Meanwhile, Ford struggled to establish a relevant new logic for its base products, which have been routinely criticized for aesthetic mediocrity. French critics, for instance, said Mays' latest Fiesta suffered from '*présentation triste*'. The lesson of Retrofuturism may be that you cannot look two ways at once. But at an exhibition of his work in 2002 it was said that Mays had made, before he was 50, a 'lasting contribution to American culture'.

Bibiography Brooke Hodge (ed.) *Retrofuturism: the car designs of J Mays* exhibition catalogue Museum of Contemporary Art, Los Angeles, 2002

2

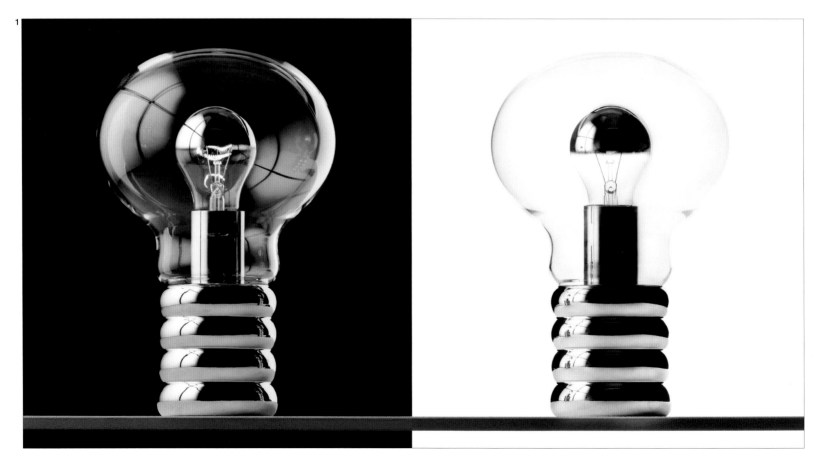

1

Marshall McLuhan 1911–81

Marshall McLuhan was a Canadian professor of English whose books, *The Mechanical Bride* (1951), *The Gutenberg Galaxy* (1962), *Understanding Media* (1964) and *The Medium is the Message* (1967), were among the first serious studies of the impact of the mass media on popular culture. McLuhan saw ephemera such as print, games and mass-produced appliances, not just as commercial products but as important aspects of contemporary culture, and thus encouraged a more critical approach towards the area of production. McLuhan coined the term 'global village' and predicted the downfall of printed information in the electronics age.

McLuhan saw ephemera such as print, games and mass-produced appliances not just as commercial products but as important aspects of contemporary culture

David Mellor born 1930

A British cutler and industrial designer, David Mellor was the outstanding British flatware designer of the twentieth century. This may sound like faint praise, but Mellor was a no-nonsense individual who with great integrity and commitment ran a workshop that produced consistently excellent products of uncompromised quality. He expressed himself with his hands rather than with words and insisted upon the essential relationship between making things and designing them.

Born in Sheffield when it was still very much a steel city, he had a natural affinity with metal perhaps arising from his father's occupation as a toolmaker for the Sheffield Twist Drill Company. To be working class in the Sheffield of Mellor's youth was to belong to a privileged class which enjoyed its status. First evidence of his commitment to the philosophy of <u>Eric Gill</u> was while on he was on National Service – he did the signwriting on his unit's main battle tanks in a light blue shade of Gill Sans.

After studying at the <u>Royal College of Art</u> he went on a scholarship to Sweden and Denmark, returning to establish a studio-workshop-factory in Sheffield in 1954. Attaching himself to the Walker & Hall business, he was among the very first to describe himself as a 'design consultant'. In his first year as an independent designer he produced a traditional service, known as 'Pride', which won one of the first <u>Design Council</u> awards in 1957. Since then he has benefited from many official commissions, principally the 'Embassy' service of 1963, designed for use in British embassies, and two years later the 'Thrift' service, intended for use in Government institutions. He has also designed other objects, including bus shelters and traffic lights, much influenced by ideas of street furniture acquired from Scandinavia, but there is something essentially English about the character of Mellor's designs: they are elegant but understated, strong in character, but unobtrusive. In addition, he fully understands the behaviour of metals and the physics of tools. He is no mere cutlery stylist.

Mellor also has strong views about the designer's role: he sees his designs as very much a way of supporting a view of life. Design, for him, is a far broader issue than even the profession's spokesmen are prepared to admit: 'It is concerned not *just* with making objects… but just as importantly with making *choices*, with choosing what we use, choosing how we live.' Since 1969 he has given form to his own particular world view in his exquisite kitchen equipment shops in London – originally as 'David Mellor Ironmonger' – and in Manchester since 1980. Here a huge range of refined working implements are offered for sale in a totally designed environment. Mellor's annual Cook's Catalogue preceded foodie cults by many years. Writing in the *Daily Mail*, Janet Street-Porter described all of this as 'super-cool', but the business nonetheless survived. Mellor and his works were hewn from the solid.

Bibliography *David Mellor – master metalworker* David Mellor Design, Hathersage, 2006

3: Marshall McLuhan in 1967. Inventor of the 'Global Village' and the talismanic 'the medium is the message'. McLuhan was first to understand the impact of electronics: 'Vietnam was lost in the living rooms of America – not on the battlefields of Vietnam'.

4: David Mellor, 'Provencal' cutlery, 1973, originally in rosewood, later in acetal resin. Mellor was the very last industrial designer still in direct touch with manufacturing technology.

Memphis

Memphis was the name of a collection of furniture, fabric and ceramics designers who gathered around Ettore Sottsass at the 1981 Milan Furniture Fair and caused a sensation in the international media. In fact, the group had grown out of Studio Alchymia, another Milanese avant-garde group, which had itself developed from the groups of radical architects and designers which flourished in Italy during the later Sixties.

Memphis provided a vehicle for Sottsass after what he described as an extended period of helplessness, and provided a forum for himself and younger designers to express ideas about furniture which he had been nurturing for 20 years. While Studio Alchymia indulged in the wilder extremes of performance art, Memphis got support from Artemide and took a showroom on the corso Europa in central Milan. It did not intend to be dangerously radical: it wanted to be a band of guerrillas, but only at the furniture fair. The group used industrial materials and mixed Fifties revivalism with an iconography simultaneously derived from ancient art and pop music. Overlaid on all of this were continuous references to the urban structure of Milan; Sottsass once said he was 'quoting from suburbia… Memphis is not new, Memphis is everywhere.' Memphis offended conservative designers like Vico Magistretti, who said: 'In my opinion this furniture offers no possibility for development whatsoever. It is only a variant of fashion.' Memphis' designers include Martine Bedin, Andrea Branzi, Aldo Cibic, Michele de Lucchi, George Sowden and Marco Zanini, but they are all, in fact or in theory, subordinated to the spirit of the genius of the group, Ettore Sottsass. When asked to explain it, he just said that 'Memphis' function is to exist,' adding ironically, 'Why should homes be static temples?'

Bibliography *Memphis Milano in London* exhibition catalogue, The Boilerhouse Project, Victoria and Albert Museum, London 1982; Barbara Radice *Memphis* Rizzoli, New York, 1984; Andrea Branzi *The Hot House: Italian* New Wave Design, MIT, Cambridge, Mass., 1984

Alessandro Mendini born 1931

Alessandro Mendini is one of the bourgeois radicals of Italian design. He was born in Milan, and until 1970 worked as an architect for Marcello Nizzoli Associati. From 1970 to 1976 he was editor of *Casabella* and since 1979 has been editor of *Modo* and *Domus*. Mendini is more politically and intellectually orientated than Ettore Sottsass, and has contributed furniture designs, which he likes to think of as 'banale', to Studio Alchymia and silverware to Alessi.

Bibliography Barbara Radice *Ologia del banale* Studio Alchymia, Milan, 1980; Andrea Branzi *The Hot House: Italian* New Wave Design MIT, Cambridge, Mass., 1984

Roberto Menghi born 1920

With Gino Colombini, Roberto Menghi was the Italian designer who developed the most sophisticated technical and aesthetic attitudes to plastics during the Fifties. For Moneta Smalterie Meridionali he produced a superb range of integrated vessels, including an exquisite polyethylene bucket, an example of which is permanently on show in New York's Museum of Modern Art. For Pirelli he has designed disposable plastic canisters (1959) and a hot-water bottle (1961): to both of these everyday objects he has brought scientific understanding and Italian style. Since the Sixties, Menghi has worked almost exclusively on architectural projects, including the Excelsior Hotel on the Venice Lido.

Bibliography 'Il Disegno dei materiali industriali' *Rassegna* 14, June 1983

1

Roberto Menghi was the Italian designer who developed the most sophisticated technical and aesthetic attitudes to plastics during the Fifties

Hannes Meyer 1889–1954

The Swiss Marxist architect Hannes Meyer was briefly the director of the Bauhaus, after Walter Gropius's resignation in 1928 and before Mies van der Rohe's takeover in 1931. Although Meyer's political ideals actually meant that he took the school nearer to its declared purpose of being a genuine industrial force than Gropius had ever done, and while he was an intellectual Marxist and not a practising revolutionary, his uncompromising politics accelerated the closure of the Dessau campus by exciting the attention of the conservative local authorities, who put pressure on the governing Social Democrats to close the school.

Bibliography Hans Maria Wingler *The Bauhaus* M.I.T., Cambridge, Mass., 1969

Giovanni Michelotti 1921–80

Giovanni Michelotti was born in Turin and at only 16 entered the body shop of Farina, before it became known as Pininfarina. In 1949 he set up his own practice. Michelotti worked for Triumph and was the first non-Japanese designer to be commissioned by a Japanese manufacturer. Michelotti's 1959 Triumph Herald was somewhat compromised by the manufacturer's lack of tools necessary to make the subtle presswork and, as a result, was presented to the public as a more two-dimensional compromise than the designer intended, but was still breathtakingly modern in appearance. His (Datsun) Prince Skyline appeared in 1961 and his Hino Contessa in 1965. Other notable designs include the Daf 44 (1966), the Alpine-Renault (1968) and the Triumph 2000 (1963).

1: Roberto Menghi, jerry can for Pirelli, 1958. One of the first utilitarian plastic objects to find its way into the sepulchral halls of New York's Museum of Modern Art.

2: Hannes Meyer, self portrait collage, 1920 and the cover of the 1929 Bauhaus brochure.

3: Giovanni Michelotti designed the body for the 1963 Triumph 2000, adding Italian flair to brute English mechanics. Only in the seventies did BMW production overtake Triumph's.

2

3

2

junge menschen kommt ans bauhaus!

bauhaus

Ludwig Mies van der Rohe 1886–1969

Ludwig Mies was born in Aachen, Germany, the son of a mason. He added his mother's name to his father's to give himself more style. Mies was trained in his father's building yard, but was also apprenticed to Bruno Paul and to Peter Behrens, so that when he began to work in the field of architectural design he practised in a restrained and severe version of the German classical school of the nineteenth century, whose most famous exemplar was the Prussian architect Karl Friedrich Schinkel, the creator of much of neo-classical Berlin.

The influence of Schinkel on Mies' work was first seen in an unrealized project for a Bismarck monument of 1912. Mies also worked on Behrens' monumental German Embassy in St Petersburg, but first came to international attention as the organizer of an experimental housing estate at Weissenhof, outside Stuttgart, for the Deutsche Werkbund in 1927. This was followed by his design for the German national pavilion at the Barcelona international exhibition of 1929. His minimal grid for the building and the fine furniture he designed for it achieved a totemic excellence far beyond the capabilities of the day-to-day architect of Modernism, constrained by practical briefs. In the same year Mies built the Tugendhat House at Brno in Czechoslovakia, for which he also designed chairs and other furniture.

Mies succeeded Hannes Meyer as the director of the Bauhaus during its last days in Dessau, and, when political pressure from the local government forced the famous school to close down, moved it to an old telephone factory in the Steglitz quarter of Berlin. When he failed to sell the idea that Modernism was authentic German design to the Nazis he was forced to close the Bauhaus completely. Unlike many of his colleagues, such as Walter Gropius, Marcel Breuer and Laszlo Moholy-Nagy, who chose to escape to England, Mies went straight to the United States, where he became professor of architecture at the Armour Institute (which later became the Illinois Institute of Technology). Here American patronage and a national longing for status symbols from European culture gave Mies the opportunity to practise an architecture which, paradoxically, had had little future in Europe even before the Nazis tried to stamp it out. In a series of buildings for the IIT campus Mies defined the visual character of the modern technological university. It is a tribute to the integrity of his designs that they still evoke the idea of 'Modern', and it is with something of a shock that one sees contemporary photos in which the new buildings butt up against their dated automobile peers, the curvaceous Buicks and Packards of the early Fifties, which were an expression of the same culture.

Mies built flats at Lake Shore Drive in Chicago between 1946 and 1959 and a monumental office building for the Seagram Corporation on New York's Park Avenue (1958).

1: Mies van der Rohe's 'Barcelona' chair was designed for the exclusive use of the King of Spain when visiting the German Pavilion at the Barcelona Exhibition of 1929, but it became a familiar status object in corporate America.

2: Model of the Mansion House Square Project, London, 1968. Mies' unrealized final project became a controversial test case for the future of city building during the Eighties. Proposed for a revered, but shoddy, part of the City of London, conservationists opposed it as 'inappropriate'. Had it been built in 1968, its fine proportions and exquisite details would have been exemplary.
3: George Nelson, 'marshmallow' chair for Herman Miller, 1956.

Herman Miller

Mies' furniture designs for the Tugendhat House and the Barcelona pavilion were licensed to Knoll. Through their marketing efforts his exquisite and expensive chairs, products of the Twenties, became the *de rigueur* status ornamentation of corporate lobbies throughout America. Just before his death in 1969 Mies designed an office block for Lord Peter Palumbo intended for a new London development to be known as Mansion House Square. The planning battle that developed over this building became a set-piece in the debate about Modernism, Post-Modernism and conservation in the early Eighties.
Bibliography Arthur Drexler *Ludwig Mies van der Rohe* Braziller, New York, 1960; Mayflower, London, 1960; Hans Maria Wingler *Bauhaus* MIT, Cambridge, Mass., 1969; Werner Blaser *Mies van der Rohe: furniture and interiors* Barron's, New York, 1982

Like Knoll, Herman Miller is one of the most respected names in American furniture, but unlike its rival, which was founded by an immigrant in cosmopolitan New York, Herman Miller was established by local businessmen at Zeeland, Michigan, near the traditional centre of American furniture-manufacturing at Grand Rapids. The company's origins date back to the early years of this century, but it did not acquire its reputation until immediately after the Second World War when it began to manufacture designs by Charles Eames first seen in exhibitions at the Museum of Modern Art.

In 1909 D. J. De Pree joined the company Miller and other local businessmen had established five years earlier. De Pree married Miller's daughter, acquired 51 per cent of the stock and changed the company's name. With De Pree the company concentrated on quality control in its reproduction designs. Modern designs only began to interest them when the cabinet-maker Gilbert Rohde joined them in the Thirties, bringing European standards of taste with him.

The company acquired an eloquent spokesman when George Nelson was appointed design director in 1946, succeeding Rohde. Nelson designed a 'Storage Wall' for Herman Miller in 1946 (see page 229), a 'Steelframe Group' in 1954 and the 'Action Office' ten years later. Eames' plywood and steel chair went into production in 1948.

George Nelson directed Herman Miller more towards the architectural market and away from run-of-the mill commercial clients. He insisted on abandoning the reproduction lines and encouraged Charles Eames to continue producing furniture designs. Under his tutelage Eames' famous lounge chair appeared commercially in 1956 (see page 134), followed by the 'Aluminum' group seating in 1958 and the 'Soft Pad' development of it in 1969. From 1952 Alexander Girard introduced more

colour and pattern into the company's merchandise. Herman Miller (UK) was set up in 1970.

Eames' work of the mid-Fifties represented for many people the last word in chair design, although Herman Miller continued to search for enhanced solutions to the problem of sitting down. It was decided that a 'cross-performance chair' was now required, one that took into account the availability of new materials and enhanced ergonomic research. In 1994 the 'Aeron' came onto the market. Its designer was Bill Stumpf (1936–2006), vice-president of Herman Miller's research department. Earlier, Stumpf had produced the 'Ergon' chair for Miller in 1976, but for the 'Aeron' he drew on research garnered while teaching environmental design at Wisconsin University. His brief to himself with the 'Aeron' was 'freeing up the body and designing away constraints'. He described the successful result as a 'metaphor of the human form'. It used advanced materials, came in three sizes and was almost infinitely adaptable, a reflection, perhaps, of the new business culture that created it. It is also very attractive to dust and dirt in the office environment.

An 'Aeron' was the first acquisition by Paola Antonelli of New York's Museum of Modern Art, immediately promoting an effective modern working chair to covetable status symbol. She described it as 'a new paradigm in office chairs'. Aerons became conspicuous in New York's dot-com boom of the late Nineties and populated the lobby of the doomed World Trade Center. After the collapse of the boom, many deflated companies who had eagerly acquired Aerons sold them off in bulk, rapidly converting a status symbol into a memento mori.
Bibliography Ralph Caplan *The Design of Herman Miller* Whitney Library of Design, New York, 1976; Bill Stumpf *The Ice Palace that Melted Away: restoring civility and other lost virtues*, University of Minnesota Press, 1998

3

Bill Mitchell 1912–88

Bill Mitchell was born in Cleveland, Ohio. He was hired by Harley Earl in 1935 and soon became head of General Motors' Cadillac studio. He had the impossible brief to follow Harley Earl's coruscating act and was GM's vice-president in charge of styling from 1958 to his retirement in 1978. Unlike Earl, who based his iconography on the race track and on science fiction, Mitchell wanted to bring to 'The General's' line-up something of the quality of low-production-run cars, like the American Duesenberg and the European Mercedes-Benz, but it was his fate to be in charge of General Motors' design during the American motor industry's most blighted years. Despite authoritative designs including the astonishing 1963 Buick Riviera, the 1965 Oldsmobile Toronado and several generations of Chevrolet Corvette, Mitchell's achievement was overshadowed by his predecessor. He explained his philosophy of design by contrasting a billiard ball with a baseball. The smooth, sleek billiard ball had no little visual or tactile interest to Mitchell. But the stitching and pattern of the baseball he found intoxicating.

1: R. J. Mitchell's Supermarine Type 300, a supremely elegant all-metal, cantilever mono-plane. By the time it first flew on 5th March 1936, the name 'Spitfire' had been chosen.

2: Issey Miyake, autumn, 2000.
3: Mies van der Rohe, Seagram Building, Park Avenue, New York, 1958. 'I don't want to be interesting, I want to be good'.

Reginald Joseph Mitchell 1895–1937

The Supermarine Spitfire was a military weapon rather than a consumer product in the strict sense (even if more than 20,000 were manufactured between 1934 and 1948), but it is often cited as a supreme example of industrial design. Mitchell had designed an award-winning plane for the Schneider Trophy and as a result was invited by the Air Ministry to submit proposals for a monoplane to replace the Air Force's ancient biplanes. The first Spitfire F37/34 flew in 1936. Mitchell's airframe was elegant, but functional: a single spar supported distinctive thin section ovoid wings and a light-alloy body was covered by a stressed skin. British historians now debate the precise military significance of the 'Battle of Britain' (which German historians do not recognize) in which the Sptifire was translated from war material into a significant component of national identity, but the craft had an unusual elegance. Its astonishing status in myth supports any arguments in favour of design being a matter of creating symbols. Yet, at the same time, the Spitfire was by all accounts a supremely functional weapon and, to its pilots, if not to its adversaries, a pure delight. In its twelve year life it evolved continuously: such evolution is often a test of inherent quality in any design.

Bibliography Jonathan Glancey *Spitfire* Atlantic Publishing, London, 2006

Issey Miyake born 1939

Hanae Mori was the first Japanese fashion designer to become an international celebrity, Kenzo was the second, but the third, Issey Miyake, is probably the most important. And an authentic genius.

Miyake was brought up in Hiroshima, but went to Tokyo to study graphics at Tama Art University. As a student he became interested in the theatre and then in fashion. However, in the early Sixties such an interest was not encouraged in Japan and to get training Miyake had to travel to Paris, where he worked with Hubert de Givenchy and Guy Laroche, and to New York, where he worked with Geoffrey Beene. By the time he returned to Tokyo to found the Miyake Design Studio in 1971 he had, for a Japanese person, an unusually cosmopolitan background.

Miyake's clothes are all inspired in their cut by traditional Japanese forms, but they have an uncompromisingly modern appearance. His great strength, however, is with materials. He specializes in rich, subtle and complex weaves, which evoke traditional values without recourse to adventitious historicism. He acknowledges that he is interested in exploring the 'limits' of clothing in particular areas such as pattern, texture and looseness. Although very influenced by youth culture with a Sixties flavour – he says he wants people who wear his clothes to know what it is like to be 'free' – Miyake has a shrewd business sense. When in the early Eighties he wanted to expand his design studio he had no hesitation in taking part in television advertisements for whisky and cars to raise the necessary funds. Miyake has helped turn Tokyo into an international city of design. His museum opens in Tokyo in 2007.

Bibliography Issey Miyake *East Meets West* Heibonsha, Tokyo, 1978; Issey Miyake *Bodyworks* Shogakukan, Tokyo, 1983

1

2

Modernism/The Modern Movement

It is delightful to note that the idea of modernity has been around for a long time. Cennino Cennini in his *Libro dell'Arte* said Giotto with his psychological realism and new-fangled perspective made painting 'modern'. Later, Vasari used the word. But essentially, the concept became firmly established in literature long before it became the imperative in architecture art and design.

In the eighteenth century, there was a debate between the 'Ancients and Moderns'. Then the 1828 Webster's Dictionary defined modernism as 'something recently formed, particularly in writing'. First mention in our current sense? Perhaps Matthew Arnold's lecture *On the Modern Element in Literature* in 1857. In Paris the Goncourt brothers coined 'modernity' the following year. George Meredith's *Modern Love* was published in 1862. A Danish literary critic called Georg Brandes produced *Det Moderne Gjennembruds Moend* (Men of the Modern Breakthrough) in 1883. By the next decade the word is a commonplace in all languages – a defining characteristic of Modernism is that it is international. And another defining characterstic is its extreme self-consciousness. As the poet Rimbaud wrote: 'Il faut etre absolument moderne!' No one was ever retrospectively construed to be a Modernist. They very well knew they were doing it.

In architecture and design Modernism meant an abrupt break with tradition: 'Its character is catastrophic,' Herbert Read wrote. In *The Unknown Citizen* (1939) the poet W. H. Auden described the utopia Modernism might provide:

Everything necessary for the Modern Man
A phonograph, a radio, a car and Frigidaire.

And when in 1954 C. S. Lewis' gave his inaugural lecture at Cambridge he said the biggest schism in culture was not between Antiquity and Dark Ages, or between the Middle Ages and the Renaissance, but between Jane Austen and the twentieth century. The reason for this? An extraordinary catalogue of technological innovation which changed the dimensions of the world and our perceptions of it.

Within a 20-year period the following things happened. Benz and Diesel discovered exactly how to exploit oil. Electricity meant that for the first time in history power could be used remotely from its source. There was Heidelberg's high-speed printing press. And radio. The telephone and sound recording. The typewriter. Lumiere's cinema, synthetic dyes and materials. Not to mention flight. Meanwhile, Henry Ford and William Hesketh Lever discovered with gasoline buggies and 'Sunlight' branded soap how to sell fast-moving consumer goods to a global constituency.

This all amounted to a change in human affairs that was brilliantly construed by Aldous Huxley, who explained that speed alone was the experience unique to the twentieth century. Speed in travel, in the manufacture of products and the generation of data. The fast new technologies offered immediate expressive opportunities

to architects and designers, but at the same time tended to marginalize fine art and literature. Mass-production was perfectly appropriate to architecture and design because everybody needs somewhere to live and products to use. Novels, by contrast, have limited appeal.

So the great and perplexing absurdity of Modernism is not the insistence that intelligent design means flat roofs for all, but the internal conflict between intellectual snobbery and consumerist democracy. While modern

architects and designers worked at making beauty, luxury and convenience democratically available, modern writers and musicians became obscurantist and inaccessible.

Styles come and go, but in the breach or the observance Modernism still defines our attitude to the world. And this is a world in which machines remain both the means and the metaphor of human ambition. Modernism was not a style prospectus, but an attitude. As Frank Lloyd Wright put it, Modernism is insistence on making the most of contemporary possibilities. I wish I had had the nerve to say that to Prince Charles as he sat on his gilt lion's claw foot cabriole chair. I might then have gone onto explain that straight lines were not the issue, but intellectual elegance, moral integrity and practical beauty were.

There was never *really* such a thing as the Modern Movement, in the sense of an association of artists and designers. It is a convenient abstraction, used by both its champions and its enemies to describe the adherents to an attitude to design which did not separate form from moral values and social purpose and which sought to create a new aesthetic for a new technological world.

The 'movement' started in Russia and was strongest in Germany, followed by France, Italy and Austria; its leaders were Walter Gropius, Le Corbusier and Mies van der Rohe. In Britain, despite the efforts of a few pioneers like Wells Coates and Maxwell Fry, the influence of William Morris created a huge obstacle to the acceptance of the Modern Movement, which only tentatively took any root at all in the UK in the late Twenties.

The chief effect in Britain was due to the wave of emigrants from Hitler's Germany. Of these Gropius, Marcel Breuer and Laszlo Moholy-Nagy moved to the United States, where at New York's Museum of Modern Art and at university campuses in Harvard and Chicago they found a more receptive audience of students and clients. Modern Movement dreams that were never fully realized in Germany or in England became reality on Park Avenue or in the showrooms of Hans Knoll.

The architect Berthold Lubetkin wrote in 1947 that the Modern Movement in architecture and design is 'a statement of the social aims of the age. Its compelling geometrical regularities affirm man's hope to understand, to explain and control his surroundings. By asserting itself against subjectivity and equivocation, it discloses a universal, purposeful order and clarity in what appears to be a mental wilderness.'

However, after some catastrophic engineering and social failures by later adherents of the movement during the Sixties and Seventies, the Modern Movement began to be widely attacked and alternative 'philosophies' such as Post-Modernism were proposed. Although the Museum of Modern Art had been at the forefront of promoting the Modern Movement, in the mid-Sixties it commissioned what became Robert Venturi's *Complexity and Contradiction in Modern Architecture*, a heterodox book which helped create the atmosphere in which Post-Modernism could flourish.

Moderne/Modernistic

'Moderne', from the French, is a term usually applied in dismissive tones to the degeneration of the <u>Modern Movement</u>'s aesthetic in superficial decorative details. It is sometimes used as an adjectival synonym for <u>Art Deco</u>. 'Moderne' became popular and successful in the United States, where the style was mass-produced on a large scale. The term now implies an exaggerated commercialism far removed from the idealism of the Modern Movement. The V&A's <u>Modernism</u> exhibition in 2006 did an excellent job of explaining the movement.

Børge Mogensen 1914–72

Børge Mogensen was a pupil of <u>Kaare Klint</u>, the Danish designer whose own study of 'classic' English furniture types fed considerable influence into the <u>Modern Movement</u> in Denmark. Mogensen became a certified journeyman cabinet-maker in 1934 before studying at the Furniture School of the Royal Academy of Fine Arts in Copenhagen. His reputation is based on work as head of the design department of the Danish Co-operative Society (1942–50) where his objective was to make quality of conception and execution available to the consumer at a reasonable price by employing the most advanced production techniques. His most celebrated design is of a sofa which folds into a simple bed.

1: Dream office for MGM by Cedric Gibbons, E. B. Williams and William Horning, 1936. Hollywood fed the public dandified versions of the 'moderne' long before such furniture was commercially available.
2: Laszlo Moholy-Nagy, design for Bauhaus exhibition poster, 1923. Moholy-Nagy believed in the hygiene of the optical.

1

Laszlo Moholy-Nagy 1895–1946

Painter, photographer, typographer, educationalist and film-maker, Laszlo Moholy-Nagy never designed anything that went into series production, but became a major influence in the world of design through his books and his teaching. He was born at Bacsborsod in Hungary, and studied law in Budapest. He began sketching while injured during military service in the First World War, and after the War founded an avant-garde group and journal called *Ma* (Tomorrow). By 1920, an ambitious artist, he had moved to Berlin, and joined the Bauhaus staff in 1922. At the Bauhaus he ran the metalwork shop, where his students included Wilhelm Wagenfeld and Marianne Brandt, made abstract and semi-abstract films, and edited the *Bauhausbücher*, a series of books on art and design theory which came out of Weimar and Dessau and whose authors included Walter Gropius, Wassily Kandinsky and Kasimir Malevich. Moholy-Nagy was one of the first 'fine' artists to draw attention to the beauty implicit in machines. His *Buch neuer Kunstler* of 1919 used photographs of aeroplanes to advance his novel aesthetic. His central belief was the visual arts should concern 'the hygiene of the optical' a typically clever bit of phrase-making.

In 1923 Moholy adopted the Platonic sphere, cone and cube as the Bauhaus logo. He was a pioneer of modern media. His 'Telephone Paintings' created by an enamelling factory when he read graph paper co-ordinates in a phone call have some claim to be the first 'ready-made'. He was enthralled by machines and explained 'Everyone is equal before the machine… there is no tradition in technology, no class-consciousness.' The most memorable artefact coming out of Moholy's metal workshop in the Bauhaus was the desk light designed by his star pupil, Wilhelm Wagenfeld. The famous 'Bauhaus' desk light was designed between 1923 and 1924 and went into production in 1927. Ilse Gropius desribed it as 'conclusive, without frills and beautiful', but this con of machine art was, in fact, expensively hand-made.

After the closure of the Bauhaus, Moholy-Nagy moved to London where he worked as a display designer for the Simpson's department store, while illustrating books for John Betjeman and doing art direction for the *Architectural Review*. In 1936 he left for Chicago and, under the patronage of Walter Paepcke, founder of the Container Corporation of America, established there the New Bauhaus, which became the Chicago Institute of Design. In Chicago Moholy-Nagy attempted to unify his ideas about art and technology into an ambitious pedagogic programme. After his death from leukaemia, his books *The New Vision* and *Vision in Motion* remain highly important texts in art education.

Bibliography Laszlo Moholy-Nagy *The New Vision, from Material to Architecture* Brewer Warren/Putnam, New York, 1928; Laszlo Moholy-Nagy *Vision in Motion* Paul Theobald, Chicago, 1946; Richard Kostelanetz *Moholy-Nagy* Allen Lane, London, 1972; Lucia Moholy *Marginalien zu Moholy-Nagy: dokumentarische Ungereimtheiten* Richard Sherpe, Krefeld, 1972

2

Mollino designed a chair that was described by *La Repubblica* as 'troppo sexy'. He was so prodigally talented that he almost defies description. And the vast range and variety of his work tempts the unwary critic to dismiss him as a dilettante. Cars and women, speed and sport were chief influences.

To call Mollino an architect describes only the poverty of language. Certainly, he trained as a building designer in Turin's famous Politecnico (where he graduated in Year IX of the Fascist Era), but he was also an occultist, photographer, racing driver, pilot, author, typographer, fashion designer and erotomaniac bachelor, as an inspiring new book explains. He was slightly mad: a favourite photographic self-portrait from about 1960 shows him in a throne (probably of his own design) wearing an orange tunic, in the style of early Jackie Kennedy, which he called the 'Riposo del Guerriero' (Warrior at Rest). Even his friends found him abrasive, blasphemous and disturbed.

The son of an engineer working for the Ansaldo conglomerate, Mollino was a typical product of Turin. A city of solid engineering and memorable masonry, it paradoxically has a metaphysical character which soothes or disturbs its citizens, depending on their cast: in Turin the tormented Nietzsche found a version of peace while its arcades made an indelible impression on Giorgio de Chirico, who continually repeated their image on his canvases. This city of planes and cars and neo-classicism (not to mention ski slopes) made Carlo Mollino. This extraordinary man was memorably described by the architectural historian Bruno Zevi as 'A man surely in league with the devil. When he opens his mouth and speaks, out come Gillette blades, razors, scimitars and splinters of glass, but also enchanted gardens and monstrous flowers in colours no one had ever seen.'

As preparation for his two most remarkable building designs, Mollino joined the Turin Flying Club to prosecute his infatuation with flight. Also, rather daringly, he climbed the vertiginous landmark Mole Antonelliano to take photographs. In the same year, 1941, intoxicated by speed and height, came his Ippica, Turin's riding school, and six years later his architectural masterpiece, the ski station at Lago Nero. This, significantly, was commissioned by Piero Dusio, the entrepreneur and ski fanatic who owned the Cisitalia car company (makers of the very first car to be shown in New York's Museum of Modern Art). Since Le Corbusier, planes had inspired architects and Mollino had been fascinated by Ansaldo's Volo Musculare Umano project (Man Powered Flight). Accordingly, the ski lodge is all swoops and curves, an amazing formal invention defying description by anyone other than Mollino himself, who said it was '*un apparecchio appoggiato sulle neve*' (a plane standing on the snow), adding that he had 'made a chalet fly'. One critic said it was the most three-dimensional building he had ever seen. Later, bi-plane struts, cross bracing and aerial shapes became a feature of his furniture designs.

Skiing remained an inspiration: Mollino wrote a book on downhill racing in 1950 (full of architecturally inspired diagrams explaining parallel turns), but cars were an even more passionate love affair. A 25-year-old Mollino had been painted as a racing driver, but his passion for speed rose to a mania after his father's death. Mollino designed a car for the 1951 Mille Miglia and another for OSCA, but the most typical Mollino automobile was the Bisiluro (Twin Torpedo), a collaboration with the engineer Nardi. Mollino raced it himself at Le Mans in 1955 and held the 750cc record for two years. In this gorgeous machine one streamlined hull contained the engine, the other the driver. But his work was not all sensuous: he also designed a technically efficient air brake.

And then there was the sex. Mollino was an obsessive photographer, the author of the now highly collectible *Il messagio della camera oscura* (1949) (Message from the camera obsura). Photography, eroticism and fashion design became one in his studio. Mollino's nudes (since 1960 mostly Polaroids) are utterly distinctive, with a potent erotic melancholy, like illustrations for Alberto Moravia's dark afternoons. Chaste by the standards of internet porn, they remain beguiling curiosities suggesting the interplay between sex and creativity. One was inspired by Man Ray's 'Violin d'Ingres': a woman, naked except for a black basque, is seen from the rear. Mollino's initials are tastefully inscribed on each buttock and the picture is propped with a bottle of Mumm Cordon Rouge and Marcello Nizzolli's 1948 Olivetti Lexikon 80 typewriter (the iPod of its day). These pictures Mollino used to develop erotic lingerie, like his hero the poet d'Annunzio (whose own underwear designs are preserved at his Lake Garda home, the Vittoriale degli Italiani, alongside his own Ansaldo biplane).

One of Mollino's last projects was an apartment on Turin's via Napione. For this he prepared drawings on an impressive, if impractical, 1:1 scale. Eclectic is scarcely the right word for the decor, but it was a combination of Napoleonic, Egyptianate, Florence Knoll's New York modernism and 'incorruptible' flowers made of maiolica. He never lived there. No one ever visited. It was never photographed for publication, but it does feature as background in some of his photographs. Perhaps, like Des Esseintes, who Mollino so much resembles in an architectural sort of way, he used the premises to prepare love philtres and celebrate the lewd rites of Bacchus.

As a professional eccentric who cultivated no favours, Mollino has never been treated entirely seriously nor acquired the reputation his very odd achievements deserve. But at a time when design is understood, if it is understood at all, as trivial posturing, his fantastic catalogue of sensuous and effective creativity restores dignity to the word. He added to inspiration the elements of persistence and execution that define authentic genius.

Bibliography Giovanni Brino *Carlo Mollino – architecture as autobiography* Thames & Hudson, London, 2005; Fulvio Ferrar & Napoleone Ferrari *The Furniture of Carlo Mollino* Phaidon, London, 2006

1

2

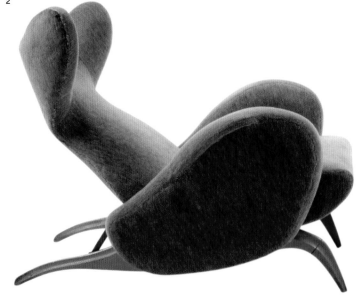

Hanae Mori born 1926

Hanae Mori can claim to be the founder of Japanese fashion and a pioneer of modern Japanese design. After being educated at Tokyo's Christian Women's College she designed costumes for movies before opening her own shop in Tokyo in 1955. The Japanese are curiously self-effacing about some of their achievements and it required Mori's example in proving that there could be excellence in native fashion design to lay the way open for other designers such as Kenzo,

Issey Miyake and Yohji Yamamoto to become major international figures.

Her designs are essentially Western in style, but employ specially woven and dyed textiles which follow Japanese traditions. This successful and influential combination of East and West has put paid to the fallacy, often heard in Japan, that 'only blue-eyed people can be creative'. In 1973 Mori opened a showroom in New York and has shown regularly in Paris since 1977.

Stanley Morison 1889–1967

While working for the Monotype Corporation, Stanley Morison persuaded Eric Gill to become a modern typographer. Gill's first face for Morison was 'Perpetua', derived from the inscriptions on Trajan's column, and he also designed 'Gill Sans' for him. Morison was himself typographic adviser to the Cambridge University Press. He also designed the face called 'Times New Roman' in 1931 for *The Times*. When it was introduced the following year, even the traditionally conservative *Times* readers considered it a masterpiece of clarity and concision; nor did they object that Morison had changed the newspaper's Gothic masthead for a classical one, so impressed were they by the improvements in legibility he brought to their paper.

Bibliography Stanley Morison & Kenneth Day *The Typographic Book 1435–1935* Ernest Benn, London, 1963

4 Perpetua
Perpetua *Perpetua 24pt*
Perpetua *Perpetua 18pt*
Perpetua *Perpetua 14pt*
Perpetua *Perpetua 12pt*
Perpetua *Perpetua 10pt*
Perpetua *Perpetua 9pt*
Perpetua *Perpetua 7pt*

1: Carlo Mollino at the wheel of his 'Bisiluro' (twin torpedo) car which he raced at Le Vingt-Quatre Heures du Mans, 1955.
2: The 'Provocative' armchair for Mollino's own office, 1948. Mollino was a late Futurist at work in the mid-twentieth century, a man of obsessions: speed, flight, shapes and sex.

3: Hanae Mori, haute couture cape dress, Paris autumn-winter, 1988–9.
4: Eric Gill, 'Perpetua' stypeface, commissioned by Stanley Morison for the Monotype Corporation, 1925.

William Morris 1834–96

William Morris was, in one way or another, an influence on virtually everybody in early twentieth-century design. His ideas became widespread, and it is with his ideas rather than his achievements that he has most influenced the history of design, but his prose and poetry were wordy and some of it is now almost unreadable.

Morris was the first to discuss the value of craft principles, such as truth to materials, which were the basis for the Arts and Crafts movement. He was a great lover of simplicity, and propagated an ideal of rustic living, writing in 1880, 'Simplicity of life, begetting simplicity of taste, that is a love for sweet and lofty things, is of all matters most necessary for the birth of the new and better art we crave for; simplicity everywhere, in the palace as well as the cottage.' The problem was, Morris had funny ideas about simplicity.

Although Nikolaus Pevsner singled him out as a pioneer of the Modern Movement in his influential book of 1936, these ideas have, in fact, had a malign influence.

Morris' anti-urban, anti-industrial conservatism undermined the basis for the Modern Movement to flourish in Britain. In fits of socialistic agitation (comfortably removed from the city) he would condemn industrialization, once telling a miner 'I should be glad if we could do without coal.'

Morris is not free from the charge of hypocrisy. He wanted his 'revolution' in values to ensure that 'the twentieth century… gets its goods wholesome and its ornaments hand-made', but made his own ornaments by machine. He spoke of craft principles, but manufactured reproduction furniture. He looked back to an idealized view of the Middle Ages, but was supported in comfort by a modern age he rigorously condemned.

Morris was, however, a talented designer of carpets, wallpapers and furniture, founding the firm of Morris, Marshall & Faulkner in 1862. He later turned to book design with the Kelmscott Press located in a Cotswold house where he could escape from the civilization which, while sustaining him, he so contumaciously despised.

1: William Morris, photographic portrait by Frederick Hollyer, 1884.
2: Kelmscott Manor, the Thames-side home where Morris escaped the 'counties overhung with smoke' and 'the snorting steam and piston stroke'.
3: William Morris, 'Anemone' textile, circa 1880.

4: Olivier Mourgue, 'Djinn' chaise-longue, 1965, polyurethane foam on a metal frame.

Motorama

Motoramas were an invention of <u>Harley Earl</u>'s as a means of showing off his dream cars to the American public. These Fifties' exhibitions were masterly marketing devices where Earl exploited his already hard-pressed designers (getting them to devise ever more extreme fantasies to titillate the public) as well as exploiting the public itself, whom Earl pumped for free market research. Although a colleague of Earl's called him a slave driver for demanding so much creativity from his design team, everyone enjoyed the successes which the Motoramas brought: most of the famous styling motifs of the Fifties were tested at a Motorama before they found their way into production.

Olivier Mourgue born in 1939

Olivier Mourgue, a French furniture and toy designer, studied at the Ecole Nationale Supérieure des Arts Décoratifs. He summarized Sixties design five years before the decade finished with his 'Djinn' zoomorphic fantasy *chaise-longue* and chair. Constructed out of polyurethane foam stretched over a tubular steel armature and upholstered in hard-to-look-at air terminal greens and oranges, they were chosen by film-maker Stanley Kubrick to suggest the future space station in *2001: A Space Odyssey*. Mourgue has recently worked as a colour consultant for Renault and now teaches at the Ecole d' Art in Brest.

Alfonso Mucha 1860–1939

Mucha was born in what is now Czechoslovakia. He became an artistic adviser to the actress Sarah Bernhardt in 1894, and was a minor practitioner of <u>Art Nouveau</u>. His strongest work was his graphic design for posters, but he also attempted some jewellery and furniture.

Olivier Mourgue summarized Sixties design with his 'Djinn' zoomorphic fantasy chaise-longue and chair

4

Josef Muller-Brockmann 1914–96

The Swiss graphic designer Josef Muller-Brockmann was born in Zürich and studied at Zürich's Kunstgewerbeschule (school of arts and crafts) before setting up his own practice in 1936. 'Sans serif as the Expression of our Age' was his motto. He worked in exhibition design from the Thirties to the Fifties and became a graphic consultant to IBM Europe, an equivalent of Paul Rand in the United States. Other clients included Geigy, Rosenthal and de Bijenkorf. His style is the Swiss school of austere minimalism – 'neue typographie' – which has enjoyed an international influence. He believed 'Quality is largely an attitude. If we insist on it in every small thing, it will permeate everything we do.'

Bibliography Kerry William Purcell *Josef Muller-Brockmann*, Phaidon, London, 2006

Peter Muller-Munk 1904–67

Peter Muller-Munk was one of the second generation of American designers, following the example of Raymond Loewy and his contemporaries, but with a degree of extra tact and discretion. He inaugurated the first professional course in industrial design at Pittsburgh's Carnegie Institute of Technology in 1936 and established his own consultancy in the steel town in 1945, specializing in corporate and product design for Westinghouse, US Steel and Texaco. He was one of the founders of the International Council of Societies of Industrial Design (ICSID), whose first president he became in 1957.

Bruno Munari 1907–98

Bruno Munari was born in time to be one of the late Futurists, although Picasso called him 'the new Leonardo'. He worked in Milan in the Thirties, mostly on graphics, in the company of Fortunato Depero and Ulrico Prampoline. Munari was involved in various ambiguous artistic movements until in 1957 he started working seriously and consistently for Danese. His work combines humour with sophistication and intellect: there was a 'Sedia per Visite Brevissime' (a Chair for Very Short Visits) of 1945; a 'Libro Illegibile' (unreadable book) of 1951 and a knitted tubular lamp of 1964. Munari was the author of many books and articles including *Design as Art* in 1987. The Munari principle was 'lucidity, leanness, exactitude and humour'. Munari was one of Milan's intellectuals, always seeing meanings in shape, colour, gesture and form. In 1963 he published a *Supplemento al dizionario italiano*, a photo guide – amusing, yet scholarly – to Italian hand gestures.

Bruno Munari was one of Milan's intellectuals, always seeing meanings in shape, colour, gesture and form

1

1

Keith Murray 1892–1981

Keith Murray was born in New Zealand and moved to England with his parents in 1906. He studied at the Architectural Association in London, but the depressed condition of the architectural market encouraged him to look for his first job elsewhere, and he chose the minor arts of glass and ceramics, working for Stevens & Williams of Brierly Hill and Josiah Wedgwood, respectively. His simple geometric designs were influenced both by what he had seen of Scandinavian design at the Paris exhibition of 1925, as well as by his own architectural training. In 1936 he became one of the first of the Royal Society of Arts' 'Royal Designers for Industry'. He found his way back into architecture in the later Thirties and designed Wedgwood's new factory at Barlaston, Staffordshire.

Bibliography *The Thirties* exhibition catalogue, Arts Council, London, 1979

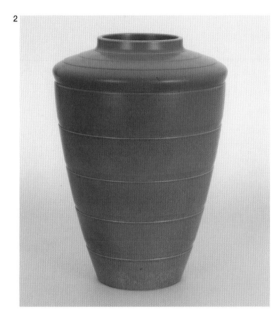

2

Museum of Modern Art

The art critic Robert Hughes wrote that 'if America is design-conscious, then the wells of its obsession were dug by the Museum of Modern Art's Alfred H. Barr'.

MoMA is a part of the New York way of life. Its staff have included Philip Johnson and Eliot Noyes, and its governing body Walter Gropius and Marcel Breuer. Its building, on West 53rd Street, finished in 1939 to the design of Philip L. Goodwin and Edward Durrell Stone, is one of America's first complete essays in the International Style, and thus was a rare case of form perfectly matching function. From the beginning the Museum set out to promote the Modern Movement, and ran a hugely influential series of exhibitions, 'The International Style' (1932), 'Machine Art' (1934), 'Organic Design in Home Furnishings' (1940) and 'Good Design' exhibitions annually during a period in the Fifties. These have firmly established MoMA as a world leader in taste.

The aestheticism of Alfred H. Barr's attitude to modern art was inherited by the Museum's design department, which collects and displays manufactured objects purely on the basis of their appearance. MoMA's architecture department has been more radical. Having done a great deal to establish the character of 'modern' architecture, the Museum then helped reverse the orthodoxy, commissioning the lectures that became Robert Venturi's *Complexity and Contradiction in Modern Architecture* in 1966 and organizing a huge exhibition about the Beaux-Arts in 1975. Ironically, both these ventures contributed to the intellectual atmosphere that encouraged the growth of Post-Modernism.

Philip Johnson added a wing to the building in the style of Mies van der Rohe in 1951, and in 1983 Cesar Pelli's Museum Tower took advantage of the 'air rights' over Goodwin and Stone's originally modest structure. In 2005 a yet more radical development by Yoshio Tanaguchi was opened. By this time, MoMA had become institutionalized and inflexible. The architecture critic of the *New York Times*, Nicolai Ouroussoff said the once influential design galleries had 'the feel' of 'a high-end furniture and design showroom'. Thus the enduring paradox of all museums of design.

Hermann Muthesius 1861–1927

Hermann Muthesius was one of the *éminences grises* behind the formation of the Deutsche Werkbund and the importation of English design ethics into Germany. He can be seen as one of the intellectual originators of the Modern Movement.

Muthesius was made superintendent of the Prussian Board of Trade for Schools of Arts and Crafts in 1903. From 1896 to 1903 he had been attached to the German Embassy in London, where he researched English housing, and wrote an article about C.R. Ashbee for the German magazine *Dekorative Kunst* in 1898. In 1904–5 he published a three-volume account of English architecture, *Das Englishe Haus* in which he particularly praised the work of the late-nineteenth-century architects, and which became a fundamental influence on German taste. Muthesius' ideas on design were widely publicized in 1914 when he was involved in an animated debate with Henry van de Velde on the approach to be followed by the Werkbund. Muthesius said that it should support the concept of *Typisierung* (standardization of objects), while Van de Velde supported freedom of artistic expression. Muthesius' main contribution to design history was theoretical.

Bibliography Joan Campbell *The Werkbund – Politics and reform in the applied arts* Princeton University Press, Princeton, New Jersey and Guildford, 1980

3

1: Josef Muller-Brockmann, 'Watch That Child' poster for the Swiss Automobile Club, 1953 and a 1955 poster for a Beethoven concert at the Tonhalle. Muller-Brockmann's collaboration with the Zurich Tonhalle began in 1950.

2: Keith Murray, engine-turned earthenware vase for Wedgwood, 1930s.
3: The Museum of Modern Art, New York.

n

Ralph Nader born 1934

A public-interest lawyer who took legal action against Chevrolet's Corvair, Ralph Nader changed the design perspectives of the American auto industry. To Nader consumer advocacy is a means of preventing the decline of civilization. He has presented American customers with a spectre of their corporations as huge, inhuman, manipulative syndicates. His goal, in his own words, is 'nothing less than the qualitative reform of the Industrial Revolution'. His attack on the Corvair on the grounds of its lack of safety provisions was made in a book, *Unsafe at any Speed*, which grew out of a paper written at Harvard. After its publication in 1965, General Motors staff spied on him, but without being able to discover anything that could undermine its success. Under the influence of the zealous, monkish Nader, Congress passed 25 pieces of consumer legislation between 1966 and 1973 that were directly influenced by his activism. A US Senator has said, 'More than anyone else, Nader made the consumer movement a considerable factor in American economic and political life.' After Nader it was impossible for a major corporation to market irresponsible products.

Condé Nast 1873–1942

With his friend, Elsie de Wolfe, Condé Nast, the publisher of *Vogue* and many other magazines, was a profound influence on American taste during the first half of the twentieth century by propagating an image of acceptable chic. His publications were targeted at the most affluent and fashionable people in America and Europe, and he flattered his public by commissioning only the best writers and the best photographers to fill not only *Vogue*'s pages, but also those of *Vanity Fair*, *House & Garden* and *Jardin des Modes*. His biographer, Caroline Seebohm, has compared Nast to his contemporary, Scott Fitzgerald: 'Both came from the Mid-West; both were brought up Catholic; both were raised in genteel poverty; and both were preoccupied by, and based their careers on, the implications and consequences of class, money, the East, and sophisticated, unattainable women.'

Bibliography Caroline Seebohm *The Man who was Vogue: the life and times of Condé Nast* Weidenfeld & Nicolson, London, 1982; Viking, New York, 1982

le jardin des modes

PUBLICATION MENSUELLE IMPRIMÉE EN FRANCE

N° 305 — AVRIL 1947
PRIX : FRANCS 60. -

1: Le Jardin des Modes, a part of Condé Nast's consumerist dreamworld.
2: Wooden model of 'Mirella' sewing machine for Necchi, 1956. The model by Giovanni Sacchi was made to a design by Marcello Nizzolli. Sacchi's skill at making drawings plastic made the ambitions of Italian designers and manufacturers tangible.
3: George Nelson, 'Storage Wall' for Herman Miller, 1946. Rationalizing the office landscape was one of the great achievements of American designers at mid-century.

Necchi

Necchi is a Milanese sewing machine manufacturer, which employed Marcello Nizzoli in the early years of Italy's post-War *ricostruzione*. Nizzoli's 'Mirella' of 1956 is a perfect symbol of the formal perfection of recent Italian industrial design. Giorgio Giugiaro is now responsible for Necchi design.

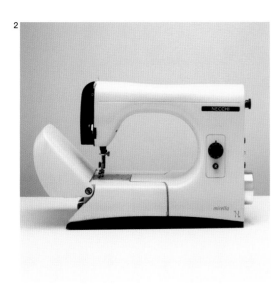

2

George Nelson 1908–86

George Nelson was perhaps the best-known American designer of what might be called the European School, a group of architects and designers more or less associated with the ideals and the educational programmes of New York's Museum of Modern Art, who repudiated the commercialism of Raymond Loewy and the other purveyors of styling.

Nelson was born in Hartford, Connecticut, and graduated in architecture from Yale University's School of Fine Arts in 1931. The winner of a Prix de Rome, Nelson travelled in Europe from 1931 to 1933 and became one of the first Americans to discover the revolution taking place in European architecture and design. He was instrumental in introducing Mies van der Rohe to the United States. On his return from Europe in 1933 Nelson, with colleagues Howard Myers, Henry Wright and Pal Grotz, founded *Architectural Forum*, a journal which, like the *Architectural Review* in England, promoted Modernism, but, unlike its English counterpart, served also as a voice of corporate power, or, at least, one part of it. From 1936 he worked on architecture and interior design projects, pioneering pedestrian malls and designing a 'Storage Wall' system, with which he first made his reputation as a furniture designer. He worked for Herman Miller from 1946, to whom he introduced Charles Eames. In 1947 Nelson set up his own offices in New York. In 1965 he designed the 'Action Office' for Herman Miller, an early attempt in pre-automation days to find a rational, ergonomic solution to the bureaucratic environment, and in 1968 the Editor 2 typewriter for Olivetti.

With his journalism, as well as his work at the International Design Conference at Aspen, Colorado, Nelson became one of the most witty and articulate spokesmen for American design. Of patronage he has said: 'It's always the same, you've either got the Church or you've got IBM.' But he is better known perhaps for appearing on committees and conference platforms all over the world, and for his books, than for his design projects themselves.

Bibliography George Nelson *The Problems of Design*, Whitney Library of Design, New York, 1957

With his journalism, Nelson became one of the most witty and articulate spokesmen for American design

3

Marcello Nizzoli 1887–1969

One of the greatest of all product designers, Marcello Nizzoli was the first and most influential of designers to work for Olivetti, the Italian business-equipment company.

He was born at Boretto and studied at the School of Fine Arts in nearby Parma. His first calling was that of painter and his first public appearance was when he exhibited two pictures at the 'Nuove Tenderize' exhibition of 1914. He began to gain a varied reputation as a poster, fabric and exhibition designer, and was hired by Adriano Olivetti in 1938 to work in the advertising office (which the company had established in 1931). He went on from there to design a series of machines which have become 'classics' of modern industrial design: the 'Lexicon 80' (1948), the 'Lettera 22' (1950) and the 'Divisumma 24' (l956). For Necchi he designed the 'Mirella' sewing-machine (1956). All shared a sculptural sophistication which found expression in organically curved body shells that hide the mechanical components; Nizzoli also paid great attention to the cut-lines in his products, as well as to the application of graphics.

Nizzoli paid great attention to the cut-lines in his products, as well as to the application of graphics

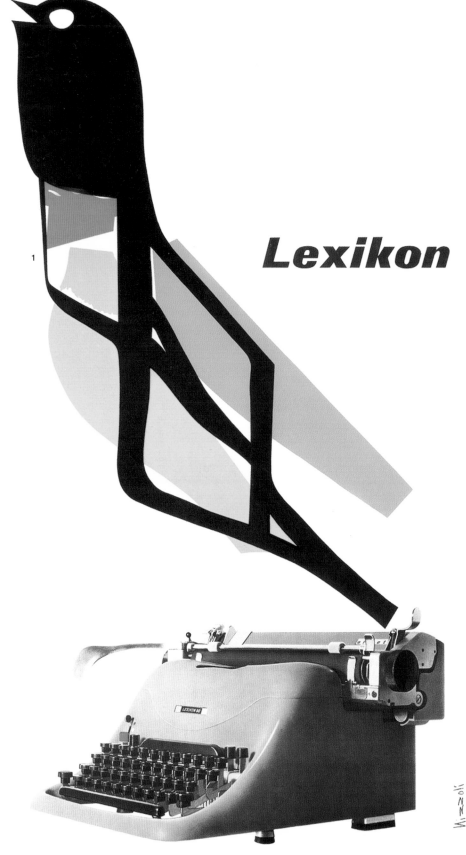

Lexikon

olivetti

Isamu Noguchi 1904–88

Isamu Noguchi is a Japanese–American sculptor who as one of the first Guggenheim fellows, went to Paris in 1927, where he met the sculptors Constantin Brancusi and Alberto Giacometti. He came to notice as a furniture and lighting designer in the Forties when both sculpture and furniture design were becoming more organic and more free. He has made designs both for Knoll and for Herman Miller, but is best known for his wire and paper lampshades whose celebrity created an internationally acknowledged stereotype. Noguchi, who made a speciality of large abstract sculptures designed to dignify corporate headquarters across America, said 'Everything is sculpture.'

Bob Noorda born 1927

A graphic designer, Bob Noorda was born in Amsterdam but since 1952 has lived and worked in Milan. After some distinguished poster campaigns for their tyres, he became art director of Pirelli in 1961. Noorda was one of the founders of Unimark, a multi-disciplinary Milanese consultancy, in 1965. He was responsible for all the signs on Franco Albini's Milan subway system, the 'Metropolitana'. At the same time, with Massimo Vignelli, Noorda designed the handsome signage for the Manhattan subway system. Typical of his approach, Noorda conducted serious research into levels of visibility and the legibility of certain letter-forms in subway conditions, but equally typically the result he achieved had a very light touch.

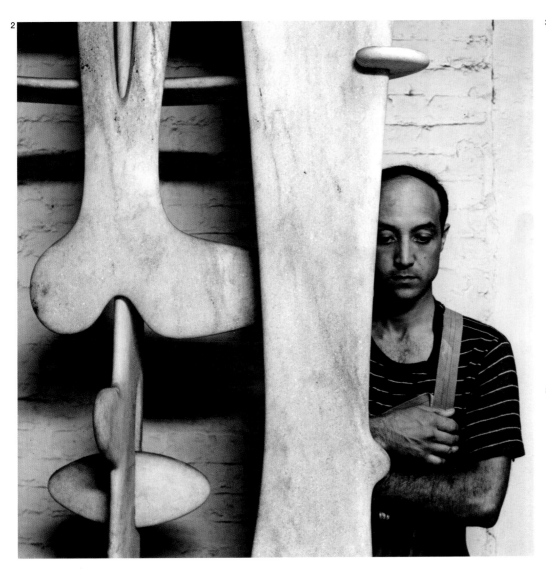

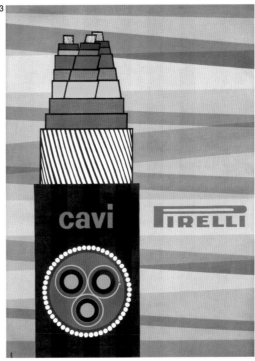

1: Advertisements and sketches for Olivetti's 'Lexikon 80', 1949. As well as products, Nizzoli, took charge of ads for Olivetti. Avian forms influenced the sculpture of office equipment.

2: Isamu Noguchi, photographic portrait by Arnold Newman, 1947.

3: Bob Noorda, advertisement for Pirelli's cables, 1957 and Noorda and Vignelli's design for the New York subway signage, late 1960s.

John K. Northrop 1895–1981

John Knudsen Northrop was a romantic aircraft engineer whose remarkable, visionary designs donated the shapes of streamlining to popular culture. A pioneer of all-metal aircraft construction, Northrop was also one of the enthusiasts for the 'flying-wing' concept, in which the wings and fuselage merge (which Norman Bel Geddes made popular in his book, Horizons). Northrop was co-founder and chief engineer of Lockheed and the designer of the 'Vega' aeroplane which Amelia Earheart used on her solo Atlantic crossing of 1932. Although his friend Donald Douglas once remarked in the 1940s that 'every major aircraft in the sky has some Jack Northrop in it' he retired, demoralized, in 1952, after the armed forces had cancelled two of his 'flying-wing' designs.

Bibliography E.T. Wooldridge *Winged Wonders – The Story of the Flying Wings* National Air and Space Museum, Washington, 1983

Eliot Noyes 1910–77

Eliot Noyes was the son of a Harvard professor of English, and was educated at Andover and later at Harvard's School of Architecture, where he met Walter Gropius and Marcel Breuer. As an archaeology student at Andover he had first read Le Corbusier's *Vers une architecture*, and Gropius's teaching confirmed his enthusiasm for the European design ethic.

Under Gropius' sponsorship, Noyes became the director of industrial design at New York's Museum of Modern Art, a post he held both immediately before and immediately after the Second World War. But it was the War itself which was to have a decisive effect on Noyes' career as a designer. In the Army Glider Program he met Thomas Watson, the son of the founder of IBM. He renewed the acquaintance in the later Forties while he was briefly working in the office of Norman Bel Geddes, who held a consultancy contract with the company, and Watson then employed him as a designer. The work he was to do for IBM, although influenced by the European

Noyes reshaped entire corporations and established new standards of integrity and efficiency in American design

1: Northrop with his YB-49 flying wing prototype, 1949.
2: Wooden model for Cummins diesel engine, 1964. In Noyes, the Bauhaus ethic, learnt from Walter Gropius, was passed straight onto American business.

3: Eliot Noyes, model for design of Mobil filling station, 1964.

example of <u>Olivetti</u>, became perhaps the most celebrated design exercise in corporate history. Telling Watson that he 'would prefer neatness', Noyes transformed the entire appearance of the huge corporation. Using <u>Paul Rand</u> to develop new graphics and hiring architects like Breuer to design buildings, Noyes himself took charge of the products and, in the words of the American journalist Ursula McHugh, 'brought the <u>Bauhaus</u> to big business'. In 1956 Noyes was formally appointed corporate design director of IBM, a role whose guaranteed access to the chief executive gave Noyes as much influence over the face of American manufacturing industry as <u>Harley Earl</u> had with his vice-presidency at <u>General Motors</u>. His products for IBM included the 'Selectric' typewriter of 1961 and the 'Executary' dictating machine of 1961. Impressed by the changes which Noyes' corporate identity programme had made on IBM's business, Westinghouse in 1960 and Mobil Oil in 1964 offered him similar appointments and briefs.

Noyes reshaped entire corporations and established new standards of integrity and efficiency in American design. In order to do this he insisted that his clients should accept the following terms of business: they should agree with his design philosophy, they should allow adequate time for the completion of each project, and they should be prepared to pay for quality. He despised market research and said that the first generation of American designers, men like <u>Raymond Loewy</u> and Norman Bel Geddes, might have proved that appearance sells, but 'simply were not motivated by a high enough intent'. Noyes' own house at New Canaan, Connecticut, a masterpiece of American <u>Modernism</u> (with its courtyard, ragstone, <u>Eames</u> chairs and matching <u>Porsches</u>), won Progressive Architecture's design award in 1954.

Bibliography *Art and Industry* exhibition catalogue, The Boilerhouse Project, Victoria and Albert Museum, London, 1982; Gordon Bruce *Eliot Noyes* Phaidon Press, 2007

Antii Nurmesniemi born 1927

The Finnish designer Antii Nurmesniemi studied interior design at Helsinki's Taideteollinen Oppilaitos (applied art school). He worked in an architect's office, designing banks, hotel and restaurant interiors, before setting up his own studio in 1956. He married <u>Vuokko Eskolin</u> (<u>Marimekko</u>'s chief designer) in the Fifties; her reputation rather overshadows his own. His clients include <u>Artek</u> and Wartsila, for whom he has designed a number of domestic objects, including cooking utensils and chairs. In the Sixties and Seventies Nurmesniemi was influential in creating a common international perception of what constituted Finnish design.

3

Olivetti

The Olivetti company was founded in 1908 by Camillo Olivetti (1868–1943) and brought to greatness by his son, Adriano (1901–60). Adriano was celebrated for cultural, social and political avant-gardism, while in more recent years his heirs have been celebrated for what has become known as design management.

Olivetti produced Italy's first typewriter, the 'MI' (using American machine tools), in 1911. In 1932 the portable 'MPI' came on the market. Designed by Aldo Magnelli with his brother, the abstract painter Alberto, this was the first typewriter to be deliberately conceived as a consumer product. That is to say, its body was styled. In 1935 the 'Studio 42' appeared, designed by the painter Xanti Schawinsky and the architects Figini and Pollini. This extraordinary machine created a stereotype for the form of the modern typewriter that took 40 years to change. In 1936 Olivetti commissioned Figini and Pollini to design a new factory in his home town of Ivrea, Piedmont, for the family business-machine company. It became one of the landmarks of Modern Movement architecture in pre-War Italy, alongside Giuseppe Terragni's Casa del Fascio in Como.

Through the enlightened patronage of artists such as Schawinsky and Marcello Nizzoli, Olivetti made his firm's products the symbols of Italian industrial design. The influence of art ran through every aspect of the Olivetti company's character and production: painters and sculptors worked in the publicity department, designed exhibitions and decided what typewriters and comptometers should look like. In 1952 New York's Museum of Modern Art recognized this by holding an Olivetti show, and the influence of this, together with the

dramatic presence of the firm's Park Avenue showroom (designed by Belgiojoso, Perresutti and Rogers), was one of the influences on IBM which inspired that company's president, Thomas Watson, Junior, to hire Eliot Noyes.

Adriano Olivetti was a pioneer of the Italian industrial revolution, a man consumed by social purpose. Not only was he the impresario of the Olivetti 'style', but he was also an influential thinker. He became a member of the Movimento Comunità and wrote or caused to be published many essays and books on social issues. He founded the journals *Zodiac* and *Urbanisticà*, and was awarded a Compasso d'Oro in 1955.

The story of Olivetti was no less than the story of Italian industrial design. At one time or another every great Italian designer has worked in some capacity for the company: Franco Albini, Gae Aulenti, Mario Bellini, Rodolfo Bonetto, Michele de Lucchi, Vico Magistretti, Marcello Nizzoli, Carlo Scarpa, Ettore Sottsass and Marco Zanuso. However, despite its international reputation for excellence, by the late Seventies Olivetti was a debt-laden, moribund company with a stagnant product line of mechanical and electro-mechanical typewriters and some uncompetitive computers. Then in 1978 Carlo De Benedetti became chairman. He still believed in a central role for design in Olivetti, but that role was now interpreted as 'forward-looking marketing input'. He turned the company around in a dramatic manner; under his guidance Olivetti manufactured the first electronic typewriter and began to establish a position as the major European supplier of office automation equipment, word processors, electronic typing systems and mainframe computers. The aesthetic excellence of the products continued, particularly with the influence of Bellini, Sottsass and de Lucchi. In 1983 De Benedetti signed an agreement with America's AT&T whereby the American concern acquired 25 per cent of the Italian company in return for Olivetti having access to AT&T's Bell Labs research facility. Neither company survived intact.

Bibliography *Olivetti* exhibition catalogue, Kunstgewerbemuseum, Zürich, 1960; *Design Process Olivetti 1908–1978* travelling exhibition, catalogue published in 1979 by Olivetti's Direzione Relazioni Culturali/Disegno Industriale Pubblicità, Milan

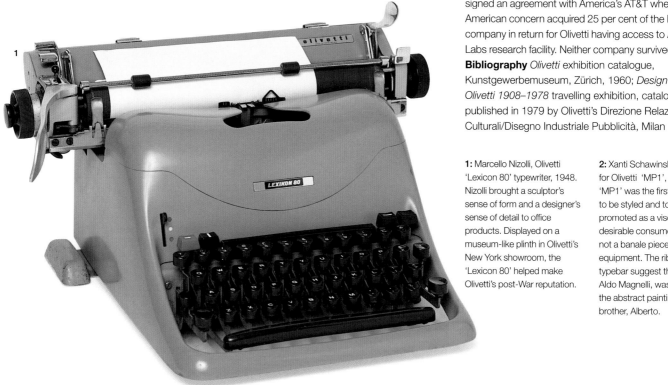

1: Marcello Nizolli, Olivetti 'Lexicon 80' typewriter, 1948. Nizolli brought a sculptor's sense of form and a designer's sense of detail to office products. Displayed on a museum-like plinth in Olivetti's New York showroom, the 'Lexicon 80' helped make Olivetti's post-War reputation.

2: Xanti Schawinsky, poster for Olivetti 'MP1', 1935. The 'MP1' was the first typewriter to be styled and to be promoted as a viscerally desirable consumer product, not a banale piece of office equipment. The ribs on the typebar suggest that designer, Aldo Magnelli, was inspired by the abstract paintings of his brother, Alberto.

Omega

The Omega Workshop was founded by the art critic Roger Fry in 1913, much encouraged by a subscription of £250 from George Bernard Shaw. The idea was to reinvent the Wiener Werkstätte and Paul Poiret's Studio Martine so that young designers could be encouraged, but Omega was Bloomsbury gone to art. It had none of the social purpose of John Ruskin and William Morris and their workshop ideals, but was from the start only a Bohemian retreat for decadent demimondaines with a taste for the decorative. Omega cared nothing for technique and strived mightily for effects alone.

For Fry, Omega represented Post-Impressionist design, and in July 1914 a room-setting showing 'Post Impressionism practically introduced into decoration and furniture' was displayed at the Seventh Salon of the Allied Artists' Association. Omega members also decorated and furnished Roger Fry's own home, Durbin's, near Guildford (1914), and Charleston, near Firle in Sussex, the home of Duncan Grant and Vanessa Bell (1916). Other members of the Omega Workshop included the architect Frederick Etchells (1886–1973), who translated Le Corbusier into English, and even Edward McKnight Kauffer showed some of his pictures at the Workshop before he abandoned painting for posters. Omega closed in 1921.

Sir Roy Strong pinpointed the amateurism of Omega when he recalled that 'any visitor to Charleston while Duncan Grant was still alive will remember the utter chaos… The Omega Workshops come across as a monument to amateurism and muddle. Running through is that deadly lack of seriousness and professionalism that has been the ruin of so much in this country. It is an attitude which goes straight on down to the Festival of Britain.'

Bibliography *The Omega Workshops 1913–1919: decorative arts of Bloomsbury* exhibition catalogue, The Crafts Council, London, 1984

The Oneida Community encouraged members to rise above the fripperies of fashion and enjoy Perfectionism in footwear

Oneida Community

John Humphrey Noyes was born in Putney, Vermont in 1811. He studied theology at Andover and Yale, but is best known for his development of a heresy he called Perfectionism. In 1834 Noyes was instructed by God, as Ann Lee of the Shakers, had been earlier, to create a millennial kingdom on earth. Noyes' version of 'Bible Communism' was also known by its adherents as 'sociology'. Noyes' Perfectionists were less aesthetically distinguished than the Shakers, despite or because of their fewer inhibitions. Besides encouraging mutual criticism, Noyes and his followers enjoyed what he called 'Complex Marriage'. This latter kept individuals in copulatory 'circulation' and predicted the Free Love movements of the Sixties. As a result of scandals arising from the enthusiastic prosecution of Complex Marriage, the Perfectionists were driven out of Vermont to Oneida in upstate New York. Here they built an architecturally conventional model community, but ran businesses making furniture and tools at an impressive profit. The Oneida Community designed the 'Lazy Susan' dining table with its revolving concentric inner element. In 1869, to encourage members to rise above the fripperies of fashion and enjoy Perfectionism in footwear, Oneida patented a design for 'The Final Shoe'. Amusingly, just as Complex Marriage predicted Sixties amoralism, so The Final Shoe predicted the Sixties Chelsea Boot.

Bibliography Dolores B. Hayden *Seven American Utopias – the architecture of communitarian socialism* 1790-1975, MIT Press, Cambridge, Mass., 1976

1

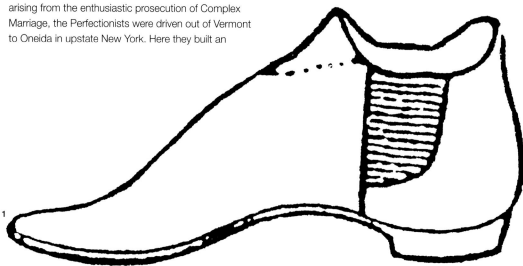

2

Orrefors

The Swedish glass manufacturer Orrefors was established at Kalmar in 1898. Among its artistic directors were Simon Gate and <u>Edward Hald</u>, who pioneered the co-operation between fine-artists, craftsmen and industry now seen as a characteristic of Swedish design. Under Hald, Orrefors produced some of the most refined decorative modern glass.

Amédée Ozenfant 1886–1966

Amédée Ozenfant was an artist who was acutely aware that in the twentieth century the legitimate concern of his vocation was to deal, in one way or another, with the machine. With his friend <u>Le Corbusier</u> he devised the aesthetic philosophy known as Purism, about which they said: 'The picture is a machine for the transmission of sentiments. Science offers us a kind of physiological language that enables us to produce precise physiological sensations to the spectator… The mechanical object can in certain cases move us, because manufactured forms are geometrical, and we are sensitive to geometry.'

He and Le Corbusier published from 1920 to 1925 the review *L'Esprit Nouveau*, which formed the basis for Le Corbusier's epochal book, *Vers une Architecture*. Their ideas were given form in the Pavillon de l'Esprit Nouveau at the Paris Exhibition of 1925.

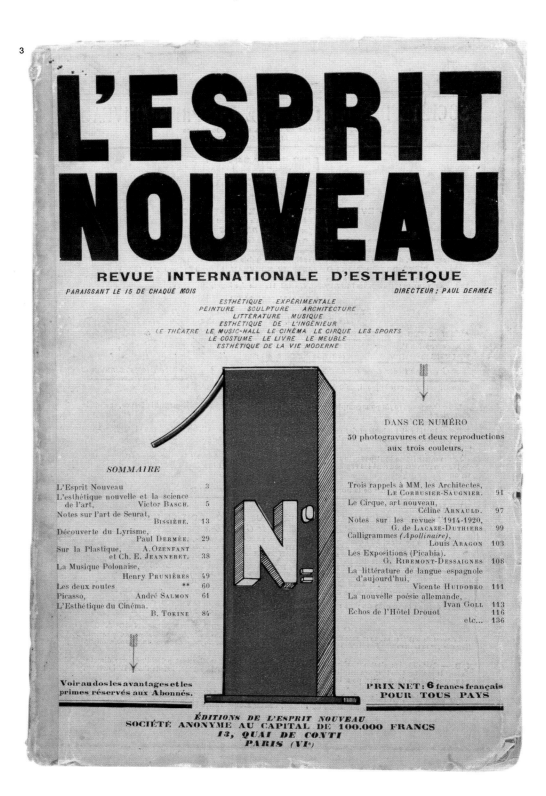

1: 'The Final Shoe' by members of the utopian Oneida Community. In its functional perfection and refusal of decorative excess, The Final Shoe was meant to stand for all time. **2:** Omega Workshops textile for A. H. Lee & Sons, jacquard weave wool and linen, 1913. **3:** Amedee Ozenfant, the cover of *L'Esprit Nouveau*, first edition, 1920.

Vance Packard 1914–96

The American writer Vance Packard studied at Pennsylvania State University and at Columbia. His first job was as a journalist on a Boston daily paper and he then moved into magazine feature writing. Before Ralph Nader he was the most vocal critic of American consumer society. Packard's study of mass psychology and his motivational research gave his books a special edge. *The Hidden Persuaders*, a book about advertising, was published in 1957, his analysis of the class system, *The Status Seekers*, in 1959, and *The Waste Makers* in 1960. Packard's target was often the profligacy he saw in Harley Earl's idea of the dynamic economy, or planned obsolescence as it is sometimes called. When trying to define a consumer 'durable' Packard suggested it was any product that would outlast the final hire-purchase instalment.

Packard lived in New Canaan, Connecticut, where his neighbours at various times included Eliot Noyes, Marcel Breuer and Philip Johnson.

Verner Panton 1926–98

The Danish furniture designer Verner Panton trained in Copenhagen as an architect, and worked in Arne Jacobsen's office before starting his own firm in 1955. He has specialized in refining and executing the idea of a one-piece stacking chair, either in plastic or in wood. The stacking chair in injection-moulded plastic that he designed in 1960 was manufactured by Herman Miller from 1967 to 1975. Later in his career, Panton has become interested in the expressive possibilities of furniture and he designed some bizarre, organically shaped plastic chairs saying, 'A less successful experiment is preferable to a beautiful platitude.' Vitra now produce Panton's one-piece chair very successfully.

Bibliography Jens Bernsen *Verner Panton: space: time: matter* Dansk Design Centre, Copenhagan, 2003

Verner Panton designed some bizarre, organically shaped plastic chairs saying, 'A less successful experiment is preferable to a beautiful platitude'

1

1
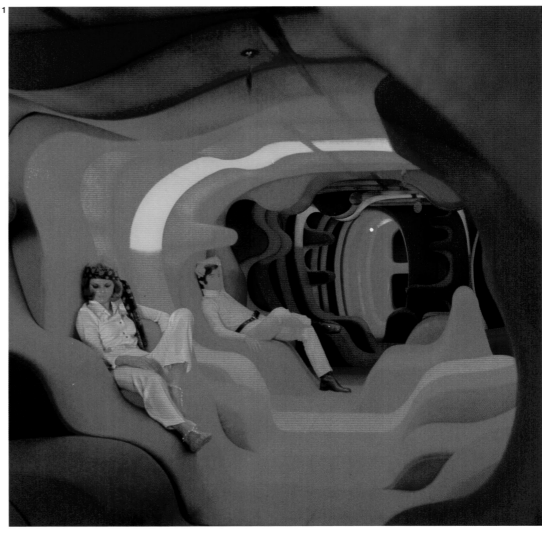

Victor Papanek 1925–98

Victor Papanek is professor of design at the University of Kansas. His book *Design for the Real World* (1967) called attention to the needs of the Third World. It was written out of a conviction that most industrial design was concerned only with 'concocting trivia', and that the world's real needs were being conscientiously ignored. He has publicized his ideas on strenuous lecture tours on all continents, describing to his audiences the need to consider the under-privileged, as well as diminishing world resources. Papanek helped make ecology and environmental awareness part of the designer's consciousness.

Parker-Knoll

Parker-Knoll is a furniture-manufacturing company established in Britain by Willi Knoll and Tom Parker. When the Knoll family split up both Willi and his cousin Hans left Germany to settle in Britain, but only Willi stayed. His contribution to the development of furniture design was a new method of springing which he submitted to Heal's. Heal's did not take it up, but Willi's innovation was noticed by Tom Parker and the two went into business together producing 'lounge' furniture characteristic of suburban Britain during the Thirties. Parker-Knoll produces in its factory in Witney, Oxfordshire, a type of furniture more than an ocean distant from Hans' company on Madison Avenue.

Gregor Paulsson 1890–1977

Gordon Russell once wrote of Gregor Paulsson, 'There are few people from whom I have learned more, or more agreeably, than Gregor Paulsson.' Paulsson was born at Halsingborg, Sweden and educated at Lund University. Studying in Germany, he witnessed the foundation of the Deutsche Werkbund in 1907 and became acquainted with the work and the ideals of John Ruskin, William Morris and C. R. Ashbee. In 1912 he was appointed keeper at Stockholm's National Museum. In 1925 he was commissioner-general for Sweden at the Paris Exhibition, and in 1930 organized the great Stockholm Exhibition. He is perhaps best remembered for two things, one his book, *Vackrare Vardagsvara* (More Beautiful Everyday Things) 1919, the quintessence of the Scandinavian design ethic, and his directorship of the Svenska Sljödföreningen (1920–34). Paulsson persuaded the Swedish Co-operative Society to employ Eskil Sundahl as chief architect and from that moment on the standards of design in Sweden were enhanced at a stroke, as the Co-operative Society was a huge patron of architecture, packaging design and shop-fitting. Much of the character of 'Swedish Modern' can be put down to Paulsson's influence.

He also wrote *The New Architecture* (1916), *The Social Dimension of Art* (1955) and *The Study of Cities* (1959).

2

Bilden överst till vänster visar en interiör från hemutställ-ningen på Liljevalchs 1917 av Uno Åhrén och därunder en interiör från Göteborgsutställningen 1923 av Carl Bergsten. Nederst till vänster en rumsinredning av Kurt v. Schmalen-sée på Stockholmsutställningen 1930.
Ovan en bild från Pavillon d'honneur på Parisutställningen 1925, där Parispokalen av Simon Gate får symbolisera det internationella genombrottet för det svenska konsthantver-ket av lyxklass. Nedan en interiör från "Kontakt med nytto-konstnären" i Göteborg med prov på dagens vackrare var-dagsvara, sammansättningsbara möbler av E. Svedberg, NK.

7

1: Verner Panton, chair for Vitra, 1968 and 'visiona 2' for plastics manufacturer Bayer at the 1970 Cologne Furniture Fair. 'Dralon' joins the artists palette.

2: An article by Gregor Paulsson in *Form* 1:1945, celebrating 100 years of Swedish design.

PEL

PEL stands for Practical Equipment Limited, an offshoot of the Accles and Pollock Group which pioneered in England the use of tubular steel for domestic furniture.

In 1929 Accles and Pollock set up a department at their Oldbury works to make steel furniture frames and 'Pel' was first registered as a company in 1931. The first catalogues were issued in 1932, but the fashionable life of tubular steel was a brief one. Pel furniture filled Marshall and Snelgrove's stores, Lyons Corner Houses and the BBC's Broadcasting House, but it never achieved real popularity. Even John Gloag, who in other contexts was a defender of Modernism, wrote that 'The metal furniture of the Robot modernist school can claim fitness for purpose, and exemplifies a just and original use of material. It expresses the harsh limitations of the movement to which it belongs.'

By the mid-Thirties more and more Finnish plywood was coming into Britain and some of the leading architects and designers preferred it to tubular steel as a medium for modern furniture design.

Bibliography *Pel and Tubular Steel Furniture in the Thirties* exhibition catalogue, Architectural Association, London, 1977

Penguin Books

The publishing imprint founded by Allen Lane in 1935 has been a great disseminator of ideas and thought amongst the general population. Lane's obituarist in *Design* magazine asked of her subject's life and work 'What other achievement in enlightenment is comparable?', and Sir Compton Mackenzie once spoke of the 'Penguin University'. Penguin Books was that rarest of things, a great Modernist project that succeeded.

Lane's career in books began in the office of his uncle, John Lane, of the Bodley Head, publishers of the *fin-de-siècle Yellow Book* which starred Oscar Wilde and Aubrey Beardsley. He said of Penguin: 'I wanted to put into the hands of people like myself the books they would have read if they had gone to university:' Paperbacks were not new: Alabatross Editions and Taunitz Verlag had published them in Germany in the nineteenth century. But Lane's achievement was distinguished by having both a sense of the consumer and a sense of design. Hitherto, book design had been a branch of the printer's craft, but Penguin Books became well-designed consumer products. Penguin rose to prominence in the Thirties, at just the time when the professional graphic designer was emerging from the muck and graft of his trade background, bringing publications on the fringes of art and culture to the ordinary reader at very modest prices. It was the decade of the mixed economy and of democratic opportunity. A new generation of commuters could enter worlds of their own while travelling on the Metropolitan Railway… rather as they do today with iPods.

It was not literature that made Penguin great. Certainly, Hemingway's *Farewell to Arms* was among the first titles, but so too was Susan Ertz' *Madame Claire*. Instead, it was design. Lane's Penguins, like the BBC's *Listener*, were influential in promoting the new modern design in Britain — a strategy which they advanced in spirit by publishing Anthony Bertram's *Design* as a Penguin Special in 1938, and in substance by ensuring their books were as well designed as possible: the original Penguins were proportioned almost exactly on the Golden Section, handy for the pocket of the gabardine mac, with all the titles set in Gill Sans. And there was colour coding: orange for fiction, blue for non-fiction, green for crime. First designs were by Lane's production manager, Edward Young, but immediately after the Second World War, when restrictions on employing foreigners were lifted, Lane employed the Swiss designer-typographer Jan Tschichold as a consultant. His influence was felt until 1961, when Romek Marber provided a new grid for Pelicans and Penguins which took the imprints through the Sixties and into the Seventies when, after Allen Lane's death, there was speculation about whether the 'noblest list in the history of publishing' would degenerate into just another softback house.

Allen Lane was a close friend of Nikolaus Pevsner and published all his most influential books. He was knighted in 1952. Pevsner appears, along with other directors of Penguin Books including philosopher A. J. Ayer and Elizabeth David's future publisher, John Lehmann, in a wonderfully evocative 1955 group portrait called *After the Conference* by Rodrigo Moynihan.

In the Sixties Penguin continued to set the standard for popular book design under the direction of Germano Facetti, one of many Italian immigrants who enlivened and enriched the art and restaurant scene of Swinging London.

Bibliography Phil Baines *Penguin by Design: A Cover Story 1935–2005* Allen Lane, London 2005

Book design had been a branch of the printer's craft, but Penguin Books became well-designed consumer products

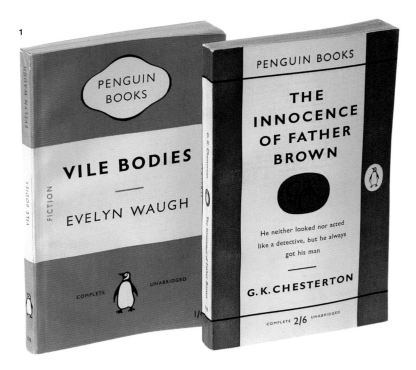

1

Pentagram

Pentagram is the London-based design consultancy founded when the offices of Alan Fletcher, Colin Forbes and Theo Crosby joined Mervyn Kurlansky and Kenneth Grange in 1972. Based on the principle of collaborative inter-disciplinary practice, Pentagram grew to a trans-Atlantic partnership of 19 individuals. For 20 or more years it was an exemplary business model, but the partnership principle was strained by conflicts of ego and generation. Abbott Miller, an Indiana-born graphic designer, described the structural problem, 'You can only add to the mixture; you can't shape it or censor it. That's the problem with democracy'. A specialist in creating corporate identities for its clients, Pentagram had difficulty maintaining its own identity after the departure of founding partner Alan Fletcher in the Nineties. It is now unrecognisable as the idealistic collaborative as originally established.

Bibliography Susan Yelavich (editor) *Profile: Pentagram Design* Phaidon, London 2004

Den Permanente

Den Permanente is a store-cum-exhibition, opened in Copenhagen by the silversmith Kay Bojesen and Christian Grauballe, head of the Holmegaard glassworks, in 1931. The idea was to create a permanent exhibition of Danish design, to act as a stimulus and as a means of raising public taste. Rigid quality standards were imposed and these, together with its popularity, made den Permanente into a genuine influence on the progress of design in Denmark.

Charlotte Perriand 1903–99

Charlotte Perriand trained in Paris at the Ecole de l'Union Centrale des Arts Décoratifs, attending courses run by Paul Follot of Le Printemps department store and Maurice Dufrene of Galeries Lafayette. Her most significant work was done with Le Corbusier in a collaboration that began after she exhibited some wooden furniture at the 'Exposition Internationale des Arts Décoratifs' in 1925, and from 1927 to 1937 she was responsible for all the fitting out in Le Corbusier's atelier.

The *chaise-longue* and armchair that they produced together in 1929 were inspired by Le Corbusier's sketches of bodies in repose. The atelier could not afford to make the chairs, so they were manufactured by Thonet. Perriand became fired with the enthusiasm of the atelier for metal furniture, so much so that she overstated its case. In reaction, frequent trips to the mountains made her familiar with the simple tastes and needs of shepherds, and their *ad hoc* furniture became an important stimulus for her after the Second World War, when the team spirit of Le Corbusier's atelier began to diminish.

Perriand designed a prototype kitchen for Le Corbusier's 'Unité d'Habitation' in Marseilles (1951), and her other late interiors included designs for the Air France and French Tourist offices in London. But during her later career her creative efforts were directed towards planning for leisure and designing for batch production.

2

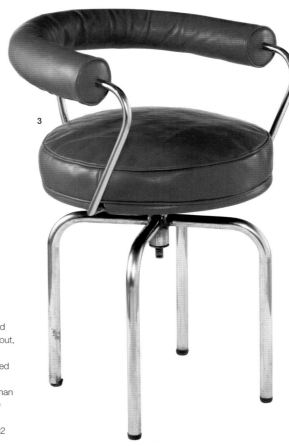

1: From the beginning in 1936, Penguin Books used stylish typography and layout, introducing successive generations to sophisticated graphic design.
2: Pentagram's David Hillman re-designed *The Guardian* in 1988.
3: Charlotte Perriand, B302 swivel chair, 1928–9.

Gaetano Pesce born 1939

Gaetano Pesce was born in Venice and studied at the university there. He was a radical designer from the outset, creating furniture that was conceptual (rather than practical). These concepts were concerned with mortality and alienation, giving his shocking, lumpy chairs and asymmetric bookcases, produced by Cassina, an existential quality. He divides his time between Milan and New York.

Bibliography Andrea Branzi *The Hot House: Italian new wave design* MIT, Cambridge, Mass., 1984

Nikolaus Pevsner 1902–83

Nikolaus Leon Bernhard Pevsner studied at Leipzig, and became an assistant keeper at the Dresden Gallery and then a lecturer at Göttingen University before being driven to England by the threat of Nazi persecution. His arrival in England changed the shape of the study of art, architecture and design in Britain. While before, such writing as there had been about art was of the *belles lettres* sort — genteel discussion of nice topics — Pevsner brought German academic method to Britain and turned the history of art into more of a science.

His books include *Pioneers of the Modern Movement from William Morris to Walter Gropius* (1936), *An Enquiry into Industrial Art in England* (1937), *Academies of Art Past and Present* (1940), *High Victorian Design* (1951), *Some Architectural Writers of the Nineteenth Century* (1973), *A History of Building Types* (1976) and his mammoth multi-volume survey of *The Buildings of England*. Notwithstanding that he actually invented the history of architecture and design as a serious academic subject, Pevsner's contribution to modern design has been much more than a merely scholarly one. His books have had such a huge structural effect on the common perception of history that his influence can be compared to John Ruskin's in moulding taste. Of the three great historians of architecture of the twentieth century, Sigfried Giedion, Reyner Banham and Pevsner, it was Pevsner who concentrated most entirely on the matter of style: with Hegelian determinism Pevsner saw the achievement of Walter Gropius as the necessary, indeed inevitable, conclusion to a series of historical developments which had preceded it.

His *Pioneers of the Modern Movement* was only a moderate success when it was issued by Faber in London in 1936, but when it was reissued by the Museum of Modern Art in 1949 it immediately became a classic. Although the arguments seem nowadays a little stilted, it is the Bible of industrial design for Modernists. Pevsner was at one time a buyer for Gordon Russell and held senior academic posts at Birkbeck College, University of London, and was Slade Professor of Fine Art at Cambridge, 1949–55. He was knighted in 1969. Because of his unfluctuating views about the moral and historical correctness of modern architecture, expressed in his books and during his period on the editorial board of *Architectural Review* during its golden years, Pevsner has come in for some sneering and jeering in recent years from the articulate right wing of the conservationist lobby, in consort with the spokesmen of Post-Modernism. In a way the wheel has come full circle; in his early days on the magazine he was known as 'Plebsveneer' and 'Granny' by some of his colleagues who could not get their minds around his 'modern' concern with social purpose. These same people conveniently ignored that Pevsner had, in 1958, been one of the founders of the Victorian Society, a body devoted to the preservation and understanding of nineteenth century architecture and design.

Bibliography David Watkin *Morality and Architecture* Cambridge University Press, 1978; Timothy Mowl *Stylistic Cold Wars: Betjeman versus Pevsner* John Murray, London, 2000

1

1: Gaetano Pesce, 'Serie Up' furniture, 1969. Pesce designs furniture in challengingly amorphous style. The polystyrene 'Up' chairs, which adapt to the sitter's contours, were made by B&B Italia.

2: The Piaggio Vespa, 1946. One of the chief symbols of Italy's *ricostruzione*, indeed, of Italy as a whole, the design of the Vespa was influenced by aircraft monocoque structures and by the needs of priests and women to step on-board while retaining modesty.

Piaggio

Rinaldo Piaggio started business at Sestri Ponente, near Genoa, in 1884. His company grew into a huge industrial concern, involving ship-building and railway rolling stock. From 1917 Piaggio became obsessed with flight, and from 1923 to 1935 his company produced no fewer than 14 original aircraft.

Piaggio's most famous consumer product, however, was the <u>Vespa</u> motor scooter, designed by the helicopter engineer <u>Corradino d'Ascanio</u>. At the end of the Second World War, Rinaldo's son, Enrico, invited d'Ascanio to design a motor scooter that could be manufactured at his factory at Biella, whose production was at the time restricted to aluminium saucepans. Announced in March 1946, the Vespa had an ingenious, but simple, technical specification and all-enveloping bodywork that suggested the influence of aircraft practice. In a sense, it was the Italian equivalent of the <u>Citroën</u> 2CV. The distinctive step-through frame was designed so that priests and women could mount it and retain modesty.

If there was one symbol of industrial Italy, it would be Piaggio's Vespa.

Bibliography Centrokappa (ed.) *Il Design italiano degli anni '50* Editoriale Domus, Milan, 1980

2

The Vespa had an ingenious, but simple, technical specification and all-enveloping bodywork that suggested the influence of aircraft practice

Frank Pick 1878–1941

Frank Pick, a solicitor who was one of the founders of the Design and Industries Association (DIA) when commercial manager of London Transport in the Twenties, instituted one of the most thoroughgoing corporate identity schemes ever by employing the architect Charles Holden and the typographer Edward Johnston to create a unified appearance for the system. It was a British realization of the theory of 'standardization' for which Hermann Muthesius had argued almost two decades before.

1: Harry Beck's Underground map of 1931 remains perfect evidence of Goethe's definition of genius: 'putting form on the indeterminate'. The reality of the tube system looks like a bowl of spilled spaghetti.

2: Pininfarina evolved from metal-bashing carrozzeria to entrepreneur of beauty. Ferrari 365 GTB4 Daytona Berlinetta, 1968. Alfa-Romeo 6c 2500 1948. Lancia Flaminia, 1958.

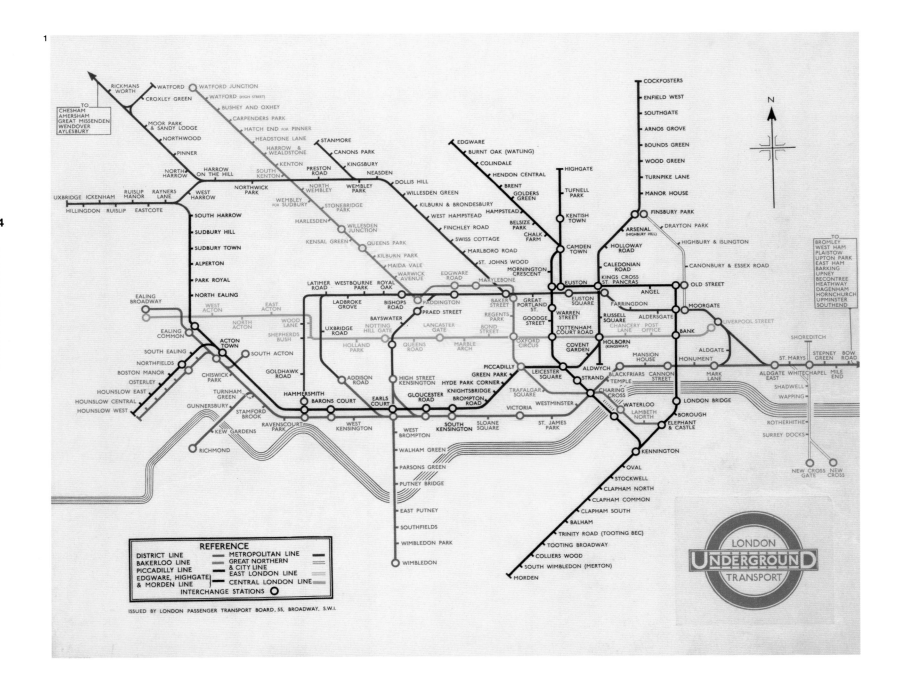

1

Pininfarina

Battista Farina (1893–1966) was born in Turin. He travelled in the United States in 1920 to learn about the new techniques of automobile production, and established his own bodywork shop in his native city in 1930. In 1959 he handed it over to his son, Sergio (born 1926). Two years later, out of respect to Battista, who was affectionately nicknamed Pinin, its name was changed to Pininfarina.

Of all the great Italian *carrozzerie* (before ItalDesign) Pininfarina has been the most concerned with research into the practical, as well as aesthetic, possibilities of car design. In addition, more than any other Italian firm of designers, it has contributed a language of form. The great cars to bear the badge with the cursive 'f' have established stereotypes it is hard to avoid, and almost impossible to surpass in beauty; the great cars include the Lancia Aurelia B20 (1952), the Austin A40 (1958), the Ferrari 330GT (1964), the Austin 1100 (1963), the Ferrari Daytona (1971), the Peugeot 504 (1968) and the Ferrari 308 GTB4 (1975). The carrozzeria worked somewhat like a studio, incubating individuals who developed their own reputations while contributing to the Pininfarina legend. These included Paolo Martin and Aldo Brovarone, responsible for the gorgeous 1965 Ferrari 365SP sports-racing car and the radically elegant 1974 Lancia Gamma Coupe.

2

2

2

Giancarlo Piretti born 1940

Giancarlo Piretti studied at the Istituto Statale d'Arte in Bologna. He has worked ever since leaving college as Castelli's director of research and design. Of all the Italian furniture manufacturers, Castelli best understands the realities of the industrial process and Piretti's classic 'Plia' folding chair of 1969 is a serious piece of engineering intended for mass-production. Although not daringly experimental, it is a superb piece of design, as Piretti made a chair with harmony and purity out of the most elemental materials and shapes. Recently he has worked with <u>Emilio Ambasz</u>' Open Ark, collaborating on the design of the 'Vertebra' chair (see page 68) and the 'Osiris' light for Erco.

Warren Plattner born 1919

Warren Plattner studied architecture at Cornell University in Ithaca, New York. He then worked in the offices of <u>Raymond Loewy</u> and <u>Eero Saarinen</u>. Throughout the Fifties Plattner worked on the design of wire furniture which <u>Knoll</u> eventually put into production in 1966. After setting up his own studio at New Haven, Connecticut in 1967, Plattner concentrated on big-budget contract interiors, the very biggest of which was the glittery and tragic 'Windows on the World' restaurant in New York's World Trade Center (where he collaborated with <u>Milton Glaser</u>).

1: Giancarlo Piretti, 'Plia' tscaking chair, 1969.
2: Ben Pon was inspired by an industrial pallet to make the Volkswagen Transporter, 1949.

3: Gio Ponti's 'Superleggera' (super light) chair, 1957, was inspired by the vernacular chairs of Chiavari on the Ligurian coast, but became a classic of sixties interiors.

1

Paul Poiret 1879–1944

The pioneer French couturier Paul Poiret was one of the great entrepreneurs of the fashion industry. He was known as the 'Sultan of Fashion', and the 'Pasha of Paris', both on account of his aggressively masculine admiration of women and because he introduced oriental influences into early twentieth-century clothes. His greatest achievement was to dispose of corsetted Edwardian formalism and replace it with 'Hellenic' dresses in a loose look that fell from the shoulders. In this he was much influenced by the exotic *bizarrerie* of Diaghilev's Ballet Russe when the company first appeared in Paris in 1908, and many critics assumed that his substitution of sombre greys and khakis with jonquils, cherry reds, Delft blues and begonia pinks had been directly lifted from the example set by Leon Bakst's costumes for them.

Poiret was an effective self-publicist, commissioning the artist Georges Lepape to illustrate a vanity publication, *Les Choses de Paul Poiret* (1911–12). He also started his own-brand line of cosmetics and perfumes and ran a craft workshop for poor girls, coyly named 'Martines' after one of his daughters. A genuinely original talent in marketing fashion and design, Poiret was also an egocentric, extravagant man. He failed to adjust to the different Europe that existed after the First World War, and died in poverty after attempting to continue living in unrepentant profligacy in his later years.

Bibliography Paul Poiret *En habillant l'époque* Grasset, Paris, 1930

Ben Pon dates unknown

Ben Pon is an unlikely hero of design, a Dutch entrepreneur from Amersfoort who was active in the British Zone of occupied Germany in the years immediately after the Second World War. At the time, the Volkswagen factory was in British hands and Army officers invited experts, including some from the very long-forgotten Humber Car Company, to offer a verdict on Dr Porsche's ingenious car design. The experts from Humber were sceptical, so control of the mad Nazi project that was Volkswagen passed back to the Germans and Heinz Nordhoff was put in charge. Nordhoff was soon visited by Pon who knew about the *Plattenwagen*, literally 'flat car' that was used in the Wolfsburg factory. This was an industrial pallet attached to a Volkswagen drive train used for moving goods round internally. Pon's proposal was to develop this into a light, forward-control van. Working with Volkswagen engineers and at the wind tunnel of the Hochschule für Gestaltung in Baunschweig, Pon developed an elegant, aerodynamic, curvaceous design, both elementally simple, yet warm and charming too. This was the original Volkswagen Transporter, a design readily adapted for campers, surfers and an astonishing variety of single-interest groups. Nordhoff said, admiringly: 'The point of departure is clean and without compromise. Only this car has its cargo floor exactly between the axles.' In all essentials Ben Pon's superbly simple Volkswagen Transporter remained in production until 1990, making it more long-lived than Dr Porsche's Beetle itself.

Gio Ponti 1891–1979

Gio Ponti founded the leading Italian architecture and design journal *Domus* in 1927. As the moving spirit behind the Monza Biennale and the Milan Triennale (as it became), Ponti was a major force behind twentieth-century Italian design.

Throughout the Forties and Fifties he worked for Arflex, Cassina and Nordiska Kompaniet, but is best remembered as architect of the Pirelli Tower, the Milanese office building of 1956 which was to Europe what the Seagram Building was to the United States. Similarly, his 'Superleggera' chair, which Cassina began to manufacture in 1957, has become a true classic and has passed into the international urban culture because of its almost universal use in Italian restaurants of a particular price bracket. Ponti got the idea from vernacular fishermen's chairs seen at Chiavari near Genoa. Despite the quality of his own actual furniture and architectural designs, Ponti's real influence has been as a propagandist. He was a moving force behind the establishment of the Compasso d'Oro awards and, as professor of architecture at Milan Polytechnic, he was able to train and form the opinions of generations of Italian designers, promoting the importance of tradition and his commitment to *la dolce vita*.

2

3

Pop

The British-based Pop movement of the Sixties helped break down the autocracy of the <u>Modern Movement</u>, introducing in its place more expressive possibilities in design. It began with fine art but embraced hitherto neglected popular culture, making it intellectually respectable. The first response was in fashion, by <u>Mary Quant</u>, and then in furniture and interiors, with a spotted paper chair by Peter Murdoch, inflatable furniture, and <u>Zanotta</u>'s 'Sacco' chair. At the same time, previously drab shop fronts began to make a colourful impact on the high street.

British Pop was a profound influence on <u>Ettore Sottsass</u> and <u>Elio Fiorucci</u>. In many ways the sense of liberation created by the Pop movement opened up numerous paths that design has taken in the past generation, from the Crafts Revival to <u>Post-Modernism</u>. Pop introduced the possibility that design might fill symbolic rather than utilitarian needs, and created wide public interest in design.

1: Willie Landels demonstrates his latex and foam 'throw away' chair for Zanotta, circa 1965. Disposability was an assumption of Pop theory.

2: Max Clendinning, Pop interior of his own house, Alwyne Road, Canonbury, London, 1969.

Ferdinand Porsche 1875–1951

Ferdinand Porsche was the designer of the Volkswagen and the founder of the Stuttgart company that bears his name. He had a strong sense of personal identity and was so proud of an honorary degree from Vienna's Technische Hochschule that it was eventually incorporated into the company name Dr Ing hc F. Porsche AG. His original consultancy business was known, less snappily, as Porsche Konstruktionsburo fur Motoren-Fahrzeug-Luftfahrzeug-und-Wasserfahrzeugbau.

He worked first for Lohner (designing a truck with a revolutionary drive system employing electric motors within the wheels), then for 23 years with Daimler. An early project included the trolley buses used in Aberdare, South Wales. His consultancy was founded in 1931 and funded by Adolf Rosenberger, a Jewish racing driver. In 1932 the Soviet Union offered him the role of chief designer of the state-sponsored Russian vehicle industry, but he preferred to go to work for Adolf Hitler. In May 1933 the new Chancellor decided to go motor racing and Porsche persuaded Hitler to split the half million Reichsmark subsidy between Daimler-Benz and Auto Union. The following year Porsche's rear-engined V16 Auto Union appeared. On 22 June the same year, Hitler (who did not drive) signed a contract to make a People's Car to Porsche's design. The specification demanded accommodation for two adults and three children, a cruising speed of 100km/h and a price of 1000 Reichsmarks. For this 'Volkswagen' Porsche adapted designs he had earlier made for Zundapp and NSU. Die Autostadt was built near Hanover as a factory town to build what the NSDAP now called the Jampf-durch-Freude-Wagen. After 1945 it was re-named Wolfsburg.

The Porsche itself came into being because Porsche, after a spell in prison (for collaborating with the Nazis during the War), and his son, Ferdinand Porsche II (born l909), known as 'Ferry', wanted to make a sports car, but as it was a state-owned firm the enterprise was considered too frivolous for Volkswagen. They decided to set up their own company, mainly using Volkswagen parts for their first car. Taking the design office number 356, this was made in 1949 at Gmund, Carinthia, in Austria. The body was designed by Erwin Komenda, who employed the experience he had gained at Auto-Union, and also, significantly, from his work in the wind tunnel at the Zeppelin docks in Friedrichshafen and in the Stuttgart tunnel operated by Wunibald Kamm, the great aerodynamics pioneer. Ferry Porsche encouraged him to keep the car as low as possible, so that the nose was only just above road level. For the engine Porsche used a flat four, designed by F.X. Reimspiess and derived from the original NSU design which had gone into the Volkswagen.

In 1969 Anatole Lapine, a General Motors designer, joined the Porsche studio in the Stuttgart Entwicklungszentrum. This marked the beginning of a more commercial phase of the Porsche company, culminating in 2006 with the acquisition of a controlling stake in the whole Volkswagen Group.

3: Porsche 356B 1600 Coupé. More so than any other manufacturer in any other field, Porsche design has been inspired by ideas of continuity and evolution. This example is from 1963.

Post-Modernism

Although the term 'post-modernism' has been familiar in literary criticism for many years (at least since the publication of Ihab Hassan's *The Dismemberment of Orpheus: toward a Post-modern Literature* in 1971), it has only more recently been applied in the context of architecture and design. The author of this usage is Charles Jencks (born 1939), an American academic-journalist living in London. Post-Modernism is the most successful of the many style-labels which Jencks has coined, but has in fact influenced journalists and publishers more than practising architects.

Jencks' idea was to find a name for a cause adopted by a number of architects disillusioned by the failures of modern architecture to redress *all* the ills which its pioneers had established as its legitimate target. Many of these reacted by adopting meretricious ornament and cheap details, or robbed exotic styles and cultures for easy effects, or else produced designs that were meant to be no more than jokey. In furniture design Post-Modernism appeared in Studio Alchymia and Memphis (which borrowed from Italian radical design of the 1960s).

The architect Berthold Lubetkin dismissed Post-Modernism as 'Transvestite Architecture' in his 1982 Gold Medal Address at London's RIBA. A year later, Bruno Zevi, the distinguished Italian architectural critic, also speaking at the RIBA, called it 'narcissistic nonsense' and declared it to be a 'minor pseudo-cultural event'. Nevertheless, some eminent architects and designers (in particular, Robert Venturi and Michael Graves) are content to be identified with Post-Modernism, while others feel it to be a temporary phase only. Despite the radical claims of cheer-leaders like Jencks, Post-Modernism is only an errant child of Modernism. In *Modernism* (1976), Malcolm Bradbury and James McFarlane saw this as true of its literary manifestation: 'The argument around Post-Modernism now adds to the abundance of versions of Modernism.'

Terence Riley, influential curator of design at the Museum of Modern Art in New York, blamed by *New York* magazine for inflaming the lust of bankers for Mies van der Rohe furniture, described his and his Museum's relationship with Post-Modernism:

'In 1984, around when I got out of school, it was the heyday of Post-Modernism. If you really wanted to lose a job quickly, you'd say you were interested in modern architecture. That was like saying you were a sex offender… I grew up in Woodstock, Illinois: redbrick courthouse, white dome, county jail nextdoor. And what's more, it actually had history. I come from a real pre-Modern town, so Post-Modernism would never have any interest to me, because of its inherent falseness.'

Jack Pritchard 1899–1992

Jack Pritchard was a furniture manufacturer and entrepreneur who had a huge influence on the introduction of modern architecture and design into Britain. While still at Cambridge, he designed and made his own chair. His first post-university job was with Michelin, but he soon left to work for Venesta Plywood, a large building materials supplier, which brought him into contact with many architects. In 1930 he was able to commission Le Corbusier and his brother, Pierre Jeanneret, to design a stand for Venesta at an exhibition, and soon after Laszlo Moholy-Nagy was commissioned to design advertisements for the firm. It was Pritchard who invited Walter Gropius to England, and Gropius stayed with him at his flats in Lawn Road, Hampstead, which he had commissioned Wells Coates to design. At this time Pritchard set up Isokon to make furniture out of moulded plywood; Gropius acted as consultant designer and Marcel Breuer designed a *chaise-longue*.

Bibliography Jack Pritchard *View from the Long Chair* Routledge & Kegan Paul, London, 1984

Ulla Procopé 1921–68

Ulla Procopé was a ceramic designer employed by Kaj Franck at the Arabia factory in Helsinki. She is most celebrated for Arabia's 'Ruska' service, a characteristically Finnish design in those rich, apparently natural textures and materials that do not compromise efficient function. In the case of 'Ruska' this means that it looks very folksy, but is oven-to-table serviceable.

Jean Prouvé 1901–84

The French furniture designer Jean Prouvé was born in Paris, the son of Victor, a painter in the Art Nouveau Nancy School who moved in the same circles as Gallé and Majorelle.

Apprenticed to a blacksmith, he worked in 'art metal'. In 1924 he opened a Nancy workshop and throughout the Twenties and Thirties Prouvé made metal furniture which attempted to redefine some of the mechanical aspects of seating. Le Corbusier, Mallet-Stevens and Pierre Jeanneret appreciated his uncompromising modernism and commissioned iron-work for building projects. In 1931 he founded the Société des Ateliers Jean Prouvé to make functional metal seating, often completely knocked down into a kit of parts, for hospitals, schools and offices.

As an architect, Prouvé was concerned to find an authentic method and technique of applying scientific methods of construction to the business of living, although he was not prepared to compromise the individual's demand for variety. His pump house at Cachat for Evian mineral water was built in 1956 and remains his architectural masterpiece. In the Fifties he experimented with prefabricated buildings, based on his wartime experience of designing portable sheds for the French army. Much taken with the practical and poetical potential of industry, he described himself as a 'factory man'. His business failed in 1952, although Le Corbusier and others continued to consult him on technical matters. In the 1990s his reputation was revived in the Paris galleries of Philippe Jousse and Patrick Seguin, turning cheap metal public service furniture into expensive collectibles. His table for the French Atomic Energy authority is for sale at $1,000,000.

Bibliography Otakar Macel & Jan van Geest *Stühle aus Stahl* Walther König, Cologne, 1980; *Jean Prouvé – the poetics of the technical object* exhibition catalogue, Vitra Design Museum, Weil-am-Rhein, 2006

Throughout the Twenties and Thirties Prouvé made metal furniture which attempted to redefine some of the mechanical aspects of seating

Emilio Pucci born 1914

Emilio Pucci, a Florentine aristocrat, was 33 when he began making sportswear for people in his own social milieu. Despite his credentials, Pucci disarmingly claims that 'It doesn't make sense to produce dresses worth as much as a round-the-world airticket.' His innovations have nevertheless often been concerned with the travel obsessions of his class: in 1954 he began to produce ultra-lightweight silk jersey dresses, patterned with his distinctive abstract designs, which looked as if they had been designed with air travel in mind. Pucci scrawled his signature on the fabrics, as well as on the wide range of accessories he marketed as desirable status symbols. He now combines political interests (he was a Liberal member of the Italian Parliament from 1963 to 1972) with making couture robes (often beaded and embroidered), while at the same time licensing his name to manufacturers of jeans, lingerie and carpets. Pucci has designed uniforms for the stewardesses of Qantas and porcelain for Rosenthal.

1: Ulla Procopé, 'Ruska' service for Arabia, 1960.
2: Jean Prouvé, 'Bridge' chair in aluminium, oak and leather, circa 1953.
3: Emilio Pucci in his Florence studio, 1959.
4: Modelling a Pucci cover-up in 1965.

A.W.N. Pugin 1812–52

Augustus Welby Northmore Pugin was a pioneer of the Gothic Revival. The first architect to associate buildings with morality and social purpose, he strongly believed that values such as 'good' and 'bad' could attach to architecture and design. In this he was a great influence on John Ruskin and thus on one whole strain of thought in the Modern Movement. (See also page 22.)

Jean Puiforcat 1897–1945

Jean Puiforcat was an Art Deco silversmith. One biographer has said of his silver tableware 'he specialized in costly simplicity'. Throughout the Thirties silver tea services that Puiforcat designed were manufactured by both French and English concerns: they are characterized by shiny surfaces and geometrical forms.

1: A. W. N. Pugin, fabric for House of Lords roller-blind, circa 1847.
2: *The Nose* is Push Pin Studio's in-house publication, each one designed by Seymour Chwast. This edition is from 2005.
3: Pyrex, an American luxury product.

Push Pin Studio

The Push Pin Studio was founded in New York in 1954 by the graphic designers <u>Milton Glaser</u>, Ed Sorel and Seymour Chwast.

Bibliography *The Push Pin Style* exhibition catalogue Musée des Arts décoratifs, Paris, 1970

Pyrex was developed in response to a demand from American railroads to find glass lenses that were tolerant of a wide range of temperatures

Pyrex

Pyrex is the trade name of a heat-and chemical-resistant borosilicate glass that was introduced commercially by the Corning Glass Works in America in 1915. Pyrex was developed in response to a demand from American railroads to find glass lenses that were tolerant of a wide range of temperatures, and Corning adapted the results to the needs of international commerce. Corning licensed the manufacture of Pyrex in Britain in 1921, in France, Spain and Italy in 1922, in Germany in 1927, and in Japan in 1930.

Pyrex products are made both by press moulding and by blow moulding. Like traditional glass, Pyrex lends itself to decoration, but not by cutting (which would impair its thermal and mechanical performance), but by transfer printing, banding and spray coating. However, these techniques were all too often used to impose witless, artless derivative patterns onto functionally efficient vessels. In 1934–5 Pyrex used Harold Stabler as a design consultant and from 1952 to 1969 <u>Milner Gray</u>. The firm's most distinguished products are the ones that carry least decoration.

Bibliography Don Wallance *Shaping America's Products* Reinhold, New York, 1956; *Pyrex: 60 Years of Design* exhibition catalogue, Tyne and Wear County Council Museums, 1983

3

Mary Quant born 1934

Mary Quant's fashion design became so much a symbol of London in the Sixties that in 1973–4 the London Museum put on an exhibition called 'Mary Quant's London'. Her clothing emphasized youth, play, fun and wit, and being cheap, comfortable and wearable, made high fashion widely available.

Mary Quant opened her first shop, Bazaar, in 1955. She was to do for fashion what Terence Conran did for furnishings, and her revolutionary concept, the mini-skirt, appeared in 1964, the same year that Conran's Habitat opened in London's Fulham Road. Both Conran and Quant were inspired by the same circumstances: the drab condition of London in the ten years or so after the Second World War. Just as Conran had abominated the goods in the furniture stores where he wanted to sell his simple modern furniture, so Mary Quant hated everything that she saw going on around her in fashion, and 'disagreed with what women did to themselves'. At the time she started out, it did not occur to her that these needs were very widely felt, but looking back in 1966 she could say, 'Although at the start we made every mistake anybody could, the need was so strong that we couldn't fail.' Shopping was about to become an entertainment, not an ordeal; when Bazaar opened people were six-deep on the pavement outside and the entire stock was sold in ten days. Mary Quant recalled: 'We wanted people to be at ease in the shop, and to be friendly. We employed the sort of girls who would never have sold in shops before…' It was more than the beginning of a new fashion in clothes, it was the beginning of the realization that the environment of the store was an essential part of retailing success. Shopping had to be an agreeable experience, not merely the selection of merchandise. Mary Quant and her husband Alexander Plunkett Greene were one of the very first modern retailers to be aware of this. Alexander had a huge influence on Mary's philosophy and style and their control over the graphics used in her shops had as much of an influence over her success as her eye for fashion.
Bibliography Mary Quant *Quant by Quant* Cassell, London, 1966

David Queensberry born 1929

David Harrington Angus Douglas, the 12th Marquess of Queensberry, was a noted ceramics designer. He was professor of ceramics at the Royal College of Art from 1959 to 1983 and has been a consultant to Rosenthal. He now works in an independent consultancy with Martin Hunt, another ceramics designer. Queensberry has designed many simple, sophisticated and practical pieces of tableware.

1: Mary Quant, circa 1964.
2: Mary Quant's first store, 'Bazaar', King's Road, Chelsea, 1955. A year before Pop Art, this was one of the starting points of a revolution in fashion and retailing.

1

Mary Quant was to do for fashion what Terence Conran did for furnishings, and her revolutionary concept, the mini-skirt, appeared in 1964, the same year that Conran's Habitat opened in London's Fulham Road

Ernest Race 1913–64

Ernest Race became one of the few English furniture designers of the twentieth century to have acquired an international reputation. He studied architecture at London's Bartlett School and worked in the design department of Troughton & Young, a lighting manufacturer, before going to live in India in the mid-Thirties, where he designed textiles to be hand woven there. On his return to London he opened a shop to sell this merchandise, but it closed soon after the beginning of the Second World War. In 1946, with a light engineering manufacturer, Race founded Race Furniture in order to make wholly modern designs. He presented two chairs at the Festival of Britain that have since become famous – the 'Antelope' and 'Gazelle'. Rather like the designs of Charles Eames, they make expressive use of the properties of steel rods. In 1954 Race won a gold medal at the Milan Triennale.

Paul Reilly said of him: 'Anyone seeking Englishness in modern English furniture would immediately think of Race, for all his work had the directness, logic, economy and sturdy elegance that one associates with the best of our eighteenth-century craftsmanship and the best of our nineteenth-century engineering.'

Dieter Rams born 1932

Dieter Rams was born in Wiesbaden and was apprenticed as a joiner, then studied architecture and design at the Wiesbaden Werk-Kunstschule (art and technical school). His first job was with the Otto Apel architectural practice; then he went to Braun, soon becoming its chief designer. While Hans Gugelot brought the discipline of the Ulm Hochschule für Gestaltung to bear on the Frankfurt factory, Rams developed an in-house style that depended in part on the severe training of the craftsman. Rams has been responsible for the major domestic machines that have made the Braun company the aesthetic epitome of Germany's 'economic miracle'. His is an austere, restrained style where graphic purity vies with sculptural presence for effect, and he has said, 'I regard it as one of the most important and most responsible tasks of a designer today to help clear the chaos we are living in.' Rams' projects include his kitchen machine of 1957 and numerous other domestic appliances upon which he bestows the same purity of form and attention to detail. (See also pages 53 and 322.)

Bibliography François Burkhardt & Inez Franksen *Design: Dieter Rams* & IDZ Berlin, 1982

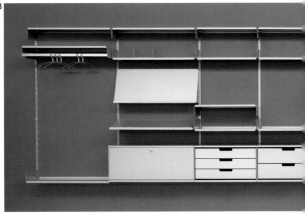

Ernest Race became one of the few English furniture designers of the twentieth century to have acquired an international reputation

Paul Rand 1914–96

Born Peretz Rosenbaum in Brooklyn, the graphic designer Paul Rand studied art at New York's Pratt Institute and at the Parsons School of Art. The re-invention of his name is itself a demonstration of how European taste infiltrated American culture. His first job was as art director of the magazine *Esquire*, and in 1959 he opened his own office. Eliot Noyes invited him to be the graphic designer on the new corporate identity programmes he was implementing for IBM and Westinghouse, and he designed a new logo and new packaging for both.

Rand wrote in 1980, 'Design clichés, so-called Post-Modern (dingbat design), meaningless patterns, trendy illustrations and predetermined solutions are signs of… weakness. An understanding of the significance of modernism and familiarity with the history of design, of painting, of architecture and other disciplines, which distinguish the educated designer and make his role more meaningful… are not always his strong point.'

Bibliography Paul Rand *Thoughts on Design* Wittenborn, New York, 1946; *Design and Play Instincts* George Braziller, New York, 1966

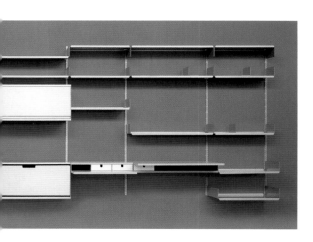

1: Ernest Race, 'Antelope' furniture, 1951. A Festival of Britain take-away.
2: Dieter Rams.
3: Dieter Rams, Vitsoe 606 shelving system, 1960.
4: Braun 'SK4' record player, 1956. Designed by Rams and Hans Gugelot, the SK4's austere appearance earned it the nickname 'Schneewittchenssar' (Snow White's Coffin).

5: Vitsoe Series 620 armchair, designed 1962, reissued 2006.
6: After Paul Rand re-designed himself as an American citizen, he set about transforming the appearance of IBM, one of America's most important corporations at mid-century. IBM film ribbon packaging, USA, circa 1959.

Rasch Brothers

The two Rasch brothers, Heinz (born 1902) and Bodo (born 1903), founded a Workshop for the Manufacture of Domestic Fittings in 1922, and published an influential book, *Der Stuhl*, in 1928. Throughout the Twenties and Thirties they made furniture designs in metal which were manufactured by L. & C. Arnold of Schorndorf. They also had a contract to design wallpapers for the Bauhaus workshops. The quality of their ideas in relation to their designs for mass-production was impressive.

Bibliography Heinz & Bodo Rasch *Der Stuhl* Stuttgart, 1928; Otakar Macel & Jan van Geest *Stühle aus Stahl* Walther König, Cologne, 1980

Armi Ratia 1912–79

Armi Ratia founded Marimekko in Helsinki in the mid-Fifties. It is a shop, a manufacturer and a consultancy all in one. Ratia drew designers from all over Finland for the store and created a strong, vivid style, part entirely original, part derived directly from Finnish folk culture: among colourful merchandise were huge vases of white lilies and tulips. Perhaps the best known Marimekko designer is Vuokko Eskolin.

Herbert Read 1893–1968

Herbert Read was the most distinguished of the English writers who popularized design in the Thirties and the country's most influential and perceptive art critic since Roger Fry.

He was born in Yorkshire in 1893, and his first job was as a clerk in a Leeds bank, but he studied at night school to gain a place at Leeds University. Although from a prosperous family background, his personal struggle to gain education encouraged him to a poetic radicalism, inspired by Tolstoy rather than Marx. Like Verdi, he said, 'I am by birth and tradition a peasant,' and added, 'I despise the whole industrial epoch – not only the plutocracy which it has raised to power but also the industrial proletariat which it has drained from the land.' After the First World War Read worked in the Victoria and Albert Museum, publishing learned works on glass and ceramics, and in 1931 became professor of fine arts at Edinburgh University. His appointment as director of a planned Museum of Modern Art came to nothing because of the Second World War. He was knighted in 1953.

Although his own enthusiasms were, perhaps, more with poetry and literary criticism, Read became well known as a champion of modern art, and his book, *Art and Industry* (1936), was the most persuasive statement by an English author to call for an awareness of the beauty of machines. The main problem it presented was whether everyday objects should be treated as art in the manner he proposed. It has been said that, despite the character and influence of his writings, Read was not, in fact, sympathetic to machine art, yet he was the first director of the Design Research Unit (DRU). Milner Gray said *Art and Industry* was 'the turning point for most of us in the clearer understanding of machine art' and described Read as 'a man of steel in his convictions, yet wonderfully moderate and gentle in his contact with his fellows… the practical poet, the design philosopher and guide'.

Read belongs to the spirit of the Thirties in his whole-hearted acceptance of Walter Gropius's principles, and is a less popular figure now than he was after the Second World War.

1

1: At Marimekko, Armi Ratia was patron of an eclectic squad of designers. 'Kaivo' fabric by Maija Isola and Kristina Isola, 1964.

2: BMW acquired the Mini brand from its misalliance with the new defunct Rover Group in the Nineties. The result was the New Mini of 2000, an adroit exercise in brainy retro. In some ways a travesty of Issigonis' original intentions, the New Mini was a superlative and successful exercise in product design and a very effective manipulation of consumer psychology.

3: Richard Riemerschmid, chair in oak, circa 1900.

Retro

The term 'retro' was first used by French journalists in the mid-Seventies to describe a tendency in popular design to look back nostalgically at recently past styles and tastes. From the early Sixties Victoriana, Art Nouveau, Art Deco and Contemporary were all revived as if to subvert the Modern Movement's obsession with the future and restore the power of psychological and symbolic meaning in design. In addition to this simple revival, another tendency also emerged which was concerned with the basic, vernacular objects associated with pre-industrial rural life. This was, in turn, associated with the larger 'back to nature' movement which, preferring natural materials to synthetic ones, and naivety to sophistication, was itself related to the Crafts Revival.

Eventually the distinction between the various 'retro' styles became eroded into a joyless, directionless eclecticism that presented the world with the alternative to Modernism sought by 'retro's various originators. As branding became a more insistent issue in the motor industry, designers began to plunder collective memory in what J Mays described as 'Retrofuturism'. Harley-Davidson's success has been to large degree inspired by the consumer's appetite for nostalgia. Equally, BMW's successful re-edition of the Mini. But to others, retro is pastiche. Audi's Walter da Silva says 'Retro one shot, Il dopo Mini, no futuro. Repetizione.' (Retro is a one shot business: there's no future for the Mini, only repetition.)

Richard Riemerschmid 1868–1957

Richard Riemerschmid founded the Vereinigte Werkstätten für Kunst im Handwerk (united workshops for art in craft) in Munich in 1897 and was, with Peter Behrens and Bruno Paul, one of the first German designers to adapt himself to the possibilities of machine production and the implications of standardization. His 'Musik Salon' flat pack chair is timeless. Like Bruno Paul, he produced furniture designs for the Werkstätten which were amongst the simplest of their day.

The term 'retro' was first used by French journalists in the mid-seventies to describe a tendency in popular design to look back nostalgically at recently past styles and tastes

Gerrit Rietveld 1888–1964

Gerrit Thomas Rietveld, a Dutch architect, was born in Utrecht and started his career as an apprentice joiner in his father's shop. He had no contact with the <u>Modern Movement</u> until Robert van t'Hoff commissioned him to design furniture in 1916. In 1917 he designed an uncompromisingly geometrical chair, which formed the basis for his 'Red-Blue' chair. From this time contact with the avant-garde Dutch group of painters who called their movement <u>De Stijl</u> was crucial. The 'Red-Blue' chair, intended to be made in plain wood, with colour used to emphasize its structure, appeared in 1919, and his 'Zig-Zag' chair in 1934. Both are now reproduced by <u>Cassina</u>. Rietveld did relatively little metal furniture, but some awkward tubular steel designs of the late Twenties and early Thirties were manufactured by the Dutch firm Metz & Co. He also produced chairs of packing-crate wood in the Depression, an upholstered chair, and chairs made of aluminium. His monument was the Schroeder House in Utrecht, which was built in 1925. This house and Rietveld's designs for it were strongly influenced by <u>Frank Lloyd Wright</u>, the American architect whose designs were enjoying a vogue in Holland at the time.

Rietveld continued to experiment with chairs all his life, but it is for his early, formalist experiments that he is remembered, even though these are illogical as structures for actually sitting in.

Bibliography Marijke Kuper et al *Gerrit Rietveld* exhibition catalogue, Centraal Museum, Utrecht, 1992

La Rinascente

La Rinascente is a chain of department stores in Italy that inaugurated the <u>Compasso d'Oro</u> design awards in 1954. It became one of the symbols of the nation's postwar *ricostruzione*. Vittorio Radice, who revolutionized Selfridges in London, has recently gone to Italy to run the chain.

Andrew Ritchie born 1948

Ritchie is the English engineer who in the early Eighties perfected the folding bicycle. Earlier attempts, including the Bickerton that inspired him, had more ingenuity than roadworthiness, but through scrupulous, painstaking development, Ritchie's design acquired both. Branded 'Brompton' because the flat where prototypes were made overlooked London's Brompton Cemetery, Ritchie's bicycle uses components from 150 suppliers, allowing a potential of several billion variations in specification.

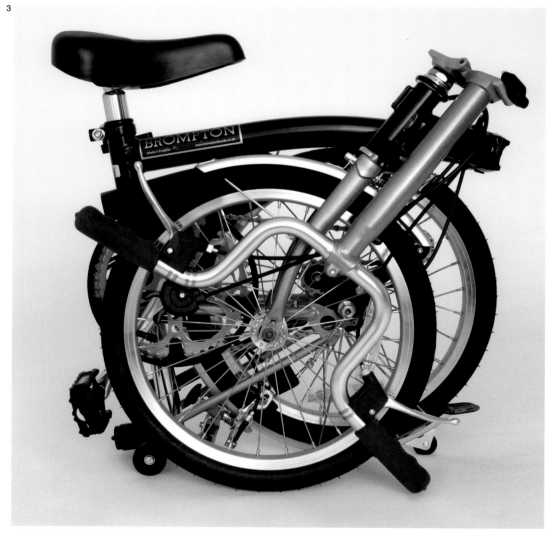

1: Gerrit Rietveld, 'Zig-Zag' table, 1934; 'Schroeder 1' table, 1922–3 and 'Red and Blue' chair (foreground), 1918. A spatial diagram of De Stijl theory with a subsidiary (and very unhappy) subsidiary use as a chair.

2: La Rinascente department store launched the Compasso d'Oro awards in 1964 and became a champion of Italian design.

3: Andrew Ritchie, 'Brompton' folding bicycle, circa 1983.

Carlo Riva born 1922

Carlo Riva was born into a boat-building family – a *cantieri* – that had been established in Sarnico, on Lago d'Iseo, since the first half of the nineteenth century. In 1962 Riva introduced his Aquarama, an elegant launch powered by a pair of mighty Chris-Craft engines. Its supremely elegant shape and luxurious appointments were a perfect physical expression of *la dolce vita* and it soon won acceptance by the nautical branch of the Jet Set. Aquarama's frame was mahogony, skinned with plywood formed using aerospace techniques. To this fine shape, lacquered to mirror-like perfection, Riva's craftsmen added seductively pleated Naugahyde upholstery, gorgeous polished metal fittings and an instrument panel that, bizarrely, took clues from both Cadillac and Ferrari. Production ended in 1996.

Terence Harold Robsjohn-Gibbings 1905–76

Cecil Beaton described Robsjohn-Gibbings in 1954 as 'the best designer of modern interiors in America today', and characterized him as 'staunchly set against the mania for antiques, for European imitation and gimcrack period creations'. His was a quest for the timeless, eternal values of the classical style in decoration. Arriving in America from England, Robsjohn-Gibbings first designed furniture of great purity and simplicity, but his most characteristic work came when he went to live in Athens for a time (where he had an apartment enjoying a view of the Parthenon). Here he designed white rooms where antiquities stood next to austere, blanched furniture that he had refined

from ancient models into idealized forms almost without substance. Robsjohn-Gibbings saw the home as a place where man confronted himself: 'Consider the alternative to the endless scrambling for ostentation,' he wrote. 'No compulsion from state, society or fashion can force a living soul to be other than himself inside the one toehold he has on this planet – his home. In equipping a house, every individual choice… will reveal… the likeness of the inhabitants.'

Bibliography T.H. Robsjohn-Gibbings Goodbye, *Mr Chippendale* Knopf, New York, 1944; *Mona Lisa's Moustache* Knopf, New York, 1947; *Homes of the Brave* Knopf, New York, 1954

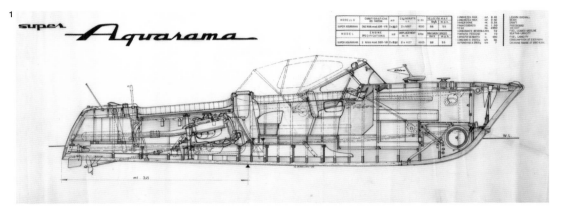

1: Riva Aquarama, 1962, cross-section and intended use. La dolce vita gets wet.
2: Walter Gropius, 'Tac 01' tea service, 1969.

Ernesto Rogers 1909–69

Ernesto Rogers was one of the partners in <u>BBPR</u>, an influential Milanese architectural practice, and the editor of the magazine *Domus* in the years immediately after the Second World War. His studio was a training camp for some of the best-known post-War Milanese designers.

Rörstrand

The Swedish ceramics factory Rörstrand was founded in 1726. In 1874 it established the <u>Arabia</u> factory in Helsinki, and in 1964 was itself bought by the conglomerate Upsala-Ekeby. Rörstrand has, like other Swedish ceramics manufacturers, maintained a long tradition of employing designers in independent studios within the factory in pursuit of the characteristic Swedish commitment to democratic values and 'good', simple design. However, in recent years Rörstrand has lost the high standards that it set in the Fifties and Sixties.

Rosenthal

The Rosenthal Porzellan AG was founded at Selb in Bavaria in 1880, by the grandfather of the present director, Philip Rosenthal, who bears the same name. Rosenthal came to prominence in the early twentieth century, marketing refined versions of <u>Art Nouveau</u>, sometimes designed by Rosenthal himself. The present Rosenthal has brought fame to the company in another way. Perhaps more than any other comparable concern anywhere, Rosenthal Porzellan hires consultant designers, and <u>Raymond Loewy</u>, <u>Wilhelm Wagenfeld</u>, <u>David Queensberry</u>, <u>Walter Gropius</u> and <u>Tapio Wirkkala</u> have all worked for the firm. Perhaps Rosenthal's single most respected product is the service designed by Walter Gropius that went into production in 1962. It is the most thoroughgoing of all Gropius's designs, and, despite its small scale, exemplifies to the full the principles which the <u>Bauhaus</u> sought to establish. Every aspect of the function of the service has been rationally reconsidered and, while formal considerations are secondary to functional requirements, the result is nonetheless aesthetically satisfying.

Like <u>Wedgwood</u> two hundred years before, Rosenthal opened a series of shops (in this case, the international 'Studio-House') to bring the firm's wares to the public.

Rosenthal came to prominence in the early twentieth century, marketing refined versions of Art Nouveau

2

David Rowland born 1924

The chair designer David Rowland was born in Los Angeles. After wartime duty as a combat pilot in Europe he studied physics at a liberal arts college in Illinois, before joining Cranbrook Academy. His first job was working with Norman Bel Geddes in the last days of his studio, and he opened his own offices in 1955.

Rowland's '40-in-4' chair of 1963, originally manufactured by General Fireproofing, is one of the great chair designs of the century and won the Grand Prize at the 1964 Milan Triennale. Its name refers to the fact that 40 of these wire chairs can be stacked in 4 feet, and it has been praised for having 'all detail refined to a point of near extinction'. This was followed by the 'Sof-Tech' stacking chair of 1979 for Thonet. Rowland tells the story that when he was starting out to sell the '40-in-4' he approached the New York representative of a large Japanese trading house. After months of delay with no reply from the head office in Tokyo, Rowland called the office again, to be told, 'I just received cable from Head Office, Tokyo, they are report latest word is that Japanese people still sit on floor.'

Royal College of Art

Like its neighbour the Victoria and Albert Museum, the Royal College of Art developed in the atmosphere of zealous reform that surrounded Prince Albert and his circle. At first called the Normal School of Design, the college was among the first products of the new design education system that was formed in Britain during the nineteenth century. However, its progress through the early years of the twentieth century was largely uneventful and the college tended, despite its early idealism, to give priority to fine artists at the expense of designers for industry.

Robin Darwin, previously professor of fine art at Durham University, became principal in 1948 and began to reorganize the college. Under him it finally acquired its own building (designed by H.T. Cadbury-Brown and Sir Hugh Casson) in 1962. For the first time since the Commons Select Committee on Arts and Manufactures reported in 1836 that they wanted to extend the principles of design among the people, the premier art school in Britain was at last housed in something more than a collection of huts in South Kensington. The year after the college's new building was opened, Lord Robbins' *Report on Higher Education* declared that the college should have university status and so, in a sense, the ideals of the 1836 Commons Committee, which had hoped to roll back the incursions of foreign imports by providing British industry with rationally trained designers, seemed to have a chance of being realized.

When Darwin arrived the college was, in all essentials, still using the educational methods established just after 1851, which by now were narrow, repetitive, unrealistic and inbred. Of this Darwin once commented, 'Looking back, it may well appear amazing that the college was able, during all those years, to maintain any kind of reputation at all... There seemed after the war very little justification indeed for the continued existence of the RCA.' As part of his rationalization of the college he introduced a new qualification, 'Des.RCA', intended to identify designers qualified for work in industry. But since Darwin's day the college has lacked a strong leader, a purpose and an identity, until newspaper magnate Jocelyn Stevens was appointed in 1984. Stevens had the wrong sort of signal to noise ratio. His successor, a vampire expert and cowboy enthusiast called Christopher Frayling, energetically manoeuvred the College into a central role in national life. A close relationship was formed with Imperial College, allowing access to technology and the development of hitherto unfeasible research projects.

Bibliography Nikolaus Pevsner *Academies of Art Past and Present* Cambridge University Press, 1940; Quentin Bell *The Schools of Design* Routledge, London, 1963

1

2

Royal Society of Arts

The Society for the Encouragement of Arts, Sciences, and Manufactures was founded by William Shipley (1715–1803) in 1754. The motivation behind Shipley's remarkable initiative was similar to that of, say, Erasmus Darwin and the provincial Enlightenment, of Josiah Wedgwood and of the numerous literary and philosophical societies which sprang up in London and the provinces in the later eighteenth and nineteenth centuries. Before the division of labour took place it was possible for men like Shipley to talk easily of arts and sciences in the same breath, and all knowledge was useful and accessible, whether concerned with archaeology or fisheries. The society was founded on the basis of such catholicity of taste and interest, and maintains it to this day. It was granted a Royal charter in 1908.

Prince Albert used the Society of Arts as a platform for generating interest in his proposed Great Exhibition. He acted on Shipley's wish that the Society of Arts 'may prove an effectual means to embolden enterprise, to enlarge Science, to refine Art, to improve Manufactures and extend Commerce: in a word, to render Great Britain the school of instruction, as it is already the centre of traffic, to the greatest part of the known world.' (See also page 17.)

Bibliography D.G.C. Allan *William Shipley – founder of the Royal Society of Arts* Hutchinson, London, 1968

Roycrofters

American Arts and Crafts community, founded by Elbert Hubbard.

Bernard Rudofsky 1905–88

Rudofsky was a curator, educationalist, designer and controversialist who also became a tastemaker. He studied architecture in Vienna, arriving in Brazil in the Thirties where he opened a practice in Sao Paolo. He settled in the United States in 1941. Rudofsky was a natural subversive and consistently argued against absurdity and for more rational, more humane design. He was especially interested in sandals. He spoke sarcastically of man's natural inclination 'to make the worst of (all) possible choices'. He believed that 'life can be less dull than we make it'. He held the standard lavatory bowl in contempt, demanding to know why it had to be a 'septic humidifier' and why such a noxious thing should be routinely placed close to the bath. At Black Mountain College in North Carolina Rudofsky gave a lecture criticizing conventional dress as anachronistic, irrational, impractical and harmful. With his wife Berta he began sandal manufacturing in 1947. One of his lectures was titled 'How Can People Expect to Have Good Architecture When They Wear Such Clothes?'

But it was with his influential exhibition and book, *Architecture without Architects* (1964), that Rudofsky made his mark. This work became part of the significant literature on the pre-history of the non-pedigree designer that also included Jay Doblin's *One Hundred Great Product Designs* (1970) and Herwin Schaefer's *The Roots of Modern Design* (1970). They have been joined by Paola Antonelli's *Humble Masterpieces – 100 everyday marvels of design* (2005).

Bibliography Bernard Rudofsky *Architecture Without Architects* exhibition catalogue, Museum of Modern Art, New York, 1964

He held the standard lavatory bowl in contempt, demanding to know why it had to be a 'septic humidifier' and why such a noxious thing should be routinely placed close to the bath

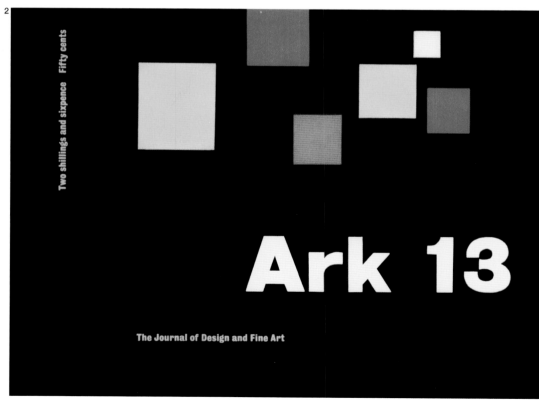

Two shillings and sixpence   Fifty cents

Ark 13

The Journal of Design and Fine Art

1: David Rowland, 40-in-4 stacking chair for General Fireproofing, 1963.
2: *Ark 13*, spring 1955. The Royal College of Art's house journal by Alan Fletcher. *Ark 36*, summer 1964, by Roy Giles and Stephen Hiett.
3: Elbert Hubbard brought William Morris' values to the United States.

John Ruskin 1819–1900

John Ruskin was the most influential art critic of the nineteenth century, and his attitudes to art, architecture, design and their relation to society and to morality had a profound effect on British culture,

Like his contemporary William Morris, Ruskin despised the industrialized world; he started writing the second volume of *The Stones of Venice* on the day the Great Exhibition opened – a display of which he had much adverse criticism to make. Ruskin had much to say about almost every aspect of the man-made world, and was a great champion of the Gothic. He despised the slick artificialities of the day, especially as apparent in the decoration of domestic villas, and railed against wood-graining and all forms of dishonesty in decoration. Every object and every gesture had a moral character for him, as is typified by his description of William Holman-Hunt's painting 'The Awakening Conscience' in his *Academy Notes* for 1854, where he drew particular attention to 'the fatal newness of the furniture' which the painter showed in the philanderer's drawing room. Ruskin's world view was of such breadth that it is not surprising that it became bifurcated.

The psychology of the Arts and Crafts was all Ruskin's. His great book was *The Stones of Venice* (1851–3). He never wrote *The Bricks of Battersea*, which is our loss. Ruskin was the last Hebrew prophet. The Library edition of his complete works has more than 3,000 index references to the scriptures, surrounded by the booming cadences of his orotund prose. The privileged – and somewhat overwrought – son of a wealthy wine merchant, Ruskin had a childhood of strict religious discipline: paintings were turned to face the walls on Sundays which habit, hunger being the best sauce, may have enhanced his appetite for art. But it was an idea of art that new conditions left wanting.

Ruskin himself soon came to realize that painting and architecture were not sufficiently large subjects to contain all of his moralizing and reforming energy. The 1857 publication of *Political Economy* had taken him a step further towards insanity. And his tenure as Slade Professor of the Fine Arts at Oxford gave him many opportunities to develop his taste for righteous work: he once made a group of undergraduates go road-mending.

Later, he personally swept the roads of London. Earlier, the discovery of female pubic hair had made him impotent. What he had lost in private sexual pistonnage, he found in public argument. And when he had finally gone mad, the Arts and Crafts continued his work.

Ruskin's influence travelled to Germany. Via Hermann Muthesius, it had a profound effect on Walter Gropius in his formulation of the ideology that moved the Bauhaus. (But through numerous translations, Ruskin's thought also influenced the German reactionaries who opposed the Bauhaus.)

Ruskin was both a profound influence on consumer psychology but also witheringly disdainful of it. 'Every new possession,' he wrote, 'loads us with new weariness.' He would not have enjoyed twenty-first century consumerism.

Bibliography Martin J. Wiener *English Culture and the Decline of the Industrial Spirit* Cambridge University Press, Cambridge, 1981

Gordon Russell 1892–1980

Gordon Russell did not actually create the Design Council, but when he became the second director of the Council of Industrial Design in 1947 it was only four years old so he was able to formulate a policy which created its character and had a significant influence on English culture during the Fifties and Sixties.

Russell's father had been a banker who became a rural hotelier, opening the Lygon Arms at Broadway in Worcestershire. It was in an antique-restoration shop in Broadway at the end of the First World War that Gordon Russell became interested in making things. He had his first exhibition of furniture designs in Cheltenham in 1922. The economic necessity of installing machinery in his Broadway workshop brought Russell face to face with the twentieth-century problem of reconciling traditional practice to modern need. While respecting the traditions of the craftsman, Russell was not afraid to use machines if they made a job easier or a shop more efficient. It was these experiences in his country workshop that Russell carried through into public life. He also had no delusions about the division of labour and was very happy simply to be the boss, having teams of toiling craftsmen executing his designs.

1: John Ruskin in John Millais' famous oil painting painted on holiday in Scotland,1853. Ultramontane Tory bigot or principled and visionary reformer, Ruskin understood the morality of design.

2: Gordon Russell, living room of his own house at Chipping Campden, Gloucestershire, early 1930s.

3: Burt Rutan, SpaceShipOne: the first private spacecraft reached an altitude of 328,000 feet in 2004.

During the Second World War Russell became chairman of the Board of Trade's <u>Utility</u> furniture panel and was a formative influence in the direction of the Festival of Britain. When he retired as director of the Design Council in 1960 he was succeeded by Paul Reilly.

Throughout his life Russell was a fanatical devotee of the concept 'skill', which was the subject of his last public address. The design of Gordon Russell Ltd furniture was, in fact, never very inspired, nor ever in touch with the reality of the popular budget, or even the dreams of advanced taste. Although always fine in quality, in spirit it was a sort of 'repro'. Only with the cabinets designed for Murphy radio in the Thirties by his brother, Dick, soon after <u>Henry Ford</u> visited the village of Broadway, did the firm begin to design for the mass market.

Gordon Russell's achievement was to bring to public and official attention the idea that making things is a serious, professional business.

Bibliography Ken and Kate Baynes *Gordon Russell* Design Council, London, 1980; Gordon Russell *A Designer's Trade* John Murray, London, 1968

'Burt' Rutan flew solo for the first time in 1959 at the controls of an Aeronca Champ. From 1965 to 1972 he was a flight test engineer at California's Edwards Air Force Base (where Captain Edward Murphy Junior coined his famous Law). In 1974 Rutan set up his own aircraft company, specializing in composite structures put at work in the service of light, conceptually unusual, energy efficient designs. The first plane from the Rutan Aircarft Factory in the Mojave Desert was the VariViggen, a two seater with a pusher propellor and with a front canard wing, a device which became

something of a Rutan signature. In 1986 Rutan's Voyager flew on a record-breaking nine-day trans-global flight. Like <u>R. J. Mitchell</u>'s Spitfire, Rutan's designs are often cited as an inspiration by other designers. And like Mitchell again, Rutan has a genius for appreciating the imaginative, sculptural possibilities inherent even within the tight envelope required by the constraints of the physics of flight. Rutan is uncompromisingly creative, both in the spirit and the letter. He says: 'If you don't have a consensus that it is nonsense, you don't have a breakthrough.'

3

3

SAAB

'SAAB' stands for Svenska Aeroplan Aktiebolaget, or 'Swedish Aircraft Company'. It was one of the many Swedish manufacturing concerns established by the banker Marcus Wallenberg. Within a few years of its foundation on the eve of the Second World War it was producing the advanced SAAB 21, the first plane to have an ejector seat. At the end of the War SAAB found itself with a lot of manufacturing plant and no demand whatsoever for warplanes, so the engineers decided to make a car. Chief engineer Gunnar Ljungstrom planned it with no preconceptions – in fact only two of the staff actually had driving licences. The company's technical illustrator Sixten Sason was called in to advise on the form and the project became

the SAAB 92, launched in 1950. It was the basis of later SAAB models, and the 96 remained in production until 1980. After Sason's death in 1969 Bjorn Envall became chief designer. SAAB popularized the forced induction ('turbo') and the middle-class cabrio, even retained a reputation for Swedish care and dash. But its acquisition as a trophy brand by a struggling General Motors in 1989 signalled the end of the idiosyncratic innovation that had been central to SAAB's philosophy. From the Nineties on, SAABs were simple General Motors mutants with curious Swedish details.

Bibliography *Svensk Form* exhibition catalogue, The Design Council, London, 1980

1

1

1: The first SAAB was designed on aerospace principles by aircraft engineers under-employed after 1945. The 92 (top left and right) appeared in 1950 and evolved continuously for the next 20 years, until SAAB decided to produce a large version of Issigonis' Mini in 1969 (bottom left). Until SAAB was acquired as a trophy brand by General Motors in 1989, it produced cars of pleasing Swedish idiosyncrasy.

Eero Saarinen 1910–61

The son of the famous Finnish architect Eliel Saarinen, Eero Saarinen was born in Finland but moved with his father to the United States in 1923. He studied architecture at Yale. Working with Charles Eames he won the Museum of Modern Art's influential 'Organic Design in Home Furnishings' competition (which Eliot Noyes had helped organize) in 1940. Saarinen then became a teacher at the Cranbrook Academy and it was through this school that he became acquainted with Hans and Florence Knoll, for whose firm he designed the 'Grasshopper' chair in the late Forties and the famous moulded plastic 'Tulip' chair in the late Fifties. Promoted by Knoll, this chair became as familiar a piece of furnishing in high-style architectural interiors as any piece by Mies van der Rohe or Le Corbusier. It was the first moulded pedestal chair, a unique sculptural design that blended all the elements of a chair into an integral whole.

Saarinen was invited by Harley Earl to be architect of the new General Motors Technical Center at Warren, just outside Detroit, in 1956, a commission which the London *Times* obituary said was 'the most distinguished application of the ideas of Professor Mies van der Rohe to the needs of American industry'. He was also the architect of the Dulles Airport at Washington (1963), the TWA Terminal at New York's Kennedy Airport (1962) and the Gateway Memorial Arch, St Louis (1964), buildings whose stressed, parabolic roofs recall the form of birds in flight and whose wilful symbolism has often led apologists for Post-Modernism to claim them and their architect as precursors.
Bibliography Jayne Merkel *Eero Saarinen* Phaidon, 2005

Giovanni Sacchi born 1913

In 1946 Giovanni Sacchi began his extraordinary career as the master model-maker of the Milanese design establishment. From his workshop in central Milan he has realized models of the product designs made by Marcello Nizzoli, Ettore Sottsass, Marco Zanuso and Mario Bellini. Almost all of the award-winning products of Olivetti, BrionVega, Necchi and Alessi were first seen in wood in Sacchi's workshop. In 1983 the Milan Triennale celebrated his achievements in promoting design by organizing an exhibition of his models.

Bruno Sacco born 1934

Bruno Sacco was born in Udine, Italy, joined Mercedes-Benz in 1958 and eventually became head of design in 1975. He trained in Turin, although he says he was inspired as a 16-year-old boy not by FIAT, but by Raymond Loewy: on a cycling trip through the Alps in 1950 he saw a metallic blue Studebaker Commander Regal de Luxe Starlight Coupe and it became a revelatory, if congruous, benchmark. One of his first jobs was on the CIII experimental car, and he was project leader for the special class of 1980 and the 'compact' 190 of 1982.

Like Anatole Lapine at Porsche, Sacco is conscious of his customers' taste for tradition. He insists that it is more of a challenge to create a new generation of car with a tangible relationship to its predecessor than to design something where anything goes (and often nothing does): 'You concentrate very hard on avoiding gimmicks… and when you do, it's fairly easy. You act in a normal, straightforward way. There are many examples of long-lasting design in other fields: in architecture and fashion. You can design a suit to last either three months or ten years. It's the same with a car.' He retired from Mercedes-Benz in 1999.

The 'Tulip' chair became a familiar piece of furnishing in high-style architectural interiors

1: Eero Saarinen, 'Tulip' chair (and tables) for Knoll, 1957, with glass-reinforced plastic seat on a cast aluminium pedestal.
2: Saatchi, Wooden model of an espresso coffee percolator, 1978.

3: Astrid Sampe, 'Persons kryddskåp' textile design, 1955.
4: Alex Samuelson, Coca-Cola bottle, 1916. The original was designed to be identifiable in the dark and became the most successful ever exercise in packaging design, both functional and evocative.

Roberto Sambonet born 1924

Roberto Sambonet was born in Vercelli, between Milan and Turin, and graduated in architecture from Milan Polytechnic in 1945. Until 1954, when he joined the family flatware and cooking-ware company, he painted and worked at the Museum de Arte in São Paulo, Brazil. His designs for Sambonet show a preference for elegant attenuated sculptural forms. Their elegance was acknowledged when a fish-serving dish he designed in 1954 won a <u>Compasso d'Oro</u> award. With <u>Achille Castiglioni</u> and <u>Ettore Sottsass</u>, Sambonet was commissioned in 1981 to design a complete new system of street furniture for the city of Turin.

Astrid Sampe 1909–2002

A Swedish textile designer, Astrid Sampe was head of the textile design department in Stockholm's Nordiska Kompaniet from 1937 to 1972. Her work is characterized by its simple decoration and excellent colour and typically Swedish lightness and humanism.

Alex Samuelson 1862–1934

A Swedish glass engineer, Samuelson won the 1916 competition for the design of the Coca-Cola bottle, perhaps the most successful packaging ever. Responding to the brief of making something recognizable in the dark, Samuelson was inspired by the contours and shape of coco leaves and cola nuts. In pursuit of even greater credibility as architect of the American Dream, <u>Raymond Loewy</u> often let journalists assume the Coke bottle had been his design.

Bibliography *Coke! designing a megabrand*, exhibition catalogue, The Boilerhouse Project, Victoria and Albert Museum, 1986

3

4

Richard Sapper born 1932

Richard Sapper studied mechanical engineering, working first for Mercedes-Benz in Stuttgart. In 1958 he left Germany to live in Milan, where he joined the office of Gio Ponti and worked in collaboration with Marco Zanuso. Sapper and Zanuso have between them been responsible for some of the most prized cult objects of the later twentieth century: the BrionVega 'Doney 14' television (1962, page 317), the folding BrionVega radio (1965), the Italtel 'Grillo' telephone (1965) and the BrionVega 'Black 12' television of 1969. On his own account Sapper has designed Artemide's most successful product, the 'Tizio' low-voltage desk light (1972) and an espresso coffee percolator.

Sapper has brought German engineering thoroughness to the Milan manufacturers, who, in turn, have given him the opportunity to produce refined and sophisticated products. However, his 'Bollitore' kettle for Alessi, which came on to the market in 1983 – a working kettle, but nevertheless a luxury product – is evidence that a wilful type of formalism overtook international designers in the Eighties. Although handsome and precious, Sapper's kettle has a handle that is too hot to hold before the water has even boiled. From 1980 Sapper was principal product design consultant to IBM.

Timo Sarpaneva born 1926

Timo Sarpaneva studied as a draughtsman at Helsinki's Taideteollisuuskeskuskoulu (school of applied arts). Since 1950 he has been a consultant designer to the Iittala glassworks and, with Tapio Wirkkala, has come to be acknowledged as one of Finland's leading glass designers, since his work first gained international attention at the Milan Triennales in the early Fifties. It is highly sculptural and expressive. He established his own office in 1962.

Sixten Sason 1912–69

Sixten Sason was born in the provincial Swedish town of Skovde. He was trained as a silversmith, a discipline which was at the time conventional grounding for a would-be designer. He became a technical illustrator, then a science-fiction illustrator and joined SAAB at the moment when its engineers were beginning to develop the company's first light car. He was responsible for the appearance of the SAAB 96, and the fame of this sophisticated car brought him more commissions from expanding Swedish industry. As a result he designed appliances for Electrolux and determined the appearance of the first Hasselblad cameras. Thus he was Europe's first design consultant to work in the American fashion on a diverse variety of products. Although his designs have all the characteristic Swedish qualities of care and responsibility, there is a strong element of Detroit style in them too.

Sason's health had been poor since a flying accident in the Thirties, but as a result he had the leisure to study engineering. Drawings and models and a prototype jet called 'Lil Draken' inspired the general arrangement of SAAB's military fighters, Sason died just as his second great car design, the SAAB 99, (inspired by Issigonis' Mini) was coming onto the market.

1

2

Ferdinand de Saussure 1857–1913

Ferdinand de Saussure was the founder of modern linguistics. His scientific analysis of language, with its inherent suggestion of the importance of structures and signs in our ways of thinking, laid the basis for semiotics, which in the hands of followers such as Roland Barthes has had a substantial effect on writing about design, and has helped bring the modern material world into the orbit of academic culture.
Bibliography R. & F. De George *The Structuralists* Doubleday, Garden City, New York, 1972

1: Richard Sapper, 'Tizio' desk light, 1978, for Artemide. Low voltage electrical power is fed through the light metal construction, obviating messy cables or chunky channelling.

2: Sixten Sason's original interpretation of the SAAB 92 design brief.

3: Tobia Scarpa. 'occhi' glass for Venini. 1962.

Sergio Scaglietti dates unknown

Scaglietti was an artisan, a master craftsman drawing down metal-bashing skills from a gene pool first stocked by Etruscans making spears and shields. Although he originally set up his workshop in 1951 for car repair, he became more creative than restorative. Saglietti worked mainly for Pininfarina. And Pininfarina worked most significantly for Ferrari. The designers of Pininfarina would create a prototype, often a wooden *mascherone*, sent to Enze Ferrari for approval. Then Scaglietti would literally 'interpret' the model in metal. Drawings were rarely involved. Instead, through exceptional skills in interpretation and perhaps even more exceptional ones in imagination, Scaglietti would make what were called 'reproductions', a term that rather confirms the status of car design as an art form. Farina had such reverence for Scaglietti's skills that he would never interfere in the process. 'They never,' Scaglietti said, 'told me how I should use a hammer.'

In this way one of the greatest cars of all time was made. This was the 1961 Ferrari 250 GTO. Pininfarina had no direct involvement. Instead, Sergio Scaglietti, Martello hammer in hand, made this exquisitely proportioned and beautifully detailed and sublimely evocative body by starting out with an idea of what Pininfarina would do and then doing it himself. It was a work of intuitive genius with no precedents.
Bibliography *L'Idea Ferrari* exhibition catalogue, Belvedere, Florence, 1991

Afra and Tobia Scarpa born 1937 and 1935

Tobia Scarpa is the son of Carlo Scarpa. From 1957 to 1961 he worked for Venini at their Murano glassworks. In 1960 he opened an independent office with his wife, Afra. Together they have designed furniture for Cassina and Gavina as well as lighting for Flos.

3

Carlo Scarpa 1906–78

Carlo Scarpa was born in Venice and in 1926 began an academic career at the University's Institute of Architecture. He designed glass for Venini between 1933 and 1947, but his speciality has been in interior and exhibition design, his major works including the Paul Klee exhibition in Venice (1948), the Venice Biennale of 1952, the Frank Lloyd Wright exhibition in Milan (1960) and the 'Frescoes from Florence' exhibition in London in 1969. Scarpa's numerous sophisticated interiors include the Olivetti showrooms in Venice, which display his interest in minimal, sculptural form, in a combination of glass, metal and marble. His greatest monument is to some lost heroes of Italy's post-War *ricostruzione*: the sombre BrionVega tomb at San Vito d'Altivole built between 1970 and 1972 just outside Venice. Scarpa, rather beautifully, said 'The place for the dead is a garden… I wanted to show some ways in which you could approach death in a social and civic way.' It was like a requiem for Italian design.
Bibliography Maria Antonietti Crippa and Marina Loffi Randolin *Carlo Scarpa: Theory Design Projects* MIT, Cambridge, Mass., 1986

Xanti Schawinsky 1904–79

Alexander (Xanti) Schawinsky was born in Basle and studied at the Bauhaus from 1924 to 1929. From 1929 to 1933 he worked in Magdeburg, but then went to Italy where he began to work for Olivetti. Schawinsky was one of an entourage of artists and creative people employed by Adriano Olivetti, and in three short years he repaid Olivetti's faith in him by designing a remarkable poster for the 'MPT' typewriter and collaborating with Figini and Pollini on the design of the 'Studio 42' typewriter. He made office equipment glamorous, seductive, aspirational and gorgeous. In 1936 Schawinsky went to live in the United States, taught briefly at Black Mountain College, and retired to spend the rest of his life painting.

Elsa Schiaparelli 1890–1973

Elsa Schiaparelli produced a paradigm of her own career as a fashion designer when she invented the colour 'shocking pink'. Translated from wealth in Rome to poverty in Paris after an unsatisfactory marriage, Schiaparelli was forced to live off her creativity. Her first fashion design was for a sweater got up in *trompe l'œil* so as to appear that the wearer was sporting a tie. Such designs quickly caught on and in 1935 she opened a shop which became a clearing house for ideas and for the people who crossed the barriers between fine art and fashion: Salvador Dali and Jean Cocteau were friends of hers and in turn they collaborated on designs for embroideries and for fabrics. As well as Surrealism, Schiaparelli also introduced various exotic influences into the repertoire of Paris couture, including Peruvian Indian colours and North African patterns. She was consistently inventive and quick to experiment with new materials, using rayon and cellophane, and was also the first couturier to use the zip fastener (which she characteristically turned into a provocative motif).

Schiaparelli was patronized by Hollywood, including Marlene Dietrich, Lauren Bacall, Gloria Swanson and Mae West (whose plaster cast provided the inspiration for the bottle containing Schiaparelli's famous scent, 'Shocking'), but her great contribution to the language of clothes was to open up fashion to a wide variety of influences, from art, folklore and science.

1: Carlo Scarpa, BrionVega family tomb, San Vito d'Altivole, 1970–72. A haunting monument to Italy's last manufacturer of consumer electronics.

2: Elsa Schiaparelli, embroidered evening coat, 1939.
3: Margarete Schuette-Lihotsky, the 'Frankfurt' kitchen, 1928. The ultimate in ergonomic practicality designed for Frankfurt's radical social housing.

Margarete Schuette-Lihotsky 1897–2000

Schuette-Lihotsky was architect of the visionary 1928 'Frankfurt Kitchen', a functional design prepared for Ernst May's ambitious socialist housing developments. These were the days when right-angles, industrial materials, space-planning and electricity promised thrilling liberation from bourgeois domestic oppression.

2

3

Douglas Scott was born in Lambeth in 1913. He studied silversmithing and jewellery at the Central School of Art and Design. A strong Arts and Crafts background led to his first job as a designer of architectural light fittings, working in provincial cinemas as well as more distinguished buildings by Sir Edwin Lutyens. But his tipping point came in 1936 when he joined the newly established London office of Raymond Loewy.

With Loewy, Douglas Scott was introduced to the commercial reality of selling creative services to often philistine industrialists. Clients included manufacturers of consumer goods, including GEC and Electrolux. Loewy's stock-in-trade was the bravura before-and-after transformation in which, with a showman's legerdemain, a clunky old machine was given smooth edges, soft contours and a dramatically 'modern' appearance. Later denigrated as 'styling', this creative catalysis became one of the defining features of business life in the middle of the twentieth century. Curved lines, as it were, went straight to bottom lines.

The Raymond Loewy London office closed and he returned to Manhattan in 1939, but not before Scott and the others had had some contact with the old Hillman Car Company for whom Loewy later transformed the drab Minx into the gorgeously profiled and ice-cream coloured Hillman Californian immediately after the War. Scott now joined the de Havilland aircraft company, adding the imperatives of aerospace technology to an already impressive personal portfolio of skills and attributes which included craft-based jewellery design, Arts and Crafts morality and commercially astute product styling. In 1946 Douglas Scott set up his own office.

This was the same year that the Victoria and Albert Museum staged a morale-raising exhibition called 'Britain Can Make it', a sketch for what became in 1951 the Festival of Britain. Here Scott showed designs for Electrolux fridges intended for use in pre-fabs, that idiosyncratic English solution to a post-War housing crisis. His first collaboration with London Transport came in 1948 when he created the Green Line coach. AEC followed with a brief that became the adored Routemaster bus. With this Scott accepted the established architecture of the London doubledecker – with its open access deck and rear stair and front engine – but, like Raymond Loewy, exercised various transformations to make it smoother and more modern.

The huge vehicle was given generous and amiable curves, wholly lacking in any sense of aggression. In its handsome shape it is irresistible not to see ghosts of Raymond Loewy's magnificent, streamlined 1937 Pennsylvania Railroad S-1 locomotive, nor indeed of the fabulous Greyhound buses which were also a product of Loewy's showy genius. Inside, the daylight openings for the passengers were generous and the seats nearly sumptuous: Scott created a signature tartan moquette coloured in 'Burgundy red, Chinese green and Sung yellow'.

Designed by a Londoner in London for Londoners, manufactured and used in the capital too, the Routemaster's proportions both pleased the eye and fitted the streets. And if, technologically speaking, it was a little crude with its lack of power-assisted driver systems, that ensured a certain courtesy and chivalry in the conduct of the vehicle, largely missing today. Some drivers had to stand to wrench the nearly horizontal Routemaster steering wheel around sharp London corners, a requirement that imposed a certain decorum. Kipling once mentioned 'That packet of assorted miseries which we call a ship'. What Douglas Scott did with the Routemaster was to get hold of that packet of assorted miseries we call a bus and turn it into something truly delightful and loved by all. Before production stopped in 1968 2,876 Routemasters had been manufactured.

Designed by a Londoner in London for Londoners, manufactured and used in the capital too, the Routemaster's proportions both pleased the eye and fitted the streets

The disappearance of Routemaster did not occur until 2005, exciting a nostalgia for the days when London Transport was not a self-exculpating association of unaccountable, politicised, incompetent time-servers, but the envy of the world – a brilliant public service with the highest standards of architecture and graphics, great morale and splendid machinery. In terms of clarity in design and fitness-for-purpose, Douglas Scott's Routemaster is at least the equivalent of London Transport's other unforgettable creation, Harry Beck's underground map.

Douglas Scott's version of 'design' had an uncontaminated sense of purpose. He knew good work would have beneficial influence and he was happy with that, never feeling any need to stimulate vulgar publicity or profess himself a fascinating creative personality with a fascinating personality disorder. Besides the Routemaster, he was responsible for a handful of other memorable objects: the old General Post Office's grey enamelled STD coin box (whose contours are so similar to a Routemaster's), the first generation Marconi Mark VII colour television camera and Ideal Standard's 'Roma' washbasin, for 30 years a familiar fixture in homes and hotels throughout the world. Scott has a reasonable claim to be one of the most successful English designers of all, yet modestly said 'I have always designed for the market… private and personal aesthetics are out of place in industrial design.'

Semiotics

Semiotics, sometimes (but particularly in France) known as semiology, is the science which studies the systems of 'signs' in language, literature and the material world. It is the linguistic part of a philosophy known as structuralism. Structuralism and semiotics evolved from the studies in linguistics by Ferdinand de Saussure and in social and cultural anthropology by Claude Lévi-Strauss, mixed together with the psychoanalysis derived from Freud. Its most highly regarded exponent was the French savant Roland Barthes, although Northrop Frye and Marshall McLuhan have also published texts which form a part of the international corpus of semiotics. Because semiotics has obvious ramifications in the media, ideas developed by Barthes and taught by his followers have had a formative influence on our awareness of structures and symbols in the modern, commercial world.

The anthropologist Edmund Leach has described the workings of semiology: 'any human creative act starts out as a mental operation which is then projected on to the external world… plays, ceremonials, religious rituals… carvings and paintings… All such creations are "designed"… The mental operations of any human designer are circumscribed, not only by the qualities of his materials and by his objectives, but by the design of the human brain itself.' It is the business of the structuralist to understand this and the business of the semiotician to analyse the details of the process.

Bibliography Pierre Guiraud *La Sémiologie* Presses Universitaires de France, Paris, 1973

1: Douglas Scott's 'Routemaster' bus for AEC, from a brief issued in the late Forties. As superb an example of enlightened public service design as Harry Beck's London Underground map.

Shakers

'There is no dirt in heaven.' Thus, Mother Ann Lee, founder of the Shakers. Lee arrived in America in 1774, aged 39, a poor girl making a physical and metaphysical escape from Manchester, England, a city at the time very busily engaged in getting its hands dirty. Her objective was to create in New Lebanon, New York, the ideal community that Lancashire so conspicuously lacked. A number of psychic drives motivated Lee: sex, perhaps because of its association with 'dirt' was banned, but ecstatic dancing – the source of the 'shaking' – was encouraged. And Lee developed a formidable work ethic that found expression in utilitarian buildings, furniture and tools of stark beauty. 'Good spirits,' she insisted, 'will not live where there is dirt.'

The Shakers were only one of a number of early American utopian communities. When Lee disembarked, the Moravians were already well established in Pennsylvania. The <u>Oneida Community</u> and the <u>Roycrofters</u> came later, also in rural New York. But the Shakers were distinguished by the astonishing integrity of their philosophy and the products they made to support their way of life. Lee was inspired by the belief that the external form of objects displayed its spirit.

With memories of Manchester's Satanic mills, Lee set about creating a heaven on earth. This is what Dolores B. Hayden called a 'paradisiac pre-occupation'. Although in one sense Lee disdained possessions, it was felt necessary for Shaker buildings and tools to be distinguished by special qualities. 'Set not your hearts upon worldly objects,' Lee said, 'but let this be your labour, to keep a spiritual sense.' Spirits of communitarianism and religious revival after the Revolution encouraged the development of Shaker communities, focused on what Lee (with touching sentimentality) called the Family.

Luxury, jewellery and ornament were disallowed, but instead pleasure was to be found in aesthetic purity. 'Let your tables be clean enough to eat on without cloths,' was one of Lee's principles. New Lebanon was founded in 1787 and set the pattern. The distinctive white meeting house with separate doors for brothers and sisters and vast open ground floor for ecstatic dancing was designed by Master Builder Moses Johnson (1752–1842). Working buildings were painted red or yellow. All Shakers buildings were distinguished by finely proportioned austerity and high-quality workmanship.

Shaker furniture followed a course of continuous refinement as Families were established in Kentucky and Ohio during the early nineteenth century. By the 1850s Shaker furniture, based on models established by Master Cabinetmaker David Rowley (1779–1855), included built-in storage. Simple cabinets became matters of organizational beauty, expressions of a world view that, despite denials, was supported by a profound sense of beauty. It was simply that the Shakers found beauty everywhere: 'A man can show his religion,' one elder wrote, 'as much in measuring onions as he can in singing Glory Hallelujah.'

Lee's heaven on earth was planned to last for a millennium, but growth was undermined by the policy of celibacy. Shaker Families could only grow by recruitment, but then new patterns of immigration and the lure of crasser forms of consumerism changed the pool of human capital. At its height, membership of the Shakers was perhaps no more than 6,000, but they left an unforgettable legacy that has been both a formal and an emotional inspiration to later designers. Shaker buildings, furniture, buckets, pails, brushes and storage boxes successfully prefigured all the tenets of classic <u>Modernism</u>. Charles Dickens visited a Family and found it ludicrous, but the painter Charles Sheeler was more positive. Shaker design 'recognized no justifiable difference in the quality of workmanship for any object'.

Bibliography Dolores B. Hayden *Seven American Utopias – the architecture of communitarian socialism 1790-1975* MIT Press, Cambridge, Mass., 1976; *Shaker Design* exhibition catalogue (ed. June Sprigg) Whitney Museum of American Art, New York, 1986

Claude Shannon 1916–2001

Claude Shannon was an extraordinary creative figure who simply 'invented' the maths he needed to establish information theory. His work both predicted and directed the merger of communications with computing. As a mathematician he was influenced by George Boole's *Laws of Thought*; Shannon stepped beyond traditional algebra to make binary code the basis of all electronics. A protegé of <u>Vannevar Bush</u>, Shannon published *A Symbolic Analysis of Relay and Switching Circuits* in 1940, a paper that helped move computing from analogue to digital. In 1948, now working at Bell Laboratories, he published another landmark paper, *A Mathematical Theory of Communication*, which made the intellectual and practical distinction between mere facts, superior data and valuable information. He juggled and rode a unicycle through the corridors of MIT. Shannon's erratic, but inspired, insights changed the shape of knowledge.

Bibliography *A Mathematical Theory of Communications* Bell System Technical Journal, vol 27, July and October, 1948; *Scientific Aspects of Juggling* unpublished typescript, circa 1980; N. J. A. Sloane and Adam Dwyner *Charles Elwood Shannon: Collected Papers*, IEEE Press, Piscataway, New Jersey, 1993

1

Joseph Sinel 1889–1975

Joseph Sinel was a New Zealand-born commercial artist who arrived in America in 1918. By 1921 he was taking on 'product improvement' jobs for the companies who were the clients of the advertising agency which was his employer.

Having set up his studio almost eight years before Raymond Loewy, Norman Bel Geddes, Walter Dorwin Teague and Henry Dreyfuss, he claimed in later life that this gave him reason to call himself America's first industrial designer. In 1923 he published *A Book of American Trademarks and Devices*.

Silver Studio

Arthur and Rex Silver (1853–96, 1879–1965), father and son, were designers of wallpapers and fabrics, the most famous of which is probably the 'Peacock Feather' pattern done for Liberty's in the 1880s. The pair also produced designs for the so-called 'sanitary wallpapers' which became available during the following decade. These were printed on a fine surface that could be easily varnished and was thus washable. This was a great asset in the days when natural coal produced so much internal pollution that wallpapers had either to be 'sanitary' or to be replaced very often.

The Silver Studio produced a huge variety of designs in many different styles from its premises at Brook Green, Hammersmith, but many went out anonymously under the Liberty name. The studio was finally wound up in 1963.
Bibliography John Brandon-Jones *The Silver Studio Collection: A London Design Studio 1880–1963* Lund Humphries, London, 1980; *The Decoration of the Suburban Villa* exhibition catalogue Broomfield Museum, London, 1983–4

Erich Slany born 1929

Erich Slany was and is almost anonymous, but he was responsible for a small range of products that nevertheless helped popularize the hard-edged German technical style. His principal client has been Robert Bosch, for whom he has designed a whole series of more or less aggressive drills, with pistol-grips and general proportions resembling those of small arms. Slany's 'style' is very refined, apparently based on engineering criteria, but in fact aesthetically determined.

The Silver Studio produced a huge variety of designs but many went out anonymously under the Liberty name

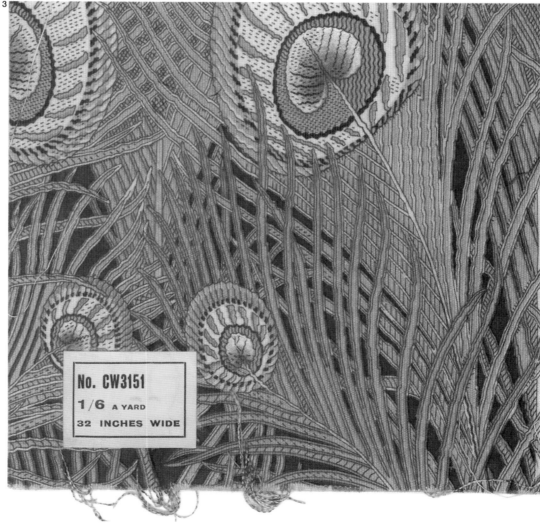

1: A Shaker interior. Mother Ann Lee, an inspiration to her followers believed 'there is no dirt in heaven'.

2: Claude Shannon, pioneer of information theory, digital crusader, designed games to test theoretical propositions.
3: Fabric designed by Silver Studios for the London department store Liberty, 1887.

Sony

In the Fifties Sony became the first Japanese consumer manufacturer to be widely known in the West, and through the Sixties, Seventies and Eighties consistently maintained a fine reputation for innovation and design. Very much under the influence of Dieter Rams and other gods of German design, Sony introduced European standards of taste into product sectors where competitors were still selling artless junk.

The origins of the company lay in Tokyo Tsushin Kogyo Kabushikakaika (TTK, or Tokyo Telecommunications Engineering), a company founded, like Honda, just after the Second World War. Its founders were Masaru Ibuka and Akio Morita, with a paid-up capital of $500. TTK started on its course of product innovation in 1950, when it designed, manufactured and marketed the first Japanese tape-recorder, the 'G' Type. This laid the foundation of the company's fortunes with guaranteed distribution through schools and courtrooms throughout the country. Characteristically, TTK found a novel way to market the machine, taking it on national tours in specially converted vans.

In 1954 TTK used Western Electric patents to manufacture the first successful transistor in Japan, and in 1955 its first transistor radio, the 'TR-55', appeared, shaped as a simple box. It was beaten to market by the American Regency TR-1 on sale for $49.95 from November, 1954, but the Japanese machine proved to be the more significant. This machine bore the brand name 'Sony', which Morita had invented after a trip to America, when he had learnt that Ford was easier to say than Plymouth, and that 'Sony' both evoked the Latin word for 'sound' and the affectionate diminutive for 'son'. In 1958 TTK adopted Sony as its corporate name.

In 1959 Sony introduced the first transistorized television, the 'TV8-301', and another wave of product innovations followed: in 1961 the first transistorized video-recorder, in 1962 a 5-inch micro TV, the 'TV5-303', in 1964 the first domestic video-recorder, in 1966 the first integrated circuit radio, in 1968 the new technology 'Trinitron' colour television tube, in 1969 the U-matic colour video-cassette, in 1975 the domestic 'Betamax' video cassette recorder, in 1979 the 'Walkman' personal stereo, and in 1980 the CD.

Although it is by no means the largest corporation in Japan, Sony became, with the possible exceptions of Toyota and Honda, the best-known globally, an achievement as much based on Akio Morita's dedication to Western ideas of marketing and public relations as on a (diminishing) talent for product innovation.

Bibliography Wolfgang Schmittel *Design–Concept–Realization* ABC, Zürich, 1975; *Sony Design* exhibition catalogue The Boilerhouse Project, Victoria and Albert Museum, London, 1982

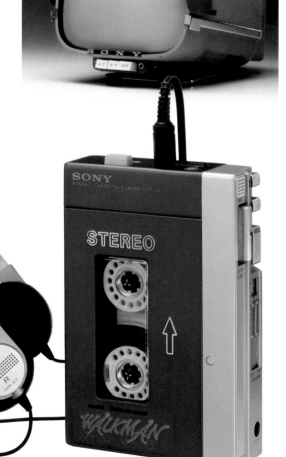

Ettore Sottsass born 1917

Ettore Sottsass, Junior, the son of an architect, was born in Innsbruck, Austria. The unusual name is a peasant corruption of '*sotto sasso*' (under the stone). Sottsass became perhaps the most outstanding Italian designer of his generation, a pioneer of the post-Second World War *ricostruzione* whose career continues to develop and take unexpected turns.

Sottsass studied architecture at Turin Polytechnic and set up his own office in the city in 1946. His first works were housing projects for the state run INA-Casa scheme, which were built in 1952–4, and he spent the following years working on interiors and small decorative objects. He was inspired both by American abstract expressionists as well as by American industrial culture. A trip to the US in 1956 taught him 'the lacquer of an automobile could be as beautiful as an abstract painting'. Later, Sottsass was one of the designers who made plastic an acceptable material for high-concept domestic furniture.

After 1957 he was most often associated with Olivetti (although he maintained his own independent identity as an architect and designer with his own practice). His principal works for Olivetti have been the 'Elea 9003' computer (1959), the 'Tekne 3' and 'Praxis 48' electric typewriters and the 'Dora' portable (1964), the 'Te 300' teleprinter (1967), the 'Lettera 36' electric portable, the 'Valentine' typewriter and 'Synthesis 45' office furniture (1973).

The Valentine is his masterpiece. Going into the shops on 14 February 1969, the Valentine in Sottsass's own description was 'the antimachine machine'. There were some technical innovations such as a carriage set at the level of the keyboard, the use of bright red plastic and an integral carrying case, but the revolution was a conceptual one. Sottsass wanted to re-invent the way people used typewriters, to bring a useful machine out of

1: Sony TV8-301, 1959. Sony 'Walkman', 1980. Sony's consistent ingenuity and policy of miniaturization continuously forced daring and unusual innovations, including a viable miniature television and a tape-recorder that did not record. With an attention to detail and finish that has its basis in traditional culture, Sony was the first Japanese manufacturer to acquire a reputation for quality.

2: Ettore Sottsass says 'I despise provincial utopias'. A restless revolutionary, he has designed both dignified office equipment including this 'Sistema 45' secretary's chair, 1973, and radical furniture which shocked conventional taste. The 'Carlton' dresser was made for his Memphis collaborative in 1981. Its inspiration Suburbia.

the office and into the street. 'Red,' he said, 'is the colour of the Communist flag, the colour that makes a surgeon move faster and the colour of passion.'

Sottsass enjoys the role of both guru and intellectual delinquent. In the Sixties he became very interested in Pop, grew his hair and went to India. This phase of his life resulted in intense and profound studio ceramics and glassware designed for Vistosi. In 1979, while still working for Olivetti and still carrying out independent commissions for Poltronova and Alessi, Sottsass became involved with the avant-garde Milanese group Studio Alchymia. He contributed some bizarre furniture designs to their collection, which was ironically called 'Bauhaus', but in 1981 broke away to form a radical group of his own which, in mock reference both to Egyptology and to rock 'n' roll, he called Memphis. This group, ironic and irreverent, but at the same time entirely serious, summarized Sottsass's attitude to design. Disciplined good taste was not of interest. Instead, Memphis was inspired by 'quoting from suburbia'.

Sottsass's work and thought is most of all characterized by formal and intellectual irreverence, although he says he is a theoretical designer, rather as Einstein was a theoretical physicist. He has enjoyed designing a typewriter which can be used in a discotheque, just as a secretary's chair for Olivetti had feet intended to suggest Mickey Mouse. These characteristics remain the same whether he is working on his own furniture, on modular systems for data processing, or on street furniture for Turin.

In 1980 Sottsass Associati was established with architects Aldo Cibic, Matteo Thun and Marco Zanini. Latterly, Sottsass has enjoyed unusual commercial success designing small, useful products for Alessi, although the great achievement of his career was to blur distinctions between art and industry, allowing consumers to enjoy in a manufactured object something of the mystical quality hitherto only available in painting.

Bibliography Federica di Castro *Sottsass Scrapbook* Documenti di Casabella, Milan, 1976; Penny Sparke *Ettore Sottsass* Design Council, London, 1982; Andrea Branzi *The Hot House: Italian New-Wave Design* MIT, Cambridge, Mass., 1984; *Sottsass* exhibition catalogue, Los Angeles County Museum, 2006

2

2

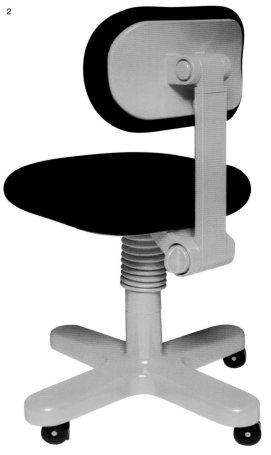

Sottsass was one of the designers who made plastic an acceptable material for high-concept domestic furniture

Mart Stam 1899–86

A Dutch architect, Mart Stam was born in Purmerend. In 1924 he was, probably, the first designer to conceive a tubular steel chair employing the cantilever principle. His initiative was taken up with more success after 1926 by the better-equipped designers of the <u>Bauhaus</u>, <u>Marcel Breuer</u> and <u>Mies van der Rohe</u>. With Emil Roth and Hans Schmidt he ran the journal *ABC* from Zürich, promoting the solution of social problems by the use of technology and modern architecture. Stam's social commitments took him from the 'New Frankfurt' he was building with Ernst May to the Soviet Union from 1930 to 1934. From 1939 to 1945 he was director of the Institute voor Kunstnijverheidsondernijs in Amsterdam. He retired from work in 1966.

Bibliography *Mart Stam – Documentizing his Work 1920–1965* RIBA Publications, London, 1970; Otakar Macel and Jan van Geest *Stühle aus Stahl* Walther König, Cologne, 1980

Philippe Starck born 1949

In spite, or because, he is a celebrity phenomenon, Philippe Starck says he is not interested in designers. A restlessly inventive son of an aircraft engineer, Starck was born in Paris in 1949 and attended the Nissim de Camondo school. Among his early clients was <u>Pierre Cardin</u>, who may have taught him the arts of self-promotion and personal <u>branding</u>. In the Seventies he made his name fitting out Paris nightclubs. As a result of this reputaton, President Mitterand had him do rooms in the Elysée Palace in 1982. This further enhanced a career already as buoyant as one of his inflatable chairs. A successful café in Les Halles for the Costes brothers in 1984 was the basis of a stellar career. A series of New York hotels introduced America to the Starck phenomenon, although he is no longer employed by their proprietor, Ian Schrager. Starck's intelligence and whimsy ('I live like a monk so there is no news') disguises manic careerism and a prodigal genius for, sometimes opportunistic, novelty. That many of his designs are absurd (the lemon squeezer for <u>Alessi</u>) or annoying (a transparent polycarbonate chair for Paris' Kong restaurant, marketed by <u>Kartell</u> as 'Louis Ghost') or misguided (a motorbike for Aprilia) has not impeded, may even have augmented, his professional progress. For good or for bad, Starck – with his energy, inventiveness, his cynicism and his smarts – is a total representation of the 'designer' phenomenon, or problem.

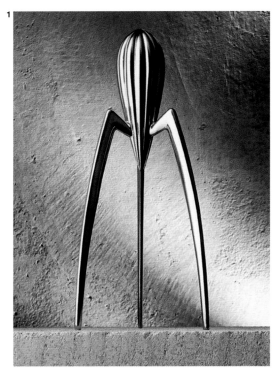

1: Philippe Starck, 'Juicy Salif' lemon squeezer for Alessi, 1990. Cheap as sculpture, expensive as a lemon-squeezer.
2: Philippe Starck, 'Louis' Ghost chair for Kartell, 2002.

3: John Kemp Starley, 'Rover' safety bicycle, 1885: the only technology with no downside.

John Kemp Starley 1854-1901

Although there are many competitors to the claim, Starley is usually credited with the final definition of the 'Safety Bicycle'. The 1880s were a turbulent and competitive time among bicycle designer-entrepreneurs. There were many advocates of tricycles while the old high-mounted 'Ordinary' (or Penny-Farthing) was becoming less and less acceptable from a health and safety point-of-view. In an essay called *Taming the Bicycle* Mark Twain described progress on a 'weaving, tottering' fashion. By 1885 Starley had settled on a successful general arrangement: his 'Rover' had a low mount, wheels of 36 inches in diameter in the front, 30 in the rear, triangular frame, chain drive to the rear. His brief to himself was to create 'the right position in relation to the pedals' at 'the proper distance from the ground.' In September of that year George Smith rode 100 miles on a Rover in 7 hours and 5 minutes. Further refinements followed, but a timeless classic had been established. In the late 1890s, Starley's business was re-named the Rover Cycle Company, ancestor of the car company. The bicycle can truly be regarded as the only technology with no down side.

Bibliography David Herlihy *Bicycle: the history* Yale University Press, New Haven, 2006

Brooks Stevens 1911–95

Brooks Stevens was the third thing that made Milwaukee famous, after beer and Harley-Davidson. He briefly left the city to study architecture at New York's Cornell University, but this was academically unsuccessful and he returned to his native city to work in stock control for a local soap company. In the best possible sense, a Mid-Western sensibility informed all his work as an industrial designer. His first job was doing labels for the soap company and in 1935 he established Brooks Stevens Industrial Design, very much on the model of the pioneer consultant New York industrial designers Raymond Loewy and Walter Dorwin Teague. A background in soap made Stevens a persuasive salesman and he successfully pitched for a vast variety of new business with a slide show called 'Industrial Design and Its Application to Industry'. Like the WASP Loewy he resembled, Stevens tirelessly made the point that design would pay for itself. Like Loewy, he specialized too in bravura transformations, turning the military Jeep into a cutely consumerized Jeepster. This was designed to 'capture the fancy of the youth of the country' and was, therefore, painted in primary colours and given chrome trim. His view of the industrial designer was 'businessman, an engineer and

a stylist, and in that direct order'. His clients included the Milwaukee Railroad, Evinrude outboard motors, Miller Brewing (its logo) and Harley-Davidson (the 1949 Hydra-glide). In 1954 in a talk to a group of advertising professionals Stevens coined the expression 'planned obsolescence'. Although this has subsequently attracted much obloquy, Stevens' own definition was relatively innocent: 'instilling in the buyer the desire to own something a little newer, a little better, a little sooner than is necessary.' Asked on retirement if he would change any of his work he said, 'Hell, yes. Everything! Because it's all out-moded.' Stevens made several other remarkable contributions to consumer psychology: putting an observation window on a washing machine (turning laundry into a spectacle), developing the wide-mouthed peanut butter jar and designing the Oscar Meyer Wienermobile, a truck shaped like a sausage.

Bibliography *Brooks Stevens – industrial strength design, how Brooks Stevens Shaped Your World* exhibition catalogue Milwaukee Art Museum, 2003

3

1

Stockholm Exhibition

The Stockholm Exhibition of 1930 was perhaps the most important activity organized by the Svenska Sljödföreningen, under its director Gregor Paulsson. Paulsson employed Gunnar Asplund to design the exhibition. Asplund turned what had been conceived as a metropolitan exhibition into an international advertisement for the Modern Movement, presenting architecture and design as essays in standardization, rationalization and availability. To English travellers like Gordon Russell and Morton Shand it was a revelation, and a whole generation of architectural students left the London and provincial schools to see what Asplund had done. Before Stockholm, international exhibitions had attracted attention by their vulgar excess or ostentatious luxury. But such was the impact of Stockholm that the Swedish glass industry abandoned engraved glass in favour of simpler forms, while the ceramics manufacturers began to think more clearly about producing tableware that was easy to stack and easy to wash. Stockholm 1930 showed the rest of the world Sweden's humane and individual interpretation of Modernism.

Styling

The term 'styling' is used dismissively (and with contempt) for an American approach to design in which a product's appearance was moulded for the purpose of increasing sales. It flourished in the Thirties and Forties. Raymond Loewy and Harley Earl were its masters.

Superstudio

Like Archizoom, Superstudio was one of the Italian avant-garde groups of architect-designers which was founded in the Sixties and which matured into something less than radical, in this case obscurity, after a brief flourish of popularity. In 1970 Superstudio collaborated with Gruppo 9999 on the foundation of the Sine Space School for the study of conceptual architecture. All three are now defunct.

284

1: The Continuous Monument Project by Superstudio, 1969.
2: Exhibition buildings by Gunnar Asplund for the influential Stockholm Exhibition of 1930: the first built expression of the ideals of the Svenska Sljodforeningen.

Surrealism

Surrealism was a movement in literature and art. A plaque in Paris' Hotel des Grands Hommes records the moment of its creation in spring 1919, when the writer André Breton and the painter Philippe Soupault invented 'L'ecriture automatique' and gave birth to a sensibility which connected Freud's investigations into the un- and sub-conscious with an artistic dreamworld. As such, Surrealism had no obvious expression in industrial design, but through its influence in film and theatre sets, interiors, fashion (especially <u>Schiapirelli</u>) and advertising helped create a mood that informed the taste of many designers. And there were occasions when the Surrealist artists themselves produced design: Salvador Dali's sofa inspired by Mae West's lips and his 'Lobster' telephone made in 1938, or Meret Oppenheim's 'Table with Bird's Legs' of 1939 are among the most frequently reproduced objects of the twentieth century. Oppenheim's fur-covered cup and saucer, produced for a Surrealist group exhibition in 1936 when she was only 23, was defiantly, hilariously anti-functional: an early example of Anti-Design. Surrealism's dream world was also an influence on art directors: *Vogue*, *Harper's Bazaar*, <u>Ford</u> and Shell all, perhaps incongruously, signed up to Breton's belief that 'beauty will be convulsive or will not be at all'.

Bibliography *Surreal Things: Surrealism and Design* (ed. Ghislaine Wood) exhibition catalogue Victoria and Albert Museum, London, 2007

Svenska Sljödföreningen

The Svenska Sljödföreningen is an art association founded in 1845. Its most important director was <u>Gregor Paulsson</u>, who ran it from 1920 to 1934. He once wrote that its purpose was to achieve 'a definitive change from the isolated production of individuals to the conscious work of a whole generation for a culture of form on a broad social basis'. It has now changed itself to Foreningen SvenskForm, or just SvenskForm for simplicity. The Sljödföreningen's greatest achievement was to organize the <u>Stockholm Exhibition</u> of 1930. It has acted as a design pressure group, being especially concerned since the Second World War with ideal sizes for furniture and with methods of rationalizing activities in smaller homes.

3: Meret Oppenheim, Objet (Le dejeuner en fourure), 1936.
4: Salvador Dali, 'Mae West' sofa, 1938. Dali wrote a 'Note to Architects: Your designs are too harsh, too mechanistic – you should cater to man's desire to return to his pre-natal abode by utilizing rounded non-rigid forms and soft protective materials'.

Svenskt Tenn

Svenskt Tenn (which means 'Swedish Pewter') is the name of a shop founded by Estrid Ericson on Stockholm's Strandvagen. Its merchandise helped popularize the idea of 'Swedish grace' throughout the world, particularly in the United States, where to many of the <u>House & Garden</u> readership Svenskt Tenn became known as 'the most beautiful shop in the world'. Svenskt Tenn became the showroom for <u>Josef Frank</u>, the Austrian architect who did much to create the Swedish style, after his arrival in Stockholm in the mid-Thirties.

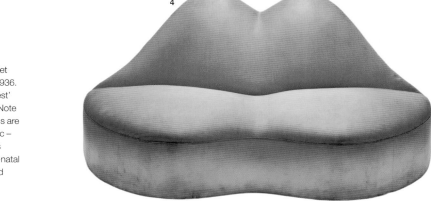

Roger Tallon born 1929

The professional institution of design does not exist in the same way in France as it does in other countries. Someone once said the French have no feel for it, just as they have no feel for jazz. Roger Tallon is one of the few identifiable, independent, living French designers.

Tallon was born in Paris. He recalled being greatly moved as a child by a visit to the 1937 exhibitions on Arts et Techniques, with its innocent visions of a cleanly designed future. He studied engineering, joining Caterpillar France in 1951, taking charge of the construction equipment manufacturer's graphics. After meeting Jacques Viennot in 1953 he joined Technes, France's original design consultancy with Viennot he had founded with Jean Parthenay in 1949. Through Viennot Tallon met Gio Ponti, Marcello Nizzolli and Le Corbusier and began visiting the Milan Triennales.

In 1957 Tallon gave the very first design lecture in France, at the Ecole des Arts Appliques and in 1963 set up the Design section of ENSAD, the Ecole Nationale Superieure des Arts Decoratifs. Indeed, Tallon introduced the French to the word design, refusing to gallicize it. 'Would it occur to you to gallicize the word jazz?' he demanded.

His first projects were all concerned with heavy industrial products: in 1954 a universal milling machine for Gambin, an airport tug for Fenwick in 1957, and electric drills for Peugeot in 1966. But Tallon is best known for his influential work on French railways. His Corail train for SNCF appeared in 1971 and the TGV Atlantique in 1983. The distinctive nose of the French high speed train was drawn by Jack Cooper, an Englishman trained by Raymond Loewy who was working at Alsthom, but Tallon retained overall responsibility for the TGV style. In 1987 he won

1

2

Ilmari Tapiovaara

the commission for design and fitting out of Eurostar. Other train projects for Alsthom and the Paris RATP followed.

According to Tallon, who is a devotee of trains, boats, planes and, indeed, cars, the Ford Model T was a major turning-point in the history of the modern world: 'It meant that people stopped copying and started inventing. Industry designed its own objects.' He also believes that 'Design is not characterized by an activity of specific conception, but by behaviour of the conceiver in the exercise of that activity.'

Tallon is loquacious, articulate, provocative and argumentative. He says the TGV is 'metal which flows into space'. In his designs Tallon combines computer modelling with aerodynamic research, combing them with a strong visual idea to create shapes that are dramatic and pure.

Bibliography Gilles de Bure & Chloe Braunstein *Tallon* Editions Dis Voir, Paris, 1999

The architect-designer Ilmari Tapiovaara was born in Tampere, Finland, in 1914. As a student at Helsinki's Taideteollisuuskeskuskoulu (school of applied arts), Tapiovaara became familiar with modern methods of furniture production, working in Otto Korhonen's factory (where Alvar Aalto's furniture was manufactured). On graduating in 1937 he got a job with the Asko-Avonius furniture factory, where his responsibility was to take creative charge of the product line. By the 1939 Finnish Housing Exhibition Asko was showing mass-produced, unpainted light wood furniture, suitable for both the urban middle-class home and the house of a small farmer. After wartime service, Tapiovaara designed furniture for a student dormitory called 'Domus Academica' (1946), and the 'Domus' chair (1946) effectively became his trademark. Because of its

success, contract furniture for schools, universities and other public buildings became the mainstay of his design work throughout the Fifties. Tapiovaara's furniture has all the 'traditional' virtues of Finnish design – elegant, simple and natural, but with subtle refinements. He has also designed various exhibitions, the Olivetti showroom in Helsinki (1954) and aircraft interiors for Finnair's Convairs and Caravelles (1957). He took part in a development project for Paraguay (1959) and designed some children's furniture for Heal's (1960).

Bibliography *Ilmari Tapiovaara* exhibition catalogue, Taideteollisuusmuseo, Helsinki, 1984

1: Roger Tallon, watches for Lipp, 1970s. Tallon's designs for the doomed French cooperative anticipated both Post-Modernism and Giugiaro's highly-evolved technical 'language'.

2: The French TGV went into service in 1983. 'Metal that flows into space' according to its designer, Roger Tallon. The distinctive architecture was inspired by English designer Jack Cooper, a disciple of Raymond Loewy's. Working for manufacturer Alstom in 1968, Cooper was briefed to 'design a train that does not look like a train'.

3: Ilmari Tapiovaara. 'Domus' chair in oak for Asko-Avonius, 1946.

3

Vladimir Tatlin 1885-1953

Vladimir Tatlin was an artist and *agent provacateur* rather than an industrial designer, but he was responsible for images and ideas which had an influential effect on Modernism's rhetoric and, indeed, on the theory of branding.

Great buildings are ideas. And just as ideas do not have to be written to be influential, buildings do not have to suffer the compromises and indignities of erection in order to be important. Indeed, many of the most influential designs in the whole history of architecture remain on paper, or at least in the imagination.

The fantastical schemes of Boullée, the scary visions of Piranesi, even Le Corbusier's coruscating Ville Radieuse were never interpreted with builder's hod and plasterer's trowel. Nor was there ever such a thing as Futurist architecture, but Sant'Elia's drawings are unforgettable. Sometimes you assume the best way to defend an architectural reputation is not to build. Tatlin's Tower is the greatest unbuilt building of them all.

Lenin demanded 'Must we serve sweet cakes to a small minority while the workers and peasants are in need of black bread?' If there was going to be Soviet art, it was going to have a social purpose. Art would be almost as important as electrification. In 1919, to exploit the creaking rhetoric of the era, Vladimir Tatlin was 'invited' to create a Monument to the Third International, an architectural commentary on Lenin's 'Plan for Monumental Propaganda'. Czarist iconography (conceited, complaisant) was to be replaced by art democratic art (systematic, pedagogic).

What to call it? The term 'Cubo-Futurism' had been coined four years before 1917 by Kasimir Malevich, the master of the black square. But such a name looked West to Paris and Milan. Two years after the Revolution, Cubo-Futurism had hardened into Constructivism. This looked east to Kharkov and Magnitogorsk. To get the sense of purpose just let the title of Lissitsky's 'Beat the Whites with the Red Wedge' take the place of hearty Ukrainian peasant women threshing in your mind's eye. Constructivism was defined by Szczuka and Zarnower: it should not be about shapes and effects (which were

bourgeois illusions), but about the actual grammar of construction. It was not, they insisted, an art that imitated the machine, but one that found its equivalent.

So, to satisfy Trotsky's demand that when the Soviet state became stable it would need monuments of its own, Vladimir Tatlin had this idea about the 66 father figures of the Revolution. And as an architectural matrix to advance their matyrology he designed the most fantastical building of all time, surging at daringly proletarian angles. Tatlin's Tower was an audacious double helix. Inside, cheerful proletarian visitors were to be moved mechanically around the structure in a nauseogenic rotating glazed cylinder in pursuit of higher levels of political awareness. Fraternal messages of solidarity from far-flung comrades were to be flashed on screens. Giant projectors would beam politically correct

Great buildings are ideas. And just as ideas do not have to be written to be influential, buildings do not have to suffer the compromises and indignities of erection in order to be important

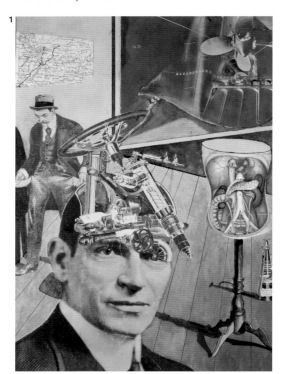

1: Vladimir Tatlin designed nothing that went into production, but was an influential propagandist of the machine aesthetic. Raoul Haussman's collage, Tatlin at Home, 1920, suggests the range of his interests.

2: Vladimir Tatlin, Monument to the 3rd International, 1919–20. Poster by Nikolai Punin.

slogans onto the cushion of cloud that sat upon Moscow. Here was a building as a brand, an ideas generator. What could not be achieved by architecture could be left to transport: Nikolai Punin suggested that from the garage within the Tower, special motorbikes and cars could rush forth in pursuit of 'agitation'.

Tatlin's Tower was never built. By 1924 Trotsky himself had his own prosaic criticisms. Why, he wanted to know, would his cheerful proletarians actually benefit from being rotated in a cylinder? Anyway, Lenin, perhaps betraying bourgeois instincts, or possibly just the travel bug, much preferred the Eiffel Tower. He was not alone: the greatest of all Soviet journalists, Ilya Ehrenburg, wrote his *Life of the Automobile* in 1929. It features extravagant coverage of André Citroën's advertisements, which illuminated the Eiffel Tower. This propaganda was real while Tatlin's Tower was fiction.

Tatlin's Tower could not be built: the structural idea was too ambitious for the available technology, but it nonetheless represented something of lasting value. Vladimir Tatlin discovered the powerful rhetoric of mechanization even before the Germans. They loved it. Widely published in Germany, Tatlin's Tower became a symbol of a future full of technological promise. At the time, the most progressive building on German soil was a factory with glass corners for making shoe lasts designed by Walter Gropius. Tatlin's Tower was stronger meat. In Berlin Dada artists stood with placards saying 'Die Kunst ist Tot, es lebe in die neue Maschinenkunst Tatlins!' It means 'Art is Dead, Long live Tatlin's new Machine Art!'

If Tatlin's Tower could have been built, it would not have survived the purges that turned the thrilling Soviet Union into a corrupt gerontocracy with antimacassars in their limousines. But it was a great idea and has become a great work of art… on paper. As Helen Rosenau wrote in her pioneering book *The Ideal City* (1959), the only true test of artistic quality is that at some point a revival will take place.

Bibliography John Milner *Vladimir Tatlin and the Russian Avant-Garde* Yale University Press, New Haven, 1983

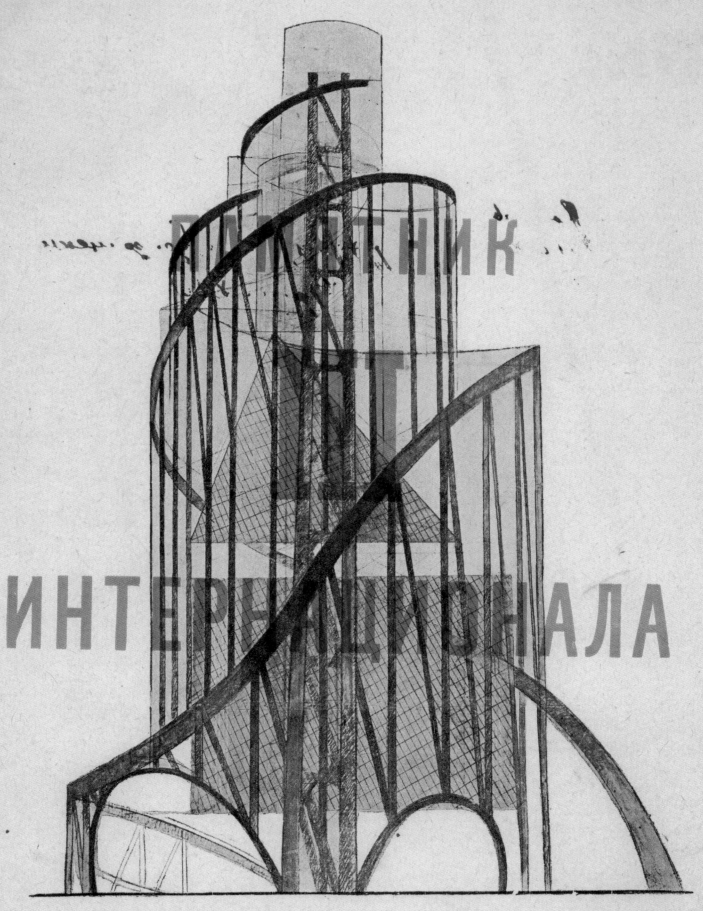

Проект худ. В. Е. ТАТЛИНА

Taylorism

Frederick Winslow Taylor was the author of *Principles of Scientific Management* (1911), a pioneering book which was an influence on Henry Ford and Le Corbusier.

Taylorism was a set of commonsense organizational principles, intended to replace authoritarianism and anarchy on the shop floor. Taylor felt it would mean 'the elimination of almost all causes for dispute and disagreement' between employers and workmen. Some of Taylor's organizational theories were picked up by the Nazis.

Bibliography Judith A. Merkle *Management and Ideology* University of California Press, Berkeley and London, 1980

Such was Walter Dorwin Teague's reputation and his firm's successes that he had attained an almost scriptural presence in American industry

Walter Dorwin Teague 1883–1960

Walter Dorwin Teague was, with Raymond Loewy, Henry Dreyfuss and Norman Bel Geddes, one of the pioneers of the consultant design profession that established itself in New York during the later Twenties.

Teague was born in Decatur, Indiana, the son of an itinerant Methodist minister. He studied at the Art Students' League, becoming an advertising draughtsman before setting up his own consultancy in 1926. This early date, despite the contrary claims of Bel Geddes, gives Teague some claim to being the very first individual to open an industrial design office.

Teague's first job was a redesign of a Kodak camera, for which he produced a set piece of styling. Teague's other clients included Ford, US Steel, NCR, Du Pont, Westinghouse, Proctor & Gamble and Texaco, and he designed six different pavilions at the 1939 New York World's Fair. His work was characterized by a restrained businesslike quality. Like his contemporaries, all eager to establish themselves as legitimate members of the community, Teague wrote a book to celebrate the accomplishments of the industrial designer. *Design This Day*, published in 1940, was the most refined and sophisticated of the first generation of industrial design books to come out of America; it had a patrician, almost sacerdotal quality. But Teague had other literary interests too: commuting to his New York offices he would read Shakespeare on the train, and in mid-life he was the author of a book on agriculture as well as a modestly successful detective story.

After the Second World War Teague's office was effectively run by his lieutenant, Frank del Giudice, whose own work concentrated on the interior design of all

Boeing commercial transports; from his Stratocruiser through his 707, 727, 737, 747 and 757 to his 767, the inheritors of a Twenties version of commercial style have moulded the world's perceptions of how aeroplane interiors should appear. The influence of the Teague office even extended to the actual appearance of the aeroplane itself – on the 707 del Giudice advised on the contours of the nose, fins and engine nacelles.

Such was Walter Dorwin Teague's reputation and his firm's successes that he had attained an almost scriptural presence in American industry.

Bibliography Walter Dorwin Teague *Design This Day – the technique of order in the Machine Age* Harcourt Brace, New York, 1940; Arthur J. Pulos American Design Ethic MIT, Cambridge, Mass., 1983

Technès

Technès is a design consultancy founded by Jacques Viennot in 1953 in Paris with offices on the Boulevard Raspail. Technès worked in both product and graphic design, and its partners included Roger Tallon. In 1975 it combined with Atelier Maurandy to form a multidisciplinary office working in retail design.

Giuseppe Terragni 1904–43

Guiseppe Terragni was born in Meda, in northern Italy. He was one of the founders of the 'Movimento Italiano per L'Architettura Razionale' and of the avant-garde Gruppo 7, all determined to modernize Italian institutional architecture. His most celebrated building, the first pure exercise in Italy of the International Style, was the Casa del Fascio in Como (1932–6). A chair he designed in 1935 in lacquered wood and steel is now reproduced by Zanotta. *Quadrante* magazine once described Terragni's Casa del Fascio as, 'The table of logarithms of construction in general, the dictionary where one could find the best solutions to the most complicated problems, a lexicon of beauty and a paradigm of wisdom'.

Bibliography Rassegna Anno II *No.4 Il disegno del mobile razionale in Italia 1928/1948* Milan, 1980; Peter Eisenmann *Giuseppe Terragni – Transformations, Decompositions, Critiques* Monacelli Press, New York, 2003

Benjamin Thompson 1918–2002

Benjamin Thompson is an American architect whose ideas about urban environment, and in particular about urban renewal, advanced in his 1966 essay 'Visual Squalor and Social Disorder', have had a profound effect on the world of design. Thompson was chairman of Harvard's department of architecture and persuaded Walter Gropius to found the Architects' Collaborative (TAC).

Thompson has also conceived and designed for his own stores. He set up Design Research in 1953 to source well-designed products. His purpose at D/R (as it became known) was 'to communicate to the viewer a sense of the world, of joy-of-living, etc.' Growing out of the day-to-day architects' business of selecting furniture and fabrics, it evolved into an expression in the mercantile world of New York retailing of some of the educational ideas which Thompson developed in his courses at Harvard: 'D/R has to do with daily life, morning, noon and night, fresh daisies on the table, a good loaf of bread – the living environment.' It was Thompson who discovered Marimekko at European trade fairs in the late Fifties, and invited Armi Ratia to organize an exhibition at his five-storey 'Design Research' store in Cambridge, Mass. Opened in 1970, this is now a branch of Crate & Barrel.

The most complete expression of Thompson's ideas about life and environment has been his rehabilitation of Boston's Faneuil Hall and Quincy Street Market into a brisk and popular urban meeting place which has restored life and business to a moribund part of the city. It was an influence on the redevelopment of London's similarly placed Covent Garden. Thompson's last great scheme has been the redevelopment of New York's South Street Seaport, an ancient wharf area on the edge of the city's financial district. His Baltimore shopping area and Aquatic centre has been influential, too.

3

1: Walter Dorwin Teague, Texaco Service Station, 1935. During the Thirties Teague's studio took charge of Texaco's corporate identity. To Teague, who had a visionary sense of design in the modern world, the garage was to the twentieth century what the temple had been to ancient Greece and Rome. The Texaco design remained in all essentials unchanged until 1983.

2: Walter Dorwin Teague, Kodak camera in the streamlined style known as 'Borax', circa 1936.
3: Giuseppe Terragni, chairs designed for the Casa del Fascio, Como, 1932–36. In Italy Modernism was not inevitably associated with left-wing politics.

Michael Thonet 1796–1871

Michael Thonet's bentwood 'Vienna' chair was one of the first examples of successful mass-production to reach the market, and has constantly been a symbol of excellence in design. Brahms used a Thonet chair at his piano, while composing. Lenin used them. Le Corbusier populated his interiors with them, because he felt they possessed 'nobility'. And they are used today in smart New York restaurants.

Michael Thonet was born at Boppard, near Koblenz, and trained as a cabinet-maker. In the 1830s he began to experiment with the technique of lamination, which was a cheaper and more effective way of making curved structures than hand cutting. Vernacular English 'Windsor' chairs already contained elements of bentwood and a US patent was given to Samuel Gragg in 1808 for an 'elastic' wooden chair, but Thonet's rationalized all the associated techniques necessary for mass-production. However, his application for a patent in 1840 failed on grounds of lack

of innovation. When his laminated chairs were exhibited at Koblenz in 1841 they were seen by Prince Metternich, who suggested he would be better off in Vienna. In July of the next year he was given an imperial monopoly on making these light, elastic laminated chairs, and duly set out for the Austrian capital. In 1842 Thonet was granted his patent. In 1849 Thonet chairs were used in the popular Viennese café, the Daum, and in 1851 Thonet exhibited in London at the Great Exhibition. In 1852 the firm Gebrüder Thonet was incorporated.

However, rising wages in Vienna started to make the labour-intensive lamination technique expensive, so Thonet continued to experiment. His next development was to bend solid wood with steam, which allowed the parts of the chair to be turned *before* they were steam-bent, and it was this technique that led to the real innovation in mass-production furniture. A new factory was built at Koritschan in Moravia in 1856 to make the

'Vierzehner' (number 14) chair, which was the model that became the classic. Thonet applied sophisticated production techniques in the Koritschan factory and took the division of labour almost as far as Henry Ford was to. Thonet also provided schools and health insurance schemes for the workers in his factories (although when Le Corbusier visited the factory in 1932 he noted in the visitors' book that working conditions were like an 'inferno').

The 'Vierzehner' was made out of six separate parts of beech. The section of each component continuously varies, according to the local demands of the structure. The flexibility and the fact that there are no glue joints or breaks is what is so important about the chair; because they are bolted together it was easy and economical to ship in parts all over the world. The chair was awarded a bronze medal at the London exhibition of 1862, where the jury declared: 'An excellent application of a happy thought… they are not works of show, but practical furniture for daily use – they are simple, graceful, light and strong.' At the same exhibition William Morris was exhibiting pseudo-medieval designs.

By the mid-Twenties it was estimated that more than 100 million examples of the 'Vierzehner' had been produced, but it was nonetheless clear to Thonet-Mundus (as the firm had become in 1906) that a new age called for the use of new materials, and the first tubular steel chairs by Mart Stam, Marcel Breuer and Mies van der Rohe were produced by Thonet in their Frankenberg factory, where the firm remains today. The original bentwood chairs are still manufactured in the old factory at Korycany in the Czech Republic (Korycany is the Slavonic of Koritschan). The 'S-64', Marcel Breuer's adaptation of Mart Stam's original design, always known as 'the Bauhaus Chair' is also still in production.

Bibliography *Ole Bang, Thonet – Geschichte eines Stuhles, Weitbrecht* Stuttgart 1979; Alexander von Vegesack *Thonet – classic furniture in bentwood and tubular steel* Hazar, London, 1996

1: As a sales promotion Thonet demonstrated that 36 knocked-down chairs could be stored in a mere cubic metre.
2: Matteo Thun, Santa Ana lamp, 1983 and Ladoga cocktail cup, 1982.

Matteo Thun born 1952

Matteo Thun is a partner in <u>Sottsass</u> Associati and contributed to the first <u>Memphis</u> collection in 1981. He was born in Bolzano, studied at the Oskar Kokoschka Academ in Salzburg and at Florence University. Since 1982 he has taught product design at the Vienna Academy of Arts.

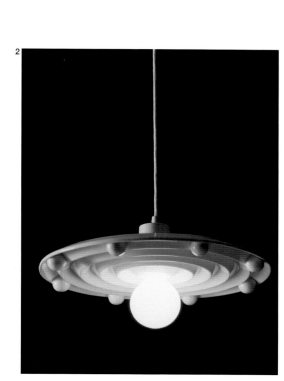

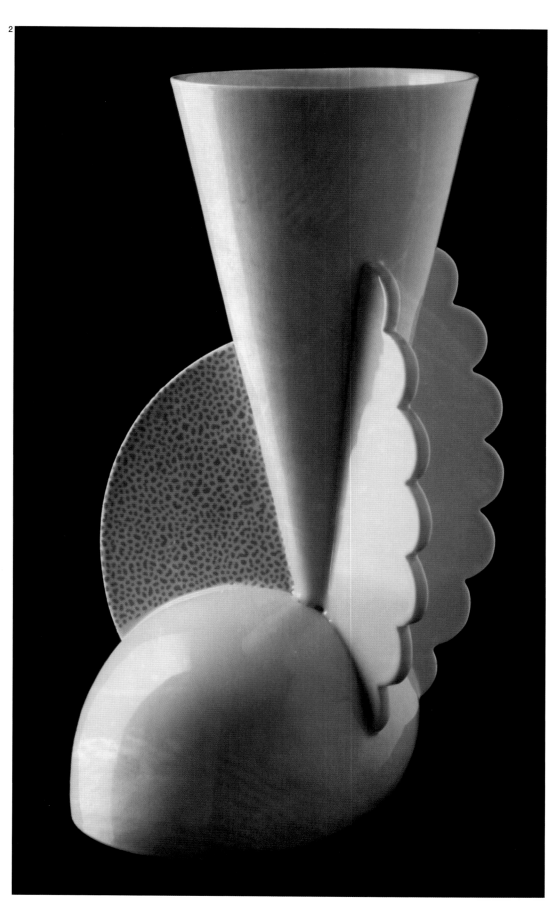

An excellent application of a happy thought… they are not works of show, but practical furniture for daily use – they are simple, graceful, light and strong

Total Design

Total Design is an Amsterdam design consultancy founded by <u>Friso Kramer</u> in 1962. His partners were Bennon Wissing and Wim Crouwel.

Its work is typical of the 'new' Dutch graphics. Although Wim Crouwel's work for Amsterdam's Stedelijk Museum shows a traditional, modern restraint, there are new elements coming into the studio's 'language'. Like other Dutch graphic designers, they tend to prefer 'grotesque' newspaper typefaces (and even newspaper layout) to the more refined 'Helvetica' of the Swiss School. Similarly, they use idioms and motifs that are deliberately anti-rational or at least dysfunctional in the old-fashioned sense.

Bibliography Alston W. Purvis and Cees W. de Jong *Dutch Graphic Design – A century of innovation* Thames & Hudson, London, 2006

Touring

Carrozzeria Touring was founded in Milan in 1926 as a partnership between Felice Bianchi Anderloni and Gaetano Ponzoni. Since its inception Touring has been particularly concerned with lightness of construction, and the shop became associated with the term it coined for its own special method of construction: *Superleggera*. This is a system, derived from contemporary aircraft practice, where hand-beaten metal panels are mounted on to a very light space-frame. Carlo Anderloni (born 1916), the founder's son, took over in 1948. One of his first designs was for Ferrari. Shown at the 1948 Turin motor show, the radical shape both dismayed and annoyed journalists who derisively called it a 'barchetta' or little boat. Properly the Ferrari Tipo 166 MM, the barchetta was a sensationally clean and uncluttered shape, a complete novelty and a new word entered the language of car design. In 1953, with flying saucer hysteria in the media, Anderloni produced a 'disco volante' show car for <u>Alfa-Romeo</u>. The company's original name was Carrozzeria Falco: the choice of the English word 'touring' in the name instead of the Italian, *turismo*, betrays the taste of the founders, and the firm's best-known body design was for the English Aston Martin DB-4. The association had begun in 1955 and the brief was 'a compact 2 plus 2 with sufficient boot'. Touring went into liquidation in 1967 and Anderloni joined Alfa-Romeo.

Triennale

The Milan Triennale grew out of a tradition of bi-annual exhibitions which began in Monza in 1923 with the 'Prima Mostra Internazionale delle Arti Decorative' (First International Exhibition of Decorative Arts). The last Biennale was held in 1930 and the first Triennale in 1933, at Milan's Palazzo d'Arte.

At the first Triennale there was a celebration of <u>Futurism</u> side by side with examples of the work of <u>Le Corbusier</u>, <u>Walter Gropius</u> and some other leaders of the <u>Modern Movement</u>. The second Triennale, in 1936, was a Fascist event, redeemed by <u>Nizzoli</u>'s participation in the design of the 'Salone della Vittoria'.

The Triennale continued after the war and by the Fifties had become the acknowledged showplace for modern design. It has contributed greatly to Milan's reputation as the leading international centre for design.

Bibliography Anty Pansera *Storia cronache della Triennale* Fabbri, Milan, 1978

1

1: Total Design, signage for PTT, the Dutch Post Office, 1978–9.
2: Jan Tschichold, 'Die Frau ohne Namen' lithograph, 1927.

3: Jan Tschichold, commercial art for Penguin, 1947–9. Tschichold also wrote the *Penguin Composition Rule*, an in-house style guide.
4: Jan Tschichold, Sabon, typeface, 1967, named after the sixteenth century Lyonais typefounder, Jacques Sabon.

GEORG JACOBYS WELTREISEFILM

PHOEBUS-PALAST
ANFANGSZEITEN: 4, 6¹⁵, 8³⁰   SONNTAGS: 1⁴⁵, 4, 6¹⁵ 8³⁰

Jan Tschichold 1902–74

With <u>Stanley Morison</u> and <u>Herbert Bayer</u>, Jan Tschichold was the most influential typographer of the twentieth century. He was born in Leipzig, the son of a signwriter, and as a young man was inspired by the first <u>Bauhaus</u> exhibition of 1923. As a result of this he published a manifesto, *Elementare Typographie*, in the same year. This polemic in the cause of new, uncluttered book design and layout was followed by a book, *Die neue Typographie*, in 1926. Like the Bauhaus masters, Tschichold had to leave Germany with the rise of Hitler, who thought that the new typography was an expression of *Kulturbolschewismus*, or Bolshevik art. In 1935 he lectured in Denmark and then moved to London, where the publishers Lund Humphries arranged an exhibition of his work. In England he joined <u>Penguin Books</u> and established the distinguished standards of typography and layout which changed the face of British publishing and did as much to educate British taste as many well-funded public and educational institutions. In 1949 he retired to Switzerland.
Bibliography Richard B. Doubleday *Jan Tschichold – The Penguin Years* Lund Humphries, 2006

THE PENGUINS ARE COMING

IF YOU WANT TO KNOW WHAT ALL THIS IS ABOUT, TURN OVER QUICKLY TO THE NEXT PAGE →

Sabon *Sabon*

U
V

Unimark

Unimark was founded in Milan in 1965 by Bob Noorda, Jay Doblin, Massimo Vignelli and others; its New York office opened in 1966. It had a distinguished client list that included Gillette, Olivetti and McCormick.

Johan Vaaler 1866–1910

Johan Vaaler was a Norwegian Patents Clerk often credited with the design of the paperclip, often cited as a perfect design: useful, elegant, inexpensive. This is an exaggeration as the English Gem Manufacturing Company was already making paperclips of bent metal before Vaaler was born. Vaaler's ingenuity lay in seeking design protection. Because Norway had poor patent legislation, he registered his design in Germany in 1899 and the United States in 1901. This secured his reputation as the inventor of this global symbol of organization: during the Nazi occupation Norwegians wore paperclips on their lapels as symbols of national unity.

Pierre Vago born 1920

A French architect and town-planner, Pierre Vago was born in Budapest and was educated at the Ecole Spéciale d'Architecture in Paris. He became editor of the influential Parisian magazine *Architecture d'aujourd'hui* in 1932, just as it was discovering the Modern Movement. At the time, Vago's magazine was the only influential French periodical to feature articles on industrial design. Vago, who left *Architecture d'aujourd'hui* in 1948, has been a prominent member of juries judging architectural competitions, and was president of the International Council of Societies of Industrial Design (ICSID) from 1963 to 1965. He has practised as an architect and town-planner in Belgium, Austria, France, Germany, Luxembourg, Israel and Italy.

Gino Valle born 1923

An Italian architect, Gino Valle gained his diploma of architecture in Venice in 1948 and then went to Harvard until 1952. With his wife Nani, and John Myer, he set up a workshop and experimented with prefabricated structures, but he is best known for the digital clocks and time-tabling equipment he has designed for Solari. His 'Cifra' and 'Dator' timepieces and giant time-tabling boards have become familiar features at railway and aircraft termini around the world. Valle's work for Solari won a Compasso d'Oro award in 1957.

Henry van de Velde 1863–1957

Belgian-born Henri van de Velde changed the spelling of his first name to its English form as a response to the Anglophilia which swept Europe in the late nineteenth century with the popularity of the Arts and Crafts movement among designers and architects.

He was influenced by William Morris as a young man, and, persuaded that art should become more directly connected with life, or perhaps the other way around, helped found a review called *Van Nu en Straks* (From Now and the Future) in 1893 to promote Arts and Crafts ideals. After his marriage in 1894 van de Velde designed his own house (and all its furniture) at Uccle. The house became a sensation and he was brought to the attention of influential taste-makers, men such as the entrepreneur Samuel Bing and the art critic Julius Meier-Graefe.

By the end of the nineteenth century van de Velde was successfully designing and manufacturing furniture in Brussels and exhibited regularly at a gallery called La Libre Esthétique. He moved to Berlin in 1900 from his native Antwerp, when he designed advertising graphics that were heavily influenced by the then current fashions in high art, in particular the symbolist style of painting practised with sinuous lyricism by Toorop and Beardsley. In 1901 he was taken on as a consultant by the Grand Duke of Saxe-Weimar, who asked him to run the Weimar Academy of Applied Arts. In this capacity van de Velde became one of the founders of the Deutsche Werkbund, but he refused to compromise what he felt to be the essential *artistic* element in design, and this led to a clash with Hermann Muthesius, who, along with most of the other members of the Werkbund, argued for *Typisierung*, or standardization and machine-manufacture of products. There was a fierce public debate at the time of the Werkbund exhibition at Cologne in 1914 and van de Velde resigned. Athough the mechanical-romantic zeal of the Werkbund vanquished his essentially nineteenth-century ideals, it was van de Velde who suggested that Walter Gropius replace him as director of the Weimar school, and so can be seen as a prime mover in the foundation of the Bauhaus.

Bibliography Alfred Roth *Begegnung mit Pionieren* Birkhäuser, Zürich, 1974; Paul Greenhalgh et al. *Art Nouveau*, exhibition catalogue, Victoria and Albert Museum, 2000; Robert Schmutzler *Art Nouveau* Thames & Hudson, London, 1960

1: Unimark, American Airlines corporate identity, 1967. Founding partner, Massimo Vignelli, has ambitions to re-design the Vatican.
2: Johan Vaaler, paperclip, 1899.
3: Henry van de Velde, advertisement for 'Tropon', lithograph, 1899.
4: Henry van de Velde, circa 1900.
5: Henry van de Velde, table, 1902.

Harold van Doren 1895–1957

Like Eliot Noyes, who went straight from working in a museum to working in American industry, Harold van Doren brought culture to bear on the raffish body of the American industrial design profession.

Van Doren was born in Chicago of Dutch antecedents, the name having originally been van Doorn. After studying languages he worked in the Louvre in Paris, and his French was good enough to allow him to become the translator of Ambrose Vollard's *Paul Cézanne* (1923) and *Jean Renoir* (1934). He also wrote an unpublished novel, *The Love Pendulum*, and played a romantic role in Jean Renoir's film *La Fille de l'eau*. On his return to America he became assistant to the director of the Minneapolis Institute of Arts, but resigned when he had a chance to become an industrial designer so that he could, in his view, make a real contribution to the modern world. His first major job was in 1934 for the Toledo Scale Company of Toledo, Ohio, which he was given by the company's president, Hugh Bennett, an Englishman whom van Doren had known since his college days. Bennett had originally approached Norman Bel Geddes to style his product and, while Bel Geddes came up with many dramatic renderings (which he published in his futuristic book, *Horizons*, of 1934) and an astonishing plan for a factory of the future, the management soon became disenchanted with Bel Geddes' lack of practicality. Van Doren's design solution was, perhaps, less visually exciting, but it was more advanced in a truer sense, as he used a new plastic called Plaskon. This product earned for Toledo Scale the distinction of being the first major user of lightweight, large-scale plastic mouldings, and was for van Doren the first of many designs in new materials. As described by Seldon & Martha Cheney in 1937 'radios and kitchen equipment, laundry and heating machines, exquisite little perfume bottles, automobile tires, a gasoline pump, a long line of streamlined juvenile vehicles are but items in the steady flow of products from his studio'. His clients were Philco, May Tag and Goodyear (for whom he styled a tyre) – blue chips, indeed, but van Doren was aware of the limitations of his new craft.

In 1940 he published *Industrial Design: a practical guide* in which he described the practical side of working with new materials and their production techniques. His health failing, he retired to Philadelphia to devote himself to music and painting and it was there that he died.

Bibliography Harold van Doren *Industrial Design: a practical guide* McGraw-Hill, New York, 1940; Jeffrey L. Meikle *Twentieth Century Limited* Temple University Press, Philadelphia, 1979; Arthur J. Pulos *American Design Ethic* MIT, Cambridge, Mass., 1983

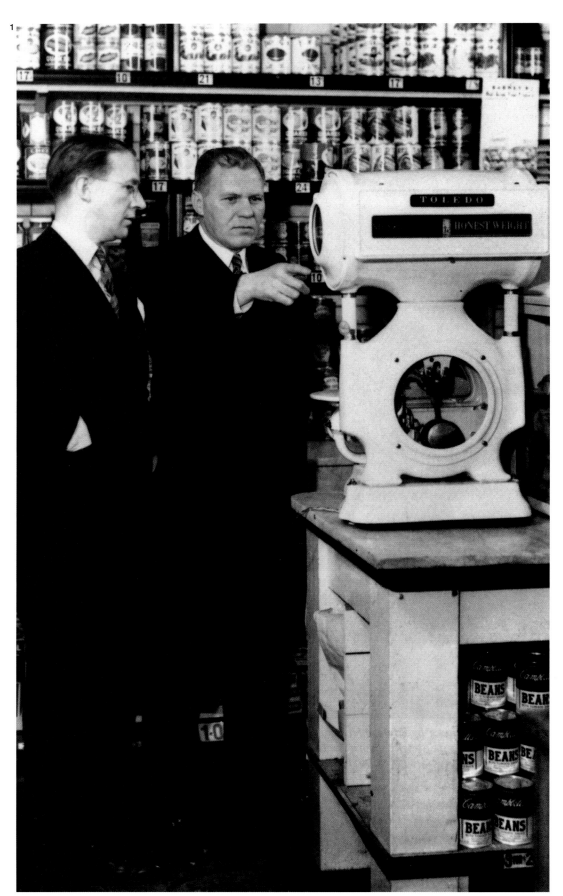

1: Harold van Doren and Hubert Bennett, 1930s. The designer is photographed with the president of the Toledo Scale Company during a store visit. Bennett had explained to van Doren that Toledo needed a new model because the old one weighed 160lbs and salesmen found it too heavy to hump around. Van Doren's new design in Plaskon, a first generation plastic, became one of the familiar set-pieces in American design propaganda.

Andries van Onck born 1928

Andries van Onck was born in Amsterdam and studied at the Hague under <u>Gerrit Rietveld</u> and at Ulm under <u>Max Bill</u>. Roberto <u>Olivetti</u> noticed him as a promising student and invited him to Italy, where he worked with <u>Ettore Sottsass</u>. He opened his own studio in Milan (with his Japanese wife, Hiroko Takeda) and became fascinated by the problem of creating interesting design at accessible prices. He has described white goods as 'a Niagara of white cubes falling over Europe', adding 'We don't want those things to be ugly cubes, do we?' His clients include the chain store Upim and the manufacturer Zanussi, to whose refrigerators, freezers, cookers and washing-machines van Onck has applied a stylized version of German minimalism. With <u>Massimo Vignelli</u> in charge of graphics and <u>Gino Valle</u> in charge of its corporate identity, the Zanussi enterprise has one of the most thorough going product design programmes in Europe; van Onck is responsible for designing three different ranges for them aimed at the different markets across Western Europe, each being replaced on a five-year cycle.

Victor Vasarely 1908–97

The French painter, sculptor and graphic designer Victor Vasarely was born at Pecs in Hungary. His geometric paintings were an influence on Op-Art, one of the fashionable styles of painting in the Sixties (which had a brief effect on advertising graphics). Vasarely designed an illusionistic, Op-Art badge for the state car company Renault in 1974, and in 1983 he designed some special bottles and labels for the private Taittinger champagne company.

> Victor Vasarely's geometric paintings were an influence on Op-Art, one of the fashionable styles of painting in the Sixties

Thorstein Veblen 1857–1929

Thorstein Veblen, an American sociologist and social critic, was educated at Carleton College, Minnesota, and Johns Hopkins and Yale universities. In 1899 he published what was to be his most celebrated work, *The Theory of the Leisure Class*. In it Veblen gave the expressions 'conspicuous consumption' and 'pecuniary canons of taste' to the language and lent dialectical form to the notions of middle-class revolt that had already been sensed in England by <u>C. R. Ashbee</u> and others. Veblen's book was the first scientific study of popular taste, written just as the professional practice of design was beginning to emerge from the late Industrial Revolution.

His later books, *The Theory of Business Enterprise* (1904) and *The Instinct of Workmanship* (1914), have been entirely overshadowed by the success of *Leisure Class*, which has been continuously in print, both in Britain and the United States, since it was first published. Yet despite its popularity Veblen's spiky personality meant that he never enjoyed academic celebrity. He spoke 29 languages and was described as the last man who knew everything.

Bibliography Joseph Dorfmann *Thorstein Veblen and his America*, Viking, New York, 1934

2: Victor Vasarely, Op-art logo for Renault, 1972. This appeared the same year Renault launched the 5, the first car with wraparound polyester bumpers.

3: Thorstein Veblen, pioneering critic of consumerism, once described as the last man who knew everything.

Venini

From 1959 the Venini glassworks was run by Ludovico de Santillana (born 1931), the son-in-law of Paolo Venini (1895–1959), its founder. Venini has had a reputation for being 'progressive' ever since it abandoned traditional Venetian forms in favour of splashed and mottled surfaces. It has produced 'art glass' designed by Tobia Scarpa, Pierre Cardin and Tapio Wirkkala. In 1986 the Venini family sold the company to the Gardini and Ferruzzi families.

Robert Venturi born 1925

Robert Venturi is a Philadelphia architect-academic whose books, *Complexity and Contradiction in Modern Architecture* (1966) – delivered originally as papers at New York's Museum of Modern Art – and *Learning from Las Vegas* (1972), persuasively argued against what he maintained was the rigid formalism of the Modern Movement in architecture and design. Instead, he sought to introduce eclecticism and variety. The doctrinaire versions of Modernism had already suffered intellectual depredations from Pop, in whose imagery and immediacy Venturi and his partners (his wife, Denise Scott-Brown, and Steven Izenour) looked for their new aesthetic.

They argued, amongst other things, for a return to native American tradition, and encouraged American architects and designers to see in the vernacular American townscape not confusion and visual chaos, but inspiration and excitement. The architectural and design culture they proposed was a reversal of and a complete reaction to the European influence of Mies van der Rohe and Walter Gropius.

In this sense Venturi can claim to be the originator of what was to be known as Post-Modernism, having written, for example, 'I like elements that are hybrid rather than pure, compromising rather than clean, distorted rather than straightforward…'

Recently he has turned his attention to furniture, and in 1984 Knoll introduced a collection of chairs and tables designed by him. The range comprises a sofa, nine chairs and two table bases. Each type, like his architecture, used historical reference; the chairs, made of laminated wood, were cut with a jig-saw so that Queen Anne, Gothic Revival, or Biedermeier features could be presented on them as flat patterns. For Knoll it was an extraordinary departure from a formalist tradition which had its roots in the Bauhaus, but Venturi had sufficient ego to see the firm through: 'Mies did one chair – I did nine,' he remarked to a journalist from New York's *Metropolis* magazine.

Bibliography Robert Venturi *Complexity and Contradiction in Modern Architecture* Museum of Modern Art, New York, 1966

1: Robert Venturi, chair for Knoll, 1984. Post-Modernist theory went into practice with high quality laminates.

2: Robert Venturi, the Vanna Venturi Hous, Chestnut Hill, Philadelphia, 1962. Venturi's practical delight in the 'symbolism of the ordinary' led four years later to the scripture of Post-Modernism.

Vespa

The Vespa motor scooter became a cult object. Its name was coined by Enrico Piaggio, derived from the Latin for 'wasp' on account of the sleek housing for its rear-mounted engine and transmission. It was the first motor scooter to break away from the basic low running-board pattern, and its wasp-like shell made for a radically new appearance.

Launched at the Rome Golf Club in 1946, the Vespa was intended as a cheap means of mass transport for housewives in the Italian cities during the post-War years of *ricostruzione*. It was manufactured by the boat and aircraft concern of Rinaldo Piaggio, to designs by Corradino d'Ascanio. Ettore Sottsass has spoken evocatively about how to his generation (which was used to the new visual language being developed for other machines by Pininfarina and Marcello Nizzoli) the Vespa seemed an especially strong symbol of a new civilization. It also became the symbol of a new outlook in England and Terence Conran delivered his first furniture on one. The step through frame was intended to preserve modesty for women and priests.

3

4

LA PLUS GRANDE PRODUCTION MONDIALE DE SCOOTERS...

Vespa

Vous

Ne courrez plus... roulez Vespa... roulez Vespa.

Victoria and Albert Museum

The Victoria and Albert Museum, in London's South Kensington, is the world's foremost museum of the applied arts. Although the present building is almost entirely Edwardian in fabric, the origins of the Museum go back to the early nineteenth century, and Aston Webb's bombastic architecture really only unites a number of separate building campaigns. Both in substance and in purpose, the V&A has grown by accretion.

The history of the Museum is inseparable from those other developments in British public life that led to the Great Exhibition of the Industry of All Nations and to the foundation of what became the Royal College of Art. Its spiritual origins lie with the *Report on Arts and Manufactures* by a Parliamentary Select Committee of 1836, which called for the setting up of exemplary collections of manufactured goods so that students and artisans might be better prepared to work to counter foreign imports. The Great Exhibition brought together all interested parties around Prince Albert including Henry Cole, who, as head of the Government's Department of Science and Art, was appointed director of the South Kensington Museum when it was established after the 1851 exhibition. The South Kensington Museum became the Victoria and Albert in 1899.

As Europe's first museum of the applied arts, the South Kensington Museum added to the international influence of Britain's Arts and Crafts movement and it was soon imitated abroad: museums in Hamburg, Oslo, Vienna and later in Zürich, all owe their origins to London's example. During the twentieth century the character of the V&A changed, and instead of being the reforming museum of the industrial arts which Cole and his contemporaries had intended, it became a vast custodian of the applied arts and fine arts. This effect was mitigated in 1981 when the Boilerhouse Project was established in the Museum's old boilerhouse yard with the intention of reviving Cole's educational and missionary purpose by showing modern design. Its lease came to an end after five years and it re-established itself as the Design Museum by Tower Bridge.

Bibliography Nikolaus Pevsner *Academies of Art, Past and Present* Cambridge University Press, Cambridge, 1940; Quentin Bell *The Schools of Design* Black, London, 1947; Fiona MacCarthy A History of British Design 1830–1970 Allen & Unwin, London, 1979; John Physick *The Victoria & Albert Museum* Victoria & Albert Museum, London, 1982

3: The Cast Courts of London's Victoria & Albert Museum: a vast memorial to Victorian enterprise, great masterpieces of sculpture and architecture copied and carried back to London for inspiration.

4: During the Fifties and Sixties the Vespa scooter became an international symbol of Italy.

Jacques Viennot 1893–1959

Jacques Viennot was a French theorist and polemicist of design. He founded the Cabinet d'Esthétique Industrielle de Technès in 1953, and was a director of La Revue de *l'esthétique industrielle*. In 1951 he established the Institut de l'Esthétique Industrielle, dedicated to informing the French people of the significance of <u>industrial design</u> in the wealth-producing cycle. It was unsuccessful.

Vittorio Viganò born 1919

A furniture designer, Vittorio Viganò was born in Milan into a family with an artistic tradition. He studied architecture at Milan Polytechnic, and after 1944 worked first with <u>Gio Ponti</u> and then with <u>BBPR</u>. In 1947 he set up his own practice and designed quiet, restrained wood furniture for the straitened mass-market. In 1949 he produced a bent plywood chair for Compensati Curvate and, in the same year, a dish-like chair in enamelled metal with a rush seat which, like <u>Harry Bertoia</u>'s similar design, was ideally suited to being pictured in the modernistic living rooms which appeared in the design magazines of the period. Viganò has also worked for <u>Arteluce</u> and contributed to the VIIth, IXth, XIIth and XIIIth Milan <u>Triennales</u>.

Bibliography Centrokappa (ed.) *Design Italiano degli anni '50* Domus, Milan, 1980; Paolo Fossati *Design in Italia 1945–1970* Einaudi, Turin, 1972; *The New Domestic Landscape* exhibition catalogue, Museum of Modern Art, New York, 1972

Vignale born 1913

Alfredo Vignale emerged as an independent coach-builder after an apprenticeship with <u>Pininfarina</u>, whose shop he had joined when he was seventeen. He founded his own firm in 1946 and produced designs for Ferrari, <u>FIAT</u>, Maserati, Aston-Martin and Rolls-Royce.

Vignale specialized in producing both small runs of utilitarian vehicles that the mass-manufacturers found uneconomic to produce, and unique designs for private clients or prototypes for industry. Among his first designs was a coupé version of the FIAT 100 of 1949. The firm produced coachwork for Ferrari racing cars throughout the early Fifties, and elements from racing cars were incorporated into the series production Maserati 3500 of 1959, which is, perhaps, Vignale's best-known design. Through one of its young designers, <u>Giovanni Michelotti</u>, the studio also produced sketches for a sports car for Standard-Triumph which ultimately became the Triumph TR-4 of 1963. The sketches of the Maserati 3500 and the Triumph TR-4 of the same year are almost identical, and a comparison of the proportion, detail and character of the sketches and the production cars makes an instructive lesson in the differences between the Italian and British car industries.

Vignale's style tended towards a high-waisted solidity, lacking the flamboyance of some of his contemporaries. After Alfredo Vignale's death in a car crash near his Turin factory in 1969 Carrozzeria Vignale was taken over by <u>Ghia</u>, which was, itself, bought in 1974 by the <u>Ford</u> Motor Company.

Bibliography Angelo Tito Anselmi (ed.) *La Carrozzeria Italiana – cultura e progetto* Alfieri, Turin, 1978

Vignale's style tended towards a high-waisted solidity, lacking the flamboyance of some of his contemporaries

1

1: Vignale, Maserati 3500GT, 1957. The first production Maserati.
2: Vignelli, *The European Journal*, 1978.
3: Vignelli, GNER (Great North Eastern Railway) Corporate Identity and interiors, London, 1997.
4: Vignelli, Stendig Calendar, 1966.
5: Vignelli, Piccolo Treatro, Milano Graphic Program, 1964.

Massimo Vignelli born 1931

Massimo Vignelli has become a social phenomenon in
American design, discussed and celebrated by people
and concerns not hitherto excited by professional
graphic designers.

Vignelli studied architecture in Venice, and then
worked for <u>Venini</u> from 1954 to 1957, before opening
an office with his wife, Leila, in Milan in 1960. He went to
Chicago in 1964, worked for the Container Corporation
of America (for which he designed a logo), and was one
of the founders of <u>Unimark</u>, a company specializing in
corporate identity. In 1971–2 he was retained by <u>Knoll</u>.
Vignelli specializes in a certain sort of supergraphics that
achieve its effects with colour planes and dramatic
variations of scale and size. He designed the graphics
for the Washington subway system.

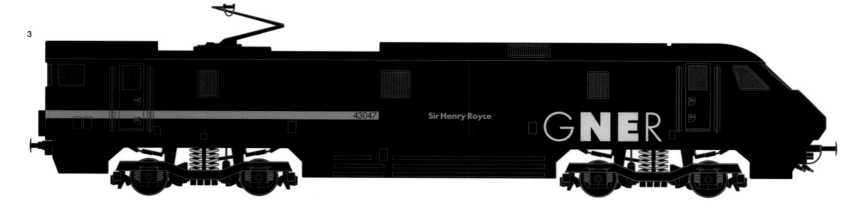

Vistosi

Luciano Vistosi is an Italian glassware manufacturer based in Murano, the Venetian home of decorative Italian glass. Vistosi produced <u>Ettore Sottsass</u>' 'Aulica', 'Diodata', 'Dogaressa' and 'Faliera' decorative glassware, using strong shapes and strong colours to achieve dolmen-like effects of intensity and presence.

Vogue

Vogue magazine was founded as a weekly paper in 1892, like its contemporary *Harper's Bazaar*. <u>Condé Nast</u> acquired it in 1909 and turned it into the leading international magazine of fashion and, to a lesser extent, design and style. Its character has been moulded by strong and determined editors, but especially by Edna Woolman Chase, who was acquired along with the weekly paper and remained with the Condé Nast group until 1952. Under her editorship *Vogue* expanded internationally: a British subsidiary was set up in 1916, a French one in 1920 and Australian, Italian, Spanish and Russian editions have all appeared subsequently.

The magazine's reputation depends very much upon the adventurous qualities of the cover design and the high quality of photography inside. *Vogue's* continuing achievement has been to introduce ideas about high fashion and interior design to a financially independent audience. The *doyenne* of American fashion, Diana Vreeland, was editor from 1963 to 1972.

Bibliography Caroline Seebohm *The Man who was Vogue – the life and times of Condé Nast* Weidenfeld & Nicolson, London, 1982; Viking, New York, 1982

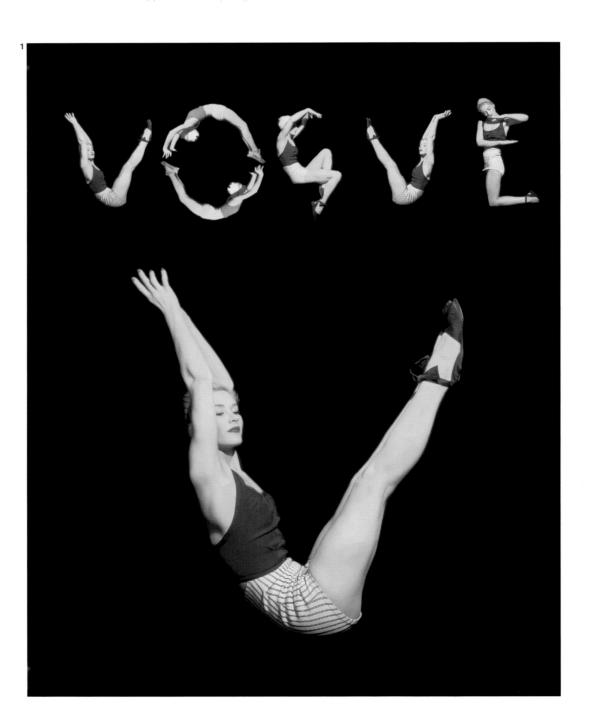

1: The model Lisa Fonssagrives forming the initial 'V', 1940, on a *Vogue* cover, 1940 photographed by Horst P. Horst.
2: A *Vogue* model in front of the McGraw Building, West 42nd Street, 1952.

Volkswagen

The first Volkswagen car is one of the greatest collaborative design exercises ever, although <u>Raymond Loewy</u> was pleased to satirise it as the 'Grdnyatstzck Four Beetle Scoopster'.

 The origins of the vehicle that became known over the world as the 'Beetle' or the 'Bug' lay in development contracts for a small car which Zundapp and NSU, both firms which were essentially motorcycle manufacturers, had placed with Ferdinand <u>Porsche</u>'s design bureau in Stuttgart in the early Thirties. In 1933 Porsche sent a memorandum to the Minister of Transport outlining his ideas for a Volkswagen, literally a 'people's car', which was to be basically a four-wheeled motorbike produced cheaply through the application of sophisticated design. The idea of a people's car appealed to the German dictator, Adolf Hitler, who thought that a Volkswagen could be an industrial counterpart to the *Volkswohnung* ('people's housing') which his ministers were promoting. Porsche's private initiative was brought under state control with the establishment of the Volkswagen Development Corporation. Test cars, employing many ideas that were first seen in sketches made for Zundapp and NSU, were running in 1936; the first experimental line was operating at the Daimler-Benz factory in 1937; and the foundation stone of the Wolfsburg factory was laid in 1938. At the ceremony, without Porsche's foreknowledge, Hitler declared that the Volkswagen would be named after the Nazi recreational organization *Kampf durch Freude* (Strength through Joy) and be known as the KdFwagen.

 The Volkswagen was built to a cost of 990 Marks, and there was to be no profit margin. This meant that hydraulic brakes could not be used because a licence fee would have had to be paid.

 Porsche settled on a flat four air-cooled engine, developed originally by Josef Kales for NSU, but adapted for the Volkswagen by another member of Porsche's team called F. X. Reimspiess (who also designed the Volkswagen logo). The body of the Volkswagen was designed by <u>Erwin Komenda</u>.

 The Second World War began exactly four weeks before Volkswagen production had been scheduled to start, and, although 100,000 military versions were built during the War, production of the People's Car did not begin until 1945, and then under the management of a British army major. Renamed the Volkswagen, with continuous development it was to replace the <u>Ford</u> Model T as the most popular car ever made, although subsequently overtaken by the Toyota Corolla.

However, its very success almost brought economic ruin to the German manufacturer because by the early Seventies Volkswagen's managing director, Toni Schmucker, was faced with the problem of revitalizing a manufacturing plant too dependent on one product with vast, but diminishing, sales. He called in <u>Giorgio Giugiaro</u> and ItalDesign to develop the Golf, a new technology front-wheel-drive, water-cooled car that replaced the Beetle in all Western markets. The influence of Porsche, an Austrian, and Giugiaro, an Italian, has provoked more than one commentator to make the wry observation that Volkswagen's most successful products have never been designed by Germans.

Bibliography K. B. Hopfinger *Beyond Expectation – the Volkswagen Story* Foulis, London, 1954

The Volkswagen was to replace the Ford Model T as the most popular car ever made

Volvo

The Swedish car and truck manufacturer was founded by Assar Gabrielsson and Gustav Larson, two employees of the SFK bearings company. Their company became 'Volvo' in 1924 (the name is Latin for 'I roll').

Volvo picked up its design principles from American cars and has concentrated on solidity and reliability, often maintaining a single model on a very long production run rather than taking risks with adventurous engineering or interesting styling. Compared with its compatriot SAAB, for a long time Volvo's interest in design was only remote. However, the conservatism of Volvo design and the reliability of the firm's products have happily combined with a dedicated safety effort since the Forties which has accelerated since the Sixties. As a result, as well as the cars being safe no one knows more than Volvo about how to make a car look safe. Volvo's head of design, Jan Wilsgaard, architect of the 'Amazon' of 1956, eschews any pursuit of 'fashion', although the Volvo Concept Car (VCC) which was developed in the late Seventies by Volvo's head of research, Dan Werbin, has been criticized for its gimmickry. Similarly, the 760 series introduced in 1982 was a blatant appeal to the tastes of the large American market.

Hans von Klier born 1934

Hans von Klier collaborated with Ettore Sottsass on numerous projects for Olivetti while working in his Milan offices from 1960 to 1968. He was born in Tetschen, Czechoslovakia and went to Ulm to study at the Hochschule für Gestaltung, graduating in 1959. In 1969 he became head of corporate identity for Olivetti.

3

C.F. A. Voysey 1857–1941

An English architect, Charles Frederick Annesley Voysey was born in Hessle, near Hull, the son of a clergyman. Voysey's whole career was to be associated with the Arts and Crafts movement. He set up his own office in 1884 and quietly developed a version of the Arts and Crafts philosophy, while remaining independent of the various guilds and societies which flourished at the end of the nineteenth century.

Voysey's place in history was established when he was claimed as a pioneer of the Modern Movement by Nikolaus Pevsner in 1936. However, the architect always denied any avant-garde element in his work, and maintained to his death that he was solely preoccupied with vernacular British traditions in architecture and design. Indeed, his trademark was a combination of strong, original forms with an inspired interpretation of traditional, vernacular details.

Voysey began to design wallpaper, textiles and silver in 1888, and each displays his characteristic concern with natural pattern. Designs like 'Bird and Tulip' or 'Nympheas' use his favourite heart-shaped motif with a general decorative treatment like William Morris's, but more stylized. Also like Morris, Voysey expounded ideals of truth to nature and truth to materials. In his most famous building, a house called The Orchard at Chorleywood, north-west of London, Voysey attempted to create a total design where the architecture, decoration, fittings and furniture all combined to create a unified effect. Voysey is significant in the history of design not because of his legacy of novel formal ideas nor for his polemics, for each of these was largely derivative, but for his sustaining influence on the tradition of the Arts and Crafts which has had such a strong influence on the development of industrial design in Britain. Despite the fine theory – as in his adjuration of 1892: 'Begin by casting out all the useless ornaments… Eschew all imitations. Strive to produce an effect of repose and simplicity' – Voysey can be held responsible for having invented the suburban style.

Bibliography Duncan Simpson *C. F. A. Voysey* Lund Humphries, London, 1979

1: Volkswagen production line, late 1940s.
2: The ur-Volkswagen, 1946.

3: Jan Wilsgaard's Volvo 120 series, 1956. Volvo management told the designer, 'it would be better if it was ugly rather than too beautiful'.
4: C. F. A. Voysey, design for Hill Close, Studland Bay, Dorset, 1896. Studland Bay is The National Trust's only naturist property.

Wilhelm Wagenfeld 1900–90

Wilhelm Wagenfeld studied at the Bauhaus, where he was a pupil of Laszlo Moholy-Nagy, but Wagenfeld rejected his Bauhaus training and, like Hermann Gretsch, remained in Germany throughout the Nazi years. He taught at the Staatliche Kunsthochschule (state college of art) in Berlin from 1931 to 1935 and from 1935 to 1947 worked at the Lausitze Glassworks. He designed utilitarian objects such as glass and cutlery, his most popular and least recognized work being his 'Pelikan' ink bottle of 1938. He created the 'Atlanta' flatware for WMF in 1954–5, a series of architectural light-fittings for Lindner throughout the later Fifties, and a melamine dinner tray and service for Lufthansa in 1955. Wagenfeld became a professor at Berlin's Hochschule für Bildende Künste, but since 1954 has run his own studio from Stuttgart. Wagenfeld has an uncompromising and unwavering commitment to both the aesthetic and to the social ideals of the Modern Movement. In 1955 he resigned from the Deutsche Werkbund as a protest against what he saw as its loss of idealism and its lack of character. His achievement has been to bring genuine Bauhaus standards to the design of readily available, mass-market glass and ceramics, although his style is severe and dry, even by the standards of contemporary German design.

Bibliography Wilhelm Wagenfeld *Wesen und Gestalt der Dinge um Uns* Eduard Stichnote, Potsdam, 1948; *Industrieware von W. Wagenfeld. Kunstlerische Mitarbeit in der Industrie 1930–1960* exhibition catalogue, Kunstgewerbemuseum, Zürich, 1960

Otto Wagner 1841–1918

Otto Wagner was one of the key figures in Viennese culture at the turn of the century. An architect and town-planner, he influenced an entire generation through his teaching at the School of Art between 1894 and 1912. His most important building was the Vienna Postsparkassenamt (Post Office Savings Bank) which he designed in an early version of Functionalist style. Wagner designed fittings and furniture for the Post Office, as well as a series of armchairs for Thonet.

2

1

Ole Wanscher 1903–85

Ole Wanscher was one of the founders of the Copenhagen Cabinetmakers' Guild, an influential society that offered the first public showing of designs by Børge Mogensen and Hans Wegner. His furniture designs, manufactured by Fritz Hansen, helped popularize Danish design.

1: Wilhelm Wagenfeld, glass teapot and cup, 1930. Wagenfeld carried the Bauhaus ethic and aesthetic with absolute consistency throughout his long life. The result was awesomely pure designs.
2: Otto Wagner, armchairs for the telegraph office of *Die Zeit* newspaper, manufactured by Jakob and Joseoph Kohn, 1902.

3: Josiah Wedgwood, 'Portland' vase, 1790. The taste for 'antiques' among the emergent middle-classes was exploited by Wedgwood. His reproduction of the famous first century BC Roman vase was a showpiece, a tour-de-force of his manufacturing prowess.

Josiah Wedgwood 1730–95

A master-potter, inventor, industrialist and retailer, Josiah Wedgwood has had his name turned into a trademark, the highest honour that industrialized culture can offer. He was a product of what the Marxist historian of the Industrial Revolution Francis Klingender called 'the Provincial Enlightenment', conquering England and France from Burslem, Staffordshire, in the West Midlands: for a while in the eighteenth century the backwaters of England led the metropolitan centres of the world. Wedgwood, together with several of his near neighbours, saw his opportunity and took it. He summed up his achievement with characteristic poetry and asperity: 'I saw the field was spacious and the soil so good as to promise ample recompense to anyone who should labour diligently in its cultivation.'

The establishment of Wedgwood's 'manufactory' at Stoke-on-Trent was the beginning of an industrial, humanitarian and artistic career that was one of Britain's most original contributions to the Age of Reason. In its various aspects, Josiah Wedgwood's life was like an overture to the nineteenth century. In all things he was an essentially practical man: he used artists like Flaxman and Stubbs, not as a precious affectation, but as a shrewdly understood means of expanding his markets and his business; and his model village at Etruria was not solely a philanthropic gesture, for, like Lord Leverhulme, he realized that happy workers are good workers (see also pages 16–18).

Among Wedgwood's practical innovations in the production of ceramics was his division of labour and of production into 'useful' wares, from his Burslem factory, and 'ornamental' wares, from his Etruria factory. His use of artists anticipated Gustavsberg by a century and IBM by two. Innovation was almost an obsession with him, leading him to develop a stoneware pyrometer that could withstand furnace temperatures and to produce his own original designs, of which the Queen's Ware and Black Basalt ranges are still in production today.

But Wedgwood's devotion to art and science did not dull his commercial instincts. Like an impresario he displayed his monumental Portland vase at his showrooms in Greek Street, offering tickets for entry to see this ceramic wonder. The large production runs that his logically organized factories made possible were such that he invented sales catalogues for the public.

A master-potter, inventor, industrialist and retailer, Josiah Wedgwood has had his name turned into a trademark, the highest honour which industrialized culture can offer

3

Hans Wegner 1914–2007

Now the designer of over 500 chairs, Hans Wegner started his career as a cabinet-maker. Until 1943 he was an employee of Arne Jacobsen, and since then has designed furniture principally for Johannes Hansen. Wegner's chair '501' of 1949, known simply as 'The Chair', turned Danish furniture into an international phenomenon. Made entirely of natural materials, it is marked by a remarkable synthesis of simplicity, elegance and care in execution. Writing in *Mobilia* in 1960, Poul Henningsen pinpointed its qualities: 'This chair is the perfect solution of a task: the light, lowbacked armchair, sufficiently comfortable. It weighs nine pounds, just like a new-born child. An architect can gain a nice reputation for himself by making this chair five times as heavy, half as comfortable and one quarter as good looking. Look at it once more. It is completely faultless. Its form is spare and harmonious. It does not have any false or mendacious pretences. It fulfills its task in society with the modest conscientiousness expected of the good citizen.' Wegner's belief was that a chair should have no back side, that it should be pleasing to view from all angles. He described Danish design as the result of 'a continuous process of purification'. Between 1941 and 1966 Wegner showed a new chair design at every annual Copen Wagen Cabinet Makers' Guild exhibition. Wegner's version of Danish Modern has given the most influential appraisal of all when President John F. Kennedy used a 1949 'Round' chair in his 1960 television debate with Richard Nixon.

Bibliography Henrik Sten Moller *Tema med Variationer* Sonderjyllands Kunstmuseum, Tønder, 1979

Weissenhof Siedlung

The Deutsche Werkbund's exhibition of 1927 was an entire housing estate, in a village called Weissenhof just outside Stuttgart. Houses by Mies van der Rohe, Mart Stam and Le Corbusier were erected together for the first time, and in them were the first examples of tubular steel furniture to be seen by the public.

Gunnar Wennerberg 1863–1914

A Swedish painter, Gunnar Wennerberg studied painting in Paris and ceramics in Sèvres before becoming artistic director of the Gustavsberg factory in 1895. Wennerberg was one of the first artists actually to work in modern industry, and his freshly observed wild flower patterns replaced the oppressive funk of the National Romantic school that had dominated Gustavsberg's production before his appointment. Wennerberg remained artistic director of Gustavsberg until 1908, and was also designing for Kosta from 1898 to 1909.

Bibliography *Art and Industry: a century of design in the products you use* exhibition catalogue, The Boilerhouse Project, Victoria and Albert Museum, London, 1982; *Wennerberg* exhibition catalogue, Prins Eugens Waldemarsudde, Stockholm, 1981

310

1

2

Wiener Werkstätte

The Wiener Werkstätte was an offshoot from the Vienna Secession. The Secession's exhibition in 1900 focused attention on the work of <u>C. R. Mackintosh</u> and <u>C. R. Ashbee</u>, and one of the Secession group, Koloman Moser, suggested setting up a workshop in Austria along the same lines as Ashbee's in London. Together with <u>Josef Hoffmann</u> he founded in 1903 the Wiener Werkstätte Produktiv-Gemeinschaft von Kunsthandwerken in Wien (the Viennese Workshops and Production Cooperative of Art Workers in Vienna). By 1905 it had over 100 craftsmen. Its forte was hand-made metalware whose reductive style belied its dependence on hand production. However, a change in style around 1915 from Hoffmann's rectilinear one to a more florid, organic approach presaged its decline; it dissolved in 1933.

Bibliography *Die Wiener Werkstätte* exhibition catalogue, Museum für Angewandte Kunste, Vienna, 1967

By 1905 The Wiener Werkstätte had over 100 craftsmen. Its forte was hand-made metalware whose reductive style belied its dependence on hand production

1: Hans Wegner, 'Ypsilon' chair, 1951.
2: The Weissenhof Siedlung, Stuttgart, 1927. A life-size exhibition of Modernist housing. This is Le Corbusier's exhibit.
3: Josef Hoffmann for Wiener Werkstätte, tray painted iron, 1905.
4: Wiener Werkstätte, exhibition poster, 1905.

Yrjo Wiherheimo born 1941

A furniture designer, Yrjo Wiherheimo has designed furniture for Haimi, Asko and Vivero, and plastics for Nokia. Wiherheimo is among the most respected of the younger generation of Finnish designers. In particular, his furniture for Vivero is admired for its combination of refined aesthetics with ergonomic precision.

Tapio Wirkkala 1915–85

A widely various Finnish designer and craftsman, Tapio Wirkkala worked for Littala after 1947 and, somewhat incongruously, joined Raymond Loewy in 1955. His work became internationally known after it appeared at Milan Triennales during the early Fifties. He worked for Venini and Rosenthal.

Ludwig Wittgenstein 1889–1951

Between 1926 and 1928 the great philosopher designed a house (down to the very last detail) for his sister, Margarethe Stonborough. Wittgenstein approached the architectural problem as if it were a philosophical one and the result is an impeccable demonstration of the intellectual basis of Modernism. The philosophical concept of 'silence' advanced in his daunting *Tractatus Logico-Philosophicus* (1922) was built in concrete and metal details on Vienna's Kundmanngasse. The house is also a pitch perfect demonstration of mathematical proportions and meticulous attention to detail: every single element is related to the whole. Frighteningly austere, the Wittgenstein House made no concessions to comfort, but remains a curious version of very high intelligence made visible.

Bibliography Bernhard Leitner *The Wittgenstein House*, Princeton Architectural Press, New York, 2000

1: Tapio Wirkkala, 'Bolle' glass for littala, 1967.
2: Wittgenstein House, Vienna, 1926–28. The 'Tractatus Logico-Philosophicus' in concrete.
3: Cover of *From Bauhaus to Our House*, Tom Wolfe, 1981.

Tom Wolfe born 1931

The American journalist Tom Wolfe has been a substantial influence in raising the level of writing about popular culture. An inventor, with Hunter S. Thompson, of what both his critics and fans call 'the new journalism', Wolfe added a satirical southern gentleman's point of view to the gallimaufry of opinions that abounded during the Sixties. He invented the name of the next ten years when he described it as the 'Me Decade'. He was first to describe how teen cults identify their values through fashion and possessions, and how cars articulate desire.

Although he was born in 1931, Wolfe thinks of himself somewhat as a modern Thackeray. His books, *The Kandy-Kolored Tangerine-Flake Streamline Baby, The Electric Kool-Aid Acid Test* (1968) and *The Right Stuff* (1979) were immensely popular, but his satire on fashions in twentieth-century architecture and design, called *From Bauhaus to Our House* (1981) raised the ire of an American establishment which was not accustomed to being mocked.

Wolff Olins

Wolff Olins was a London-based design consultancy, founded in 1965. The founders were two very different personalities – Michael Wolff (born 1933), a romantic who describes his recreation in *Who's Who* as 'seeing', and Wally Olins (born 1930), who says he is the 'first design consultant who couldn't draw'. Wolff and Olins had had patchy careers before forming the consultancy, Wolff as a designer for the BBC and Olins as an executive for the advertising agency Geers Gross.

Wolff Olins specialized in corporate identity and was an English equivalent of American firms like Lippincott & Margulies and Anspach, Grossman, and Portugal. The Wolff Olins style veered between a specialized whimsy, characterized by Michael Wolff's suggestion that the Bovis group of companies choose a humming bird as their corporate symbol, and a hard-edged slickness which the firm produced for BOC, Aral and VAG. Michael Wolff left the firm in 1983. Olins left in 1997.
Bibliography Wally Olins *The Corporate Personality* Design Council, London, 1978

Although he was born in 1931, Wolfe thinks of himself somewhat as a modern Thackeray

Frank Lloyd Wright 1869–1959

Frank Lloyd Wright was an immensely successful architect who has influenced the whole world of design through the novelty and power of his vision. Chris Bangle of BMW calls him 'a god'. Because he stood outside, way outside, the Euro-centric vision of the Modern Movement, Wright has been adopted as a hero by many diverse vested interests: Tom Wolfe, who perhaps sees him as an authentic American hero, and the historians of Post-Modernism, who see him as some kind of anticipator of the garish Kitsch that clogs the colour supplements.

Frank Lloyd Wright was born in rural Wisconsin, where his Welsh grandparents had emigrated 100 years earlier. He studied engineering in Madison, the state capital, and then went to Chicago in 1887 to work as a draughtsman. He soon entered the architectural offices of Dankmar Adler and Louis Sullivan, and his career had begun. Sullivan's theories about organic building were a fundamental influence on Wright, and when he left the Adler & Sullivan office to set up his own in 1893 he took with him what he had learned from his first years as an architectural apprentice. He combined this with an appreciation of the traditional building of Japan and his own vision of the universe into an authentic, original philosophy of design. His house designs worked from the functional requirements of living accommodation towards the outside, and Wright never imposed a style robbed from reference books onto a predetermined structure. He thought about what he wanted his building to be and then worked it out from first principles. He was also always anxious to integrate any building into its natural environment, so it is no coincidence that the long, low Wright buildings, covering huge areas of ground, grew out of his experience of the vast plains of the Mid-West, later fortified by experience of the vast emptiness of the Arizona desert. He once said that no building should ever be made on a hill; it should be of the hill.

Wright also made many technical innovations in his buildings: his Larkin office building in Buffalo, New York (1905), was among the first anywhere to use plate-glass doors framed in metal, air-conditioning and bizarre metal furniture – which was made to Wright's own designs. In 1909 Wright travelled to Europe and his contact with German and Dutch architects gave a new dimension to the inchoate fermentation that we now see as the beginning of the Modern Movement. Drawings and photographs of his buildings were extensively published in Holland and Germany.

Wright never imposed a style robbed from reference books onto a predetermined structure. He thought about what he wanted his building to be and then worked it out from first principles

Wright took from his Welsh ancestors a prophetic, bardic, and chthonic interest in nature and folklore, naming his own houses after the druid Taliesin, and praising vernacular architecture at the expense of the formal. He wrote that 'humble buildings are to architecture what folklore is to literature'. It was this element of his thought, together with his insistence that architecture should be based on contemporary possibilities, that interested the Europeans. J. J. P. Oud, the Dutch architect, praised Wright for proposing buildings that were economically possible and socially responsible (while criticizing him for never having produced any, save for some exquisite examples for rich men). Wright's vision of the future was that there should be houses spread across the United States, each integrated into its natural environment and each in an acre of ground, with 'the future city… everywhere and nowhere'.

C. R. Ashbee, who met him, did much to publicize his work in Britain.

Bibliography F. Gutheim (ed.) *Frank Lloyd Wright on Architecture* Duell Sloan & Pearce, New York, 1941; Charles Jencks *Kings of Infinite* Space Academy Editions, London, 1983

Russel Wright was an American institution – of sorts – Modernism's Martha Stewart, a branded celebrity distributing own-name merchandise to the dinner tables of middle America. His work was seen first in Macy's store in New York and then in the Museum of Modern Art's 'Machine Art' exhibition. In the words of Russell Lynes, author of the influential book *The Tastemakers*, 'Russel Wright was the answer for those of us who were brought up to accept the Bauhaus doctrine… but who could not afford to buy the expensive imports of Le Corbusier and Mies van der Rohe and Marcel Breuer.' Wright managed to balance in an odd, but effective, way, Functionalism, Art Deco and the vernacular Mission Style which so many American first-time buyers had picked up from junk and antique shops in the years between the Wars.

He was born in Lebanon, Ohio into a family of Quakers, and his values have always been located both in Puritanism and the Mid-West (although each was somewhat adapted to meet the demands of consumption). He studied sculpture at the Art Students' League in New York and law at Princeton, but did not last the course in law, being drawn to the theatre. Norman Bel Geddes offered him a theatrical job that Wright turned

down on the basis that the wages were too low (they were nil). Under the influence of his wife, Wright began to move away from the theatre towards a novel form of sculptural caricatures which, celebrated in *Vogue*, sold well. His first essay in industrial design was a set of spun aluminium bar tools, which also sold well, and which launched him on his new career. Wright enjoyed metals because of 'their easy workability' and 'permanent integral coloring', and began to design entire table settings in spun aluminium and spun steel. His wife would present these at department stores and trade shows throughout the Thirties. In 1932 Wright did a classic transformation job on a Wurlitzer radio, turning a solemn piece of funereal table architecture into a Raymond Loewy casket, and in 1934 introduced a 60-piece range of furniture (manufactured by Heywood-Wakefield) at Bloomingdale's. In 1935 his hugely successful 'Modern Living' furniture line, with its characteristic blond maple, was introduced at Macy's. His wife's sense for public relations and his own theatrical background helped 'Modern Living' ease into a rut in the American imagination, together with the designer's name. He was the first designer to persuade Macy's to use his name in their advertisements, for which he became so celebrated that in 1951 *Advertising Age* ran an article headed 'Russel Wright Does Not Advertise, But Many Ads Give Him Top Billing'. In 1937 Wright began to concentrate on ceramics, his greatest success being the 'American Modern' line for Steubenville Pottery, which ran for 20 years after its launch in 1939.

Bibliography Donald Albrecht and Robert Schonfield *Russel Wright: creating American lifestyle* exhibition catalogue, Cooper-Hewitt Museum, New York, 2001–2002

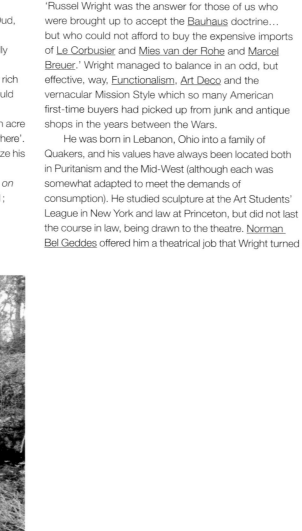

4

1: Frank Lloyd Wright, Solomon R. Guggenheim Museum, 5th Avenue, New York, 1959. A high-concept museum which dwarfs the art it houses.
2: Frank Lloyd Wright, 'Falling Water', Baer Run, Pennsylvania, 1934. The roof leaked.

3: Frank Lloyd Wright, chair in oak, 1908. This chair was designed for Wright's assistant, Isabel Roberts, who worked in his Oak Park, Chicago, office.
4: Russel Wright, American Modern pitchers for Stenbenville, 1939.

Sori Yanagi

Yanagi was born in Tokyo in 1915, but came into early contact with European modern design while he was an assistant in <u>Charlotte Perriand</u>'s office in Japan. In 1952 he founded the Yanagi Industrial Design Institute, and since 1977 he has been director of the Japan Folk Crafts Museum in Tokyo, two moves which suggest his dual commitment to the cultures of both East and West. His approach to <u>industrial design</u> has an oriental, somewhat mystic quality: 'basic concepts and beautiful forms do not come from the drawing board alone'. His most famous design is a plywood and steel 'Butterfly' stool of 1956, a delightful mediation between modern techniques and ancient ideals.

Zagato

Ugo Zagato (1890–1968) was originally a mechanical engineering apprentice in Cologne, and set up his own bodyshop, Carrozzeria Zagato, in Milan. After his death it passed into the hands of his sons, Elio (born 1921) and Gianni (born 1929). Zagato has often produced exaggerated, even ugly, body designs that derive much of their character from the symbols and necessities of the racetrack. In particular, the firm has worked for <u>Alfa Romeo</u> and Lancia; for them it has produced the Lancia Flavia Sport (1963) and the Alfa Romeo Guilia TZ2 (1964).

1

Marco Zanini born 1954

Marco Zanini, a partner in Sottsass Associati, studied architecture at the University of Florence, travelled in the United States, and joined Sottsass as an assistant in 1977. He contributed to the first two Memphis collections.

Zanotta

Zanotta is one of the leading firms of Milanese furniture manufacturers, producing side chairs, easy chairs and tables. Based at Nova Milanese, Zanotta abandoned the traditions of Italian furniture manufacture and turned to design patronage in the early Fifties, devoting itself to the search for aesthetic and functional solutions to the problems of the modern interior. Zanotta is a commercially astute company and has an important presence at the annual furniture fairs in Milan, Paris, Cologne and Kortrijk. It produces Giuseppe Terragni's 'Follia' chair of 1935 and Achille Castiglioni's 'Mezzadro' stool of 1957.
Bibliography Stefano Casciani *Furniture as Architecture – Design and Zanotta products* Arcadia Edizioni, Milan, 1988

Marco Zanuso

Marco Zanuso was born in Milan in 1916 and graduated in architecture from Milan Polytechnic in 1939, then joining its staff. He was editor of *Casabella* and designed all the Milan Triennales from VIIIth to XIIIth. His product designs have a remarkable sense of form which, while minimal, always achieve strong presence: for both his 1956 Borletti sewing-machine and his 1962 BrionVega television he won a Compasso d'Oro award, and he continued this sculptural tendency with his 'Black' television for BrionVega and his 'Hastil' and 'Thesi' pens for the Aurora company. He has designed factories and offices for Olivetti at Segrate, São Paulo, Buenos Aires and Caserta, and children's plastic furniture for Kartell.

1: Sori, Yanagi, 'Butterfly' stool, 1956.
2: Achille Castiglioni, 'Sella' stool for Zanotta, 1957. Castiglioni's trademark improvisation.

3: Marco Zanuso, BrionVega 'Doney' 14 television, 1964. Zanuso used high-quality injection-moulded plastics to create this elegiac memorial to European consumer products.

2

1: Wells Coates, Isokon flats, Hampstead, London. This international style building was a cultural landmark for Modernist entrepreneur and furniture-maker Jack Pritchard. Perhaps incongruously, Walter Gropius and Agatha Christie both lived here. In 1946 *Horizon* magazine, a literary ghetto, called it Britain's ugliest building.

2: Elizabeth David, *Mediterranean Food*, 1950. A taste-making book in every sense.

Anything that is made betrays the preoccupations and beliefs of the people who made it. You can, as Henry Ford once said, read any object like a book… if only you know how. The distinctive cultures and philosophies of the industrial nations find their way into manufactured goods, adding semantic richness to functional objects.

British design is ever associated with William Morris and the Arts and Crafts movement. The dual emphases on 'right making' and 'fitness for purpose' remained from the Design and Industries Association in the Twenties to the Council of Industrial Design and its successor, the Design Council. Although these are worthy principles in themselves, the tradition of Morris and the consequential 'Cotswold effect' (which is anti-urban and anti-industrial, even anti-commercial) advanced craft-based activities while retarding the progress of design in mass-production. For example, at the height of its influence in the Sixties, London's Design Council would not acknowledge that Detroit's Ford Mustang was the most successful car in the world. A product of marketing and styling, it did not conform to the dominant ideology of polite formalism and social responsibility. In other word, it was crass and dangerous, if undeniably sexy.

For similar reasons, Modernism was never widely accepted in Britain. For so long as it was unthreatening, a mere fashion, Modernism was tolerated, even by so conservative a character as the poet John Betjeman (who worked on the *Architectural Review* in the Thirties). But as soon as Modernism threatened to be influential, it was criticised as German, Bolshevik and possibly even Jewish too. Maverick products, including the radios designed for E. K. Cole by architect Wells Coates, were an exception. While the Festival of Britain of 1951 encouraged experimentation (especially in the work of Robin Day and Ernest Race), the best work of the mid-century was really little more than a synthesis of Italian, Scandinavian and American ideas. The mood of Britain's elite was reactionary.

The development of mass travel in the Fifties produced the first breakthrough in changing British taste, and hence design. An important influence in this change was the cookery writer Elizabeth David, whose first book, *Mediterranean Food* (1950), expanded the area of choice to the British consumer nurtured on traditional ideas of food made worse by the Second World War and rationing. (Its illustrations, by John Minton, also anticipated fashions in restaurant design that were to erupt in coffee bars, bistros and *trattorie* over the next decade: acceptance of European interior design came through licensed premises.) A distinguished series of other cookery books followed from Mrs David, and from the availability of *salade niçoise* and *ratatouille* it was only a short step to the wholesale adoption of the Provençal kitchen and French provincial cookware in the repertoire of interior design. Cooking enhanced the nation's palette.

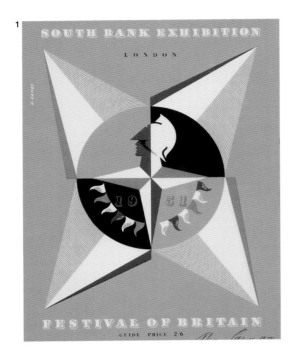

However, it was only with the advent of the Pop revolution of the Sixties that Britain established a position of international significance in design. In the liberal atmosphere of that decade Archigram, Terence Conran and Mary Quant became famous and were successful in establishing 'design' as an accessible force. A new type of professional design consultancy – including DRU and Pentagram – was established in the Sixties and Seventies, but they specialized mostly in graphics and interiors, an inevitable conclusion to a story that began with William Morris detesting industry. It is elegiac that architects Norman Foster and Richard Rogers, working in a culture that has disdained manufacturing, are inspired by technology. Equally, Britain's last remaining designer–entrepreneur–manufacturer, James Dyson, caused controversy when he moved his production lines to Asia.

In the United States there were two movements of design during the last century: the first was the industrial design movement, established in New York in the Twenties and peaking in the Fifties. This was driven by consumerism and aimed to satisfy mass markets by using streamlining and other styling clichés to stimulate demand. The second was a movement more influenced by European emigrés, and more oriented towards Europe, which found expression in furniture and interior design.

The industrial design movement brought individuals trained perhaps as advertising draughtsmen, window dressers or stage designers into contact with the manufacturers of hard goods such as washing machines, refrigerators and cameras which, at the time, were status symbols. Caught by the Depression of the late Twenties, an extra quality was needed stimulate demand. The style that emerged from this flirtation was essentially commercial and created a mass aesthetic that was the first democratic style of the twentieth century. Henry Dreyfuss, Raymond Loewy and Walter Dorwin Teague were widely imitated (both as stylists and business models) across the world, although the British generally found it meretricious and vulgar and refused to have any association with it.

In contrast, the second American design movement was enthusiastically accepted by both the American social and commercial establishment, fascinated by all things European, and by the Europeans who were lost in admiration for the Americans' ability to implement their own ideas with such effect. The second movement is characterized by the exhibitions and the personnel of New York's Museum of Modern Art. The Museum gave Charles Eames a major exhibition and selected furniture manufactured by Herman Miller and Knoll as winners of prizes offered in its 'Good Design' competitions of the early Fifties. The spindly legs and bent plywood of this furniture style soon became a familiar sight in many interiors and, combined with plants and 'organic' coffee tables, populated many features in *House & Garden* magazine.

The later Fifties, America's most prosperous years, are, perhaps, best remembered by the extravagant automobile designs of Harley Earl, Virgil Exner and Brooks Stevens. Using the imagery of space rockets, Earl proved H.L. Mencken's dictum that 'nobody ever went bust underestimating the public's taste'. However, the rise of consumer protection and conservation movements led by Ralph Nader, the bullish exuberance of American automobile styling was condemned as immoral and American design lost its primitive dynamism.

In the later Sixties American design became a predominantly corporate matter. After Eliot Noyes left the Museum of Modern Art to transform the entire image of IBM, leading American designers concentrated on identity and branding rather than products or furniture. This reflected a decline in the US manufacturing of consumer goods, symbolized in the early twenty-first century by the near bankruptcy of Ford and General Motors and by IBM selling-off its hardware to Chinese interests. The sole exception to a general decline has been the work of Jonathan Ive at Apple Computers.

1: Abram Games, Festival of Britain publicity material, 1951.
2: Charles Eames, stacking chairs for Herman Miller in zinc-coated steel tubes with moulded polyester seats.

3: US automobile production and national confidence peaked in 1955 when it was said that anything wrong with Detroit was wrong with America. This 1954 cadillac was a perfect symbol of a nation's preoccupations.

3

In the United States there were two movements of design during the last century: the first was the industrial design movement, established in New York in the Twenties. The second was a movement more oriented towards Europe, which found expression in furniture and interior design

The Scandinavian countries are more socially cohesive than Britain or the United States (which is to say more 'middle class') so it was easier for an early generation of designers to impose a single level of taste across an entire continent. The term 'Danish Modern' (although it could just as easily be 'Swedish Modern') was coined in the Fifties to describe a style of furniture and interior design that depended on spare, sculptural forms and natural materials (particularly teak and canvas).

Furniture design in twentieth-century Denmark grew from formal schools of cabinet-making: Kaare Klint reworked the deck chair and Mogens Koch the campaign chair. After the Second World War, Børge Mogensen, Hans Wegner, Finn Juhl and Poul Kjaerholm designed furniture that was progressively more striking and sculptural. By the Fifties Danish furniture had established an international reputation for impeccable craftsmanship and meticulous attention to detail. By the Sixties and Seventies, David Lewis at Bang & Olufsen was applying similar principles to consumer electronics.

While furniture is the most important component of Danish design, in the other Nordic countries there was a consistent interest in the applied arts, particularly those associated with the kitchen and the table. Flatware is most readily associated with Georg Jensen and with Kay Bojesen, who established Den Permanente in 1934. For many years this continuous exhibition of Danish products made high standards public, although in a world where design is the environment, not the competition, Denmark has lost its special identity and descended into limp self-parody.

Alvar Aalto excepted, Finland exported its greatest designers. The Saarinens were more influential in New York than in Helsinki. Finland was late to establish a distinct design identity, additionally because the manufacture of consumer goods was not so well advanced. A Finnish language of design emerged only in the early Fifties when Tapio Wirkkala and Timo Sarpaneva began to show art glass at the Milan Triennales. Since then Finnish design has continued to be both more sculptural and more exclusive than its other Scandinavian counterparts. In addition to glass, Finnish furniture, ceramics and textiles also have special qualities. From Aalto to Kukkapuro, Finnish furniture combines respect for the nature of

1: IKEA, modernism
goes global.
2: BMW Isetta microcar, 1956.
An Italian design made in
Germany.

3: Lucio Fontana, a space-
light structure in neon,
9th Milan Triennale, 1951.

Simple shapes, undecorated
surfaces, and purity of colour
and detail became the tokens
of German design

materials with a subtle sense of proportion and a feeling for quality. But it is with printed cotton textiles of Marimekko and Vuokko that Finland most recently excelled. By 2000 Finland's most successful manufacturer was not Arabia or Artek, but mobile phone maker Nokia. Yet at this stage in the history of portable telecoms, possibly at this stage in civilization, progress is driven more by technological features than design.

Since the emergence of the modern kingdom, Swedish design has been associated with a respect for tradition, a sense of humanism and a concern for democratic values. This last commitment in particular lay behind the dominant 'beauty for all' principle, first announced by the writer Ellen Kay and picked up by Gregor Paulsson in 1915, who turned it into the motif of the Svenska Sljödföreningen. These ideas provided the ideological background against which companies such as Gustavsberg, Rörstrand and Orrefors initiated their policies, widely imitated throughout the Nordic area, of having practising artists work in their factories.

The Modern Movement in Sweden took a softer and more natural form than elsewhere and the style that became known as 'Swedish Modern', with its predominant use of beech, simply patterned textiles and small wooden objects, was described by a jaded American journalist visiting the 1939 New York World's Fair as 'a movement towards sanity in design'. The appeal of 'Swedish Modern', or what The Beatles called Norwegian Wood, was widespread in the Fifties and Sixties, but since then the Swedes have found no formula of similar international appeal (although the nation's industries still dominate world markets in their production of factory-made crafts goods and, through IKEA, of mass-market Modernism).

Trade and education have had as much influence on German design as *Formgebung*. The German commercial tradition, for example, confers real status on tradesmen through an apprentice system that depends on a mixture of *Berufsschulen* (vocational schools) and factory training. This tends to produce higher-skilled workers who demand and get status; thus your *metzger* (butcher) or *zimmerman* (carpenter) does not feel socially inferior to your accountant or dentist. And he gets vehicles and tools and graphics to prove it.

Similarly, a systematic approach to education and to understanding drawing as a sort of intellectual exercise, going back to Heinrich Pestalozzi's *Anschauung* (Perception) and the contemporary belief that in *Hauptformen* (key forms) there were the essential characteristics of product types, had a clear influence on the evolution of a design tradition that emphasized clarity and order.

Thus, German products have a 'rational' style. Simple shapes, undecorated surfaces, and purity of colour and detail became the tokens of German design. This approach has its origins in the Deutsche Werkbund, an organization that sought to ally art with industry and to impose standardization. This concept of standardization had aesthetic and organizational implications that formed the basis for all subsequent German design.

It was Germany that responded most enthusiastically to the ideas about scientific management established in the United States by F. W. Taylor. The Bauhaus (although it had an early phase that was expressionistic) supported rational forms, while companies such as AEG, Arzberg, Bosch and Rosenthal evolved a simple, rational aesthetic for their products.

In the years after the Second World War Germany was quick to re-establish its industrial supremacy, while maintaining its pre-War design concerns. At the Hochschule für Gestaltung in Ulm and with Braun, the German ideal always seemed to be reason and purity in front of emotion and complexity. An engineering tradition, exemplified by Porsche, has given esoteric support to this national preference, and has also tended to mean, with the exception of global stars such as Dieter Rams, that the designer is an anonymous figure.

In Germany after 1945 means were desperately limited. There was not enough metal to make saucepans, but with characteristic genius Germans managed to make cars. The humbled optimism of the advertisements and brochures is as touching as the amazing ingenuity, variety and restraint of the designs themselves. The Champion 400 microcar had a door with a pure <u>Bauhaus</u> glazed semi-circle above a rectangle. This semi-circle pivoted for storage, but offered infinite variety of segmental variations of ventilation aperture en route. The Lloyd Alexander of 1958 had ruched door pockets. <u>BMW</u>'s Isetta was made between 1955 and 1964, 160,000 units in all, each with a forward-entry front door somewhat reminiscent of a coffin lid. An Isetta brochure used Swiss typography and declared 'Fur die Wohlfhartspflege Deutschland!' (For German Welfare). Cary Grant and Elvis Presley promoted the Isetta in the United States and it was sold with the hilariously ambivalent slogan 'The most exciting car on the American highway'.

The German contribution to the mechanics of the twentieth century has been huge. The best tools, the Bauhaus, Porsche, BMW all demonstrate the qualities of clarity, integrity and reason on which the reputation of German design is founded.

Since the Second World War Italy has enjoyed an international reputation for excellence in design, although the homeland of Palladio and Michelangelo has fewer art schools than Cheshire. Still, the influence of the Renaissance cannot be eradicated by a few deficiencies in higher education. During the period of *ricostruzione* after the War, design was seen as an important element in Italy's industrial regeneration. From the beginning it was associated with the names of certain architects – including the <u>Castiglioni</u> brothers, <u>Ettore Sottsass</u> and <u>Marco Zanuso</u> – who had trained during the Thirties and who were employed on a consultancy basis by the newly founded or reorganized firms based around Milan and Turin: <u>Olivetti</u>, <u>Cassina</u>, <u>BrionVega</u> and <u>Artemide</u>.

In the Forties and Fifties the visual source for Italian design was contemporary 'organic' sculpture, mixed with late <u>Futurism</u>, and this, combined with new production techniques used for the new metals and plastics, created a unique aesthetic. Design emerged as an element in marketing policies that emphasized exclusiveness and *la dolce vita*: the Riva Aquarama speedboat is a perfect example here. In Italy design was part of a national bid for a share of world trade and was supported by Milan's <u>Triennale</u> exhibitions, a vast variety of magazines and <u>La Rinascente</u>'s <u>Compasso d'Oro</u> awards.

By the mid-Fifties Italian chic had been accepted as an international style by the wealthy, while a diffusion version became fashionable at a popular level with espresso coffee and the <u>Vespa</u>. However, by the Sixties there was among the intelligentsia a growing dissatisfaction with this national image and some architect–designers who wanted a stronger social base for their work proposed a protest movement called anti-design. Ettore Sottsass was a principal influence in this, together with <u>Superstudio</u> and <u>Archizoom</u>, and his Pop furniture and ceramics were an inspiration to many young Italian designers keen to work outside the constraints of manufacturing industry. The irreverent spirit was revived (or possibly survived) into the Eighties in <u>Memphis</u> which reclaimed for Italy the avant-garde.

Of all the great manufacturing nations, the Japanese have most in their traditional culture to encourage excellent practice and fine appreciation of design. The *sakoku* was the voluntary period of seclusion when trade and travel were discouraged. While the *sakoku* inhibited economic development, it left Japan with an integral culture that had not been violated by colonialism. More significant still, it encouraged the Japanese to think of themselves as functionally distinct to other people.

Looking at a Nikon or a sushi lunch box you can see Japan in miniature: physical beauty and practical discipline, standardized and miniaturized

There are three ways of understanding Japanese design. Its historic traditions, its voracious appetitite for assimilation and its occasionally surreal experiments and innovations (some years ago a leading furniture designer made a sofa out of shards of broken glass). But this being Japan, where Western models are admired but have to take their place in a unique culture that had sophisticated packaging and corporate identity when native Americans were still chewing bark, they are all mixed up. A sophisticated dualism defines Japan: the best book ever written about the culture was Ruth Benedict's *The Chrysanthemum and the Sword* (1948), describing a nation where refined aestheticism sat next to ferocious martial arts. It has been said that the Japanese have a great sense of beauty, but no sense of ugliness. For every traditional *riyokan* admired for its austere geometrical perfection, there is a fluorescent pink love hotel with disco balls and heliotrope strobes. For every set of Momoyama period tea ceremony utensils, evoking a Zen-like sense of transcendence, there is an Edwardian baroque lacquer cocktail cabinet. Still, the traditional crafts of Edo period lacquer and ceramics are as much an expression of Japanese culture as the motorbikes, cars, cameras, electronics and other industrial products that created the Japanese economic miracle.

A bonsai is much more than a miniature potted tree, more an expression of the universe. Equally, the classic Nikon F is more than just a camera: it is a demonstration of a belief system, a diagram of mechanical perfectionism, miniaturization, order and hierarchy. The traditional Japanese blending of art, religion, philosophy and practicality aided the processes of industrialization. But the Western concept of 'design' was only introduced in the second half of the nineteenth century when Otto Wagner and Christopher Dresser travelled there. After the Second World War, with the restructuring of the economy under the American Marshall Plan (which also, for the first time, gave the Japanese street names), new firms like Sony and Honda joined the older established giants of Japanese manufacturing industry, most of whom had their origins in textiles or heavy engineering. Circumstances forced Sony and Honda to innovate: Sony's first product was a tape-recorder produced to satisfy Civil Information and Education division of the US Occupation Forces. Honda strapped small industrial engines to push-bikes.

At first the emphasis was on high-volume production. This is where the misunderstanding about Japanese copying arose. Japanese manufacturers aped Western models, but this was because their concerned was to invest in process technology rather than capricious invention. This investment later gave them the flexibility to innovate. Creativity came out of the factory floor, not out of the studio.

As the market for high-volume goods became saturated, the Japanese government encouraged flights up-market. Edward Deming taught quality control and Western designers, including Giovanni Michelotti and Count Albrecht van Goertz, found work in the automobile industry. Results were at first mixed. Only when the Japan Council of Industrial Design organized an exhibition of Western electrical goods in 1965 did the Japanese get very thoroughly exposed to Western taste. Equally, because of the dominance of flat graphics in the history of Japanese art (they have no very great tradition of sculpture-in-the-round), only when computers able to handle complex surfacing became available in the late Eighties did Japanese car design break out of its sometimes awkward two-dimensional effects.

There are important concepts in Japanese thought which have inhibited the development of the 'designer' as the sort of stand-alone, autonomous, creative professional known in the West. *Haragei* is a sort of non-verbal communication: the Japanese attach special value to an introspective understanding of personality. Discretion is valued above extroversion.

At the same time, a term borrowed from arboriculture, *nemawashi* (literally 'root binding') is used to describe the preparations made before meetings to make sure everyone agrees. This leads to *ringi*, or consensus decision-taking. Because of *nemawashi* and *ringi*, the Japanese tended to resist personalities, but with increasing confidence and globalization, creative personalities began to emerge. First in architecture with Kenzo Tange, then in fashion with <u>Hanae Mori</u> and <u>Issey Miyake</u>, then in furniture with <u>Shiro Kuramata</u> becoming global figures.

Traditional concepts have given the Japanese a highly sophisticated response to manufactured objects. There are ideas that simply do not exist in European languages. For instance *ne*, which means a sound – like the chirruping of cicadas – that is somewhere between a mere noise and self-conscious music. If you possess notions of such sophistication, it is inevitable that you will find sophisticated solutions to problems. From Zen the Japanese have also acquired a concept known as *ke*, or the beauty that is inherent in something, not the sort of beauty that is a surface effect. But together with this mysticism there is a strong practicality. The regularized tatami mat (in Kyoto strictly determined as 2 inches thick, 6.3 feet long and 3.15 feet wide) is a cognitively standardized unit that aids a systematic approach to design.

Looking at a Nikon or a sushi lunch box you can see Japan in miniature: physical beauty and practical discipline, standardized and miniaturized. The same confidence that has allowed Japanese designers cautiously to step forward as personalities is also encouraging them to explore national characteristics. Manufacturers are wondering very seriously whether there is such a thing as a distinctive Japanese style.

There is certainly a distinctive Japanese approach to objects and it is based in a religious spirit. Even when you are contemplating a plasma screen in the back of a chillingly air-conned Lexus, it is important to know that Japanese design is essentially Buddhist. Theirs is an aesthetic view of the world, which is to say a philosophy that is based on physical sensation. But, equally, they do not make the same distinction as the West between 'art' and 'design'. Instead, the single word *katachi* describes the totality of an object's character. And this applies to a samurai's katana blade as surely as it does to a Global kitchen knife.

But there are three other concepts essential to understanding Japanese products. The first is *wabi-sabi*, the term for harmony. *Wabi-sabi* encourages an appreciation of simplicity, even a delight in the incomplete, and has its basis in Zen mysticism. It affects every Japanese designer.

An even more important concept is *bi*, which more or less means details. *Bi* was a cultural source of the Japanese genius for miniaturization and applies to details as well as things. The sense that an individual is a part of a larger community finds expression in product design where the details are construed to contain the whole. Lastly, there is *ma*, or vagueness, a quality difficult to describe in physical terms, but eloquent of the sophisticated relationship Japanese have with objects.

Globalization and the dematerialised priorities of the Information Age may have blurred our perception of national characteristics in design, just as they have diminished our appetite for acquiring more stuff, but the essential truth remains: objects have meanings and values that are quite independent of price. But design is not necessarily art. Designed objects begin with a functional purpose. If they are any good, they endure. And then, to paraphrase Charles Eames, they become art, or, at least, they usurp the conventional role of art, which is to say they can be read not at one, rather at several different levels. But whether a functioning device, or a something worthy of contemplation, there is always one definition of design, wherever it comes from and whenever it was made. Good design is… as Le Courbusier said, intelligence made visible.

1: The Nikon 7, the world's last mechanical camera was manufactured between 1959–1974. Its disciplined details and compact form betray an ancient inheritance.

2: Kenzo Tange, Yoyogi National Stadium, Tokyo, 1964. A new Japanese national self-conciousness.

3: Playing Pachinko in Kyoto: not every Japanese tradition is minimalist.

4: Hanae Mori, shirt inspired by Japanese prints, circa 1970.

Museums & Institutions

The universal nature of industrial production has made design into an international subject. There are a number of museums, societies and other institutions in all parts of the world which either have permanent collections or can make available specialist material for students of design.

Australia

Standards Australia Limited
286 Sussex Street
Sydney
NSW 2000
www.standards.org.au
actively promotes excellence in Australian design and innovation through the Australian Design Awards

Austria

Museum für Angewandte Kunst
Stubenring 5
1010 Wien
www.mak.at
permanent collections

Belgium

Design Museum Gent
Jan Breydelstraat 5
9000 Ghent
design.museum.gent.be
an eclectic collection of design products

Canada

ICSID
455 St-Antoine W. Suite SS10
Montréal
Quebec H2Z 1J1, Canada
www.icsid.org
The International Council of Societies of Industrial Design promotes better design around the world

Czech Republic

Czech Design.CZ
o.s., K Safinů 562
149 00 Prague 4
www.czechdesign.cz
exhibitions and collections

Museum of Decorative Arts
Ulice 17
Listopada 2
Staré Mesto
Prague 1
www.upm.cz
permanent collections

Denmark

The Danish Arts Agency
H.C.Andersens Boulevard 2
DK-1553 Copenhagen V
www.kunststyrelsen.dk
exhibitions and awards

Danish Design Centre
27 HC Andersens Boulevard
1553 Copenhagen V
www.ddc.dk
showcasing new design talent

The Visual Arts Centre
Kongens Nytorv 3
DK-1050 Copenhagen K
www.kunststyrelsen.dk
exhibitions and awards

Finland

Alvar Aalto Museum
Alvar Aallon katu 7
Jyväskylä
www.alvaraalto.fi
permanent collection of Aalto's work

Design Museo
Korkeavuorenkatu 23
00130 Hensinki
www.designmuseum.fi
exhibitions, permanent collections

France

Bibliothèque Forney
Hôtel de Sens
1, rue du Figuier
75004 Paris
documentation of textiles and wallpapers

Centre Georges Pompidou
Place Georges Pompidou
75004 Paris
www.centrepompidou.fr
exhibitions

Musée des Arts Décoratifs
107, rue de Rivoli
75001 Paris
www.lesartsdecoratifs.fr
the applied arts department of the Louvre; exhibitions

Germany

Bauhaus Archive / Museum of Design
Klingelhöferstraße 14
D-10785 Berlin
www.bauhaus.de
permanent collection on Bauhaus design

Design Center Stuttgart
Haus der Wirtschaft
Willi-Bleicher-Straße 19
D-70174 Stuttgart
www.design-center.de
exhibitions

Deutsches Museum
Museumsinsel 1
80538 München
www.deutsches-museum.de
permanent collection

German Architecture Museum (Deutsches Architektur Museum)
Schaumainkai 43
Frankfurt 60596
dam.inm.de
exhibitions

Rat für Formgebung/German Design Council
Dependance/Messegelände
Ludwig-Erhard-Anlage 1
60327 Frankfurt am Main
www.german-design-council.de
information about design, competitions, awards

Hungary

Musuem of Applied Arts
Address: IX. Ülloi út 33–37
1450 Budapest, Pf.3.
www.imm.hu/angol/index.html
museum of applied arts with an interest in industrial design

Ireland

Kilkenny Design Centre
Castle Yard
Kilkenny
www.kilkennydesign.com
exhibitions and documentation, largely about craft-based design

Israel

The Israel museum
POB 71117
Jerusalem 91710
www.imj.org.il
exhibitions

Italy

Associazione per il Disegno Industriale (ADI)
via Bramante 29
20154 Milano
www.adi-design.org
documentation, competitions

Triennale di Milano
Palazzo dell'Arte
Viale Alemagna 6
20121 Milan
exhibitions

Japan

Japan Industrial Design Promotion Organization (JIDPO)
4th floor Annex, World Trade Center Bldg.,
2-4-1 Hamamatsucho,
Minato-ku, Tokyo 105-6190
www.jidpo.or.jp/en/
permanent collections, awards

Netherlands

Stedelijk Museum
Paulus Potterstraat 13
Amsterdam
www.stedelijk.nl
permanent collections, exhibitions
(closed for renovation until Autumn 2008.
A temporary location can be found at Post CS-building,
Oosterdokskade 5, 1011 AD Amsterdam)

Norway

Kunstindustrimuseet (Musum of Applied Arts)
St. Olavs gate 1
N-0165 Oslo
permanent collections, exhibitions

Nordenfjeldske Kunstindustrimuseum
(National Museum of Decorative Arts)
Munkegaten 3-7
N-7013 Trondheim
www.nkim.museum.no/
permanent collections, exhibitions

Sweden

Form / Design Center
Lilla Torg 9
Malmö
www.formdesigncenter.com
exhibitions, awards

National Museum
Södra Blasieholmshamnen
11148 Stockholm
www.nationalmuseum.se
permanent collection

Rohsska Museet (Museum for Design and Decorative Art)
Vasagatan 37–39
SE-400 15 Göteborg
www.designmuseum.se
permanent collections, exhibitions

Svensk Form (the Swedish Society of Crafts and Design)
Holmamiralens väg 2
SE-111 49 Stockholm
www.svenskform.se
promotes Swedish design at home and abroad,
exhibitions, documentation

Switzerland

Alliance Graphique Internationale
c/o Mrs. Erika Remund Jagne
Limmatstrasse 63
CH-8005 Zurich
www.a-g-i.org
an élite club of the world's leading graphics designers and
artists

United Kingdom

Design Council
34 Bow Street
London WC2E 7DL
www.design-council.org.uk
the national strategic body for design

Design Museum
Shad Thames
London SE1 2YD
www.designmuseum.org
designers, architects and technologies of modern and
contemporary design

V&A South Kensington
Cromwell Road
London SW7 2RL
www.vam.ac.uk
permanent collections, exhibitions

United States of America

Cooper Hewitt National Design Museum
2 East 91st Street
New York, NY 10128
ndm.si.edu
museum devoted exclusively to historic and contemporary
design, permanent collections, exhibitions

The Museum of Modern Art
11 West 53 Street, between Fifth and Sixth Avenues
New York, NY 10019-5497
www.moma.org
permanent collections, exhibitions

Index

Page numbers in **bold** refer to main entries;
italic numbers refer to the illustrations

Acknowledgements

The publisher would like to thank the following photographers and agencies for their kind permission to reproduce the following photographs:

Special photography: 8-9, 336 Mark Harrison/Conran Octopus; 12, 59 above Héloïse Acher/Conran Octopus; 21 (Courtesy of Unilever), 107, 121 left, 164 above, 234, 235, 240, 286, 310 left, 314 above right Clive Corless/Conran Octopus; 66 above, 90-91, 117, 270 right Nicola Grifoni/Scala/Conran Octopus; Conran Octopus p3, 96 left & right, 253, 271 right, 296 right

4-5 Fiat; 6 Steve Speller/Heatherwick Studio;10-11 Terence Conran; 14 Oxford Science Archive/Heritage-Images; 15 By permission of the Founders' Library, University of Wales, Lampeter; 16 Private Collection/Bridgeman Art Library; 17 above Royal Society of Arts; 17 below The Trustees of the Weston Park Foundation, UK/Bridgeman Art Library; 18 above & below Courtesy of the Wedgwood Museum Trust, Barlaston, Staffordshire, UK; 19 left Angelo Hornak; 19 right Deutsche Technikmuseum Berlin © DACS, London 2007; 20 R.A Gardner; 22 V&A Images/Victoria & Albert Museum; 23 Royal Armouries/Heritage-Images; 24 Linley Sambourne House, London/ Bridgeman Art Library; 25 above Sears Archives; 25 below Rischgitz/Hulton Archive/Getty Images; 26 William Morris Gallery/London Borough of Waltham Forest; 28 left & right The De Morgan Centre, London/Bridgeman Art Library; 28 centre Fitzwilliam Museum, University of Cambridge/Bridgeman Art Library; 29 Albertina, Vienna; 30 left Carl Larsson-garden; 30 right English Heritage Photographic Library; 31 Angelo Hornak; 32 Allan Macintyre, President & Fellows of Harvard College/Harvard University Art Museums, Fogg Art Museum, Louise E.Bettens Fund; 33 Bauhaus Archiv, Berlin © DACS, London 2007; 34 Michael JH Taylor; 35 Centraal Museum, Utrecht © DACS, London 2007; 36 above The Estate of William Heath Robinson; 36 below Stapleton Collection, UK/Bridgeman Art Library © DACS, London 2007; 37 Bettmann/Corbis; 38 Boeing Images; 39 AB Electrolux; 40 The Art Institute of Chicago; 41 Courtesy of AT&T Archives and History Centre, San Antonio, Texas; 42 V & A Images/Victoria & Albert Museum; 43 left Courtesy of the Eliot Noyes Archives; 43 right Teague Associates; 44 Fiat; 45 Alessi; 46 Fox Photos/Hulton Archives/Getty Images; 47 Fornasetti; 48 Sottsass Associates; 49 Arflex; 50 Gaetano Pesce; 52 a-d Braun GmbH; 53 Sony; 54 above Keystone/Hulton Archive/Getty Images; 54 below Ford Motor Company Limited; 55 Chaloner Woods/Hulton Archive/Getty Images; 56 Courtesy of Apple Inc.; 57 akg-images; 58 above & below Droog Design; 59 below Google Inc; 60 Studio Job; 61 China Photos/Getty Images News; 62 Artek; 63 above left Adelta; 63 below left Artek; 63 a-b Deutsche Technikmuseum Berlin; 63 c Deutsche Technikmuseum Berlin © DACS, London 2007; 63 d Deutsche Technikmuseum Berlin © DACS, London 2007; 63 e Deutsche Technikmuseum Berlin © DACS, London 2007; 64 left © 1976 by ERCO Leuchten GmbH; 64 right Bridgeman Art Library/© The Joseph and Anni Albers Foundation/VG Bild-Kunst, Bonn and DACS, London 2007; 65 Studio Albini; 66 below left & below right Alessi; 67 above & below Alfa Romeo; 68 Emilio Ambasz & Associates; 69 left Arabia/littala; 69 right Peter Cook/Archigram Archives; 70 left RIBA Library Photographs Collection; 70-71 Copyright of Christie's Images 2006; 71 The Museum of Modern Art, New York/Scala, Florence; 72 David Lees/Time & Life Pictures/Getty Images; 73 above RIBA Library Photographs Collection; 73 below Private Collection/Bridgeman Art Library; 74 left Martine Hamilton Knight/Arcaid; 74 right Spectrum/HIP/Scala, Florence; 74 centre Erich Lessing/akg-images; 75 left & right Artek; 76 left Courtesy of Archivio Flos Arteluce; 76 above right & below right Artemide; 77 above Ferenc Berko/Berko Photography; 77 below The Museum of Modern Art, New York/Scala, Florence; 78 left Swedish Society of Crafts and Design; 78 right Architectural Press Archive/RIBA Library Photographs Collection; 79 left Herve Champollion/akg-images; 79 right Archivo Storico Olivetti, Ivrea, Italy; 80 above Eric de Mare/RIBA Library Photographs Collection; 80 below British Motor Industry Heritage Trust; 81 left V & A Images/Victoria & Albert Museum; 81 right Gjon Mill/Time & Life Pictures/Getty Images; 82 left BMW AG; 82 right Leica Camera AG; 83 The Museum of Modern Art, New York/Scala Florence; 84 & 85 left The Kobal Collection; 85 right Saul Bass & Associates 1974/United Airlines; 86 Bauhaus Archiv, Berlin © DACS, London 2007; 86-87 Bauhaus Archiv, Berlin © DACS, London 2007; 87 ph: Markus Hawlik/Bauhaus Archiv, Berlin © DACS, London 2007; 88 left The Museum of Modern Art, New York/Scala Florence © DACS, London 2007; 88 right RIBA Library Photographs Collection; 89 Deutsche Technikmuseum Berlin © DACS, London 2007; 90 left V & A Images/Victoria & Albert Museum; 91 Stuart Cox/V & A Images/Victoria & Albert Museum; 92 above Bauhaus Archiv, Berlin © DACS, London 2007; 92 below Geiger International; 93 Knoll, Inc; 94 Citroen Communication; 95 left & right Bestlite; 96-97 RIBA Library Photographs Collection; 97 above The Museum of Modern Art, New York/Scala Florence; 97 below National Motor Museum/MPL; 98 left & right BMW AG; 99 above Knoll, Inc; 99 below left & below right Renault Communication/Photographer Unknown/All Rights Reserved; 100 right The Philadelphia Museum of Art/Art Resource/Scala, Florence © ADAGP, Paris and DACS, London 2007; 100 above BMW AG Group Archives; 100 below BMW AG; 101 above Michelin Tyre Public Limited Company; 101 below Arnold Newman Collection/Getty Images; 102 above left Bauhaus Archiv, Berlin; 102 above right & below Braun GmbH; 103 above National Motor Museum/MPL; 103 below left Bauhaus Archiv, Berlin; 103 below right Bauhaus Archiv, Berlin; 104 above Bettmann/Corbis; 104 below BrionVega; 105 above Airstream Inc; 105 below Archive Holdings Inc/The Image Bank/Getty Images; 106-107 Barbara Burg & Oliver Schuh,www.palladium.de; 108–109 & 109 Buyenlarge/Time & Life Pictures/Getty Images; 110 left ph: Mario Carrieri/Cassina Collection (out of production); 110 right Zanotta SpA; 111 left Pictorial Press Ltd/Alamy; 111 right National Motor Museum/Heritage-Images; 112 left Michael Halberstadt/Arcaid; 112 right & 113 left Chermayeff & Geismar Studio; 113 right National Motor Museum/MPL; 114 left & right Citroen Communication; 115 left P.Louys/Citroen Communication; 115 right Courtesy of Sotheby's Picture Library; 116 above Morley von Sternberg; 116 below V & A Images/Victoria & Albert Museum; 116-117 Rosenthal AG; 118 above & below Courtesy of Studio Joe Colombo, Milan; 119 The Museum of Modern Art, New York/Scala, Florence © DACS, London 2007; 120 Design Council Slide Collection, Manchester Metropolitan University, Design Council; 121 Anthony Crane Collection, UK/Bridgeman Art Library; 122 above Danese srl; 122 below National Motor Museum/MPL; 123 Hille; 124 left Michele De Lucchi Archive; 124 right Zanotta SpA; 125 left Haags Gemeentemuseum, The Hague, Netherlands/Bridgeman Art Library; 125 right Campari Group; 126 left Donald Deskey Collection, Cooper-Hewitt, National Design Museum, Smithsonian Institute; 126 right Rheinisches Bildarchiv Koln; 127 Loomis Dean/Time & Life Pictures/Getty Images; 128 left akg-images; 128 right K.Helmer Petersen/Nanna Ditzel Design A/S; 129 RIBA Library Photographs Collection; 130 Margaret Bourke-White/Time & Life Pictures/Getty Images; 131 Private Collection/The Fine Art Society, London/Bridgeman Art Library; 132 right Robert Yarnall Richie/Time & Life Pictures/Getty Images; 132 above left Thomas Gustainis/Courtesy of the Polaroid Collections; 132 below left Eric Schaal/Time & Life Pictures/Getty Images; 133 Dyson Ltd; 134 Herman Miller Inc; 135 above London College of Communication (formerly Printing); 135 below National Motor Museum/MPL; 136 left Swiss Army Tools; 136 right Ercol Furniture Ltd; 137 above Marimekko Corporation; 137 below Jerry Cooke/Time & Life/Getty Images; 138 a-c & 139 left Penguin Group UK; 139 right Copyright of Christie's Images Ltd 2006; 140 left & below right Fiat; 140 above right National Motor Museum/Heritage-Images; 141 above Citroen Communcation; 141 below Minox GmbH; 142 left & centre Alan Fletcher; 142 right Flos; 143 Hulton Archive/Getty Images; 144 Fornasetti; 145 left Svenskt Tenn; 145 right BMW AG; 146-147 RIBA Library Photographs Collection; 147 Estate of Buckminster Fuller; 148 Marius Reynolds/ Architectural Association; 149 right Private Collection/Bridgeman Art Library © DACS, London 2007; 149 above left The Museum of Modern Art, New York/ Scala, Florence; 149 below left Sanden/Hulton Archive/Getty Images; 150 Private Collection/Bridgeman Art Library; 150-151 & 151 left Estate of Abram Games; 151 right Zanotta SpA; 152 Hillbich/akg-images; 152-153 Lake County Museum/Corbis; 153 right Bettmann/Corbis; 153 above left Knoll, Inc; 154 Le Grandi Automobilie; 155 above National Portrait Gallery, London; 156 left Cheltenham Art Gallery & Museums, Gloucestershire, UK/Bridgeman Art Library; 156 right Herman Miller Inc; 157 above left & below left Barilla; 157 below right Volkswagen AG; 158 left & right Milton Glaser; 159 RIBA Library Photographs Collection; 160 Guildhall Library, City of London/Bridgeman Art Library; 161 above Daniel Brooks Collection/Henry Ford Heritage Association; 161 below Corbis; 162 Bauhaus Archiv, Berlin © DACS, London 2007; 163 10-gruppen/Ten Swedish Designers AB © DACS, London 2007; 164 below AB Electrolux; 165 left Marion Kalter/akg-images; 165 right Swedish Society of Crafts and Design; 166 V & A Images/Victoria & Albert Museum; 167 Orrefors Kosta Boda AB; 168 left Bauhaus Archiv, Berlin © DACS, London 2007; 168 right Private Collection/Fine Art Society & Target Gallery, London/Bridgeman Art Library; 169 above left Nikolas Koenig/ Heatherwick Studio; 169 above right Len Grant/Heatherwick Studio; 169 below left, below centre & below right Steve Speller/Heatherwick Studio; 170 left Ericsson; 170 right Danish Design Centre; 171 left V & A Images/ Victoria & Albert Museum; 171 right Museum of Modern Art, New York/Scala, Florence; 172 left The Estate of David Hicks; 172 right Dell & Wainwright/ RIBA Library Photographs Collection; 173 Museum of Modern Art, New York/Scala, Florence; 174 left ph: Georg Riha/Hans Hollein Studio; 174 right Hans Hollein Studio; 175 right Elbert Hubbard-Roycroft Museum, East Aurora, New York; 175 above left & below left Honda Motor Co. Japan; 176 left & right IBM; 177 Ikea; 178 above right V & A Images/Victoria & Albert Museum; 178 below Edifice/Corbis; 179 above right, centre right & below left British Motor Industry Heritage Trust; 179 below right ALH Dawson/MINI; 180 left Bauhaus Archiv, Berlin; 180 right Bauhaus Archiv, Berlin © DACS, London 2007; 181 above left, above right & below Courtesy of Apple Inc.; 182 left & right Fritz Hansen; 183 left & right Georg Jensen; 184 above Judson Brohmer/ Lockheed Martin; 184 below Lockheed Martin; 185 above Bill Pierce/Time & Life Pictures/Getty Images; 185 below Bill Maris/Esto; 186 London's Transport Museum © Transport for London; 187 Private Collection/Bonhams/Bridgeman Art Library; 188 left Vladimir Kagan Design Group; 188 right Swedish Society of Crafts and Design; 189 above right, below left & below right Kartell; 190 Simon Rendall/Shell Art Collection/National Motor Museum; 191 above & below left Studio Tord Boontje; 191 below right Fritz Hansen; 192 left & right Knoll, Inc; 193 © J.Paul Getty Trust. Used with permission. Julius Shulman Photography Archive, Research Library at the Getty Research Institute; 194 above Georg Jensen; 194 below National Motor Museum/Heritage-Images; 195 left Aram; 195 right Rauno Träskelin/Design Museum Finland; 196 Keystone/Hulton Archive/Getty Images; 197 left Lalique © ADAGP, Paris and DACS, London 2007; 197 right Express Newspapers/Hulton Archive/ Getty Images; 198 Crafts Study Centre; 199 above left Fondation Le Corbusier; 199 above right Ernst Haas/Hulton Archive/Getty Images; 199 below left Boris Horvat/ AFP/Getty Images; 199 below right Cassina I Maestri Collection; 200 above right, below left & below right Ivan Margolius/Tatra Technicke Muzeum; 201 above & below Renault UK Ltd; 202 above Bang & Olufsen; 202 below left With kind permission from Liberty plc; 202 below right National Motor Museum/MPL; 203 above right & below right J & L Lobmeyr; 203 below left Swedish Society of Crafts and Design; 204 above Bernard Hoffman/Time & Life Pictures/Getty Images; 204 centre Advertising Archives; 204 below Greyhound Lines, Inc; 205 above Courtesy of the Herb Lubalin Center at The Cooper Union; 205 below Tim Benton; 206 left Victoria & Albert Museum/ Bridgeman Art Library; 206 right The Museum of Modern Art, New York/Scala, Florence; 207 left Victoria & Albert Museum/ Bridgeman Art Library; 207 right Heller; 208 Croix, France/Bridgeman Art Library; 209 left Cleto Munari Design Associati srl; 209 right Marimekko; 210 above Estudio Mariscal; 210 below London's Transport Museum © Transport for London; 210-211 Courtesy of Sotheby's Picture Library; 211 V & A Images/Victoria & Albert Museum; 212 above Volkswagen AG; 212 below Ingo Maurer GmbH; 213 left Bernard Gotfryd/Hulton Archive/Getty Images; 213 right David Mellor Design; 214 The Museum of Modern Art, New York/ Scala, Florence; 215 above left Bauhaus Archiv, Berlin; 215 above right National Motor Museum/MPL; 215 below Bauhaus Archiv, Berlin; 216 Vitra Design Museum © DACS, London 2007; 216-217 RIBA Library Photographs Collection; 217 Herman Miller Inc; 218 left Science Museum/Science & Society Picture Library; 218 right Christopher Moore; 219 Ezra Stoller/Esto; 220 The Kobal Collection; 221 Bauhaus Archiv, Berlin © Hattula Moholy-Nagy/ DACS, London 2007; 222 left Elirio Invernizzi/Courtesy of Museo Casa Mollino, Torino; 222 right Private Collection, USA/Courtesy of Museo Casa Mollino, Torino; 223 Pierre Vauthey/Corbis Sygma; 224 left Private Collection/The Stapleton Collection/ Bridgeman Art Library; 224 above right Private Collection/Bridgeman Art Library; 224 below right Society of Antiquaries/ Simon Randall Photography; 225 The Kobal Collection; 226 left & right Museum für Gestaltung, Zurich; 227 left Courtesy of the Wedgwood Museum Trust, Barlaston, Staffordshire, UK; 227 right Floto+Warner/Arcaid; 228 Fonds Jardin des Modes/Archive Imec; 229 above Necchi; 229 below Herman Miller Inc; 230 Archivo Storico Olivetti, Ivrea, Italy; 231 left Arnold Newman Collection/Getty Images; 231 above right Archivio Storico Pirelli; 231 below right Vignelli Associates; 232 left Northrop Grumman Corporation; 232 right & 233 Courtesy of the Eliot Noyes Archives; 236 below V & A Images/Victoria & Albert Museum; 237 Fondation Le Corbusier © FLC/ ADAGP, Paris and DACS, London 2007; 238 left Vitra Design Museum; 238 right Verner Panton Design; 239 Swedish Society of Crafts and Design; 241 left Guardian News & Media Ltd; 241 right V & A Images/Victoria & Albert Museum; 242 Gaetano Pesce; 243 left Archivio Storico Piaggio; 243 right Piaggio; 244 London's Transport Museum © Transport for London; 245 above & centre National Motor Museum/MPL; 245 below Fiat; 246 The Museum of Modern Art, New York/Scala, Florence; 247 left Volkswagen AG; 247 right Cassina Collection; 248 left Zanotta SpA; 248 right RIBA Library Photographs Collection; 249 Porche; 250 above Arabia/littala; 250 below Christie's Images © ADAGP, Paris and DACS, London 2007; 251 left David Lees/Corbis; 251 right Henry Clarke/Conde Nast Archive/Corbis; 252 V & A Images/Victoria & Albert Museum; 252-253 Push Pin Studio; 254 Everett Collection/Rex Features; 255 Ray Moreton/Hulton Archive/Getty Images; 256 left Courtesy of Race Furniture Ltd; 256 right Braun GmbH; 256-257 Vitsoe; 257 right Matt Flynn/Cooper-Hewitt, National Design Museum, Smithsonian Institute; 257 above left Vitsoe; 257 centre left Braun GmbH; 258 Marimekko; 259 above Bethnal Green Museum, London/Bridgeman Art Library; 259 below MINI; 260 right, above & below Cassina I Maestri Collection; 261 above Studio Albini; 261 below Brompton Bicycle Ltd; 262 above & below Riva SpA; 263 Rosenthal AG; 264 left Vitra Design Museum; 264 right Royal College of Art; 265 above Elbert Hubbard-Roycroft Museum, East Aurora, New York; 265 below Royal College of Art; 266 Private Collection; 266-267 The Gordon Russell Trust; 267 above & below Courtesy of Scaled Composites, LLC; 268 above & below Saab GB Ltd; 269 Saab GB Ltd; 270 left Knoll, Inc; 271 left Almedahls AB; 272 Artemide; 272-273 Saab GB Ltd; 273 Venini SpA; 274 Scala, Florence; 275 left ph: Lynn Rosenthal Philadelphia Museum of Art: Gift of Mme Elsa Schiaparelli, 1969; 275 right Bildarchiv Foto Marburg; 276-277 Steven May/Alamy; 278 Canterbury Shaker Village, Inc., Canterbury, NH; 279 left Reprinted with permission of Lucent Technologies Inc/Bell Labs; 279 right With kind permission of Liberty plc; 280 above & below Sony; 281 left & right Sottsass Associates; 282 left & right Agence Starck; 283 Science Museum/ Science & Society Picture Library; 284 left The Museum of Modern Art, New York/Scala, Florence; 284 right Swedish Society of Crafts and Design; 285 above Courtesy of the Trustees of the Edward James Foundation/V & A Images/Victoria & Albert Museum; 285 below The Museum of Modern Art, New York/Scala, Florence © DACS, London 2007; 286-287 Pitchal Frederic/ Corbis Sygma; 287 Tapiovaara Design; 288 Moderna Museet, Stockholm, Sweden/Giraudon/Bridgeman Art Library © ADAGP, Paris and DACS, London 2007; 289 The Museum of Modern Art, New York/Scala, Florence; 290 above & below Teague Associates; 291 above & below Zanotta SpA; 292 Vitra Design Museum; 293 left & right Matteo Thun & Partners; 294 Total Identity; 295 left The Museum of Modern Art, New York/ Scala, Florence; 295 right Penguin Group UK; 296 left Vignelli Associates; 297 above left The Museum of Modern Art, New York/Scala, Florence; 297 above right & below right Adelta; 299 left Renault Communication/ Photographer Unknown/All Rights Reserved; 299 right Bettmann/Corbis; 300 left Matt Wargo/Venturi, Scott Brown & Associates; 300 right Rollin La France/Venturi, Scott Brown & Associates; 301 above V & A Images/Victoria & Albert Museum; 301 below Archivio Storico Piaggio; 302 National Motor Museum/MPL; 303 a-d Vignelli Associates; 304 Horst P. Horst/Conde Nast Archives/Corbis; 305 Ernst Haas/Hulton Archive/Getty Images; 306 above & below Volkswagen AG; 307 above Volvo; 307 below RIBA Library Drawings Collection; 308 Bauhaus Archiv, Berlin © DACS, London 2007; 308-309 Sotheby's/akg-images; 309 right Courtesy of the Wedgwood Museum Trust, Barlaston, Staffordshire, UK; 310 right John Donat/RIBA Library Photographs Collection; 311 left V & A Images/Victoria & Albert Museum; 311 right Austrian Archive/Scala, Florence; 312 Venini SpA; 313 left Albertina, Vienna; 313 right Courtesy of Farrar, Straus & Giroux; 314 below left Nathan Willock/View; 314-315 Richard Bryant/ Arcaid; 315 Russel Wright Design Centre; 316 The Museum of Modern Art, New York/ Scala, Florence; 317 left Zanotta SpA; 317 right BrionVega; 318 Arcaid/ Alamy; 319 John Lehmann Ltd; 320 above Estate of Abram Games; 320 below Herman Miller Inc; 321 Hulton Archive/Getty Images; 322 Ikea; 323 above BMW AG; 323 below Photo Archive Foundation la Triennale di Milano; 324 above Nikon; 324 below Andrew Morse/Alamy; 325 above Karen Kasmauski/Corbis; 325 below Gianni Penati/Conde Nast Archive/Corbis

Every effort has been made to trace the copyright holders. We apologise in advance for any unintentional omissions and would be pleased to insert the appropriate acknowledgement in any subsequent publication.

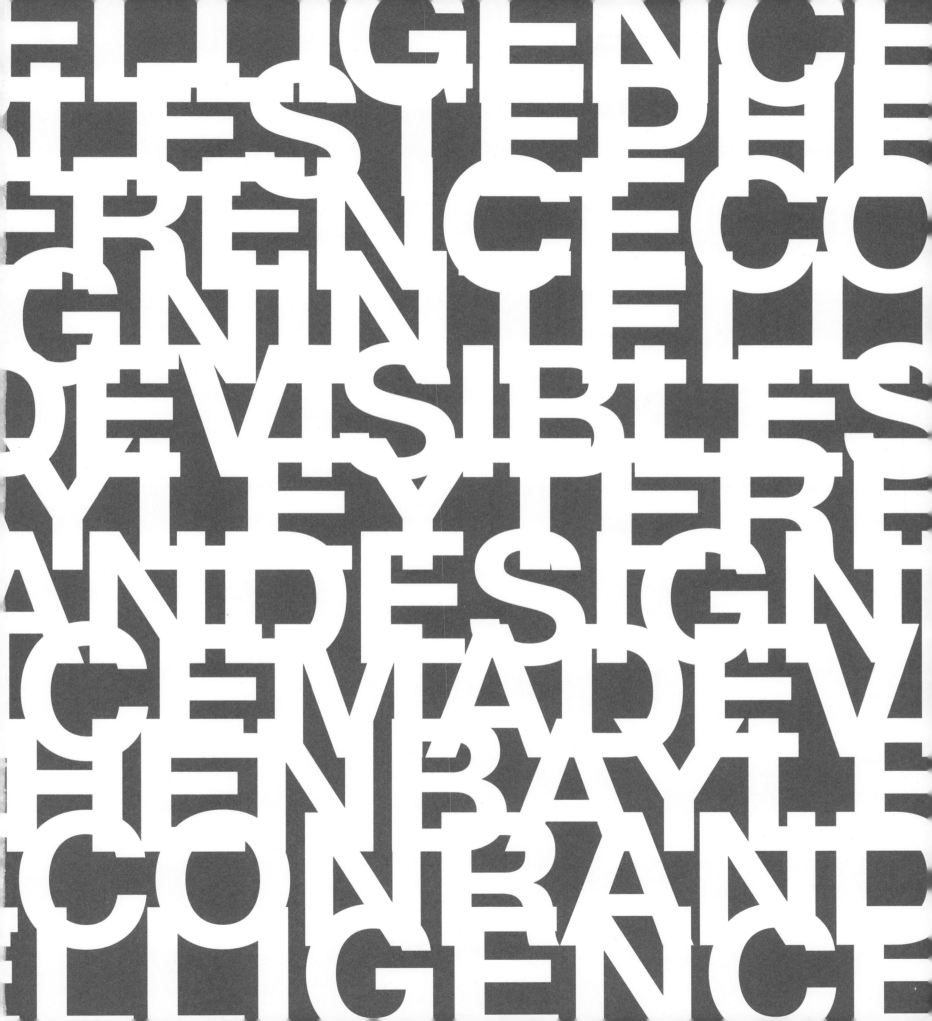

Terence Conran on Stephen Bayley

'I first met Stephen Bayley when I was looking for somebody to run the Design Museum project which my Foundation had set up in 1980. We decided to have a trial run in a dilapidated space offered to us by the V&A Museum. It was called the Boilerhouse Project. He reminds me that in fact he had interviewed me for the *Architectural Review*'s Jubilee issue in 1977.

Stephen organized about 25 outstanding small exhibitions which were very well received and became an invaluable trial run for the Design Museum proper in Butlers Wharf, London. Stephen planned the new museum and became its first director. Unfortunately he found the administrative aspects of a large organization not to his taste. There is no doubt he knows more about design, designers and design movements than anybody else I know that is why I was so happy to cooperate with him on this book.

You might find something of a bias to car design – this is because Stephen is besotted with automobiles and to a lesser extent so am I, cars are indeed one of the most complex products any designer can work on. If you can design a good car you can design practically anything would be our excuse.

I hope Stephen's quirkiness, high spirits and humour and our joint obsession with the importance of design, comes through clearly in this book.

P.S. To write a book with somebody and remain friends is something of an achievement and to do so with our passion for the subject matter and still be friends is remarkable.'

Stephen Bayley is one of the world's best-known authorities on design and popular culture. He has been a design consultant working on imaginative communications projects for clients including Ford, Absolut Vodka, The Coca-Cola Company, Volkswagen Audi, Marks & Spencer, Penhaligon's, Foster Associates, Harvey Nichols, BMW, Piaggio and the V&A amongst others.

He is also well-known as an outspoken commentator on art and design, contributing regularly to *The Times*, *The Daily Mail*, *The Observer*, *The Evening Standard*, *The Guardian*, *The Spectator*, *The Los Angeles Times*, *High Life*, *New Statesman*, *The Independent* and *GQ*. He often broadcasts and appears on various popular programmes including *PM*, *Today*, *Newsnight*, *Start the Week*, *Channel 4 News*, *London Tonight*, and *Any Questions*.

In addition, he has lectured in universities and museums throughout Britain as well as around the world. He has also been a judge of many national and international design competitions, including Campaign Press Awards, RIBA Architectural Awards, The Building Awards, Louis Vuitton Concours d'Elegance at Hurlingham, Cartier Style et Luxe at Goodwood and BBC Good Food Awards.

In 1989 he was made a Chevalier de L'Ordre des Arts et des Lettres, France's top artistic honour, by the French Minister of Culture.